Media in Society

Richard Campbell
Miami University

Joli Jensen
The University of Tulsa

Douglas Gomery
Emeritus, University of Maryland

Bettina Fabos
University of Northern Iowa

Julie Frechette
Worcester State University

Bedford | St. Martin's
Boston • New York

For Bedford/St. Martin's

Publisher for Communication: Erika Gutierrez
Developmental Editor: Jesse Hassenger
Production Editor: Kellan Cummings
Senior Production Supervisor: Dennis J. Conroy
Marketing Manager: Stacey Propps
Copy Editor: Steve Patterson
Indexer: Melanie Belkin
Photo Researcher: Susan McDermott Barlow
Permissions Manager: Kalina K. Ingham
Art Director: Lucy Krikorian
Text Design: Castle Design
Cover Design: Donna Lee Dennison
Cover Art/Cover Photo: (top) ©TongRo Images/Alamy; (bottom) Darrin Kilmek/Getty Images
Composition: Cenveo® Publisher Services
Printing and Binding: RR Donnelley and Sons

President, Bedford/St. Martin's: Denise B. Wydra
Presidents, Macmillan Higher Education: Joan E. Feinberg and Tom Scotty
Editor in Chief: Karen S. Henry
Director of Development: Erica T. Appel
Director of Marketing: Karen R. Soeltz
Production Director: Susan W. Brown
Associate Production Director: Elise S. Kaiser
Managing Editor: Shuli Traub

Manufactured in the United States of America.

8 7 6 5 4 3
f   e   d c   b   a

For information, write: Bedford/St. Martin's, 75 Arlington Street, Boston, MA 02116 (617-399-4000)

ISBN 978-0-312-17986-1

Acknowledgments
Acknowledgments and copyrights are continued at the back of the book on pages 318–19, which constitute an extension of the copyright page. It is a violation of the law to reproduce these selections by any means whatsoever without the written permission of the copyright holder.

About the Authors

Richard Campbell chairs the Department of Media, Journalism, and Film at Miami University in Oxford, OH. He is the author of *"60 Minutes" and the News: A Mythology for Middle America* (University of Illinois, 1991) and coauthor of *Cracked Coverage: Television News, the Anti-Cocaine Crusade, and the Reagan Legacy* (Duke University, 1994); *Media & Culture*, ninth edition (Bedford/St. Martin's, 2014); and *Media Essentials*, second edition (Bedford/St. Martin's, 2013). He holds a PhD from Northwestern.

Joli Jensen is the Hazel Rogers Professor of Communication at the University of Tulsa. She is the author of *Is Art Good for Us? Beliefs about High Culture in American Life* (Rowman & Littlefield, 2002); *Redeeming Modernity: Contradictions in Media Criticism* (Sage, 1990); and *The Nashville Sound: Authenticity, Commercialization and Country Music* (Vanderbilt, 1998) as well as book chapters and research essays on media criticism, communication technologies, communication theories, the social history of the typewriter, and fans and fandom. Dr. Jensen received her PhD in 1985 from the Institute of Communications Research at the University of Illinois.

Douglas Gomery is the coauthor of *Who Owns the Media?*, third edition (Lawrence Erlbaum, 2001) and author of *Shared Pleasures* (University of Wisconsin, 1991). He continues to research the history and economics of the mass media as Resident Scholar at the Library of American Broadcasting at the University of Maryland's Philip Merrill College of Journalism.

Bettina Fabos is an associate professor of Visual Communication and Interactive Digital Studies at the University of Northern Iowa. She is the author of *Wrong Turn on the Information Superhighway* (Teachers College, 2004) and coauthor of *Media & Culture*, ninth edition, and *Media Essentials*, second edition. Her areas of expertise include critical media literacy, Internet commercialization, digital media archives, libraries in the digital age, and media representations of popular culture. A former print reporter and award-winning video maker, Dr. Fabos is now actively involved in digital media production. She holds a PhD from the University of Iowa.

Julie Frechette is a professor of communication at Worcester State University, where she founded and codirected the Center for Teaching and Learning. Her book *Developing Media Literacy in Cyberspace: Pedagogy and Critical Learning for the Twenty-First-Century Classroom* (Praeger Press, 2002) was among the first to explore the multiple-literacies approach for the Digital Age. She is the author of numerous articles on media literacy and feminism; has served as an inaugural member of the editorial board for the *Journal of Media Literacy Education;* and was selected by the National Telemedia Council for the special journal series, Emerging Scholars in Media Literacy.

Brief Contents

Preface

The media are everywhere. Take a look around: Media products are on our phones, on outdoor advertisements, and on every screen in our homes. In today's fragmented, niche-driven market, we no longer all absorb the same media content at the same time; broadcasts, songs, blogs, videos, and other media products reach us in more individual, but also more inclusive, ways. Our new digital world itself can be seen as a product of the media.

The media have transformed the way we communicate in the Digital Age and, as such, the sharp distinction between media and society seems to have blurred. Because we understand their relationship to be symbiotic, *Media in Society* does not analyze media and society as separate entities but instead seeks to understand how media and society create and affect each other. As our title indicates, we believe that the media are best understood as elements *in* society. *Media in Society* demonstrates that the key to unlocking the media/society relationship is through investigating an aspect of the media that has remained a constant throughout time and across cultures: storytelling. All media tell stories.

In writing *Media in Society*, we sought an alternative to ponderous media theories and theorists and to quickly outdated efforts to celebrate or bemoan what is new about the Digital Age. We wanted to produce a more interactive, accessible book for media and society courses that could help students understand the variety of ways that media stories, in and about media, operate in their lives.

We hope that our own affection for media in all its forms comes through in our analysis. We believe that the best place to begin discussion of the role of media in society is with the appreciation and analysis of our favorite TV shows, social media sites, music, and other facets of contemporary media culture. We offer examples and exercises that help students describe, evaluate, and interpret their own media experiences in order to help them become more engaged consumers and citizens in the Digital Age.

As authors, we identify ourselves as narrativists: We believe that the media are best understood as social, cultural, political, economic, and technological storytellers. Obviously media audiences are engaged at the level of story, whether by the romance and melodrama of *Downton Abbey*, the mythic grandeur of a *Star Wars* movie, the rising and falling melody in a Mumford & Sons song, or a thirty-second TV ad for beer—media stories of all kinds tell us about who we are and what we value. But our commitment to narrative goes deeper and wider than the stories that our media tell.

Media in Society also looks at the stories that we, as a society, tell *about* the media. These stories can range from inspiring narratives chronicling the role of the free press in a democracy to horror stories about the influence of violent movies or addiction to video games. To represent the range of stories we tell about media, we also bring into play a broad range of well-established theoretical approaches to studying media, including constructivist and reflectionist criticism. Though we always focus on the power of stories, we think the best way to analyze storytelling, from and about the media, is through a balance of narrativist, reflectionist, and constructionist perspectives.

Media in Society examines the complex relationships between media and society through three thematic lenses: *technology*, *democracy*, and *capitalism*.

- Technology has been the driving force behind the digital turn, a convergence and reshuffling of media forms that has profoundly reshaped the delivery and consumption of media stories across platforms; these changes have simultaneously reshaped the economics of media industries—and, in turn, the world's economies.

- As digital media become more participatory and politics continue to revolve around the creation and harnessing of specific narratives, media affects the way a democracy functions.

- Political narratives, fueled by capitalism, influence the economics of media outlets large and small.

Connections among these themes are drawn throughout *Media in Society*. Discussion of narrative modes in Chapter 4, for example, leads into the application of those modes to election narratives in Chapter 5, and an explanation of how journalists create their own narratives in Chapter 6. The visual literacy lessons in Chapter 3 resonate in the discussions of advertising, both commercial (in Chapter 7) and political (in Chapter 5). Chapter 9's exploration of representation in media relates to Chapter 11's rundown of cross-cultural media and globalization.

Our hope is that students will recognize these connections and relate them to their own mediated lives.

FEATURES OF *MEDIA IN SOCIETY*

An engaging approach to media and society that examines media storytelling and actually tells stories *about* the media to inspire student participation and discussion. We're media scholars who draw on a variety of perspectives and theorists to help students become conversant with media studies issues and ideas. Through examples from reality television, online fan communities, popular advertising, Disney animation, and more, *Media in Society* understands not just the content but the pleasure we get from media narratives—and how that pleasure relates to the meaning and effectiveness of media narratives.

Comprehensive coverage that students and instructors need for a study of media and society in a concise, accessible package. *Media in Society* discusses constructivist, reflectionist, and narrativist perspectives throughout chapters on media criticism, visual literacy, politics, journalism, globalization, media representations, and the growing influence of technology—tying together classic media studies themes with a fresh, student-friendly point of view.

An innovative critical approach to media literacy that introduces students to five stages of critical thinking—description, analysis, interpretation, evaluation, and engagement—and applies those stages with **critical process exercises** at the end of each chapter.

A thought-provoking and diverse array of significant topics like semiotics, narrative formulas, the evolution of the news media, pop culture and fandom, presidential election discourse, and gender in the media—with relevant and eclectic examples from throughout media history, including today.

| RESOURCES

Book Companion Site at bedfordstmartins.com/mediasociety

The Web site for *Media in Society* offers RSS feeds with headlines from major media outlets, a portal linking to the best media-related sites on the Internet, and an index of media-related job sites and opportunities.

VideoCentral: Mass Communication

With over forty clips, this collection of short videos gives students an inside look at the media industries through the eyes of leading professionals. Each three- to five-minute clip discusses issues such as the future of print media, net neutrality, media convergence, and media ownership. The videos contain unique commentary from *Media in Society* author Richard Campbell, as well as some of the biggest names in media: Amy Goodman, Clarence Page, Junot Diaz, Anne Rice, and more. *Video-Central: Mass Communication* can be packaged for free with the print book.

Media in Society Bedford e-Book to Go

The Bedford e-Book to Go version of *Media in Society* includes the same content as the print book and provides an affordable, tech-savvy PDF e-book option for students. Instructors can create a custom version that includes their own content and the chapters they want. Typically half the price of the print book, the e-book makes it possible to include multiple books in the course without the financial stress. Learn more about custom Bedford e-Books to Go at **bedfordstmartins.com/ebooks**.

Other e-Book Options

A variety of other digital versions of *Media in Society* are available to for use on tablets, e-readers, or computers. For more information, see **bedfordstmartins.com /ebooks**.

ACKNOWLEDGMENTS

We'd like to thank everyone at Bedford/St. Martin's who supported this project through its many stages of development and production, including Macmillan Higher Education Presidents Joan Feinberg and Tom Scotty, Bedford/St. Martin's President Denise Wydra, Director of Development Erica Appel, and Marketing Manager Stacey Propps. We are especially grateful to Publisher Erika Gutierrez for her leadership and Executive Editor Simon Glick for his creative input, as well as Development Editor Jesse Hassenger and Editorial Assistant Caitlin Crandell. We also appreciate the tireless work of Managing Editor Shuli Traub; the careful and exacting eye of Project Editor Kellan Cummings, who made sure we got the details right with help from copy editor Steve Patterson and proofreaders Julie Nemer and Will Rigby; and Senior Production Supervisor Dennis J. Conroy, who kept the book on schedule.

We also want to thank the many thoughtful reviewers who contributed feedback and ideas as we developed this first edition of *Media in Society*: Frank Absher, *St. Louis University*; Kevin Taylor Anderson, *University of Massachusetts—Amherst*; Alan Barton, *Delta State University*; Mary Blue, *Tulane University*; David Burns, *Salisbury University*; James Burton, *Salisbury University*; Rod Carveth, *Western New England University*; Preston Coleman, *Gainesville State College*; Michelle Delery, *Tulane University*; Greg Downey, *University of Wisconsin—Madison*; Samuel Ebersole, *Colorado State University—Pueblo*; Tara Emmers-Sommer, *University of Nevada—Las Vegas*; Michael Ensdorf, *Roosevelt University*; Thomas Grier, *Winona State University*; Margaret Haefner, *North Park University*; Rebecca Hains, *Salem State University*; Jarice Hanson, *University of Massachusetts at Amherst*; Allison Harthcock, *Butler University*; Curt Hersey, *Berry College*; Nina Huntemann, *Suffolk University*; Claire Sisco King, *Vanderbilt University*; Elana Levine, *University of Wisconsin—Milwaukee*; Jeremy Littau, *Lehigh University*; Brenton Malin, *University of Pittsburgh*; Melissa Meade, *Colby-Sawyer College*; James Mueller, *University of North Texas*; Michael Newman, *University of Wisconsin—Milwaukee*; Darrell Newton, *Salisbury University*; Michael Palm, *University of North Carolina at Chapel Hill*; Ronald Rice, *University of California—Santa Barbara*; Ann Savage, *Butler University*; Lance Strate, *Fordham University*; Christine Von Der Haar, *Indiana University*; Scott Webber, *University of Colorado—Boulder*; Bruce Wickelgren, *Suffolk University*; Evan Wirig, *Grossmont College*; and Bill Yousman, *Eastern Connecticut State University*.

This book has been a labor of love for us and we hope you find it rewarding. Please feel free to e-mail us at mediainsociety@bedfordstmartins.com with any comments, concerns, or suggestions!

Contents

3 Visual Literacy and the Truth behind an Image   53

4 Narrative Formulas and the Cycle of Storytelling   79

5 Political Stories and Media Messages   103

6 News, Culture, and Democracy   133

10 Technology, Convergence, and Democracy 251

11 Media Globalization   277

Media in Society

1 | Introduction

Understanding Media in Society

Today we take for granted what used to seem miraculous—our ability to use mass media to extend communication across time and space. For thousands of years we lived in an oral culture with only speech and memory to record and share our experiences. Although writing systems allowed us to "mediate" face-to-face communication, it was not until the invention of the printing press that we entered an era of mass mediation in which ideas could be speedily reproduced and then widely disseminated.

But books and newspapers still needed to be physically carried from place to place and mass communication remained reliant on traditional means of transportation and channels of distribution. Electronic forms of communication changed all that. Many theorists believe that the advent of electronic broadcasting and its ability to communicate information almost instantaneously to almost anywhere in the world began to dismantle the limits of time and space.

Now, in the Digital Age, we seem to have eliminated these boundaries on communication altogether. Online newspapers, freed from space constraints, can print unlimited letters to the editor in the form of user comments, and TV networks, released from the time limits of traditional broadcasting, can run entire news interviews on their Web sites. Almost anyone with a cell phone and a Web page can record images, video, and sound to create, disseminate, and preserve his or her own personal reality.

The Internet emphasizes how mass communication in all its forms is central to our lives—psychologically, socially, culturally, economically, and politically. Never before have so many people been aware of the various forms of communication or as concerned about their influences.

That we have begun to take these Internet-era advances for granted should not be surprising. Older mass media like print, sound recording, radio, movies, and television were once fresh and amazing too. As developing technologies they offered new ways to frame stories, and as the "new media" of their era they sparked both extravagant hopes and extravagant fears in their time. In the twentieth century, movies, radio, and television raised concerns about how accurately the media depicted reality, how appropriately the media were shaping us and our culture, and what kinds of stories the media were telling us about our common life.

Nonetheless, the Internet seems to defy categorization in a way that other media have not, in part because it is new—and in part because it isn't. Never before have so many people had the ability to create as well as consume a near-endless variety of mediated content. But what exactly is the Internet? It is a text-based medium like a newspaper or magazine, but it is also an audio medium like radio and a visual medium like film or television. As such, one way to understand the Internet is to see it as the latest example in a long line of media forms.

But the Internet is also a hybrid medium where all previous mass media converge and combine. It demands print media skills in that users need to be able to read to navigate its sprawling terrain; it's also an explosion of sound and sight to which people themselves can contribute. It is not a classic mass medium because users can set limits to the scope of their communication—they can e-mail selected friends or post entries in a blog that can be read by anonymous strangers. The filtration process that once stood between media creation and media consumption—selection, evaluation, editing, revision, distribution, marketing, and promotion—is collapsing. Interestingly, one of the Internet's most successful ventures, Amazon.com, blazed its trail on the one of the newest mass media by selling the world's oldest mass medium—the book.

So when we seek to understand the role of media in society, we need to be aware of the established technological forms that today's media incorporate, as well as of the origins of the content that today's media purvey. We must also know more about the kinds of criticism that accompanied older as well as current media forms and content. By exploring the history of our efforts to make sense of media's role in society, we can see how today's hopes and fears about the Internet are just the latest version of an ongoing conversation.

UNDERSTANDING MEDIA FORMS: USING TECHNOLOGY, DEMOCRACY, AND CAPITALISM

Historically, the ways we communicate (by speech, writing, print, electronics, and now also digital technology) have shaped the ways we think, feel, and live. If we were living in an age before writing, with speech as one of the only ways to create and transmit our thoughts, we would be spending much of our time telling and retelling stories to one another, hoping to retain, in memory, all that we need to know. If we were living during the rise of writing, we might be writing or studying manuscripts as memory supplements, to tell or read stories about the world.

What can truly be called mass communication began to emerge in the mid-fifteenth century with the rise of the printing press, which, along with other communication technologies, revolutionized thought and society. The opportunity to print and disseminate words relatively cheaply and easily supported an ever-increasing (but sometimes controversial) democratization of knowledge. Before that time, when only a small elite portion of the literate population—mostly men from the aristocracy and clergy—controlled information, monopolies of knowledge were easier to maintain. With the printing press, these monopolies were challenged by wider, more inclusive, and more inventive ways of telling stories and recording information about everyday life. It is easy to forget how controversial this kind of increased access was, and it is important to realize that concerns about the Internet were first raised with printing.

As printing became the dominant form of communication, the world changed both economically and politically; both capitalism and democracy can be seen as print-based phenomena. Once people could be contacted and controlled across time and space, via the "new" mass medium of print, nation-states could emerge, international markets could develop, and we could learn to think of ourselves as "modern" citizens and as consumers. Printing made it possible to communicate more things to more people, but it also made it harder to control what was being communicated. The print age brought with it the easier circulation of pornographic pamphlets as well as political opinion, of scandal and ridicule as well as erudition and art.

The next great leap forward came with the electronic revolution, a transformation begun by the telegraph and electric light in the nineteenth century, and continuing with radio and film. Electricity and data gave way to transmitting sound, then sound and image together, finally arriving at the interactive sounds, sights, and print of the Internet.

While print communication is still a crucial part of the Internet, today we are living in a late phase of the electronic revolution and in what some believe is an early stage of a new digital era. The dots and dashes of the telegraph's Morse code have become the zeroes and ones of today's digital binary code.

This book explores media forms and content in relation to three themes: democracy, capitalism, and technology. We as authors believe that understanding media in society first requires paying attention to the ways that media technologies are linked to democratic politics and capitalist economics. Then we need to move from considering technology (media forms) to deciphering content (media narratives), to explore not just how stories are told but what those stories are telling us.

Because understanding media in society involves content, not just form, we offer in this chapter a critical process that encourages systematic exploration of all media content and experiences. Then we explore three traditional types of media criticism—reflectionist, constructivist, and narrativist—that have characterized claims about media influence in society. Finally, we note some of the familiar complaints in media criticism that are currently reemerging in relation to the Internet.

Media Technologies

The media are always technological forms, not just narrative content. And technological forms aren't just the gadgets we use to access the media but the mass communication networks we use to stay connected to others. From this perspective, writing can be considered a communication technology, as can printing, film, radio, television, video, cell phones, and the Internet. Our latest phase of communication technology is broadly referred to as digital, encompassing the Internet, mobile technology, and everything that's now become interrelated.

So we have moved from oral, to written, to print, to electronic, and now to digital technologies—but what is interesting to us is not how these technologies work but how they work on us. Communication theorists Harold Adams Innis and his student Marshall McLuhan first drew attention to the ways that the media shape our understanding of time and space. McLuhan defined media technologies both as "extensions of man" and (famously) as "the message."[1] In McLuhan's perspective, media technologies are interesting not because of their technical traits and capabilities but because of what they make possible—particular styles of thought and particular kinds of social relationships.

So when we focus on the theme of media technologies, we do so to explore how new media forms shape us personally, socially, culturally, politically, and economically. Always, communication technologies enable some possibilities and constrain others. Whenever we consider the influence of new media technologies, we need to sort out what is being enabled and what is being constrained, if we are to understand the consequences of our ever-changing media environment.

Democracy

The role the mass media play in the maintenance of modern democracy is this book's second theme. Early Greek democracies relied on speech—in public spaces among particularly privileged men—in order to thrive. But the more modern democratic ideals of America's founders were imagined in relation to the printing press and its burgeoning potential for the free circulation of opinion and ideas. It was clear to the framers of our Constitution that effective self-government depended on quick and easy dissemination of information. It became clear to later thinkers that democracy requires a public equipped with the skills and resources needed to take part in the democratic process. A free press, along with public libraries, schools, and literacy, is believed to be a necessity for civil society in modern democracies. As democracy becomes the avowed goal in countries like Egypt, academic critics, concerned consumers, and ordinary citizens are debating just what kinds of media content—news, advertising, and entertainment—a successful democracy needs.

They are also debating the role that current forms of media—especially the Internet and social networks—played in fostering democratic hopes and making the overthrow of unelected leaders possible. For example, the spring 2011 uprisings by Arab peoples against dictatorships in Tunisia, Egypt, Libya, Bahrain, and Yemen, among other Middle Eastern countries, offer a striking example of democratic organizing enabled by new media forms that helped bypass government control and abusive dictatorships. Taking its lead from the Arab Spring protests, the Occupy Wall Street movement in the United States also demonstrates that new media technologies can be instrumental in fostering and sustaining democratic practices.

Capitalism

The influence of new forms of media technologies on democracy links to a third theme: the relationship between media and capitalism. Commerce is inextricably linked to our contemporary media. Not only does advertising support news and entertainment programming, but we are categorized by media as consumers and as markets. We are sold media products just as we are sold soap: Our media are products of capitalism, as well as purveyors of it. Throughout the twentieth century, media consumers were "sold" as audiences to advertisers, and this continues even in today's more fragmented, specialized media. Most of the time, the bigger or wealthier the audiences, the more the media seek to serve them.

There are connections and contradictions between democracy and capitalism. Through mass media, we enact a particular role in the marketplace of ideas. Rather than meeting as equals in a public square, as early democratic theorists like John Stuart Mill imagined, we seem to have become consumers of other people's images and ideas. The mass media address us for their purposes, not necessarily ours. And their purposes are often economic, rather than political, cultural, or social.

When we think about the connections among media technologies, democracy, and capitalism, we can see how new forms of media embody and enable both democratic and capitalist processes. What exactly is embodied and enabled by current media, and what we should do about it, matters to us and, we hope, to you. For example, while YouTube, blogging sites, and other form of digital communication have made it easier to reproduce images and ideas, it is uncertain whether the Internet will greatly improve democratic discourse, or simply make it easier for us to consume products, or just introduce additional noise to the cultural atmosphere. In spite of some early hopes for a democratized, noncommercial World Wide Web, it seems possible that the need to make money from the Internet, and reach consumers through media content, may deepen rather than refigure the connections among media, capitalism, and democracy that have been with us since the print era.

UNDERSTANDING MEDIA CONTENT: THE CRITICAL PROCESS

Understanding media in society, and the connections among technology, capitalism, and democracy, requires understanding and exploring media content. Content is what media technologies purvey and how the media work their narrative magic.

We believe that content exploration involves learning how to be *critical* rather than *cynical*. Here is the difference: A cynical point of view usually involves intolerance and dismissal. For example, we could be intolerant of all the ads that stream through our lives, we could reject certain kinds of music as unlistenable, we could roll our eyes at reality TV programming, or we could snub mainstream media as mere propaganda. We wouldn't be the first to do so. But rejecting entire media forms, styles, and practices as trivial, "trash," ideological misinformation, or even "evil" is in the end a cynical perspective.

Rather than cynically dismissing entire media styles and practices, the critical approach attempts to understand the institutional and interpretive processes through which media are made, distributed, and interpreted. To be critical, then, is to gather information, look for patterns, figure out what the patterns mean, make an informed judgment, and then, if possible, act on that knowledge.

In short, to become critical in the fullest sense of that word, we subscribe to a method of media analysis we call **critical process**. This is an uncynical effort to understand "how media mean" by focusing both on the stories they are telling us and the stories that we are telling about them. The critical process involves five overlapping stages that build on each other:

1. *Description*: paying close attention, taking notes, and researching the subject under study.

2. *Analysis*: discovering and focusing on significant patterns emerging from the description stage.

3. *Interpretation*: asking and answering the "What does that mean?" and "So what?" questions about one's findings.

4. *Evaluation*: arriving at a judgment about whether something is good, bad, or mediocre, which involves subordinating one's personal taste to the critical assessment resulting from the first three stages.

5. *Engagement*: taking some action that connects our critical perspective with our role as "global citizens" in order to question media institutions, adding our own voice to the process of shaping the cultural environment.

Reality shows like Bravo's *Real Housewives* franchise follow a different sort of narrative from shows like *The Amazing Race*, *Catfish*, or *Storage Wars*.

To apply the critical process, let's take the example of reality TV. Since the 1990s, with the emergence of *The Real World* on MTV, many have accused reality television of exploiting ordinary peoples' personal travails for fun and profit. Criticisms have further suggested that the only reason these shows litter the TV landscape is because they are much less expensive to produce—since it's easier and cheaper to use nonactors in their "natural habitat" than to pay for expensive sets and professional writers who craft coherent narratives that aspire to depict something significant or interesting about the human experience. While certainly some forms of reality TV may seem to fit a negative stereotype, should we draw cynical conclusions about this type of raw and ragged storytelling by placing an entire TV genre with its many offshoots into a single category? After all, this sprawling genre now ranges from *The Real World*, *Catfish*, and *The Biggest Loser* to *Ice Road Truckers*, *Monster Garage*, and *Deadliest Catch* (the 2011 Emmy winner for Outstanding Reality Program) to *Dancing with the Stars*, *The Voice*, and *American Idol* (the most popular and highest-rated TV program in the United States from 2004 to 2011—a record). Rather than dismissing the genre as a whole, we can begin a more critical analysis.

Description

We will start by describing current terrain that encapsulates reality TV and by identifying various subgenres that encompass these types of narratives. For example, programs that throw ordinary people into competition (*Survivor, The Amazing Race*) could constitute a category. Another category might include what some TV producers call "dude television"—shows about vehicles, mechanics, or hunting (*Pimp My Ride, Monster Garage, Dog the Bounty Hunter*). Yet another category could be what producers call "treasure TV"—about finding valuable things or weird stuff in storage units or at auction sales (*Storage Wars, Auction Hunters*). Do some background research at this stage—including both academic research and popular media critiques—about reality TV to try to get an idea of the genre's history and in what directions its many categories and subgenres seem to be going.

Analysis

Now that we have amassed some data, we can turn to the second stage of the critical process. In the analysis stage, we isolate patterns that call for closer attention. For example, figure out patterns in the kinds of storytelling that emerge in these programs and their various subgenres. Who are the central characters? What are the main plots? What constitutes the conflict in these narratives? Do the producers of the program try to convey a central theme or message to viewers? Investigate too the economic patterns that help explain why these kinds of programs are so prolific, especially today. After all, reality programs like this have been around since radio (*Candid Microphone*) and the earliest days of television (*Candid Camera* and *Arthur Godfrey's Talent Scouts*, the No. 1 show in the United States in 1951–1952).

Interpretation

In the interpretive stage, we try to determine the meanings of the patterns we have analyzed. The most difficult stage in criticism, interpretation demands an answer to the "So what?" question: an attempt to understand the significance of what we are studying. For instance, if we look at the story of reality TV and have determined perhaps that some of these programs do indeed exploit their participants while others reveal some meaning about human experience or are more socially relevant, the answer to the "So what?" question may be that reality TV is far more complicated than its critics imagine.

Evaluation

The fourth stage of the critical process focuses on making an informed judgment based on the previous stages. While interpretation has us determining meanings, evaluation encourages us to form an opinion about the value of those meanings. As such, building on description, analysis, and interpretation, we are now better able to evaluate the reality TV genre. At this stage, we can grasp its strengths and weaknesses and make critical judgments measured against our own frames of reference—what we like and dislike, as well as what seems good or bad about various reality TV subgenres. Knowing the story of reality television is important to making a judgment that might go something like this:

> A diverse and seemingly limitless range of TV programs—that depend not on professionally trained actors and writers but on the lives of "ordinary" people—challenges the hegemony of the Big Networks by offering less expensive programs that appeal to a wide audience who identify with these programs and the stories they tell. These stories are often about characters following their dreams and perseverance in the face of adversity. They are often morality plays about the consequences of behavior—in biblical terms, "reaping what we sow." They are also about emotions—cautionary tales about showing too much or too little feeling.

Thus, in this fourth stage we make a more informed judgment: not dismissing an entire category or genre of TV storytelling, but evaluating the reasons why this genre has proliferated and what these narratives tell us about themselves and ourselves. In short, some critics and cynics aren't entirely wrong in finding fault with reality TV— like any other TV or film genre, there are a lot of bad stories out there—but they are wrong in dismissing all of it.

Engagement

To be fully media literate, we must actively work to create a media world that represents broad interests and tastes—the fifth stage of the critical process. In our study of reality TV then, engagement might involve identifying particular shows that seem to exploit participants or challenging producers with critiques and offering suggestions about ways they might improve storytelling practices. For example, we could work with our own college communities to plan panels— even a conference—on reality TV programs, inviting producers of the genre, scholars who study media, people who have participated in these programs, fans of the show, the general public, and students/faculty interested in serious media criticism about the cultural, political, social, and economic influences of this TV genre. We could also work with local and regional media to draw coverage to our events and further extend the influence of our work. Finally, we could offer our own critical writings about reality TV to various media outlets—from new online venues to traditional print media trying to find ways to better connect with audiences.

TYPES OF MEDIA CRITICISM

The media are praised, and blamed, for all kinds of things, by all kinds of people. As media consumers, we can worry about the impact of hip-hop music on our siblings or bemoan the amount of time we waste on video games. We can believe that advertising makes us buy things we don't need or think that magazines full of super-thin models contribute to eating disorders. We can believe news stories about addictions to the Internet and editorials suggesting that violent video games lead to school shootings. This combination of personal belief and journalistic coverage, which sometimes quotes (and misrepresents, or oversimplifies) academic expertise, provides a kind of daily running media commentary—and it is what many people often accept as "true" about media influence.

In this section we explore the stories critics and scholars tell about the media rather than how the media themselves tell stories. We describe the beliefs that dominate media commentary, so that you can recognize the variety of ways that media influences are imagined and understood. As authors, we hope to strike a balance between offering our own take on these matters and representing other perspectives fairly so that you can develop and locate your own perspectives.

We also make a distinction here between media criticism (what we are up to) and social science-based studies of media that use traditional content analyses, surveys, or experiments and other quantitative methodologies to conduct formal research on media. Doing media criticism represents a *cultural* approach to media. It is essentially interpretive work that draws on a variety of critical perspectives (which we discuss more fully later in this chapter).

Communication scholar James Carey, in his own work, addressed the limitations and strengths of this kind of interpretive approach. He contrasts the qualitative, ritual view of communication with a more quantitative, transmission view of communication. A cultural approach to communication, he argues, "does not seek to explain human behavior, but to understand it. It does not seek to reduce human action to underlying causes or structures but to interpret its significance. It does not attempt to predict human behavior, but to diagnose human meanings."[2] Cultural anthropologist Clifford Geertz has argued that such a cultural perspective is not "experimental science in search of law" but instead "interpretive" work "in search of meaning."[3]

Like all academic fields, communication includes ongoing disagreements about how to study the media. These arguments are about theory (what concepts we use to study the media) and about method (what techniques we use to study the media). While we are open to information gathered from a more social science-based transmission point of view, we ally ourselves with interpretive methods and therefore with a cultural approach to communication. The cultural approach defines communication as the creation of meaning in time rather than the transmission of messages across space. Our preferred methods involve "interpreting interpretations" using critical practices, rather than doing experiments or surveys.

By articulating our point of view as part of a larger, ongoing conversation about media influence in academia and in popular discussions, we hope to help you sort out the merits and limitations of different theoretical and methodological approaches to media in society.

Of course, when most people hear the term "media criticism" they think of what appears in newspapers, magazines, and Web sites. These are typically short columns in which the writer reviews or previews a particular TV program, movie, or Web site. This form is sometimes interesting and useful, but it's not really media criticism as we work with it in this book.

Reviews and previews are written under tight deadline pressure, and a healthy dose of personal evaluation—"this is a great show" or "this is piece of trash"— typically dominates the review. This kind of writing has its place, but it often lacks the substantive analysis, interpretation, and engagement that the best media criticism provides and that we described earlier in this chapter. Moreover, media review and preview articles usually deal with a current single text—a TV show or one movie. Most of this kind of reviewing represents a personal kind of writing that promotes one writer's individual cultural tastes.

Media criticism as we define it here comes from a theoretically informed perspective, making explicit or implicit interpretive assumptions about how media operate in society. It tells a story about what media are, what they mean, how they mean, what roles they play in our lives, and how we should think and feel about them. True media criticism analyzes the media as social, cultural, historical, political, and economic content and form. It is not about whether the writer likes or doesn't like a particular genre or show, but about what the writer thinks the media are and do—in particular and in general.

Three common approaches to media criticism characterize our field:

- reflectionist criticism
- constructionist criticism
- narrativist criticism

Reflectionist Criticism

A **reflectionist** perspective focuses on how well—or badly—the media represent the real world. This reflectionist approach offers content analyses of media, often using quantitative measures, and claims that the media present an unrealistic or distorted picture. This charge is most often leveled at television (especially news and advertising), but it also applies to music, video games, and other media forms. Media

Reflectionist criticism might claim that most advertising does a poor job of reflecting real people and real concerns.

fare, reflectionist criticism argues, is more violent, more sexual, more formulaic, and less diverse than everyday life. The media do not accurately mirror the world as it is. From this perspective, the media are inadequate sources of information because they offer us distorted messages.

While various nonprofit watchdog groups, like Fairness and Accuracy in Reporting (FAIR) or Accuracy in Media (AIM) regularly monitor both print and TV media to offer "reality" checks, television still draws the most critical attention for its inability to properly reflect reality. While other forms of media are not subject to this same critique nearly as often, it is worth pointing out that TV's visual aura and near ubiquity makes the medium seem—among all mass media forms—best suited to reflect real images of daily life with the most accuracy.

Still, critics may not demand that book publishers, magazine editors, or film directors make "reflecting reality" their primary objective. Given that television is mostly in the business of telling stories, it is a truly demanding imperative to ask that our culture's central *fictional* storyteller over the past fifty-plus years be realistic.

Similarly, advertising is in no way loyal to accurate depictions of reality, yet it is frequently castigated, from this perspective, for harmfully unrealistic portrayals of feminine beauty. Media critics like Jean Kilbourne have made a career of showing how advertising messages are supposedly "killing us softly" by using varieties of techniques to distort women's actual looks in order to sell products.

The reflectionist perspective calls our attention to distortions and discrepancies in the way various media represent the world. It does so by focusing on the media as "message senders." Drawing on an American heritage of mass communication research, it tends to understand communication using statistical content analysis techniques, drawing on a sender-message-receiver model of communication. How many and what kinds of representations are being sent to us by the media? How accurate or complete or fair are these representations? This linear model, with messages being sent from senders to receivers, has been described as a "transmission" model of communication.

Demonstrating how over-, under-, or falsely represented particular groups (women, the working class, lawyers, parents) are is important work. But a reflectionist approach mostly documents message content and has little to tell us about how and why media messages are what they are, or what those messages actually mean to us in everyday life. The focus is on how inadequately a media message represents a seemingly unproblematic reality.

But this assumes a single, simple, objective reality—one that is known to and preferred by the critic. Perhaps reality is never singular or simple; in fact, it may not be fully depictable. Evaluating the media on their ability to reflect or encompass reality seems less useful to us than the deeper interpretive issues addressed in constructionist and narrativist criticism.

Constructionist Criticism

A second type of media criticism adopts a **constructionist** perspective and focuses on the ways the media shape—or "construct"—individuals and society. This approach emphasizes what it means to live in a heavily mediated environment. Under this perspective, the critique focuses on media form and content, and on who we become when we spend time with media. This perspective emerges from the Frankfurt School of media scholars, most of whom emigrated from Nazi Germany and knew firsthand how the media could be used to create or shape a toxic reality.

The Frankfurt School perspective, along with Marxist and structuralist concepts, helped inform the development of what has come to be called critical theory. Critical theory transformed the study of literature and other forms of media in the 1970s.

Developing as post-structuralist and neo-Marxist theory, it helped energize a generation of literary theorists and media scholars, who drew on scholars like Jacques Derrida, Roland Barthes, and Michel Foucault to develop a critical approach to media.

The constructionist perspective focuses on ideology and power and asks how the media participate in creating and sustaining power relationships. A constructionist is interested in how ideology (organized sets of ideas and beliefs) supports hegemony (ideologically enforced power relations) and how it is that the media are part of this constant process of maintaining the status quo.

A constructionist critique might begin by exploring the ideological consequences of spending hours in front of a television making fun of bad performances on *American Idol*, or connecting with old high school friends on Facebook, or playing *Grand Theft Auto* and blowing up digitized bad guys. Using interpretive methods, the critique would connect this process to larger ways that we as media consumers are "structured in dominance"—unwittingly reproducing hegemonic values and beliefs through our participation in media content.

Constructionist criticism centers around what it means to live in a media culture— a world saturated in commercially successful messages. As such, it concentrates less on the media as transmitters and reflectors of information and more on the media as ideological conditioning. The constructionist perspective defines media more as an encompassing environment than as a series of messages. It often finds that our media environment is toxic and self-serving, and calls for us to break through the ideological messages that we are unwittingly absorbing.

Not all constructionists are critical theorists; belief in the conditioning role of media—that the media make us into what they need us to be—is widely held by critics across the political spectrum. Constructionist critiques of popular media can be found in books with alarmist titles such as *Four Arguments for the Elimination of Television, All Consuming Images, Amusing Ourselves to Death*, and *The Death of Literature*. This perspective may be best documented in Allan Bloom's influential 1986 book, *The Closing of the American Mind*. Here, as a deeply conservative academic critic worried about the undermining of cultural authority and traditional aesthetic standards, Bloom laments the influence of contemporary rock music on young people, particularly its alleged power to distract students from reading great works in philosophy and literature:

> The issue here is its effect on education, and I believe [rock music] ruins the imagination of young people and makes it very difficult for them to have a passionate relationship to art and thought . . .
>
> . . . I suspect that the rock addiction, particularly in the absence of strong counterattractions, has an effect similar to that of drugs. The students will get over the music. . . . But as long as they have the Walkman on [Today he might cite the iPod], they cannot hear what the great tradition has to say, and, after its prolonged use, when they take it off, they find they are deaf.[4]

Bloom imagines that we, the media consumer, are being shaped and formed by media culture in ways that displace or prevent us from being shaped and formed by high art. Notice that both options are constructivist—seeing both popular and high art as shaping us into what they need or want us to become.

In the past fifty years, constructionist criticism has highlighted some of the most interesting and important issues in media in society. By drawing our attention to how the media naturalize power relations, circulate ideology, and enforce the status quo, they have helped generations of students become conscious of, and willing to reappraise, their eager participation in mainstream media. But constructionist criticism doesn't give us, the audience, much credit for how we actually participate in and through contemporary media. It tends to see us as constructed rather than constructing reality. This is why, as much as we can learn from constructionist criticism, we prefer a narrativist approach.

Narrativist Criticism

As authors, we respect (and share) many of the concerns that these two perspectives address. We want reliable access to truthful and realistic accounts of the world, and we want to be aware of how we are being shaped by mediated culture. However, we also believe that there is a missing piece in reflectionist and constructionist perspectives—one often addressed in reviewing and previewing. Rather than understand the media mostly as inadequate reflections or as worrisome shapers, we seek to understand popular media at the level of pleasurable storytelling.

Storytelling is the cultural level that engages most media audiences. A **narrativist** perspective toward media criticism views the media as society's central storytellers. We argue that people experience the media (and everything else) chiefly through *stories*—the dominant symbolic way we make sense of daily life. These stories can be fact, fiction, or some combination; they can be a short story or a book, a song lyric or a blog post, a single image in a magazine or Internet ad, a tweet, a political speech or a PR release, or a complex ongoing TV series.

Even if media stories are designed only to sell us something or to provide a platform for commercial pitches, they tell us important things about who we are and what we value. Stories can be simple or complex, shallow or deep, confirming or challenging, depending on the context in which they are told. What matters most is that there are many and often contradictory stories being told in the media—far more than at any other time in human history.

What the authors of this book have most in common—and what we hope we share with our readers—is an avowed affection for many of the stories that circulate in the media. We like to watch television; go to movies; listen to music; read newspapers, books, and magazines; and use the Internet for these and other purposes. We appreciate the diversity of content in today's media that ranges from mainstream media narratives on network television to the cornucopia of alternative views available on the

Internet. Each of us can cite media fare we love and, of course, media content we hate. But we think that, on balance, and even with all their flaws, today's media offer us more benefit than harm. We see the promise rather than the doom, and this can sometimes put us at odds with many other knowledgeable media critics.

We remain aware of the many social changes enabled by the printing press and the first mass medium—the book. Literacy, consumer culture, mass production, modern individualism, nationalism, and representative democracy are all aspects of print culture that are now being deepened or refigured in an electronic age. Changes in the technologies of storytelling, as well as changes in the stories we tell, are vital to what we can be and become, individually and collectively. The media really matter, but we need to understand them narratively, we believe, to understand what they are actually up to in our lives.

CURRENT ISSUES IN MEDIA CRITICISM

Both academic and popular media criticism share tendencies. We draw your attention to them here so that you—and we—can be aware of how some media assumptions can be taken for granted, especially in discussions of the current and future effects of the Internet. These tendencies in media criticism need to be recognized so we can make better arguments about the role of media in society.

Media: Single or Multiple?

Some media critics imagine the diverse media in our culture to be a single force, a monolithic entity—"The Media"—capable of enormous impact. Part of this is a grammatical problem. The single form of the Latin term *media* is *medium*, and it is grammatically correct if we refer to one particular medium or different kinds of media. It is technically incorrect to say "The media is . . ." when we mean "The media are. . . ." This mistake in usage reveals a deeper problem—the tendency to imagine "The Media" as a single influential unit, causing problems in society.

For example, in Bloom's *Closing of the American Mind*, the critic used only two examples to stand in for all of rock music—Mick Jagger and Michael Jackson.[5] English professor Alvin Kernan filed a similar complaint in his 1990 book, *The Death of Literature*: "Television is a nervous, continuous collage, always ramshackle, never put together with much care, quickly and soon discarded, . . . produc[ing] not classics but entertainment consumables that seldom have any existence beyond their brief moment on the screen."[6]

It sounds as if Kernan refers to all television programming here; it is difficult to tell from his book since he offers *no* examples for critique, preferring to treat television programs as a singular noun with a single identity. In doing so, Kernan ignores television's rich and complicated history.

Treating media as a single entity makes it easier to identify them as the main cause of key social problems. By transforming a multiplicity into a singular phenomenon, all forms of popular culture are reduced to the same demonizing villain at the heart of any number of controversies: from the Dixie Chicks' 2003 criticism of President Bush's leadership to the enabling of Charlie Sheen's public series of meltdowns in 2011.

When media then are lumped together in a monolith narrative, we are less able to distinguish media work that questions or challenges the dominant stories told about terrorism or Wall Street. Remembering that the media are plural and contradictory helps us explore major media's connections to power and the ways they capitalize on the dramas they construct, whether it be presidential elections, natural disasters, financial collapse, or Kim Kardashian's latest celebrity misadventure. Rather than falling into the media monolith tendency—a recipe for cynicism—we believe that the best media criticism treats media as plural, making careful distinctions among the range of media and contributing to a social conversation in which we help investigate how decisions get made and how power is wielded.

Media: Scapegoat or Mediator?

Some media criticism treats various forms of popular culture as scapegoats for social or political ills. In doing so, the media are blamed for causing what they may only mediate or reflect. For instance, when electronic and visual media are condemned for lowering test scores among college students, critics can ignore possible social and institutional factors like the democratization of college campuses after World War II. Once the media are identified as a cause of a problem, no one needs to explore alternative explanations.

Similarly, when a young middle-school student injures another over a name-brand jacket or pair of sneakers, critics can simply condemn ads that glamourize clothing. If they scapegoat advertising (or the media), they never need to dig deeper to examine consumer-oriented culture and the growing disparity between rich and poor. Ads choose and use narrative themes that "work" in contemporary culture, and from a narrativist perspective, we seek to explore the connection between mediated narrative meanings and larger social ills and patterns.

Scapegoating the media usually leads to a dead end—the media become the imagined cause of all that is wrong in modern life. Instead, we believe that hopes and fears about the media effects should be analyzed as narratives—the stories we tell ourselves about what is going wrong and right in contemporary society. The most valuable thing about media criticism may be what it tells us about what we are really worried about when we blame the media for problems in modern life.

Media: Junk Food or Health Food?

A common paradox that surfaces in media criticism is a deep mistrust of the very same things that are most pleasurable and popular. We spend amazing amounts of time, energy, and money on the mass media, we give them affection and loyalty—yet we may also believe they are harmful to us. On one hand, many condemn the sexual themes in the CW's *Vampire Diaries* or the pointlessness of *Angry Birds*; on the other hand, many of us watch these programs and play digital games each week. Our attraction to media seems at odds with the widespread suspicion of them.

This paradox helps to explain why so many people, including experts, compare the media to drugs or junk food. All of us, of course, look for ways to resolve the contradiction between our desires and our beliefs; a junk-food or drug metaphor can help explain why we spend so much time with media forms that are supposedly bad for us. As individuals, we are deeply attached to certain music, movies, programs, magazines, social network sites, or celebrities, but we may feel uneasy about or embarrassed by the strength of our attachments, as when people refer to particular media products as "guilty pleasures." We "shouldn't" like some media so much, the reasoning goes, because it's not good for us.

How can these connections coexist with such mistrust? One explanation is that our choices and habits (and love/hate relationship with media) result from the limited selection provided to us by the predominant commercial media. So while we like our favorite media, we also complain about a lack of good stories or serious journalism, or new music, or alternative voices that aren't constrained by commercial demands. If only there were more good stuff out there, we say, the public would flock to it. But this belief is less and less plausible as the Internet expands our access to all kind of options and shows us what we actually click on.

Another way to resolve the media mistrust/media affection paradox is to consider that perhaps popular media forms are not automatically bad for us. We may want to acknowledge longstanding public choices for entertaining, escapist, formulaic, sexual, and violent fare, in spite of the equally longstanding critical disdain for popular culture. We might want to explore our own affection for our own choices. Why do we like what we like? Why do other people like what they like?

We may explain our affection by pointing out that the media can be hypnotic, seductive, even addictive. This gets us off the hook, personally; it also gives the social critics, who think that the media are ruining personal and public life, a way out too. However, media mistrust is so widespread that we usually just live with the paradox—liking our own personal choices of media content while deploring general media influences on other people.

Media and the Third-Person Effect

As we investigate our own relationships with the media, we may conclude that years of cartoons, TV ads, and video games haven't hurt us personally. But there persists a worry among both social critics and concerned citizens about the influence of the mass media on *other* people, especially children. This argument notes that today's cartoons, video games, movies, TV shows, and Internet sites are much more graphic and potentially harmful than the ones that older generations grew up with. By this logic, dangerous media influences that today's adults have more or less escaped are still lurking out there for the next generation, more toxic and influential than ever.

Many media commentators extend this line of thinking toward the paradoxical belief that the media are dangerous to others but not to themselves. In fact, formal mass communication research has a documented name for this. Identified as the **third-person effect** in a 1983 study, this phenomenon suggests that people believe others are more affected by media messages than they are themselves.[7] We can consider ourselves safe from the worst effects while still worrying about the younger or less educated or informed who, we fear, take the tabloids seriously, or imitate violent movies, or get addicted to the Internet.

Just as social science discussions in college classrooms often presume the worst effects to be happening to other people, the same is true in media criticism. When some critics describe the ways in which media shape and deform consciousness, they assume that they have somehow managed to escape and "see through" media influences. It seems fair to ask how this is possible, how media critics or "we" escape the effects we worry are hurting "others."

One way to explain how media are bad for others but not for ourselves is to believe that our personal protective shield is forged from intelligence, education, family, or training that otherwise shelters us from the advertising, cartoon violence, or other bad media that so influence others. This logic works for many media critics concerned for the more vulnerable members of a population, making it easy to believe that the media are bad for lots of other people, but okay and actually kind of fun in our own individual cases. But consider whether those "other" people are really so gullible and whether "we" are really so unaffected. If critics believe that media are shaping people in bad ways, they have to explain why other people are more at risk.

Another way to explain the paradox of the third-person effect, and our personal protection from this effect, is to imagine that things are getting rapidly and dramatically worse. But critics have been saying that media are becoming more and more graphic, sexual, violent, and immoral for many generations. Can media content really be getting worse and worse week by week, year by year, since the nineteenth century? Of course, media content of 150 years ago depicted less explicit sexuality and violence, but did this reflect a less sexual, less violent, more moral society—or is

Media can affect different people in different ways, but imagining that it will be harmful to others who are less savvy than yourself is key to the third-person effect.

the worsening of the media just another component of an ongoing story we like to tell about the good old days?

Rather than trap ourselves in this nostalgia narrative, the best media criticism questions, investigates, and interprets the changes that have occurred historically, politically, and economically in order to better understand how capitalism, ratings and audience research, advertising, and profits—in addition to changing personal and social tastes—have systematically altered the cultural landscape.

Media as Stories

One of the criticisms of our narrativist approach is that it focuses too much on particular shows, genres, or stories—on what individual narratives are up to. This can be so fruitful and engaging that we ignore the ideological, institutional, and economic contexts that determine and shape the narratives and us. But if our media criticism skills are honed as they should be (and we are describing, analyzing, interpreting, evaluating, and engaging fully the media we study), this tendency in narrativist media criticism can be tempered. In the chapters that follow, we examine media texts, industries, and issues through a set of questions that aim to identity the main patterns that underlie media and help anchor our narrativist perspective in a larger social, cultural, economic, and political context. Our hope is to connect narrativist perspectives with reflectionist and constructionist concerns.

- Who gets to tell the stories of our culture? (institutional and political analyses)
- What are the goals and objectives in producing our culture's stories? (economic and ideological analyses)
- What is the content of these stories, and how do they represent individuals and communities and give us a common language for understanding our world? (textual/narrative analyses)
- How do these stories influence audiences, and how do audiences interact with these stories? (audience analyses)

TOWARD MEDIA LITERACY

In this book, we focus on what the media are actually doing—telling stories—and what we are actually doing—telling stories about what we think the media are doing. The narrativist approach focuses both on the media as storytellers and on the media as something about which we tell stories.

Concerned citizens and watchdog groups—both liberal and conservative—work toward media reform: everything from promoting Internet software that blocks porn to demanding less strident partisanship on twenty-four-seven cable-news channels. Communication researchers continue to search for convincing social science evidence of media effects or write about how that search will be unsuccessful because of the complexity and multiple variables at play in trying to pin down evidence of media causing actual effects. The public, meanwhile, continues to engage in all kinds of media experiences, with various levels of mistrust, ambivalence . . . and pleasure.

We offer ways to explore the form and content of the media simultaneously: technology and story together. But we also offer ways to uncynically understand the stories that draw us to the media, in whatever technological forms we choose. We want you to learn how to describe, analyze, interpret, evaluate, and then engage—a critical interpretive process that can be applied to particular media content as well as particular stories *about* media content, because the media are always, simultaneously, telling and being told about. And media criticism is how we tell ourselves stories about the roles that the mass media may play in our common life.

Our goal in writing this book is to help you become media literate. Media literacy identifies symptoms and conditions for what really worries us when we worry about modern life. Now that we have a better sense of the nature and traits of media criticism, we can begin to explore how media actually operate and learn how to ask deeper and wiser questions about their role in society.

In developing a media-literate perspective, we are challenged to acquire the critical standards necessary to judge our culture, recognizing the links between cultural expression and daily life and monitoring how well media serve democratic practices. It is important to keep in mind that media criticism is not conducted through a scientific search for laws and rules that govern media but through acts of interpretation that search for how media—and society—create meaning.

A healthy democracy requires the active involvement of its citizens. Part of that involvement means engaging with and watching over media—not always deferring to our elected legislators, paid media critics, watchdog organizations, and the shouting-head pundits on cable. A media-literate critical perspective demands that we think broadly about media: not just in the ways we use them in our own lives but about the ways that the media operate in our community, nation, and world.

CRITICAL PROCESS 1 | Media Autobiography

The goal of this exercise is to explore "how media mean" as well as how to do the critical process. Choose a media-related experience that has been important in your life, one that is interesting enough to you to describe in detail, analyze, and interpret.

Describe [what?]: Choose (from childhood or now) a favorite show, movie, video game, or media-related family ritual—basically any media content or experience that was important to you as a child or now. Describe this so that any reader can understand what it involves.

Analyze [how?]: Go deeper into what was memorable or appealing about your media experience. What made/makes this experience so interesting or important? What was/is it that you learn or gain or enjoy about this particular form?

Interpret [why?]: What does your analysis tell you about yourself, your situation, your role, your life? Go as deep as you can into the meaning that this form has/had for you.

Evaluate [with what consequences?]: What kind of judgments could others make about this media form, and what do you say/feel/believe in response? Do you believe it is valuable and worthwhile? Why or why not?

Engage: [toward what greater ends?]: Given your analysis, interpretation, and evaluation, what can you say about the wider social, political, and cultural value of this particular media form or experience? Does it encourage any kind of public action?

CRITICAL PROCESS 2 | Media-Free Day

The goal of this exercise is to become aware of how much of your life is media-connected. Spend twenty-four hours with as little media as possible. Pick a regular day, but try to eliminate as much media as you can, for as long as you can, even if it's not realistic to go the entire day. If you need to maintain interpersonal contact through your cell phone, for example, limit it to necessary communication rather than entertainment. Try also to avoid the Internet, iPods, video games, TV, radio, magazines, newspapers, movies, or even books. Just spend a day (or even four or five hours) without print, electronic, and digital influences for as long as possible.

Describe [what?]: How long were you able to last without media, and what happened to you during this period?

Analyze [how?]: What was the same and what was different about this day? What patterns stayed the same? What was disrupted?

Interpret [why?]: What does this tell you about the various roles that the media play in your life? What can you now say about these roles?

Evaluate [with what consequences?]: What do your analysis and interpretation tell you about how media work in your life? Should you think about changing your media use to reflect your experience during the media-free day?

Engage [toward what greater ends?]: Are there things you learned from this experience that make you want to help other people understand and act differently in relation to their media use?

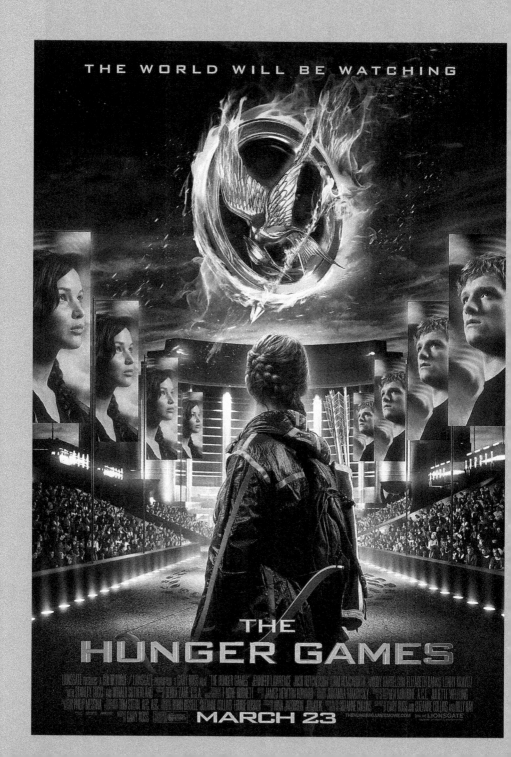

2

Media Metaphors

To understand the complex ways media work in society, we can look at media not just as narrative structures (the ways our culture tells stories) but also as something we tell stories about. In this chapter, we directly explore the stories we tell about the media—in our everyday life, as well as through academic inquiry. When we analyze how we tell stories about the media, we are exploring how we use the media as metaphors.

Often, when we tell stories about the media, we use them as stand-ins for all that worries us about modern life. We think we are talking about the media, but we are really talking about the larger contemporary experience. Accordingly, the first section of this chapter explores how we understand the media as a metaphor for modernity. These "big picture" concerns are organized around our themes of democracy, capitalism, and technology.

But we also use metaphors to understand how media influences us. We imagine them as outside forces that invade, persuade, impose, distract, and demean us, while we also believe they could educate, respond, enrich, and enliven us. We metaphorically imagine the media as "bad company." The second portion of this chapter explores some of these "influence" metaphors: the ways we can imagine and tell ourselves stories about the media as forms of invasion, information, propaganda, commerce, distraction, education, and art.

Why spend a chapter talking about the metaphors we use to talk and think about the media? In the influential 1980 book *Metaphors We Live By*, linguists George Lakoff and Mark Johnson show how metaphors don't just "describe or reflect reality" but actually construct it.[1] Metaphors aren't just figures of speech; rather, they work at a deeper conceptual level, central to how various cultures assign meaning. As Lakoff and Johnson argue: "Since much of our social reality is understood in metaphorical terms, and since our conception of the physical world is partly metaphorical, metaphor plays a significant role in determining what is real for us."[2] By focusing on metaphors, we can explore what kind of "reality" we construct when we treat the media as a metaphor for modern life and when we treat the media as particular kinds of influence. What stories are we telling ourselves about the media, and with what consequences?

27

MEDIA AS CURRENT EXPERIENCE

Critiques of media tend to deal with larger issues of society. Media become metaphoric stand-ins for submerged, perhaps even unconscious concerns about where we are headed as a social collective. For both everyday people and academic types, making claims about media influence becomes a way to express hopes and fears about what has been lost, what is happening now, what may happen in the future.

The problem with this kind of metaphoric thinking, as we suggested in Chapter 1, is that the media often become misidentified as the cause of everything that is wrong in today's world; the media become scapegoats for modernity.[3] This means we call for media to change, hoping that if we change the media we can change the world. A better understanding of media metaphors can help us correctly identify which social, political, economic, and cultural changes we hope for, and figure out more effective ways to support and foster them.

One advantage of analyzing this habit of mistaking media for the contemporary experience is that we can use media criticism to access our collective conversation about what we think is wrong and right about our current life and collective experience. We can explore what our claims about the media can tell us about the complexities of democracy, the influences of capitalism, the risks of totalitarianism, and the costs of technological progress. By applying elements of description, analysis, interpretation, evaluation, and engagement to the metaphor of media as modern life, we can bring these deeper concerns to the surface.

The Complexity of Democracy

It is easy to forget that democracy remains a daring, rather new experiment. Letting ordinary people govern—people without special training, wealth, or inherited position—was a radical step in the eighteenth century, and it remains a radical perspective in global society. Participatory democracy goes against centuries of assumptions about the need for specially trained and influential elites to run society. Democracy also goes against centuries of elite mistrust of those less wealthy, educated, and sophisticated than themselves, often connected to centuries of monarchy, religious orthodoxy, or colonial rule.

Most people, even staunch egalitarian types, seek reassurance that "the people" truly have the wisdom and skills to guide society. The worry that the masses are far too easy to mislead is persistent, and some look to institutions like education, the arts, and news media to help make the public reliable enough to self-govern. Schools are institutions designed to turn children into good citizens, arts are created to uplift and refine us as good citizens, and journalism is designed to educate and inform us as good citizens.

Journalism especially plays a pivotal role in our faith in modern democracy. In the twentieth century, journalists as well as social commentators emphasized the vital role of the nonpartisan press in keeping government accountable to the citizenry, and in creating and sustaining a unified and informed public. The ideal of the mainstream press was to offer relatively neutral information so that—it was hoped—citizens could make wise political and social decisions. If the people know what their elected representatives are doing, as well as what is going on in the world, then they have the information they need to make democracy function well. What the public deserves, from narrativist, constructionist, and reflectionist perspectives, is relevant information packaged in news stories and presented as clearly, fully, and fairly as possible.

As such, concerns about censorship are constant and intractable. Freedom of the press and freedom of speech were imagined by the founders of democracy as ways to ensure that all citizens have insider knowledge and the ability to freely form and express opinions. This guaranteed, for them, the possibility of rational self-government. When there are social movements to curtail a free press or free speech—in the name of decency, morality, national security, or profit—alarms go off, signaling questions about whether these movements attempt to undermine democracy by directing us toward a more repressive, less representative, more secretive, more authoritarian, or less tolerant social order.

This is also why charges of press bias, from the right and from the left, are of such concern. Conventional wisdom suggests that if journalism is slanted toward particular political parties, ideological perspectives, or interest groups, then citizens don't have the full range of information they need to become rational, self-governing citizens. When mainstream journalism is dismissed as liberal or conservative or capitalist propaganda, and more partisan sources are believed instead, the populace becomes mistrustful and polarized. If that keeps happening—as it has during the recent conversations about wealth disparity between rich and poor, health care, national debt, and other issues—some fear we will be less able to engage in the kinds of rational public discourse that social theorists believe to be the cornerstone of the democratic experiment.

As these fears linger, the role of the press continues to change. Since the 1700s, dominant forms of journalism have shifted from announcements of commercial interest, to partisan accounts of political parties, to stories of urban life, to more professional, dispassionate models of information sharing, to twenty-four-hour cable news and Internet blogs that provide, on demand, information, stories, and partisan confrontation. But there is nothing intrinsic to news that says it must be objective and must foster rational decisions, or even that it should cover politics and world events.

After objectivity became an ideal for U.S. journalistic practice in the twentieth century, though, we came to expect journalism to be more scientific—that is, neutral and value free. But that expectation is a cultural construction and a function of journalism trying to ride the coattails of the prestige of twentieth-century science.

Today, when news media are castigated for their many inadequacies—including their failure to be objective (even though all journalism is selective in its storytelling and certainly not a science)—the deeper fear is that they aren't doing what they need to do to make everyone into informed, educated, and discerning citizens. Rather than simply blaming media for failing to provide that service, we could and should explore what kind of media form and content we actually need to become effective citizens in a democracy.

We don't often think of that democracy as fragile, nor do we usually think of tyranny as a genuine threat. But at least since World War II, there has been an ongoing fear in the United States that democracy would give way to some form of authoritarian rule. With U.S. troops still stationed in Iraq, our post-9/11 world, and global economic crises, we are increasingly aware that not everyone sees our way of life as ideal, or desirable, or trustworthy.

The fear is that a rigid, rule-bound, authoritarian regime—using media as a tool to control its messages—will find a way to replace or threaten our current relatively free, relatively improvised, relatively egalitarian system. In general, critics from the left and the right share this concern about the rise of totalitarian rule. While it is often obvious when a tyrant tries to take over by force or with threats or terror, it is also possible for us to elect our own tyrants, as the Frankfurt School scholars who fled Nazi Germany reminded us in the mid-twentieth century. To some, the media in the hands of either Evil Government or Big Business seem to increase the risk of a totalitarian state: They can be used by tyrants and elites to brainwash us because they can inflame our passions, satisfy our desires, and dull our reason. On the other hand, more centrist critics argue that—using the Occupy Wall Street movement or the Arab Spring uprisings as examples—the Internet is such a decentralized (and disorganized) communication system that it is harder and harder for business or government to control content on Twitter, Facebook, and independent blogs. Even so, fears remain: The media can theoretically distract us with entertainment to the point of not noticing democracy, freedom, or autonomy dissolving under our feet. In popular culture, the Hunger Games trilogy, for example, reflects this fear that entertainment will turn into a cruel distraction, manipulated by sinister forces. As Aldous Huxley warned earlier in *Brave New World*, we can be willingly seduced into submission. Even with the new decentralized digital landscape, then, the demise of democracies still seems possible. The fear is that we, as citizens, are letting media sap our powers of discrimination. These are powerful and persuasive arguments in their own right, and we will examine them in some detail later in this chapter.

The Influence of Capitalism

Critiques of capitalism, as an economic and social system, abound. These criticisms come not just from alternative systems, like communism or socialism, but also from people who support democracy. The link between capitalism and democracy is tricky: One is an economic system and the other a political system, and there can be capitalist monarchies and socialist democracies. Yet often in public discourse, capitalism and democracy are fused and confused, treated as if they are synonyms. It is possible to be deeply committed to individualism, self-government, and democracy, but feel that an unregulated free-market economy leads to and supports inequity and injustice. Capitalism has been criticized, especially in the wake of the 2008–09 economic crisis and its enduring fallout, for fostering self-absorbed individualism, rampant greed, and amoral acquisition, as well as economic and social inequality. But it has also been praised for its ability to foster a strong work ethic and produce capital that supports volunteerism, philanthropy, and projects that could not be sustained by purely market-driven profit goals.

For constructionist critics of capitalism, media are extensions of the economic system. They are ideological tools that tie us ever closer to capitalism, in the guise of merely informing or entertaining us. Constructionist critics might argue that, while we are reading the news, listening to music, or watching a movie or TV show, we are actually functioning as unreflective dupes for the captains of capital and their corporate greed.

These arguments are not unsupported; well before the most recent recession, the media naturalized consumption of consumer goods. Consumerism permeated print and electronic media forms throughout much of the twentieth century. After all, given all our choices in the plentiful marketplace, commonsense wisdom says who would ever want another system? In general, the media made it seem that consumption was the only option—simple, easy, accessible . . . and natural. Media do this both in their forms and in their content. Media forms have mimicked the allegedly free market, which critics of capitalism argue is in actuality a limited selection of things that those in power want to offer us. In other words, although we appear to have lots of choices, we do not directly participate in determining what those choices and goods will be. Nor do we easily imagine the possibilities of not consuming them.

In addition, mainstream media content usually has not challenged this naturalized status quo but has instead offered us repetitive messages about how we can solve most of our everyday problems through product consumption. In this way, media offer us the cure for the disease that they themselves help to foster, especially through the ubiquity of advertising. The mainstream media offer us an illusory way out of the bind that capitalism causes. We are dependent on an economic system that seduces us with commercialism, and we can't imagine alternatives since capitalism—as the natural state of the economy—seems like the only option.

Marxist and Marxist-influenced critics want us to learn how to see through mediated ideology and recognize the underlying economic mechanisms that are structuring our society. They write to wake us up. They hope that their criticism can raise our consciousness and help us free ourselves from media domination, or hegemony (see Chapter 4), that serves the interests of the powerful rather than the powerless. At the very least, these critics hope to prove to us that the media are instruments of mass persuasion that keep us from questioning the flaws in capitalism.

From this perspective, mainstream media, along with the state and large corporations, convince us to participate in our own oppression and subordination to powerful interests. We may think we are truly free, and freely choosing, but we are not. Sometimes these concerns move beyond Marxist media criticism: The global economic recession that began in late 2008 undermined faith in the self-regulated capitalist system. News media became more critical of capitalism, and many stories have emerged, even in mainstream media, to help explain why companies went under, why people lost their jobs, how global markets failed, and why wealthy CEOs still got bonuses even after their banks received government bailouts.

We need to explore these important underlying issues about links among capitalism, ideology, and power rather than just blaming the media. Again, the metaphor of media as stand-in for the problems of contemporary society can lead us to believe that changing the media will solve all of our problems. Once we understand this misplaced metaphor, however, media criticism can help us describe, analyze, interpret, and evaluate our current economic, political, and cultural conditions in order to engage more effectively in improving them.

The Costs of Technology and Progress

The media, especially when regarded as new technologies, are heir to both hopes and fears. Embedded in these hopes and fears are deeper concerns about the inevitable costs of progress. Modern technologies must offer us something we want, or they wouldn't become part of our lives. Most often they offer some combination of ease, comfort, pleasure, and efficiency—but many would agree that there is also a cost. The smart phone, for example, lets us talk to distant loved ones, but it keeps interrupting us, even as we go to our classes or to our offices—we are rarely free from social network notifications, e-mails, or calls and texts from those who have our number. The automobile gives us mobility and freedom, but we could also say that it has replaced inner city residences with tangled concrete freeways, fostered the rise of safe suburbs as escapes from city problems, spurred the growth of ugly strip malls, and killed the potential for robust public transportation systems in most U.S. cities. Finally, radio, television, and the Internet have brought entertainment into our homes, but they may have also led to a decline in reading, physical exercise, family dinner conversation, shared hobbies, and porch sitting with neighbors.

The story of progress, then, is frequently told as a story of loss—the loss of a world that seemed simpler, kinder, and somehow more authentic. This lost past may be described as less rushed, more personable, and more communal. Even if that is true, however, perhaps the past had its own pitfalls. As Stephanie Coontz documents about our impressions of the 1950s, much of what we imagine to be true of "back then" is bunk. Nostalgia paints the past in a rosy glow, and it is easy to attribute to it all the things we wish were true in the present. But Americans have been complaining about hectic, unfair, impersonal "modern" life and longing for the worlds of their forebears since at least the 1830s.[4]

Much has of course changed in modernity, including the media. Modernization is an ongoing process that is mediated, but the media are neither the cause nor the cure for whatever we think is wrong with modern life. But because we so often, and so easily, displace our concerns about contemporary life onto the media, the metaphor of media as contemporary experience can illuminate what we are actually worrying about when we worry about the influence of media in society.

As we discuss in the final section of this chapter, the media metaphor we find most useful is to imagine the media as narrators—narrators that themselves can grow and change, even as they narrate social, cultural, political, and economic changes. By telling us stories about how the world was, is, and could be, they narrate the stories that we as citizens construct. This means, in short, that the media are, in a sense, us: They don't simply influence or reflect our society but participate in it and change along with the rest of us. In a broad sense, this change is difficult to resist; it's a part of society. But as we describe in the next section, much media criticism uses other metaphors that imply that the media are outside influences, forces, and agitators that can and should be resisted.

MEDIA INFLUENCE METAPHORS

Media serve us as stand-ins for our deeper concerns, and we can explore the more specific concerns that we project onto the media. The key metaphors that we address here include:

- Media as interloper
- Media as information
- Media as propaganda
- Media as commerce
- Media as distraction
- Media as curriculum
- Media as art

It is important to remember this cautionary tale from Lakoff and Johnson: "the metaphor highlights certain features while suppressing others."[5] Each of these media metaphors provides an angle of vision—a way of looking at the media that fosters particular aspects, questions, and concerns but suppresses others. They are not necessarily wrong or right, but each one is a lens that both highlights and suppresses. And in doing so, they may miss or misrepresent the narrative, mediating role of media in society.

Once we understand these various angles of vision, we can spot them in media analyses and everyday conversations, as well as figure out which ones are most limiting or deceptive, or most useful or accurate. The reason for these multiple metaphors has much to do with how complex media actually are—and metaphors provide us with ways of creating some categories of understanding that help make sense of complexity. But we hope that, in becoming media critics and scholars, we all learn to recognize and evaluate the often invisible metaphors being used to understand the media.

Media as Interloper

Media are easy to imagine as outside forces. They are perceived by critics and citizens as interlopers, influences that come into our culture from "out there" to shape our lives. For example, during the 2008 and 2012 presidential elections, many campaign strategists invoked "Hollywood" (meaning violent or sexually charged TV shows and movies) or "East Coast elite media" (meaning news people hopelessly out of touch with small-town virtues) as metaphors for aberrant values that stand in opposition to the "moral values" of decent, hardworking folks everywhere. When we imagine the media as interlopers, we are suggesting that if the alien media would just disappear, we'd all be better off.

Because the media are commercially based, technologically connected, and mass produced and consumed, they can seem to come from some unidentified place outside of our own communities and culture. Especially for older generations, newer media like the DVD, the DVR, the iPod, and Twitter can feel crucially different from the stories and songs of a predigital era, feeling less natural or real. But in the premedia and premodern age, local cultures were often shaped by trade routes, invasions, travelers—outsiders, in other words—and culture has always had a technical component, be it paintbrush, stylus, printing press, or hard drive. Just because something originates elsewhere and is technologically sophisticated, does not make it alien or inhuman.

Similarly, people can form deep personal connections to particular performers, songs, movies, and games, even if they are designed by technologically advanced for-profit companies. A contemporary songwriter and artist like Adele, who started out as an eighteen-year-old MySpace phenom, became wildly popular internationally through a recording deal with an indie label, Beggars Group, which helped her music reach much larger audiences, many of whom connect intimately with her stories and very personal lyrics. Even if alternative forms of media are passionately designed primarily to express deep personal feeling, they can later be exploited and commercialized. For example, music that sounds like it was recorded live by a teenage band in their parents' garage can become co-opted later by corporate music labels or international advertising campaigns and transformed into a genre called "garage rock." Still, people can connect with music on a personal level, despite the commercial process, complicating the notion that for-profit co-option is always somehow sinister.

Singer/song-writer Adele became a worldwide star through a combination of intimate, personal songs and a global marketing campaign. Her album *21* was the best-selling album in the United States for both 2011 and 2012.

Media are also metaphorically imagined as interlopers through fears about new and changing technology. Historically, with the emergence of each new media form, anecdotes and tales emerge to support these fears of technology—from cheap dime novels corrupting the newly literate working classes in the nineteenth century to Saturday morning cartoons seducing our children in the twentieth century. Then the next new twenty-first-century media forms—such as Internet social networks exposing our teenagers to predators—make dime novels and network cartoons seem quaint and even benign.

Fears of the newest technology, then, will eventually fade, and technology may eventually be seen as contributing to positive change. The revolution in satellite transmission and home computing, in combination with the development of the Internet, has made it possible for individuals to sift through vast stores of information, write each other, join support groups, make and distribute movies and albums, create and download personalized digests, access alternative news sources, and much more. All of these options were developed in connection with enthusiastic new users who chose to participate. There was no invasion that imposed this new technology on an unwilling and unwitting public.

As a new communication technology and our newest mass medium, the Internet—compared to books or newspapers—may be faster, more interactive, easier, more fun, and more efficient than library research, reading newspapers, shopping via catalog, writing letters, and using the personals column in newspapers to get a date. However, issues related to privacy, government surveillance, pornography, blocking software, and other invasive outcomes are particular to new technologies and require careful scrutiny. Rather than fear or blame the Internet for the same influences we have worried about for generations, though, the best forms of criticism will instead examine the range of consequences and influences that have arisen from new media. This can include noticing how, when, and why we tell stories that cast new technologies as alien invaders. We can then ask how the Internet is changing the ways we tell stories to each other. Then we will be much better able to explore the consequences—good, bad, and indifferent—of those changes.

Media as Information

When we talk about media in terms of journalism, we are imagining the media as agents of information. We usually mean the news media here, not all media, acknowledging that the *New York Times* is not the same thing as *World of Warcraft*. This kind of criticism and conversation imagines news media as primarily information purveyors addressing us as interested citizens. Much of the time, though, we accuse media of being biased in a variety of ways, of being sensationalistic, of being shallow by focusing more on image than on substance.

News, as a form of culture, has been invented and reinvented. It has a history that can be studied. With the growth of various forms of new media and despite the decline of traditional newspapers, more information outlets exist than ever before. We might ask what role the emerging news media are playing in providing information we need as citizens of a democracy. We might also question the apparent increase in punditry and partisanship in media, especially on cable news and on the Internet. Ideally, answers would include investigating the cultural, economic, and professional constraints that news media practitioners face, the kinds of stories they tell and how these have changed over time. We can also examine the technological shifts that have influenced reporting and storytelling, as well as the economic developments that have destabilized the ground upon which the news media operate.

What we now have, in news and other forms of information, is not the ideal, dispassionate, rational, objective data that many critics and citizens seemed to want throughout the twentieth century. But to blame media as inadequate and biased information purveyors is to imagine them as faulty data conduits and to compare them to a nonexistent past when news was somehow "pure." As media sociologist Michael Schudson has noted in telling the story of journalistic values:

> Objectivity is a peculiar demand to make of institutions which, as business corporations, are dedicated first of all to economic survival. It is a peculiar demand to make of institutions which often . . . are political organs. It is a peculiar demand to make of editors and reporters who have none of the professional apparatus which, for doctors or lawyers or scientists, is supposed to guarantee objectivity.[6]

This science-like information metaphor assumes that free-flowing idealized information would somehow make the world a better place, but it also forecloses discussion on the news media's role as cultural storytellers. Audiences, after all, experience the news primarily as selected and constructed stories, not as neutral data. But if the news media are storytellers first, then it is up to us not only to demand better stories but to help create the stories we think need to be told, and the participatory structure of the Internet makes this more possible.

Beyond these important individual concerns, it is crucial to consider economic constraints and technological changes that shape the news media role as information conduits. For example, various news media outlets have changed the size of their operations over the past decade. In the past ten to twenty years, major newspapers have gone under, and newsrooms have cut staff to the bare bones. In 2009, the *Seattle Post-Intelligencer* and *Ann Arbor News* both became predominantly online papers. Online journalism is growing rapidly, but it is still unclear how well it will be funded, how carefully it will be edited, and how effectively it will harness and reward the energies and talents of journalists. If storytelling is what the media do, and journalism is in major transition, who will be telling the stories, for what purposes, to which audiences, with what effects?

Using a refurbished "media as information" metaphor, we could even make an argument that today's news environment is extremely rich, subtle, and compelling, more democratically accessible than ever before. Such a case would involve comparing this environment with previous eras, and recognizing the improvement, over time, in the public's access to all kinds of information—mainstream and alternative, serious and humorous, edited and unedited—told in a variety of narrative forms, including news. It would also involve examining various economic constraints that reshaped traditional news and technological innovations like the Internet that have befuddled and challenged the old news business. After all, more people read news produced by newspaper outlets at any time in U.S. history, but many are reading these news stories online—for free—with audiences delivered to newspapers' online sites by aggregators like Google.

Media as Propaganda

In ideological terms, if we consider some news media as propaganda serving society's elites by selectively reporting their interests, then we should also consider how other media help us become more aware of—and less vulnerable to—the various modes of persuasion in our lives. As such, another angle of vision on the media—another metaphor—has been to construct them as transmitters of persuasive messages. This is especially true of media criticism that has focused on the negative influences of advertising and public relations. For many from this perspective, living in a media-rich world means that we are being bombarded with persuasion, awash in material designed to convince us of something we might not otherwise believe or need.

From this persuasion perspective, we are constantly preyed upon by unscrupulous message senders. The widespread belief in, and fear of, hidden messages is linked to this metaphor. A classic 1950s account of "subliminal seduction" is Vance Packard's *The Hidden Persuaders*. More contemporary influential visual documentary versions include Jean Kilbourne's *Killing Us Softly* series about gender representation in advertising and Sut Jhally's *Dreamworlds* about sex, power, and gender in music videos. For these critics, media appeal to our darkest impulses, getting us to do their bidding. This perspective maintains that the media are able to semi-hypnotize us and appeal to us on an unconscious level, as sociologist Stuart Ewen argues in the widely circulated 1990s educational documentary *The Ad and the Ego*.

For all the billions of dollars spent on ads, it's difficult to fully determine whether they make people do things they don't already want or plan to do. As media economists point out, only about 10 to 15 percent of new products succeed in the marketplace in any given year—and this includes new TV programs, songs, and movies as well as new sodas, cereals, or deodorants. It's one of the more surprising elements in some media criticism and among the general public: how much stock we put in the enormous persuasive power of advertising. Michael Schudson argues in his book *Advertising: The Uneasy Persuasion*, "Advertising is much less powerful than advertisers and critics of advertising claim, and advertising agencies are stabbing in the dark much more than they are practicing precision microsurgery on the public consciousness."[7]

When we reduce media to a propaganda metaphor, we miss other cultural, institutional, and personal influences that explain advertising's ubiquity and storytelling function. After all, advertisers, like journalists, create narratives, which are powerful when combined with political and economic imperatives. This kind of narrative analysis helps us understand how advertising tells the story that happiness and success (not to mention good grooming) comes from consuming products. The best forms of criticism explore how advertising tells us convincing and unconvincing stories about ourselves and our world.

In balancing a continuum of views that run from advertising as powerful propaganda to an industry position that regards ads as mostly benign—and central to capitalist enterprise—what are the counterarguments and alternative questions? We could argue that living in an ad-saturated age makes us more skeptical and less gullible to all forms of persuasion—better citizens, ultimately, because we know how to see through spin. Today's media-savvy audiences are aware, when confronted with elaborate and subtle ad campaigns, that "they just want our money," or that "they just want our vote."

To promote the best in media criticism, we suggest studying media narratives related to purchasing products through advertisements across annual ad campaigns, not just on a one-by-one basis, to explore the patterns that emerge across advertisements in different historical periods. With political campaigns, a narrative approach could also include questioning the types of stories told (negative or positive) in political ads, how television and other forms of media alter our understandings of politics, on what basis voters make their choices about the candidates they select, and how the media's use of polls and sensationalism become storytelling devices that affect elections.

If we compare today's advertising to the belief systems of people born in premodern, preindustrial times, ads do seem like a fairly benign, even weak, form of persuasion. In premodern times (and in many fundamentalist nations or communities today), people didn't have much choice over what to believe because they were born into a single, monolithic perspective—a feudal hierarchy, a religious indoctrination, a clan or tribal system—that dictated "the way things are and always must be." While some might argue that we should return to those times of unquestioning faith in whatever tradition we were handed at birth, others believe in the more modern and cosmopolitan possibility of searching for our values, choosing our commitments, and finding our faiths. It is important to stress that this doesn't mean that we are impervious to advertising's ability to privilege capitalism over other economic systems, such as socialism, or that we don't come to accept certain world views over others as families might have done in monolithic cultures. This is where a study of power is crucial. A good critical approach allows us to examine changes in society and to explore the storytelling qualities and power of media ads and Public Relations as influential social forces.

Another alternative angle to the propaganda metaphor might be to focus on the ways in which overt persuasive techniques are more widely available in contemporary life—that the "good guys" (e.g., nonprofit organizations, grassroots movements) can use advertising too. In this way, media offer us an ongoing persuasive context that trains us by example to be savvy—albeit skeptical—participants rather than passive onlookers. The media not only offer us varieties of persuasive encounters, but they also give us access to the very processes of persuasion being used on us.

So, rather than seeing the media as propaganda, we can explore how the media help us feel like insiders, privy to the persuasive ploys being used. The key point here is that deploying a narrow type of propaganda metaphor as the main way to understand media limits what we can ask in the critical process.

Media as Commerce

This metaphor sees the media as extensions of the marketplace, penetrating our homes just to sell us products, addressing us only as consumers and not as citizens. That this is bad is taken for granted; why this is taken for granted is less clear.

"Commercial" is often employed as an epithet; the assumption is that economic ties—being impersonal, individualistic, and institutional—are less valuable and worthy than ties of the personal, the sentimental, or the traditional, which are imagined as being more intimate or communal. Many critics fear that, as we transform into consumers, we become more individualistic and less social, more shallow and less humane. This critique of consumer culture often suggests that, in today's media environment, we are being trained to think mainly of buying and selling, of acquiring more for ourselves, with little thought of such things as the public good, long-term outcomes, or traditional customs.

The media are without a doubt commercially motivated. But an alternative angle on this metaphor is that the consumer orientation of corporations also makes them responsive to us. By trying to sell us on themselves, the media must offer us content that we actually want; the marketplace is impersonal, but it is also designed to please. After all, many of us who are critical of the commercialization of culture still buy numerous products and expect our capitalist system to provide us with an array of choices. While we may be critical of the choices we have, the lack of imagination in product (or story) innovation, or the disparity in wealth that consumer culture has wrought, a connection exists between societies that have relatively open consumer marketplaces and those with open spaces and outlets for circulating diverse ideas and viewpoints.

The market's potential impersonality is also its freedom and its accessibility. Under capitalism, for example, race, class, gender, nationality, and religion don't matter so much to corporations, as long as people are buying products. We can choose not to buy—to say no to the system—far more easily than we can choose not to believe political, social, or religious doctrine, or pay taxes to a monarch, or do what our family demands. In what Karl Marx termed the "cash nexus," purchasing power becomes more important than race, class, gender, and so on. Unfortunately, things like character, integrity, and loyalty become less important too, and many of us rightly worry about the shallow values and amoral self-interest that capitalism—and consumer culture in general—can foster.

One danger of media-as-commerce is the threat of monopolies. But, in fact, this is technically inaccurate since most of our traditional commercial media are organized not as monopolies but as oligopolies (see Chapter 7 on media economics). That means that a single company like Sony or Disney does not dominate particular industries like music or movies, but usually competes with a handful of other giant media companies, like Viacom and News Corp. Fears of media monopoly are fueled by media stories of corporate mergers and the ways in which news and entertainment industries have reorganized themselves in recent decades so just a few major companies compete with each other. Given that a handful of companies do control much of the production, distribution, and exhibition of media, these companies can often set—or even fix—prices (as in the case of the music industry and CDs). They can also limit the range of what kinds of stories get told, music gets played, movies get shown, and information gets reported.

Still, many major media mergers (e.g., AOL–Time Warner, *Chicago Tribune–Los Angeles Times*) have not worked out—and most new commercial media products introduced every year actually fail. This happens to new TV programs, new music, new movies, and new books, which often do not make up the costs of their production and distribution in spite of wide promotion and distribution. Interestingly, given this commercial system, innovation, diversity, and fragmentation still exist in the marketplace. And the Internet, with user-created content like YouTube, eludes (for now) corporate control under an oligopoly structure.

Because so many new ideas and products do fail, the commercial media must generate a lot of new products to try to see which ones will catch on with consumers. Those in charge of the media are mainly trying to make money by telling stories; the media are as much servants of, as they are creators of, the complex, diverse, contradictory desires of the populace. This means that ownership doesn't dictatorially control content—at least not in a corporate, capitalist society. For example, J. K. Rowling's *Harry Potter* series was rejected by more than twenty publishers before the then tiny Scholastic—the publisher of *Weekly Reader*—took on the project and became one of the world's top publishing houses as the *Harry Potter* books went on to outsell every other book in history except the accumulated versions of the Bible. One of the more curious aspects of capitalism (which also helps explain its ability to adapt) is that it survives by producing what consumers want—even if what they want is a critique of capitalism itself. *The Simpsons*, for example, one of the longest-running shows in prime-time TV history, frequently satirizes its corporate owner Fox. The mainstream system seems happy to circulate and promote movies, music, books, and magazines about the evils of the current system, as long as they make money selling those views. Outside that mainstream, there are also alternative sources for stories and information—independent, underground, and partisan sources and now fully accessible to anyone on the Internet—that express nonmainstream views, views that question corporate culture.

The *Simpsons* entered its twenty-fifth season in fall 2013 and has logged countless jokes about its corporate owner, Twentieth Century Fox, along the way: The show has mocked the Fox Network that airs it in addition to Fox News and movies from Fox's studio.

Further exploration of the media-as-commerce metaphor should examine commercial issues across various media and their different funding mechanisms. If we're talking about mainstream, for-profit media, these outlets do not necessarily always provide us with what we want but instead with products that are profitable, cheap, or pleasing to advertisers. For example, the rise in violent media portrayals in movies or video games may be a result of global marketing imperatives that make violent representations cheaper to produce and easier to translate across markets. Programs like *The Simpsons* or *The Daily Show* that provide a critique of powerful corporate or political interests may not survive if they can't demonstrate that they reach a desirable audience and, as such, maintain commercial sponsorship. As media-literate consumers, then, we must decide whether the media really do construct us as consumers and, if so, to decide if being a consumer hurts or helps us as we attempt to be better people and democratic citizens.

Media as Distraction

Many of us experience media as a form of escape—as a good way to spend our leisure time. When we watch TV, play video games, listen to music, go to the movies, read comic books, and look around online, we often think of ourselves as relaxing or taking a break. But to some critics, and maybe even to ourselves, relaxation becomes something darker—"vegging out," growing into couch potatoes, wasting time, and generally failing to contribute to the greater good. Is it okay to zone out and escape into our favorite media, or are we spending too much time watching TV, shopping online, playing video games, or tracking friends on Facebook.

This metaphor of media as distraction, whether it comes from scholars, teachers, or parents, usually begins by quoting statistics or authorities about how much of our waking hours we spend watching TV, surfing the Internet, or playing computer games. This metaphor invites alternatives: Let's spend our leisure time doing something more productive—out in nature, or with art, or in the service of others. It implicitly prescribes idealized alternative ways to spend our time—attending a ballet or concerts, exploring nature, exercising, or helping the less fortunate. Under this distraction metaphor, the media are imagined as luring us away from worthwhile ways to spend our leisure hours.

But this metaphor sets up a dichotomy between popular media—considered trivial— and refined culture—considered worthy of our leisure pursuit. This runs the risk of creating a false or limited choice between "good" culture and "bad" media. This metaphor also implies that it is not possible to enjoy media while also analyzing and questioning it. Instead, we can ask what we are up to when we spend time with our favorite cultural forms. Maybe we don't totally zone out when we escape into entertainment but instead use the media to refresh or restore ourselves, to listen, watch, or make stories that give meaning and routine to our lives.

For example, a parent and child may watch *Project Runway* or a football game together, or might bowl or golf with the latest version of Wii. Some families might make fun of contestants on *American Idol* on Fox or follow the adventures of *The Mentalist* on CBS. Other families might share reading Harry Potter or Hunger Games novels. Because few complain about how much time kids spend in school (often, as we know, a traumatic experience), or people spend practicing musical instruments, or professors spend reading books, characterizing all media as a distraction is pretty clearly not about media use, per se, but about the alleged quality and value of what we spend our time on; it relies on unexamined assumptions about what constitutes a "right use" of our time.

To become media critics in the best sense of the word, we do need to recognize the broad spectrum of media in the culture competing for our attention. We can enjoy favorite media at the same time as we engage it as critics. We do this all the time when we evaluate the lyrics of a new pop song, consider a performance on YouTube, criticize an updated version of a favorite video game, or talk back to the opinions of a cable news commentator. When we use the media-as-distraction metaphor, we are adopting a modern belief about the difference between work and leisure. In this familiar dichotomy, work and an accompanying work ethic are associated with being productive members of society, while leisure is typically associated with escape or laziness.

Another critical angle on media-as-distraction goes so far as to argue that our modern "play" is harming us—it is turning us into passive, gullible people. This powerful line of thinking, represented best in Adorno and Horkheimer's *Dialectic of the Enlightenment* (1947), argues that escapist leisure available in formulaic media is what keeps us numb to the conditions of our own oppression, willing to continue to work for, and support, a social system that exploits our needs—using media to keep the whole thing going, unquestioned. Adorno and Horkheimer viewed mid-twentieth-century culture industries as obstacles to genuine critical reflection by filling the social landscape with diversions and distractions, by creating false needs and satisfying them through product consumption.

This important critique, originating in Marxist theory, is a constructionist perspective, suggesting that most of us are being harmed by the very media that give us pleasure. To question how individuals and society spend time is important, but perhaps we can't automatically assume that the time others spend with stuff we don't like or understand is wasted time for the people who choose it.

To condemn the media for turning others into passive blobs misses the complex ways in which work and leisure have been redefined in modern life and the ways in which we reduce options to a binary choice—productive or unproductive. In the best forms of criticism, we should question the ways in which our time is being spent overall—at work and at play—and then sort out whether the media are enhancing or harming our ability to spend time wisely and well.

Media as Curriculum

Many critics talk about the media as a dysfunctional learning environment, in competition with the schools to socialize us into the world and train us as valuable citizens, centering on the question of what the media are teaching our children. Constructionist criticism sometimes sees the media as inadequate forms of cultivation, misshaping the cognitive and emotional environment of all of us, but particularly children. Reflectionist criticism addresses the ways that reality is represented, especially on television. When the TV world does not match certain numbers in the real world, in terms of violent incidents, sexual content, and racial, gender, and class balance, the media are faulted. From this media-as-curriculum perspective, media promote inadequate socialization because they offer inadequate mirrors of society.

But while allowing that the media cultivate and socialize us in these ways (and surely we live in a world that includes but is not only made of mediated stories), we can also point out that never before have so many people had access to so many different—and contradictory—assessments of the world. It may not be a perfect reflection, but maybe no "single" true story about the world exists. Maybe the world is best represented by many plausible, fanciful, accurate, inadequate, valuable, and goofy stories. The sheer variety of stories and experiences that contemporary media tell run the gamut from the trivial to the sublime. The best media criticism teases out the differences, remaining conscious of the nuances of meaning, the multiplicity of stories, and the differences among getting our "media education" from a newspaper, a magazine, a TV station, a movie theater, or online.

Imagining the media as an inadequate curriculum assumes that theoretical "good" media would exactly reflect a simple, unified reality and socialize our children into that reality. But reality is not singular or binary but multifaceted, and cultural representations of reality can be experienced very differently by people depending on their race, age, class, gender, ethnicity, education, and sexual orientation. Culture has never been a perfect replica of reality, an exact reflection of the world; culture is always an imperfect dramatization of everyday experience, one that puts key issues up for contestation and reinterpretation. Perhaps a better way to explore the media-as-curriculum metaphor is to ask how the media sustain, enhance, or diminish the ways we come to know and understand the world.

Media as Art

Another conventional metaphor that circulates about media claims that we are being poorly served by the low aesthetic quality of most mainstream media fare. This view characterizes media not as inadequate information or education but as inadequate culture. We will explore this approach in much more detail in Chapter 8, "Entertainment and Popular culture." For now, we note that this metaphor imagines that the media's love of trash so ruins our taste that we can no longer appreciate real or high culture when it appears. But if we instead view media as varied forms of a complex cultural landscape that includes art, then we can ask if, and how, media enhance the aesthetic landscape of contemporary life.

Since the rise of the novel, there have been culture critics troubled by the formulaic plots, easy laughs, simplistic values, and shallow escapism they find in most commercially successful media fare. For example, Matthew Arnold (*Culture and Anarchy*, 1869) viewed popular culture in the nineteenth century—best represented in his day in cheap dime novels—as pandering to the lowest common denominator rather than serving as a civilizing force for the masses in the manner of great poetry and classical education. Similarly, for many years network television has served as the main symbol for the "vast wasteland" of what passed for popular culture. TV critics, high art connoisseurs, literature professors, among other caretakers of high culture, dismissed widely popular programs like *The Beverly Hillbillies, Green Acres, Dallas,* and *Dynasty.* While audiences still have affection for these old shows that now circulate on cable, many new programs in prime time today draw critical praise, a testament both to the Internet displacing television as the newest mass medium we should fear and the evolution of storytelling on series television. Look, for example, at the narrative dimensions and character representations of commercial network programs like *Lost, The Good Wife,* or *Parks and Recreation.* Even long-running hit *The Simpsons* is packed with references to both popular and high culture, constituting a complex narrative that challenges its young audience to keep up. In discussing a narrative strategy called "multithreading"—the ability of contemporary series television to keep multiple plot lines and character studies going in the same episode—Steven Johnson has acknowledged "the public's willingness to tolerate more complicated narratives in the success of shows such as *ER* and *24.*"[8]

High culture aficionados are often blind to the subtleties of unfamiliar forms, just as so-called low culture enthusiasts are. The differences between good and bad opera can be as invisible to the country music fan as the differences between good and bad country music are to the opera buff. "It all sounds alike" is what the outsiders say about a genre they don't enjoy or know. Most cultural genres are a combination of formula and innovation (like an Elizabethan sonnet): The outsider perceives only the formula, while the insider appreciates the variations. This is as true in hip-hop, Bollywood films, and graphic novels as it is in classical music, Shakespearean tragedy, and postmodern literature.

If we learn how to analyze popular culture with the same tools and zeal that literary scholars use to analyze high culture, we find that there may not be as many essential narrative differences in the content or in the overall impact of high, popular, commercial, and folk art. Of course, while there are narrative similarities, tremendous variations still exist in the political and economic motivations and influences among these art forms. The best criticism covers both their narrative nuances and ideological underpinnings.

In the end, it seems disrespectful to insist that only some kinds of culture are good enough to be studied, taught in schools, or supported by tax dollars. Instead, maybe we can work on ways to democratize access to all levels of culture—help people appreciate the full range of stories—from other places and times as well as our own. In fact, with all their flaws, new media technologies and Internet sites like YouTube and *Wikipedia* are facilitating media access to information and stories in new, important, global ways.

MEDIA AS NARRATORS

There is no perfect media metaphor out there; as media scholars, we hope our perspectives are analyzed, interpreted, and evaluated by readers so that they can be

The movie *Bride and Prejudice* (2004) combines genre elements of Jane Austen novels with Bollywood musicals, fusing familiarity with invention.

revised and improved. Our hope is that this discussion of dominant metaphors helps clear away some of the debris that we think prevents productive thinking about media in society.

We believe that the best metaphor for understanding media in society, one that encapsulates aspects of all of the aforementioned perspectives, involves seeing the media as modulating or mediating change through narrative. Many of the most common ways of looking at the media—as interloper, information, propaganda, commerce, distraction, curriculum, and art—are negative assessments of the media as a single outside force. From our perspective, it is instructive but ultimately unproductive to see the media as outside forces. It is instructive because these metaphors give us vital information about what we fear and hope for, but unproductive because these metaphors ignore that we are always creating new media forms; participating in different media stories; imagining what is past, present, and future; and telling ourselves stories in and through the media.

Thinking of the media as narrators and moderators of change offers us a metaphor that we believe is a more accurate and productive description of what the media are actually up to. This metaphor treats the media as truly mediating or moderating cultural, social, political, and economic processes and change. Important and difficult questions about ownership and control, cultural quality, and audience vulnerability raised by the other metaphors can still be asked, and how the media shape us and are shaped by us can be studied in relation to stories and styles that are ever-changing, partly in response to the mediating process itself. One of the most profound questions we can ask about contemporary media is about the speed and direction of change.

With the media-as-narrator metaphor, then, we foreground the creative narrative process while acknowledging the economic processes that constantly seek to recognize, distribute, and profit from stories and styles. This changing cultural process anoints some things as new and interesting, others as boring and old hat, some things as relevant, others as out of fashion. What this metaphor relies on is the still understudied phenomenon of the substance of style.

If we understand the media as narrating and moderating change, we recognize how, as a system, the media "coolhunts," to use Malcolm Gladwell's term. Every element in the system is part of a search for whatever might be the next new musical style or TV story form to capture our imaginations—and consumer dollars. But the media also "pasthunt" in that they return to past styles and beliefs (like hip-hop samples from old rock and roll, jazz, or R&B standards). And they "otherhunt" in that they review and recirculate symbolic material from other cultures (like U.S. reality programs or sitcoms copied from British and other European shows).[9] The media—and their many producers and audiences—are all about revising and circulating stories and styles.

If, as media scholars, we take storytelling cycles as central to media processes, we can then explore the ways that the media find and foster the new and the different, as well as recirculating and recycling the reassuring and the familiar. They are simultaneously challenging us with new stories and reassuring us with old ones. Just as we use fashion and style to forge individual identities, we use media forms to tell us who we are and who we can be.

So this is the dominant metaphor we develop in the rest of the book, and we offer it as a productive way of imagining the media in society. We see media content as a collection of changing cycles and story forms, which have been enabled and constrained over time by various communication technologies. These cycles and stories always exist in power structures in society that can both encourage and limit the range of choices, but our focus is on the stories, not the structure.

Mediated stories are an ever-fluctuating, interchangeable process of cultural meaning, created and sustained by people making sense of their lives in modern times and by people making profits from change. Things move in and out of fashion in ways that mean a lot to some people and very little to others. This is also true of news stories, car colors, celebrities, television shows, sports, curricula, jobs—almost any cultural form we can think of. We need to understand why this happens and figure out why we care about, and participate in, this constant flux of shifting meanings in modern cultural forms.

Contemporary culture is a consumer culture, and media-circulated styles offer identity and connection in compelling ways. Taste is not "intrinsic" to us—we aren't born with certain tastes in, say, music, clothes, ideas, or movies. We instead construct our preferences in interactions and conversations with family, friends, teachers, clergy, bosses—and with a media-circulated array of choices. These may feel like natural preferences, but they are really socially constructed cultural alliances. What we choose is in relation to what is available, what we can afford, and what people like us—and perhaps more importantly, not like us—choose too.

To see media as narrators of change captures much of what is interesting and complicated about media influence. It allows us as media scholars to focus on some key elements of media in society, elements that we cannot address as well with the other metaphors. It includes the interactive and synergistic relationship between consumption and production. Under capitalism, media companies usually try to give us what they think we want. But not all media have the same goals, funding imperatives, or economic constraints. If we're talking about the mainstream commercial media, the process between consumption and production takes place within capitalism, which is different from what may occur in the construction of alternative and non-profit media.

Mainstream media aren't forcing us to like the stories they offer. They are not directly beaming messages into helpless, empty minds. Instead, a constant and sometimes messy feedback cycle operates, where what media offer are responses to change—in what people will read, watch, listen to, participate in, and finally buy.

Seeing media as narrators of change takes into account the complexity of various social groups constantly seeking, selecting, and discarding various cultural forms. We aren't identical and isolated, mere message recipients responding in similar ways to neutral media information. We have "our" cultural forms, and other groups have "their" cultural forms, as marketers and demographers can now document in extraordinary detail. We are active participants—we too narrate change—in the construction of media meanings, in relation to self-created social and cultural groups. Both mainstream and alternative media forms don't address all of us in the same way but cater to different groups in different voices while allowing others to listen in. Understanding this requires an understanding of media as always IN society—shaping and expressing our ideas, values, and beliefs. The media are always participants in modern cultural, social, political, and economic processes.

Finally, this media-as-narrator metaphor also helps us see the cultural, social, political, and economic substance of style. We sometimes presume style to be insubstantial, a trivial or shallow process. But changing ideas, values, and stories are like changes in the style of hair, or pants, or sounds. In fact, one way to understand the modern decline in overt sexism, racism, and homophobia is to understand that it is now "uncool" to be sexist, racist, or homophobic, at least in many communities, especially among young people. Slowly, over time and generations such change becomes custom rather than style.

In his classic 2000 study *Bowling Alone: The Collapse and Revival of American Community*, sociologist Robert Putnam faults the media (particularly television) and new technology for taking us away from our communities.[10] But, on the other hand, his study discovered that younger generations today are more socially tolerant than previous generations. Maybe the changing stories that we tell and circulate in mass media—about women working, about African American families, about gay people—have had something to do with our increased tolerance toward others.

When things go in and out of fashion, there can be longer and deeper shifts in what is acceptable and unacceptable. Media may help us compare options, not just in clothes but in how we act and what we believe. In a modern, democratic society this can be a valuable function. However, in more traditional societies, where technological transformations and social change come more slowly, this process can be viewed as dangerous and destabilizing.

This is where many critiques of the global influences of mass media begin, and we discuss these concerns in detail in Chapter 11, "Media Globalization." But for now it is enough to understand why we have chosen this metaphor. By focusing on how film, television, music, journalism, and others mediate and narrate change, we can capture the problems, promise, and complexity of global media influence. As educated thoughtful participants in modern life, when we move outside ourselves, we explore the possibility of becoming informed critics of media, culture, and society, asking far better questions about what is wrong with contemporary life and what we can do about it.

| CRITICAL PROCESS 1 | Vernacular Metaphors

In this exercise, interview at least three people about what they think about media influence on people and society. These should be open-ended interviews, recorded if possible, so you can analyze the implicit metaphors that may be underlying what your friends and family believe is true about media influence. Your job is to ask questions that focus on news, entertainment, advertising, and the Internet in ways that help your informants make claims about what they think the media are up to in today's society. You might also ask them to evaluate how media influences have supposedly changed in the past twenty years. From their comments:

Describe any metaphors that are being deployed to discuss media. Start a list of words and phrases used to describe media. Are they using the same ones as suggested in this chapter? Are they inventing new metaphors?

Analyze the function of the metaphors. Do you see patterns and similarities in these media discussions? How do your interviewees organize and make sense of the concerns about media influence?

Interpret the usefulness and meaning of the metaphors. How do they help your informants come up with a point of view, set of beliefs, or critical position?

Evaluate the metaphors. How interesting, useful, or right do you think these metaphors are? Why?

Engage with other students, parents, friends, and teachers to figure out which metaphors and terms seem to dominate, and whether or not you agree with them. Did anything you found out surprise you?

| CRITICAL PROCESS 2 | Metaphors in the Media

Read an article about media (such as the cable news wars); watch a movie that addresses various issues related to media, such as *Network, The Truman Show,* or *Natural Born Killers;* or watch a TV series where media play a central role, such as HBO's *Newsroom,* or Netflix's *House of Cards,* or the BBC's *The Hour.* Take notes, and from these notes:

Describe the metaphors that are being deployed. Are they using the same ones as suggested in this chapter? Are they inventing new ones?

Analyze the function of the metaphors. Who seems to be the intended audience(s), and how do creators or producers of your media product organize and make sense of the concerns about media influence for their audiences?

Interpret the usefulness and meaning of the metaphors. How do they help tell the stories that the media in question are trying to tell, whether fiction or nonfiction?

Evaluate the metaphors. How interesting, useful, or right do you think these metaphors are? Do they enhance your watching, listening, or reading experience?

Engage with other students, parents, friends, and teachers about how they think "The media" are portrayed in the media. How do newspaper critics critique and evaluate TV. How do movie directors portray the news business or celebrity culture? Cite examples.

3

Visual Literacy and the Truth behind an Image

If every picture tells a story, what's the story in this photo? The photo itself reveals only certain information. It appears to be two soccer teams in a ceremony, presumably before the game begins, in a huge outdoor stadium filled to capacity (at least in the part of the stadium we can see) on a sunny day (evidenced by the shadows). Both teams—one in white jerseys, one in dark jerseys—are giving a raised arm salute. The photo's black-and-white graininess tells us this is an archival photo, and we can also tell the photo was taken by a photographer at field level.

But there is a lot more to understand in the story of the photo. What is it about the composition that makes it so striking? What does it mean when a row of soccer players raise their arms in a uniform salute? Does the time and place of this photo, and our time and place as viewers of the photo, make a difference in how we understand the gesture? What is the truth behind the photo's story?

Here's what the historical record tells us about the image: The two soccer teams weren't crosstown rivals but instead the national teams from England (in white) and Germany. The event was an exhibition match in Berlin's enormous Olympic Stadium. The date was May 14, 1938. The era was a time when sport, especially soccer, was increasingly becoming a commercial spectacle (the first World Cup was played in 1930, and the third one would come to Paris in June 1938, just one month after this match in Berlin).[1] It was also an era of sociopolitical drama and heightened tensions in Europe. Hitler's Germany had just invaded and annexed Austria two months earlier in the *Anschluss*, a violation of the Treaty of Versailles signed at the end of World War I. In England, the government of Prime Minister Neville Chamberlain, terrified of Germany's growing power and grasping for ways to avoid war, took a cautious approach of diplomatic appeasement.

The English team was entering Berlin at a moment laden with international politics. In the locker room just minutes before England's team entered the field, British Football Association officials ordered the team to perform the salute during the German national anthem to "ensure a friendly reception by not only the huge swastika-waving crowd present in the Berlin stadium" but also by the even larger radio audience in Germany and beyond.[2] What the photo doesn't show is that the English players voiced their strong opposition in the locker room. Although they may look like Nazi sympathizers in the photo, none of the English players were saluting willingly as they faced the dignitaries' box, which included top Nazi officials such as Goebbels, Goering, and Hess.

Interestingly, the photo also tells us nothing about the game itself. Going into the match, Germany had been undefeated for twenty-six straight games (one ended in a tie). The team had undergone an unprecedented two weeks of intense training in the Black Forest and had an overwhelming home advantage: 110,000 fans in a stadium filled to capacity. Meanwhile, the English team had just finished an exhausting league season and had undergone no special preparations. Nonetheless, England performed brilliantly, beating Germany 6 to 3. But a big win for the English team is not how the exhibition match of May 14, 1938, is remembered. It's not the story told by this photo.[3]

Versions of this photograph appeared in nearly every British newspaper the next day. The British public was outraged by the image and what they believed to be Germany's demand that their soccer team perform the "Hitler salute."[4] In his 1946 autobiography, former English team captain Eddie Hapgood said the salute and the subsequent public indignation disturbed him for the rest of his career. The photo disappeared from public view but emerged sixty-five years later in a BBC documentary, *Football and Fascism* (2003), to renewed British outrage in news outlets and blogs as a "moment of shame" that still haunts British sport.

In this chapter we will investigate how images tell a story, which in turn connects to a larger narrative about our culture, values, and society. We will explore an image's narrative on multiple levels: on the level of composition, on the level of symbolic meaning, and also in terms of its ability to evoke realism. In doing so, we will visit the themes that guide our critical process: communication technology and the constantly changing media environment, democracy and the role images play in fostering democratic thought, and capitalism—how our image comprehension and construction are inextricably linked to the visual languages of advertising and photojournalism.

COMPOSITION: THE VISUAL'S AESTHETIC POWER

Composition is the creative activity of placing objects within a frame. When painting a picture, we're choosing where to place shapes and dots and lines on a two-dimensional plane. When we create a book or Web page design, we arrange images, words, and graphic elements, most typically filling some sort of rectangle. Whether we do this using construction paper and glue or digital software, we're directing viewers to notice certain elements within a frame, purposefully communicating our ideas through visual language. When taking a photographic or video image, we arrange external objects within the dimensions of a viewfinder, panning left and right or crouching down to get the desired perspective. As visual communication scholar Herbert Zettl points out, understanding the aesthetics of composition does not necessarily mean knowing how to create a beautiful image; it means knowing how to structure both still and moving screen images for "maximally effective communication."[5] The best photographs and graphic designs do that: They dictate a reader's comprehension. Michael Rabiger discusses good composition this way:

> While it interests and delights the eye, good composition is an important organiz-
> ing force when used to dramatize relativity and relationship, and to project ideas.
> Superior composition not only makes the subject (content) accessible, it heightens
> the viewers' perceptions and stimulates his or her imaginative involvement, like
> language from the pen of a good poet.[6]

To understand this "organizing force," then, we must understand the various elements we need to organize when creating images: color, form, line, and movement. Every choice can be a powerful way to both convey and understand meaning.

Color

Color choices have great impact on an image. We consciously and unconsciously respond to color every day, and we are constantly making aesthetic choices related to color. We decide to wear a blue T-shirt over a yellow one, pick an orange cereal bowl over a white one, or choose a pen with blue ink over black ink. Most of us have a favorite color or are drawn continuously to the same color palette. We also have intense emotional reactions to color. We may love the color orange but hate the color blue. We may walk into a room that makes us feel uncomfortable, feel the intense urge to leave, and then realize upon reflection that its color was the thing that turned us away. Virginia Kidd, who teaches media production at California State University, has an emotional response to Room 317, the room in which she holds her classes:

> I have a theory that the University obtained paint for this room at an enormous
> discount because nobody with any choice in the matter would have purchased
> it. Three walls are battleship gray. The impact is dismal. I am reminded of bat-
> tered aluminum cooking pots and galvanized garbage cans. Apparently in an effort
> to counter this, the fourth wall was painted yellow; not, however, a soft banana
> yellow, which happens to be my favorite color, but a glaring mustard yellow that
> could have come straight from a French's jar; this covers an entire classroom wall

and oppressively dominates whatever is happening. If nothing else, the choice of paint for room 317 at least graphically demonstrates the power of color.[7]

The power of color was also evident during "tulipmania" in seventeenth-century Holland. The Dutch were so taken by the vivid colors of tulips (an import from Turkey) in the gray Dutch landscape that they became intoxicated; a frenzy of financial speculation followed and a single tulip bulb could cost a thousand Dutch florins (the average annual income was 150 florins).

The fact is, humans are physiologically programmed to respond to color, and we respond to certain colors in particular ways. We see red especially easily, not because it's a bright color but because our eyes are designed to block the opposite of red: ultraviolet electromagnetic waves that can be harmful to our retinas. Red and orange light wavelengths pass through our retina more easily, making these colors the most noticeable: Stop signs and traffic lights are red for a reason. Correspondingly, violet is the least noticeable color. Thus, as we make our own images or respond to the images of others, we can understand how color works for maximum effect. Red works well as an accent color to draw attention to a certain part of an image. Photojournalists are pleased, for example, when a person in a crowd they are documenting happens to be wearing a red scarf or shirt, allowing them to use that individual as a focal point in their frame: "Look here."

Advertisers are also keenly aware of red's power: The color will lead a viewer to a particular corner of the page, clarifying a message or saying "this is important." Consider how red is effectively deployed in corporate logos, signage, and national flags.

Red juxtaposed with blue simulates depth—the warmer color will appear closer (more noticeable) while the colder blue tones will recede (appear less noticeable). This is why intense blue and red fields on the same two-dimensional surface will seem to pulse back and forth in a third dimension. Thus, color helps to bring three-dimensionality to the two-dimensional frame.

Colors can also be used to generate more emotional responses. If red can agitate or provoke, then green can soothe; blue can yield to emotions of melancholy and coolness; gray can lack emotional commitment. Because light colors have soft and cheerful associations, we tend to surround babies with various shades of pastel; we tend to demonstrate dark and moody emotions through dark colors. This all makes color a powerful, if sometimes ambiguous, tool for directing visual messages.

Form

Form has to do with the object inside the frame, how big it is, and where it is placed. The simplest form is a dot, and placing a dot within the four walls of a frame commands attention: We look at the dot before we look at any blank space within a frame. (Even if a form does not have an explicit frame—imagine a sculpture in the middle of a vast plain—it is still implicitly framed by our field of vision.) Moreover, with the act of framing, something rather magical happens, something we refer to as **frame magnetism**. When a dot is closer to one side of a frame, that side seems to pull the dot toward it. Notice the diagram below.

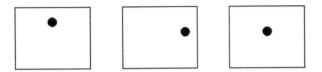

The dot is being pulled upward in the first panel. In the second panel, the dot is being pulled to the right. The result, not surprisingly, is a bit of agitation, or at least interest. Place the dot in the absolute center of the frame and it becomes inert—all four sides of the image are pulling equally at the dot, making for a rather boring composition.

Depending on how large the dot is and where it is placed, the four sides of the frame impact form (in this case, the dot) in significant ways. Consequently, we can use the pull of the frame to add drama or significance to our message. We can create tension between two individuals, for example, by placing them close to the edges of each frame. Or we can do the opposite, framing figures so they are not pulled by the sides of a picture but are comfortably balanced within the frame. TV producers usually strive to achieve this kind of balance: They routinely make talk show hosts and their guests sit (or stand) uncomfortably close to each other so that they aren't pulled apart by the sides of the video frame. The result is to have them fake their comfort in order to make *us* comfortable: As viewers we feel as if these individuals like each other and are having a pleasant conversation, not pulling away from

The interview pair on the left look uncomfortable in part because the frame's magnetic forces are actively pulling them away from each other; the pair on the right stand uncomfortably close to each other (in real life), but the shot itself is more balanced and centered, causing us to perceive a "friendly" relationship.

The rule of thirds

each other. If we return to the Nazi salute photograph, we can also see that the two dominant shapes (in this case, each soccer team) are cohesively clumped without being pulled to one side of the frame or another, creating a sense of pictorial balance.

The realities of frame magnetism have led to certain framing conventions. One is **headroom:** framing an image so an individual has a bit of space over her head to convey that she is not cramped by the frame or pulled upward by frame magnetism. Headroom creates the illusion that the figure is in a larger setting rather than a box. Another framing convention is the **rule of thirds,** a well-known principle of photograph and image composition. By breaking an image down into thirds (both horizontally and vertically), and by placing elements on the points of intersection, we can avoid both the uncomfortable pulling when the form is too close to the frame and the boring inertia when the form is too central.

Knowing the rule of thirds is to create images that are balanced yet interesting. However, knowing when to break the rule—to add tension—is also an essential part of the artistic vocabulary and a means for conveying narrative.

Shape is tied to form. The most basic shapes—square, circle, and triangle—are often connected to the three basic (primary) colors, red, blue, and yellow. Each shape in turn has an expressive quality. Squares convey stability, solidity, support, confidence, and strength but also boredom. They carry a heavier weight in the frame than circles or triangles and tend to be imposing, dominating an image. Rectangles—part of the square family—usually feel slightly less stable and slightly more interesting than squares. In contrast, circles are fluid instead of solid, expressing wholeness, completion, happiness, unity, and motion. Circles are more interesting than squares, but nowhere near as interesting as triangles, our most dynamic shape. Triangles are stimulating because they *point,* leading one's eyes to various areas within the frame, adding tension with diagonal lines and energy to the entire visual composition. Like the color red, triangles are useful in isolating ideas and identifying the significance of an element within the frame. For example, a photograph of two basketball players jumping up toward a ball completes the shape of a triangle and dramatizes the ball's significance. A photograph of a bird landing on a gutter—the bird's wings outstretched—shows two triangles: each one pointing in a different direction and asking the viewer to follow the direction of both invisible lines. In the Nazi salute photograph, the flags in the stadium point upward, lifting our eyes out of the narrative. As designer and theorist Johannes Itten commented about shapes, "The square is resting matter, the triangle is thought, and the circle is spirit in eternal motion."[8]

Line

A line embodies a narrative significance of its own. Horizontal lines evoke calm and stability; vertical lines convey energy and upward thrust. Diagonal lines, like triangles, are dynamic, exciting, somewhat unstable, and for these reasons are advantageous toward visually communicating complicated ideas. It's an important strength, when creating an image, to be aware of how lines divide a frame. For example, telephone lines can slice a frame into numerous boxes and rectangles against the sky, or dramatically slice a frame at a diagonal, directing viewers to various points of interest. Photographers can also intentionally create diagonals by cocking the camera—making what we call a Dutch angle— and destabilizing an otherwise sturdy image to make a visual point. In advertising, Dutch angles are used constantly to add excitement or to juxtapose instability (e.g., discomfort in the doctor's office) with stability (e.g., relief after taking a certain pill).

A tilted horizon or a flagpole make obvious lines within a frame, but lines can also be inferred: A look between two figures—gaze meeting gaze—creates an invisible line linking characters. A person (or in the case of the Nazi salute photograph, a group) pointing in a particular direction produces a directional force that we can follow, perhaps even beyond the frame. Two figures working in a vast field, one in the foreground and another far off in the background, are invisibly connected by a diagonal line; we look at the foreground figure first and then are drawn to look at the second. Thus, diagonal lines both offer directional force and convey depth. Lines, whether visible or invisible, help us understand spatial arrangements and the corresponding relationships within the visual narrative.

The angle from which the image is taken offers more invisible lines and another means for communicating depth—the more extreme the angle, the more intense the feeling of depth. The invisible lines that angles create are also infused with meaning. A very low angle intensifies the stature of a figure or inanimate object. A child portrayed from below can look like a giant, a monster can appear even more scary and powerful, and an armed tank all the more menacing. When shooting *Citizen Kane*, for example, Orson Welles was so intent on portraying Kane with as much grandeur as possible in certain scenes that he dug holes in the floor of sets and shot from below the floorboards, creating extreme low angles for maximum effect.

Shooting at a low angle also tends to create directional lines toward sky, clouds, windows, and the vigorous thrust of buildings, all of which can bring powerful associations. The opposite is true for high angles. People shot from above tend to look weaker, diminished, and victimized; a high angle correspondingly leads one to focus on ground, dirt, feet, and litter, all of which can bring a negative energy to an image. Line thus helps define perspective and lead a viewer to points of emphasis within a frame. Other ways to communicate spatial organization in an image include high-contrast lighting, sound, and, as we discuss next, the temporal elements of motion.

Movement

Western cultures tend to read lines (and other images) the same way we read this text, left to right. This has compositional implications, giving lines additional energy that we read into them; we automatically assign movement to lines.

Because of our Western left-to-right orientation, our eyes tend to rest or linger on the right side of the frame, so whatever appears on the right side seems to dominate the image. This is why advertisers and graphic designers typically place product logos on the right, the last place a viewer's eye will rest. We read diagonal lines according to this left-right orientation as well. For example, we understand a slope that starts at the bottom left-hand corner of a frame and ends at the top right as an "uphill" slope; we easily interpret a slope that begins from the top left and ends at bottom right as "downhill" (even though it could easily be uphill).

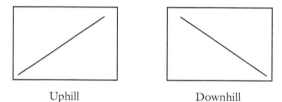

Uphill   Downhill

In Western cultures, then, placing critical elements on the right side rather than the left can become a forceful tactic in planning visual compositions. If we grew up speaking and reading Arabic, we would learn to read images from right to left, and we would plan our visual compositions differently.

With these directional forces—also called vectors—at play, lines within a frame can either compete with our natural desire to read left to right, causing tension, or flow with the left-right momentum. For example, car advertisers use these tendencies to their advantage: If the message is "speed," they might show a car driving left to right and preferably downhill, as if to increase the speed of the car: The car is traveling in the same direction our eyes are naturally traveling. If the message is "rugged and powerful," advertisers might show the car (or more probably, truck) traveling right to left and uphill: By going against the grain it appears that the truck is working harder and is twice as tough.

The image on the left conveys speed, while the one on the right focuses on power.

These kinds of *continuous* vectors extend beyond the frame and cause anticipation: We don't know if the motorcycles will crash at the bottom of the hill or if the Chevy truck will ever reach the top of the mountain. In the Nazi salute photo, arms raised and flags pointing upward also cause anticipation, leading our eyes outside of the frame. *Converging* vectors, where two forces converge together in the same frame, tend to evoke a sense of calm because the forces are pulling together and a sort of resolution is taking place. *Diverging* vectors—two forces moving away and out of the frame—can be deeply troubling. Indeed, the directional force of lines, combined with our left-to-right orientation, can yield considerable drama and storytelling to a still image.

When that image moves, as in film or video, the narrative possibilities multiply. Panning (horizontally swiveling from one side to another) to the right tends to evoke a sense of panic; we are already reading to the right and the rightward sweeping pan doubles the speed of our reading. Panning to the left, on the contrary, has a more calming effect.

Similarly, following a character moving left to right within the frame is invigorating but troubling if the filmmaker or videographer doesn't supply enough *lead room*—the extra space to suggest a character is traveling toward something outside the frame and not slamming into the frame's edge. To frame an individual in the most flattering conditions, a videographer might pose a subject—say, the president—walking left to right (i.e., "forward," not backward), walking with extensive lead room (i.e., they are open, comfortable, and in control of their environment), and at a low angle (i.e., they are powerful). In contrast, a videographer also has the power to do the opposite, portraying a political official in extreme close-up, walking left or against the edge of the frame, and looking up at the camera rather than down, as if to portray the official as cramped, uncomfortable, squirming under pressure, and belittled.

Narrative structure in film and video is, of course, propelled forward through editing: the juxtaposition of long shots, medium shots, and close-ups. Perhaps it's easiest to think of individual shots as sentences and sequences of shots as paragraphs. Each shot delivers a new idea to a cohesive storyline: A **long shot** (sometimes called an "establishing shot") establishes place and context; a **medium shot** draws attention to a particular character or object; and a **close-up** describes that character/object in terms of emotions, actions, or other details. Think of these first five sentences in Rohinton Mistry's novel *A Fine Balance* (1995)—a story about India in the 1930s—as a series of five edited film shots:

1. (long shot) The Morning Express bloated with passengers slowed to a crawl, then lurched forward suddenly, as though to resume full speed.

2. (medium shot) The train's brief deception jolted its riders.

3. (medium shot) The bulge of humans hanging out of the doorway distended perilously, like a soap bubble at its limit.

4. (close-up) Inside the compartment, Maneck Kohlah held on to the overhead railing, propped up securely within the crush.

5. (extreme close-up) He felt someone's elbow knock his textbooks from his hands.

Similarly, a fully edited film could be broken down, shot by shot, into a stream of descriptive sentences and paragraphs.

The pacing of editing combined with shot size can also dramatically affect meaning. Quickly edited shots and sequences accelerate tension, especially if the shots are all close-ups, conveying a feeling of entrapment or suspense. In contrast, numerous slow-paced long shots side by side slow down the narrative and give room for reflection. Finally, the juxtaposition of extreme shots—long shot to close-up, slow-paced to fast-paced, moving to still—is a chance to create a jarring scene in the narrative, one where the viewer has to work extra hard to figure out what the story is.

Indeed, juxtaposition is a way to induce meaning not through the actual content of individual shots but through the coupling of two or more shots. The famous Russian film theorist Lev Kuleshov demonstrated the power of juxtaposition by coupling the same expressionless headshot footage of a prominent actor, Ivan Mozzhukhin, with three completely different film segments: first, a bowl of soup; then a coffin in which a dead woman lies; and finally, a little girl at play. Kuleshov presented the three juxtapositions to an audience. According to Kuleshov's colleague V. I. Pudovkin, the viewers commented on Mozzhukhin's superior acting ability: "the heavy pensiveness of his mood over the forgotten soup," "the deep sorrow with which he looked on the dead woman," and "the light happy smile with which he surveyed the girl at play."[9]

Even though the headshot never changed, the Kuleshov group concluded that "with correct montage, even if one takes the performance of an actor directed at something quite different, it will still reach the viewer in the way intended by the editor, because the viewer himself will complete the sequence and see that which is suggested to him."[10] In other words, authors of visual material can create meaning by connecting two or more separate elements, providing competent continuity, and asking viewers to fill in the blanks. "The challenge," writes visual theorist Gretchen Barbatsis, "is to theorize, study, and create visual narrative in ways that we appreciate its sense-making function as a way to better understand disordered, raw experience; as a powerful way of constituting reality and not a way of merely recording it."[11]

While the Nazi salute photo is not a moving image edited in relation to other images, it effectively communicates meaning and movement through its composition. The photograph's color contrasts (black and white), spatial organization of subject matter within the frame, use of line, and sweeping vector movements suggest a controlled drama of binary opposites and leading lines. This is a story of opposites, order, and balance. Both teams balance each other in terms of frame placement and contrasting uniform colors (dark vs. white). The flags are equidistant. The stadium line and the row of athletes—particularly their waistlines—rest comfortably on the horizontal thirds, suggesting interest but little tension, until one considers the vectors. With arm and gaze vectors pointing out of the frame and flags pointing up to an open sky, there is an edginess to this picture, a story of anticipation: We don't know what's going to happen.

If the photograph had been cropped or taken from a different angle, meaning would change drastically. Indeed, different versions of the photograph, such as the example below—unearthed in a German archive in 2008—are cropped and angled in ways that don't communicate the same conflict, balance, and anticipation. Without the context of the opposing German team and evidence of a crowded stadium, the image is more passive, less oppositional. The outstretched arms have less potency from the frontal perspective.

SEMIOTICS AND SYMBOLIC MEANING

Beyond a pure compositional reading, we can also read deeper into the image and acknowledge that every element in the frame conveys an independent symbolic meaning. In other words, we can add more narrative layers through our understanding of the signs implanted within the image.

What is a sign? A **sign** is simply something that conveys meaning beyond the object itself. Flowers are a sign of spring; dark clouds are a sign that it might rain; yawning is a sign indicating fatigue or boredom. We know these things because we are familiar with weather and human nature.

Other signs are not quite so obvious, requiring more knowledge of cultural norms to understand their meaning. For example, what does a child dressed in a princess costume, holding a bag of candy mean? If we live outside U.S. culture, we could probably deduce that this costume represents some sort of event or festival. But one has to know more about the special role of Disney characters in U.S. culture and the cultural traditions surrounding Halloween in order to clearly decipher the true meaning of the costume: that the child has gone trick-or-treating as Cinderella. Similarly, different cultures read gestures, like publicly spitting or picking one's nose, in different ways. These actions are perfectly acceptable in many countries, but in the

United States, they often mean improper personal hygiene, a sign of being distasteful, antisocial, and unclean. A child might not know this, however, unless he or she learns it from parents or teachers. A right arm raised at an angle above one's head may be someone's way to say hello or hail a taxi, but it is mostly a gesture loaded with negative meaning, symbolizing Nazism, one of the most appalling political ideologies of the twentieth century.[12] "For something to be a sign," Paul Lester writes, "the viewer must understand its meaning. If you do not understand the meaning behind the orange color of a jacket, it isn't a sign for you."[13]

Semiotics, the study of signs, was developed in the early twentieth century by Ferdinand de Saussure and Charles Sanders Peirce. Both studied signs by breaking them down into their fundamental parts—the word, image, gesture, or sensory cue ("signifier") and the concept ("signified")—and asked important questions about how something comes to stand for something else, and how a sign is connected to the object to which it refers. For example, English speakers call a four-legged domesticated animal with a wagging tail a "dog"—here, the word "dog" is the signifier—and we associate this word with our concept of a dog, the thing signified. Together the signifier and signified constitute the sign, which is differentiated from the object—in this case, the dog—out there in the world. Now suppose that our language had developed differently and the signifier "cat" signified the idea of a dog instead? This wouldn't change the nature of dogs, just the word we use to talk about them. The relationship between language and meaning is arbitrary and learned and this is what interested both Saussure and Peirce. Visual communication scholar Sandra Moriarty notes that Peirce's work has become particularly helpful in reading images because he emphasized *representation* as "a key element in how a sign 'stands for' its object."[14] Peirce formulated three different types of representation, "iconic," "indexical," and "symbolic," which range from the most easily interpreted signs (iconic) to the most complex (symbolic).

Iconic signs are the most basic sign types because they closely resemble the thing they represent: a photograph or film, or a pictogram like those shown below.

Because iconic images represent a tangible gesture, action, or thing, they are easily understood across cultures. They also can be a part of more complex indexical or symbolic images.

One step up in complexity, **index (or indexical) signs** are less straightforward but still logical representations of an object. A deer hoofprint in the woods is a sign that a deer passed by. A bullet hole is a sign that both a bullet and a gun were present at a certain time to create the hole. The whistle of a tea kettle is a sign that water is boiling inside. A map is not as literal as a photograph but is a logical representation of a landscape nonetheless—an index sign pointing to a terrain. As literary theorist and semiotician Roland Barthes described index signs, "they point but do not tell."[15] One has to have a certain amount of lived experience to recognize indexical representations: experience boiling water in a tea kettle or going to the woods looking for deer, for example, to fully understand what a tea kettle whistle or a hoofprint mean.

When reading index signs in media images, we also borrow from our own lived experience to determine how the signs contribute to the overall narrative. If a car advertisement, for example, cuts from an image of a shiny new car to some black-and-white, grainy, flickery footage of cars not recognizable on today's roads, we can read that footage—based on our own experience with today's cars and the media—to mean "old" or "historical." Even though the black-and-white footage may have been shot recently and overlaid with special-effect filters to look archival, it still signifies "old." If we see an image of a person smiling as they hold up a beauty product, we can deduce that the smiling gesture is an indexical sign associated with the product: The smile points to the act of using the product (even though we don't actually see the product being used). "Before" and "after" images are good examples of index signs; we never see the product being applied but are led to infer that the product shown had something to do with the result displayed.

Symbolic signs are the most complex of all signs because they are determined by culture and therefore in need of a higher level of interpretation. For this reason they tend to be the most interesting for semioticians (and us) to analyze. Language and words are good examples of symbolic signs: One has to learn the language before he or she is able to interpret the sign.

Besides their inherent connection to spoken and written words, symbolic signs include other cultural indicators: socially defined gestures, collective practices, styles of dress, national emblems, and cultural innuendo—all the things that are learned through one's upbringing education, and interactions with specific social groups. In the category of socially defined gestures, for example, one hails a taxi differently in Paris (point down) than in the United States (point up); one has to learn through cultural practice whether to point up or down. Similarly, in the United States and elsewhere, red, white, and pink together signify Valentine's Day; orange and black mean Halloween; and red and green mean Christmas. As cultural studies scholars Jessica Evans and Stuart Hall have observed, the meaning of an image "is not in the visual sign itself as a self-sufficient entity, nor exclusively in the sociological positions and identities of the audience, but in the articulation between viewer and viewed, between the power of the image to signify and the viewer's capacity to interpret meaning."[16] What Evans and Stuart recognize is that an image (or any text for that

The Semiology of "Heil Hitler"

- Compulsory greeting enforced by Nazi regime in 1933
  - Civil servants were legally obligated to use the salute as a formal greeting and to end all paper correspondence with "Heil Hitler."
  - Greeting was considered a "civic duty."
  - Nazi SA (storm troopers) said "Heil Hitler" while clicking their boots.
- Understood as *hail* but also indicated *health, safety,* and *best wishes,* and thus implied "Health to Hitler"
  - The greeting framed Hitler as a "Supreme Being" who could in turn grant *good health to a greeter's recipient.*
- All people of Jewish descent banned from saying "Heil Hitler" by 1937
  - Through racial exclusion, the salute became symbolically linked to German unity and racial superiority.
  - Posters throughout Germany proclaimed "Germans use the German Greeting!" So if a German didn't use "Heil," then he or she was "not German." Since Jews were forbidden to say "Heil Hitler," Nazi propaganda implicitly stated that a person could not be both Jewish and German.

Allert Tilman, *The Hitler Salute,* trans. Jefferson Chase (New York: Macmillan/Picador, 2009).

matter) has the possibility for multiple readings, with each reading dependent on a person's culture and his or her own personal interpretations.[17]

For example, advertising images in Japanese business magazines routinely depict men in groups holding hands—an image understood by many Japanese as heroic, representing teamwork, strength, and togetherness. A different culture might read homophobic meanings into such images or consider men holding hands a sign of weakness rather than a sign of strength. U.S. advertising images, for instance, tend to frame men as "independent" and "individual" doers and thinkers.

Symbolic Storytelling

Symbolic signs can be highly charged and emotional simply because they reflect or comment upon culture. As such, they can be a very powerful means of storytelling, bringing a deeper meaning to an image as viewers are asked to make cultural connections to understand the symbolism. Beer advertising, for example, is often loaded with phallic and sexual imagery that are symbolic indicators for a highly sexualized beer culture (particularly in the United States but also evident in other countries), not so subtly connecting beer (and, given the advertising context, the purchasing of beer) to male sexual conquest. The advertisements that represent this culture have also become part of the culture itself: Beer foam, the sweat on the beer bottle, the angle and direction a male model holds the bottle of beer, allusions to the cultural practice of bachelor parties, the disappearance of wedding rings—all are typical narrative symbols to connect male sexuality to beer.

Symbolic signs can be so charged with meaning, however, that they can easily be misinterpreted.[18] Take a Danish print ad for Tuborg beer that attempted to represent a bachelor party with beer bottles standing in as men. In the ad, seven beer bottles with labels *on* (signifying dressed men) encircle a beer bottle with no label (signifying a woman just completing a strip tease). The words "bachelor party" are intended to clarify the scene. But the label-less beer bottle might be understood as an undressed *man*—an awkward message for the heterosexual target audience Tuborg is intent on reaching.[19]

Like any textual message, visuals can thus be complicated and fraught with controversy. They can be extremely evocative, but also extremely vague. Therefore, context is always a critical part of the story and meaning behind any visual message. Let's consider the context of this Carl's Jr. Western Bacon Thickburger commercial, starring *Top Chef*'s Padma Lakshmi. (See the ad online at http://www.youtube.com/watch?v=mQDit9-z1Xw.)

The commercial, which was created and released in 2009,[20] shows Lakshmi (who is originally from India, was raised a vegetarian, and is known for her discerning palette) walking through a food market to her own voice-over: "I've always had a love affair with food. And after traveling the world and writing two cookbooks, I think I've tasted every flavor imaginable."[21]

Then the commercial cuts to Lakshmi on the steps of a brownstone, taking huge, lusty bites out of a Thickburger. Sauce drips on her leg, she wipes it with her finger and licks it off, and licks more sauce from the burger, letting her tongue curl up in pleasure. She is sweaty, and hikes up her skirt as her voice-over says, "But there's something about the Western Bacon. It reminds me of being in high school, sneaking out before dinner to savor that sweet, spicy sauce, and leaving no evidence behind."[22] The semiotic meaning is not subtle: She's having a sexual liason with the burger, as the burger (coded "male") drips its "sweet, spicy sauce" on her—a near-pornographic story served up for the male, teenage target audience for Thickburgers. Lakshmi could be any woman wearing a sheer, low-cut, and clingy dress on a hot summer day. But the fact that she's a celebrity, and also someone known for being on a food show about high cuisine, and a famously self-controlled *Top Chef* judge at that, gives an ironic intertextual context to the ad, which strategically exploits the notion that she is losing herself sexually over a Carl's Jr. Western Bacon Thickburger.

Padma Lakshmi in an ad for Carl's Jr.

Another powerful layer of context we can examine is the ad's authorship and distribution. Who created the ad and why? This 2009 Carl's Jr. ad was produced by CKE Restaurants Inc. (owner of Carl's Jr. and Hardee's), a company that has been associating their burgers with sex and gearing their product toward "young, hungry, [presumably heterosexual] guys" for over a decade.[23] By 2012, Carl's Jr. was spending about $60 million a year on its racy, memorable advertising. "When you see our ads, you see them once, and you remember it," says CKE CEO Andrew Puzder.[24] So the Lakshmi ad is part of a larger, long-running campaign that features famous female personalities (Kim Kardashian and 2011 *Sports Illustrated* Rookie of the Year swimsuit model Kate Upton are recent Carl's Jr. talent), routinely pushes the line of indecency, and influences the way an entire generation thinks about hamburgers.

The Lakshmi ad is also notable in that it was directed by Chris Applebaum, the same person who directed the "infamous" 2005 Carl's Jr. ad depicting hotel heiress Paris Hilton wearing a low-cut black bathing suit and suggestively soaping up a Bentley in a garage, shooting a hose toward the camera (more overt sexual innuendo), and finally lunging into a Carl's Jr. hamburger during the commercial's final seconds.[25] The commercial, with music reminiscent of a vaudeville striptease act, slyly referenced Hilton's notoriety for being in an Internet-released sex tape (more context) two years earlier. Banned from airing during the 2005 Super Bowl, this Carl's Jr. ad became the most talked-about commercial of that year. The Lakshmi ad has an historical context by being a part of a larger ad campaign and also by referencing other commercials that have reached iconic stature. An examination of these contextual elements significantly adds meaning to the visual text.

Therefore, a semiotic analysis includes the social and economic circumstances that enabled the image to be produced, an examination of its circulation, and the image's historical background and iconic stature.[26] Let's also not forget the speed at which one is expected to digest (or has to digest) a visual text—the Lakshmi commercial was released as a thirty-second commercial on television, with a sixty-second extended version on the Web—nor the different viewing experiences.[27] For example, seeing the ad on TV is a completely different experience from seeing it on YouTube, where it exists (in various forms) alongside other Carl's Jr. ads and numerous Padma Lakshmi videos, and is accompanied by strident commentary, from soft porn to genuine critiques of the commercial (including Lakshmi's "hypocritical" role in it) and of the Carl's Jr. burger itself. This is the context of interpretation: Audiences will be reading and interpreting (and often misinterpreting) the image, and these multiple (polysemic) interpretations all play into our understanding of the image's larger meaning.

REALISM: TRUTH AND PHOTOGRAPHY

One of the most controversial aspects of visual imagery is the relative truthfulness of images and the ease with which images can be manipulated—the question of whether visuals can be trusted. Some visual theorists, like Walter Benjamin and Susan Sontag, have repeatedly raised suspicions over the merit of visual representation as an illegitimate replacement for the "real thing." Writing in the 1930s, German cultural critic Walter Benjamin was appalled, for example, that films could replace live theater. For him, "fake" screen performances in front of a "mechanical contrivance" were no match for authentic theater performances, where actors could respond and adapt to a live audience.[28] Sontag made a similar argument with photography. For her, taking a picture was the same thing as capturing something live and committing "sublimated murder."[29] In other words, photographers rendered something real into a representation and thus detached it from the truth. Both of these cultural theorists were deeply troubled by mass production and consumerism—brought on by industrial-era technology such as film and photography—and the potential for erosion of authentic experience. Photographs are mere mirrors of the real scene at hand.

But what if the people in a scene are not even being truthful in their actions when a photograph was taken? For example, in performing the Nazi salute the English soccer team was not being truthful to their real positions about the Nazi regime. French literary theorist Roland Barthes talks about the nature of the pose and how the presence of a camera—and the fact that one is aware of being photographed—affects the captured image, even if the intent is absolute realism.[30] But what is a "real" pose? Is it a smile?

If you look at photographs from the mid-1800s, particularly daguerreotypes, you'll notice that people's typical expressions are serious: They don't smile. In the early days of daguerreotype technology, photographic subjects had to keep very still for up to twenty minutes so the image could fix on the copper plate. Apart from this technical limitation, there were also social reasons. Since photography was so new, it was also scary, and many people had their photographs taken with the underlying fear that the camera was capturing their souls, serious poses marking their inner panic. Smiling was also considered vulgar and lower-class. In fact, a popular expression before a picture was about to be taken was "Say prunes."[31]

This all changed, at least in the United States, when Kodak—trying to aggressively market their new $1 Brownie camera in 1900—sought to make cameras less intimidating and more integrated into people's everyday life. Kodak did this by celebrating the ease of new technology ("You press the button, we do the rest"), associating the consumer camera with the Kodak girl ("so easy even a girl can do it"), teaching Americans to take pictures of happy events in their lives (celebrations, vacations), and suggesting that the "normal" pose to assume when having one's picture taken was a smile.[32] Kodak brought a new era of documentation into our lives. But what kind of documentation? Even today, we don't tend to take pictures of unhappy moments such as people crying, arguing, or attending funerals, and we tend to smile when people point a camera at us, even though we're not necessarily happy. Are many of the snapshots in our albums, then, fake? On the other hand, the photographs taken before Kodak introduced the smiling standard could also be read as a misrepresentation of reality.

Image Misrepresentation and Manipulation

Photographers, in fact, have been intentionally misrepresenting reality since the earliest days of photography. One of the first concocted photographic poses dates back to the 1830s when Frenchman Hippolyte Bayard, bitter that his photographic process wasn't recognized before Daguerre's (who created the now famous daguerreotypes), posed as if he committed suicide.

The very earliest photographers also altered backdrops (and thus altered reality). Civil War photojournalists dragged corpses to different locations and added props to magnify the drama of the battlefield. Early art photographers dangled items from imperceptible threads so that objects seemed to fly into the frame, and photographers used all sorts of props to enhance their photographs. Many of the famous Farm Security Administration photographs taken by Arthur Rothstein, Walker Evans, and Dorothea Lange to document the Dust Bowl and the extreme poverty of the Great Depression were staged, albeit in very subtle ways.[33]

Still, as Barthes noted, even if photographs are a mere representation, at least they do offer some sort of proof that the people or objects photographed were there. For example, even if we weren't at the stadium in 1938 to witness the pregame ceremonies and the infamous Nazi salute, the photograph of the English soccer team at least offers some documentation that the English players were *there*, in Berlin's Olympic

Which image is manipulated and which isn't?

Stadium. Or were they? Perhaps the stadium was fake—the real backdrop was really just a field in England, and the football players were digitally pasted into the stadium.

In the left-hand photo above we have done the opposite: using digital manipulation to place the British team onto a 1926 soccer match between England and Jamaica/Haiti. The point is that with the proliferation of programs like Photoshop and other digital image manipulation techniques over the past twenty years, what constitutes reality in photographs has become anyone's guess.

But while most people associate photo manipulation with new digital technology, it also dates back to the earliest days of photography. This 1917 photograph, for example, fooled many people who actually thought the fairies, which were superimposed using clever dark-room techniques, were real.

The two photographs of Charles Dickens above illustrate that, even in 1867, photographers were altering and tidying up publicity photos. Dickens looks disheveled and fatigued in the original photo (left), taken originally in 1861. He was transformed into a quaffed gentleman in 1867 after numerous touch-ups in a photography studio (right).[34] Additionally, Stalin, Hitler, Mao, Fidel Castro, and Mussolini all saw the value in retouching photographs to adjust the truth. In many cases they retouched people out of photographs who had fallen out of favor with them.[35]

Retouching photos by hand has, of course, been replaced by far more sophisticated digital techniques. Part of reading images today means reading *against* the likely possibility that a photograph has been "Photoshopped," or digitally altered. In advertising and promotional imagery especially, nearly all photographs are altered: Bodies

Stalin circa 1930: The man to the right of Stalin is eliminated in the second photo.

Hitler, 1937: Joseph Goebbels was removed from the photo on the right.

are elongated, slimmed, arched, retextured, and colorized. Men's biceps and pectoral muscles are inflated, women's arms and legs are thinned, wrinkles are ironed out, teeth are altered and whitened, and separate heads are often placed onto different bodies.

These practices have generated vigorous discussions about the ethical nature of Photoshop manipulation. Slimming down already too-thin female models or adding more pronounced washboard abs to perfectly fit male models creates false ideas about beauty. Weight obsession and steroid use among teenagers should not come as a surprise given that we are awash with highly distorted images of what it means to be attractive, which build up our anxiety levels and encourage us to buy beauty and health products to "fix" the problem, which is ultimately our inability to ever measure up. Digital manipulation in advertising plays into the most egregious aspects of our consumer culture: Products marketed under false pretenses. How ethical is it for a beauty product company to fake antiwrinkle cream results in their before and after images?

Digital manipulation is also used prolifically in public relations materials and, as with advertising, stirs up controversy about the ethical nature of digital manipulation. Consider the ethics, for example, of a university's public relations department that adds images (via Photoshop or other software) of minority students in their admissions brochure in order to sell the notion of campus diversity to donors or prospective students. Consider too the ethics of a government publicly releasing an image of a missile launch that has an additional missile image digitally inserted (as in the case of Iran in 2009).[36] Today, these practices are routine.

The largest area of concern, however, involves photojournalism, which is based on the notion that a photograph is real. In recent years, some photojournalists have been caught tweaking images for various reasons. Some have strived for a more dramatic composition (and thus front-page status) by compositing two photographs together or eliminating unwanted elements from the frame, thus altering reality. Others have color-corrected photos to, as they say, more closely reflect what their eye actually saw at the time they snapped the picture. Since cameras can't as easily adapt to the green hue of fluorescent lights, for example, or for the competing exposures of a dark inside and a brighter outdoors, some photojournalists defend the use of Photoshop because it makes their images *more* realistic. To date, the mainstream press has responded to these practices by adopting a zero-tolerance position on any kind of digital manipulation or posing—so as to protect the integrity of their product.[37] Indeed, numerous media establishments have fired photojournalists for tampering with their photos—even those who have tried to make their photos more realistic. For example, the *Charlotte Observer* suspended Patrick Schneider in 2006 for adjusting the background of a silhouetted firefighter against the morning sun. Schneider argued that he had underexposed the original photograph and was trying to recapture what his eyes really saw. The *Observer,* however, cited a strict policy against altering colors from the original scene photographed. Meanwhile, the blogosphere has exploded with "fake or photo" or "fauxtography"[38] detection Web sites, ratting out unethical photojournalists or uncannily manipulative public relations firms and alerting readers to the easy of manipulation of journalistic photos in the media.

All of these concerns have led Fred Ritchin of the New York School of Photography to create an icon for digital manipulation and to advocate that all photographers acknowledge any image tampering in their advertising, publicity, art, or photojournalism. The icon is meant to represent a camera lens and should be placed, according to Ritchin's guidelines, "outside the bottom perimeter of the image, either on the left or right corner."[39]

"Not a lens": manipulated image

"Lens": nonmanipulated image

But perhaps the real problem is simply the intent to mislead. As filmmaker and photography critic Errol Morris notes, the extreme response from the mainstream press to ban any kind of photo manipulation is grounded in the notion that there is something true about photography in the first place. "It allows the false assumption: if we can just determine that this photograph wasn't Photoshopped, then it must be 'true,'" he writes. "But Photoshop serves as a reminder to us of something that we should have known all along: photographs can deceive."[40] Indeed, an unaltered photograph, like the "objective" treatment of a news story, is no proof of a particular reality. Like any text, it is an interpretation reflecting both the photographer's point of view and the subject's. The opposition to digital manipulation—while helpful in developing a critical eye in reading images—also gives us a false sense of consciousness about the supposed truth of any visual image that has not been perceptibly tampered with.

Images in Context

To fully read an image, then, we need to understand the context in which the image was produced, as well as the context in which it continues to exist. Context can include the way the photo or image was made; who made it and why; the historical circumstances under which it was made; the extent to which the image was circulated, altered, and reconfigured; and the way the image continues to be interpreted and reinterpreted by individuals and publics. For example, when George W. Bush, as the governor of Texas, was videotaped in the mid-1990s flipping his middle finger to the cameraman as he sat in a local television studio, the real meaning of the clip was lost as it circulated (without proper context) over the next decade. The image was true (it happened), but it was also false. Without proper context, one couldn't understand the real story: that Bush was joking around before (not during) a live public television appearance and before he thought the cameras were rolling.

More often than not, the context surrounding a photograph or image exists in written form. (Barthes has argued that an image is forever dependent on verbal text for comprehension.)[41] As such, an image's context often appears as a caption below or beside it, or within the pages of a book, the news media, or a Web site. The Nazi salute photograph, for example, first appeared in newspapers with various captions and accompanying articles explaining the event. It was later reinterpreted (and given deeper meaning) through the autobiographies of at least two people who were there: national team caption Eddie Hapgood, and younger player Stanley Matthews.[42] Without these verbal accounts—for example, if we were to discover the Nazi salute photo in a box somewhere—we might be at a loss to what the story is. We could infer that the black-and-white photo is a historical record of the Nazi era, assuming we know something about that era. On its own, however, the solitary photograph does not adequately communicate the historical turmoil in which it was created.

The photograph would also not communicate the fact that it went out of circulation for sixty-five years and was resurrected for public consumption by a BBC documentary in 2003. Again, the image took on new meaning. Recast as the "Moment of Shame" in the British news media and in the blogosphere, the picture and the story behind it have become a reference point for understanding government conciliation in the face of power and authoritarian rule. "That picture of impressionable footballers obeying orders from mutton-headed apparatchiks went round the world and became a lasting source of shame to this country," wrote British columnist David Mellor in 2008.[43] Without mooring or a backstory, a photograph is thus a slim measure of evidence that something happened, and it can have a huge range of interpretations.

If interpreting a photograph is often dependent on verbal descriptions, we must be critical readers of these accounts as well. Captions, accompanying articles, and autobiographical accounts surrounding a photograph can be misleading or utterly false, and quotes can be taken out of context. For example, Eddie Hapgood's personal recollections about his team's locker-room dissent before the 1938 soccer match, which appear in his published autobiography (1946), may have been shaped by historical hindsight. Was his own visceral protest what *really* happened, or did he perhaps alter his story after the photograph was published, after the British press made a big deal out of the photo (initially blaming Germany for requiring the salute) and after World War II revealed the horrible truths about Nazi Germany?

To successfully read an image, we need to understand:

- the *compositional forces* (either intended or unintended by the image's creator);
- the various *signs* within the image that are either evident, learned, or culturally imbued;
- the possibilities of *posing* or *digital manipulation* (especially when photographs are concerned);
- and perhaps most important, the *context* in which these images were produced, as well as the context in which they continue to exist.

Every choice a creator makes in terms of framing, content placement, manipulation (whether ethical or unethical), and textual mooring affects the way the image operates in our social discourse. Visual literacy is thus a way toward interpreting the stories behind the image and attempting to make sense of our image-laden culture.

CRITICAL PROCESS 1 | Composition in Photography

This exercise is about aesthetics and the power of the photographer, videographer, or film director to create emotion and meaning through framing choices alone. Select a professional photograph from a Web site, newspaper, or magazine or, if you want to be slightly more ambitious, a three-to-four shot clip from film or TV. Your goal is to think about how this visual text uses the principles of composition described in this chapter. What choices did the photographer make in terms of depth, arrangement of space, and other aesthetic principles?

Describe the choices the author of the image made. Think about the use of color, form, line direction, depth, foreground versus background, frame magnetism, and rule of thirds. If it is a moving text, describe the movement and shot juxtaposition. Do these uses conform to the principles of composition described in this chapter? If they do, what principles do they use? If they don't, how do they differ?

Analyze the function of the choices made in presenting the image. What is the intended audience of the image, and how do the aesthetic choices affect that audience? Did the photographer want the audience to feel a certain way?

Interpret what the photographer or artist might have meant in creating these feelings or audience reactions. Why do you think the photographer wanted to make the audience feel this way?

Evaluate the photograph or image—how interesting or striking or telling is it? How well does the photograph accomplish what you think it is trying to accomplish?

Engage with other students regarding the images they picked. Would you have come to the same conclusions?

| CRITICAL PROCESS 2 | Semiotic Analysis of Visual Texts

Undertake a semiotic textual analysis of a magazine advertisement showing how meaning is constructed. Choose an ad with people in it, one that is rich with cultural meaning. The more interesting and complex the ad, the more there is to talk about. Forget that this is an advertisement created by an ad agency trying to sell you something, and just focus on the image as a complicated visual text.

Describe the composition of the ad; then describe the various signs (icon, index, symbol) and the way the ad is anchored (or not anchored) through text. What ideologies do you think are communicated through the advertisement?

Analyze the patterns of meaning: How do the cultural signs you identify point to a general message?

Interpret what the individual signs mean (and ultimately what the general message of the entire image means). Start with individual signs: If the ad contains a woman with blond hair, then describe the meaning of blond hair in our culture. If the ad portrays a man with a muscular physique, then what does that say about our attitudes toward masculinity and the pressure men are under to stay in shape? If someone has a crew cut, then what does this say about that person? Does this image make you think "military," and can you address the "military culture" that seeps into U.S. culture at large? Do you think James Bond? State trooper? Rock star? Are there any intertextual references to other media texts within the image? If so, what might they mean? In short, dig deep into the core signifiers of your culture and explain what they signify, as if you are talking to aliens who know nothing about our culture.

Evaluate the meaning of the image. To what extent is the ad manipulated, either by photo-editing software, or in terms of a manipulated rendering of reality? Does this image reflect or challenge mainstream values? Is it sexist? Is it racist? Does it convey positive or negative body-image or gender-role connotations? What can you say about the ideology behind the image and its relation to your own ideological position?

Engage in a discussion with your classmates about your semiotic interpretations. Did your image communicate the same kind of "common sense" narrative as many of your peers' images? Why? How?

4

Narrative Formulas and the Cycle of Storytelling

During the run-up to the 2012 presidential election, candidates campaigning against the incumbent president took on "Big Government," influential lobbyists, and, to a lesser extent, Wall Street greed. Never mind that most of the candidates running against President Obama served in government, worked as lobbyists, and/or received campaign money—as President Obama also did—from Wall Street. The stories that presidential candidates told about themselves during TV debates and in political TV ads often had little to do with their real-life behavior and actual work history. Instead, these stories belonged to an enduring genre—similar to detective mysteries or western adventures. The candidates appeared as rugged individualists, as Middle American characters who "we the people" identify with—intrepid detectives and tough cowboys who are ubiquitous stock characters in our national depository of shared stories and myths.

This is not an accident. By associating themselves with characteristics found in fictional forms, presidential candidates can conceal many of the contradictions—for example, former governors running against government, or former lobbyists trashing lobbying—that emerge in the swarm of stories that inundate any contemporary presidential race. The mainstream news media—as they also did in the 2004 and 2008 elections—played their role in the larger political narrative by drawing little attention to the actual narrative strategies of political campaigns. Instead, most news media overemphasized polls, which often reduced the story of an election to a two-dimensional "who's winning/who's losing" racehorse narrative, obscuring complex policy issues like the Afghanistan war, economic growth, and wealth disparity. The racehorse narrative has been bolstered by the proliferation of presidential polls and Internet sites that track these polls daily (e.g., realclearpolitics.com) and critique polling data (e.g., fivethirtyeight.com). Back in 2008, Clark Hoyt, then public editor of the *New York Times,* reported that, of the 270 political articles published in the *Times* during the last few months of the election, just "a little over 10 percent were primarily about policy substance." These data were similar to election coverage for much of mainstream media. Hoyt noted that other studies reported that in fall 2008 the vast majority of election stories were about "the horse race, political tactics, polls, and the like."[1] These nonpolicy narratives often pitted conservatives against liberals in dramatic good guy/bad guy intrigue that many in the voting public, who are moderate in their politics, found wanting.

This example of national presidential elections helps establish one major assumption of this book: understanding metaphors and stories as a key to understanding why our society and politics work the way they do. So, the underlying and dominant structure of most of our everyday media, whether it is a *Harry Potter* book, the latest episode of *NCIS*, a new Taylor Swift CD, a Chevy truck magazine ad, a political TV ad, or a news story reporting poll results, is the narrative. As our dominant symbolic structure, narratives help us make sense of experience and articulate what we value. Film and literature professor Frank McConnell puts it in strong terms at the outset of his book *Storytelling & Mythmaking*: ". . . stories matter, and matter deeply, because they are the best way to save our lives."[2] Psychologist Jerome Bruner reminds us that we are storytelling creatures, that as children we acquire language to tell stories that we already have inside us. In his 2002 book *Making Stories: Law, Literature, Life* he says, "Stories, finally, provide models of the world."[3] As powerful archetypal models, narratives replicate (and reduce) the rhythms of the birth-life-death in daily experience, representing them in the beginning-middle-end cycles of media-generated storytelling.

This book acknowledges the centrality—and limitations—of stories in our daily lives and how they provide the models through which we understand the world. Our perspective here aims a critical lens at the narrative as that cultural space where we work out what's important and meaningful. Historically, other critical perspectives have searched for meaning in other places: Literary studies once focused on the writer/author as the locus of meaning, Marxist perspectives looked at economic arrangements as the foundation for meaning, and "reader response" or audience studies relocated the center of meaning to the audience. We argue here that meaning certainly can emerge from all three, but particularly at the intersection among an author's text, a reader's (or viewer's) response, and an industry's choices. Our critical choice here is to focus on common ground, the shared territory that intersects these multiple critical perspectives: the narrative. Our view here is that authors create stories, industries produce them, and audiences need them.

The common denominator between our entertainment and information cultures is the narrative. With narratives as their chief currency, most authors and most mass media are in the business of telling and selling stories, making the lines between fiction and news blurry and complicated. In this chapter we investigate the sociopolitical implications and limitations of narrative forms and genres. We will also analyze the types of narrative formulas that dominate our social landscape, their chief tendencies, and why they matter so much.

HEGEMONY, COMMON SENSE, AND STORYTELLING

To understand the power of stories in our culture, it is crucial to first understand power in general. Toward that end and in order to lay out the social relationships among politics, culture, and democracy, this book grounds a view of power in the concept of hegemony. As defined by the *Oxford English Dictionary*, the Greek term *hegemony* originally meant "the leadership or predominant authority of one state of a confederacy or union over the others: originally used in reference to the states of ancient Greece...." British cultural theorist Raymond Williams in *Marxism and Literature* discussed this "traditional definition" of hegemony as "political rule or domination, especially in relations between states."[4] In the 1920s and 1930s, Italian philosopher and activist Antonio Gramsci worked out a more complex notion of the concept (what Williams called "one of the major turning points in Marxist cultural theory"[5]) during his imprisonment by Mussolini's fascist government. For Gramsci, hegemony explained how a ruling class in a society maintains its power, not simply by military or police force, but more commonly by citizens' consent and deference to power. He offered an explanation for why people who are without power—the disenfranchised, the poor, the disaffected, the unemployed, exploited workers—do not more routinely rise up against those in power. For Gramsci, "the rule of one class over another does not depend on economic or physical power alone but rather on persuading the ruled to accept the system of beliefs of the ruling class and to share their social, cultural, and moral values."[6] **Hegemony**, then, as it is used here, means the predominance of elite classes and the acceptance of the dominant values in the culture by those who are subordinate and less influential than those who hold economic, cultural, and political power.

Writing in the 1970s, Raymond Williams notes the fluid nature of hegemony:

> A lived hegemony is always a process. . . . It is a realized complex of experiences, relationships, and activities. . . . Moreover, . . . it does not just passively exist as a form of dominance. It has continually to be renewed, recreated, defended, and modified. It is also continually resisted, limited, altered, and challenged by pressures not at all its own.[7]

So how then does this process actually work? How do ruling classes and political parties come to convince its citizens to consent? How do the interests and values of the dominant and powerful groups in a society come to be seen by the subordinate and less powerful as common ground, as shared territory?

Common Sense

Edward Bernays, who set down many of the defining principles of modern public relations in his 1923 book *Crystallizing Public Opinion*—and whose client list ranged from the American Tobacco Company to President Calvin Coolidge—defined public relations as the "engineering of consent."[8] Bernays believed that companies and rulers couldn't lead people—or get them to do what they wanted—until they consented to what those companies or rulers were trying to do, whether it was convincing them to support going to war or women smoking cigarettes. To pull this off, Bernays had to convert clients' desires and plans to "common sense"; that is, he tried to convince consumers and citizens that his clients' interests were the natural or normal way to do business—*just the way things were.* Bernays believed that if companies or politicians could convince consumers and citizens that the interests of the powerful were "common sense" and therefore normal or natural, they created an atmosphere and context in which there was less chance for challenge and criticism. Common sense, after all, repels self-scrutiny ("that's just plain common sense"—end of discussion). Status quo values and conventional wisdom (e.g., hard work and religious belief are rewarded with economic success) or political arrangements (e.g., the traditional two-party system serves democracy best) become taken for granted, viewed as natural and commonsensical ways to organize and see the world.

One prominent element of the hegemony process then is the idea and influence of commonsense. Such sense can be instrumental in allowing citizens to come to agreement, even if it's not necessarily in their best interests. Yet common sense is not usually natural but rather socially constructed, its definition shifting over time. For example, it was once common sense that the world was flat, that black people shouldn't be allowed to vote, or that women shouldn't play sports. One persistent "commonsense" argument that became a big part of conservative state and presidential politics in the early 2000s was selling the idea of homosexuality as deviant and unnatural. Historically, once such views become the norm or widely accepted as common sense, then local ordinances, federal laws, and even constitutional amendments can be enacted that penalize certain groups for being outside the bounds of the normal. Common sense is particularly powerful because it contains no abstract strategies for criticizing dominant points of view and therefore certifies class, race, or sexual orientation divisions, or mainstream political views, as received conventional wisdom. To buy uncritically into common sense, then, inadvertently serves to maintain such divisions as natural; to cling to commonsense positions shuts down a discussion before there is any reasoned assessment about the ways in which social divisions, cultural taboos, or political hierarchies are not natural and given. Commonsense withstands definition, analysis, and close examination, as Stuart Hall has argued, "precisely because what is 'common' about it is that it is not subject to tests of internal coherence and logical consistency."[9]

So when political candidates run for office, the stories they tell about themselves espouse their connection to Middle American common sense and shared values—for instance, a George W. Bush photo-op in working-class jeans clearing brush on his

Texas ranch or Barack Obama playing basketball with his buddies in a high school gym. These symbolic ties to common values connect the powerful to the everyday, making their interests appear common and shared. They are like us.

Examining how common sense is woven into our cultural fabric is key to understanding hegemony's connection to storytelling. The narrative, as the dominant symbolic way we make sense of experience and articulate our values, becomes the vehicle for delivering the commonsense goods. Therefore, ideas, values, and beliefs are carried in our mainstream media stories—the stories we tell and find in daily conversations; in the local paper; on the evening news or online; or in books, magazines, movies, and favorite TV shows. This makes the narrative the normative structure or container whereby ideas, values, and beliefs are converted into "common sense"—the way things are. As the most familiar and accessible structure we have for understanding our world, narrative is the obvious and formidable medium for rendering the world commonsensical. It is why every four years our two main political presidential candidates/characters spend a billion dollars or more in national elections, trying to tell and sell stories about themselves that align them with the main values of their constituencies and the bulk of Americans who would vote.

In 2012, Barack Obama and Mitt Romney both tried to align themselves with the values of voters—and create negative narratives about each other. Obama was portrayed by Romney as a failed leader, while Romney was portrayed by Obama as out of touch with the middle class.

Consensus Narratives

Not all stories, of course, carry common sense and the dominant values of a society. Stories can also—in the words of Raymond Williams—"resist, limit, alter, and challenge" our commonsense notions of the world. However, those sorts of stories are less likely to become part of a cultural consensus. Media scholar David Thorburn called these popular centrist stories "consensus narratives"—narratives that take place on prime-time television, in Hollywood movies, and in mainstream newspapers and magazines. He argued that such narratives operated across different times and cultures—in "the oral-formulaic of Homer's day, the theater of Sophocles, the Elizabethan theater, the English novel from Defoe to Dickens, . . . the silent film, the sound film, and television during the Network Era."[10] The job of such narratives "is to articulate the culture's central myths, in a widely accessible language, an inheritance of shared stories, plots, character types, cultural symbols, and narrative conventions. Such a language is popular because it is legible to the common understanding of a majority of the culture."[11] Consider enormously, popular, artists like Adele and Mumford & Sons and how their songs construct narratives by pairing lyrical conventions and accessible song structures that can be easily understood by the dramatic rise and fall of their melodies.

The reason that consensus narratives work is that they identify with a culture's dominant values—particularly the theme in most of these stories that individual character can triumph through adherence to a set of taken-for-granted Middle American virtues such as allegiances to family, common sense, honesty, hard work, religious belief, capitalism, democracy, competition, moderation, loyalty, fairness, authenticity, modesty, heterosexuality, and so forth. Again, these kinds of traditional Middle American virtues are the ones that our major politicians frequently align themselves within the political ads that tell their stories. The term *middle* in "middle class" or "Middle American" signifies the middle ground between a variety of contradictory and central cultural tensions: nature vs. culture, individual vs. institution, public vs. private, liberal vs. conservative, authentic vs. artificial, or tradition vs. change. Consensus narratives also appear to solve—or mediate—a number of difficult conflicts. So, for example, many of our Hollywood and TV westerns, operating as consensus narratives, have celebrated the individual integrity of the lone rugged hero, seeking the middle ground between the brutal forces of nature or uncivilized enemies and the civilizing influences of the small town and westward expansion. This, in part, explains the importance of political strategists tying candidate images to values that resonate with such stories and their triumphant themes.

Media Narratives: Responding and Resisting

So as readers and viewers, as consumers and citizens, how do we react to this media landscape where power plays out and values are articulated in the stories we tell? Stuart

Hall has offered one influential model that partially helps explain our relationship to media narratives, one that works particularly well in understanding how we view news stories and political ads. Hall has argued that as readers and viewers, as consumers and citizens, we take three positions (with multiple variations) with regard to media stories. First, there is a dominant stance where we might identify fully with and accept a story's intended meaning, which seems normal and commonsensical to us. For example, in 2008 or 2012 if we held traditional Democratic or progressive views, the political ads for Barack Obama seemed to replicate and articulate our own view of the world. Second, there is a "negotiated" position, which means that we might partly share the messages and values of the ad, but may object in part and need to alter it in a way that is in keeping with our beliefs. We may have supported Hillary Clinton back in the 2008 primaries but needed to transfer our allegiance to the chosen candidate Obama, modifying our views and tempering our criticisms of him because we came to believe that he had the best chance to win. Third, Hall argued that we could also read a media story in an oppositional way. For example, Obama supporters watching a Mitt Romney ad in 2012 might have totally rejected the dominant set of values and the story told in Republican ads because they ran counter to their own views and values. (More likely, an Obama supporter may have resisted the ad completely and simply changed or muted the channel, just as a Romney supporter may have done the same for an Obama ad.) In this reading, we might have understood the dominant reading that seemed intended in the GOP ad, but we read against the text and rejected the story being told.[12]

Let's look at an example of how people respond to a political issue and the narratives surrounding it. In the early 2000s, Tennessee was one of nine states (and still is) without a state income tax, relying mainly on a high sales tax—around 10 percent—on many services and most goods, including food. The outgoing Republican governor of the state, who initially opposed an income tax, came to believe that such a tax would be fairer, placing a greater burden on wealthier citizens and allowing the state to reduce the sales tax and eliminate taxing food, a particularly heavy burden for poorer and low-income working people. His attempts ultimately failed as the majority of Democratic and Republican lawmakers in the state all ran on "no state income tax" platforms. Polls conducted in the state routinely reported that the majority of citizens opposed an income tax. When the economy slumped badly in the early 2000s and state surpluses vanished, rather than consider an income tax (which the incumbent Republican governor now supported, to the dismay and opposition of the majority of Tennessee legislators), the state raised its sales tax again and eventually approved a state lottery, another system of raising money that relied heavily on poorer to middle-income groups for revenue.

What is fascinating about this story is that studies done in the state showed that more than 60 percent of adult taxpayers—mostly from low- to modest-income brackets—would pay less taxes overall under a state income tax system (because the sales tax would decline and they would pay just a small percentage or nothing at all under the proposed graduated income tax). Yet these income groups were often the ones most firmly opposed to the new more progressive tax system. Many state university students—raised by parents who traditionally opposed an income tax—also resisted supporting what amounted to lower taxes, even though their tuition kept increasing by 10 to 15 percent a year as the state's ability to support higher education diminished, particularly during a recession. The key question here is: Why would poorer people and many working college students oppose an income tax when it clearly was in their best economic interest to support it? In other words, how did those in power convince less wealthy people to maintain the status quo position that helped more affluent and powerful citizens pay less tax?

One answer is found in an examination of the most popular story that circulated during this time, mainly told by talk radio personalities interviewing lawmakers and influential citizens who opposed an income tax. According to their story, a vote for a state income tax meant that individual citizens would have to turn over more money to government; even if this didn't happen right away, the new tax system would give the government authority to raise the income tax levels whenever it needed to (and remember, this is a state in which the local lawmakers already routinely raised sales tax every two years). These radio talk show hosts and anti–income tax lawmakers, most of them affluent and from the more conservative suburbs that surrounded Tennessee's two largest cities—Memphis and Nashville—constructed a powerful narrative that was very persuasive. In this narrative, ordinary citizens are set upon by state "revenue men" (an old Southern epithet for government agents from romanticized moonshining and bootlegging days), who act as a sinister force threatening ordinary people's most cherished value, individualism, which is compromised in the hands of a bureaucratic, heartless, and greedy institution—state government.

With the common man as the good guy and the demon government as the bad guy, this powerful tale—with themes similar to those found in our movie westerns and TV police dramas—dominates each year that Tennessee income tax discussions resurface. The appointed heroes of this ongoing tale, then, are the radio talk hosts who seem to take the middle ground between citizens and government, staking claim to the commonsense view that a state income tax is abnormal; this view apparently solves the conflict between the individual and the institution or state. Of course, what is ultimately going on is that affluent talk show hosts, citizens, and lawmakers, who represent the dominant ruling class in the state and would have to pay more under an income tax plan, sold a story to less powerful and less affluent citizens: the story that *all* their mutual interests would be served by opposing the government's new tax system.

The key idea is that as citizens both watching the democratic process and participating in this process, understanding the relationships among power, values, and storytelling offers insights into how culture works and how we construct meaning. According to hegemony theory, power is partially maintained and managed through news stories and political ads that make claims that the values of ruling parties and the values of ordinary citizens are one and the same. Sometimes this may actually be true, but many times, it may not be. As citizens, our responsibility lies in understanding this process in order to "resist, limit, alter, and challenge" those stories that we think are misrepresenting actual experience, our interests, and democratic practices.

DEFINING NARRATIVE FORMS

Making the case that power is maintained and values are transmitted through common-sense stories requires an examination of the common ways that narratives manifest themselves in our culture. When we enter a video store or access Netflix online, for example, we routinely see movies categorized by genre or narrative formulas: comedy, drama, action/adventure, romance, mystery, westerns, science fiction, or musicals. With television we also tend to place programs into commonsense categories: comedy (or sitcoms), dramas, game shows, news documentaries, and reality shows. While critics and consumers might prefer slightly different designations—or larger generic subdivisions (as in music: hard rock, indie rock, punk, pop, metal, techno, etc.)—the fundamental point is that media "texts" are grouped together because they share common features that allow media industries to sort them for consumers who prefer particular, differentiated, and identifiable kinds of music and stories. For example, if we watch a movie from the urban thriller listings on Netflix, we assume that the story will take place in a city environment, contain dramatic tension between forms of good and evil (often involving cops and criminals), and wring suspense from life-and-death situations. Not every urban thriller will necessarily contain all these elements, but it would not be unreasonable to expect them.

American filmmakers from D. W. Griffith to Steven Spielberg to Christopher Nolan have understood the allure of narrative, which always includes two basic components: the **story** (or plot—what happens to whom) and the **discourse** (or narration—how the story is told).[13] For example, sporting events are fundamentally narrative in their structure. In a televised football game, then, the story is the chronological unfolding of the action over time, while the discourse is the description and analysis of the game provided by announcers and commentators who use technology like replay and slow motion to alter or retell the chronological action of the game's unfolding plot. When NBC in the 1990s tried an experiment by taking away the announcers and letting fans just watch the story of the game, the network robbed the event of half its narrative—the discourse. Viewers and fans, even those annoyed by inept or offensive commentators, missed the narration, and NBC's experiment lasted for only one game. Even when we attend live sporting events, we sometimes take radios to provide the discourse, we spin out running commentaries during the game in conversations with friends and other fans, or we simply add the discourse in our own heads and imaginations.

Although most of us use the terms *narrative* and *story* interchangeably, narrative scholars generally regard "the story" as one ingredient in the larger narrative structure, as a subcategory of narrative. Most movies, like most TV shows and novels, feature a number of stories, or plot lines, that play out within the larger narrative of the entire film. For example, in Sam Mendes's Academy Award–winning film *American Beauty* (1999), the narrator is a character who is already dead—middle-aged father and husband Lester Burnham (played by Kevin Spacey). In this dark comedy, Lester recounts how his seemingly perfect suburban life was for him phony and unbearable. The movie's subplots—Lester's disconnected relationships with his daughter and wife, the unusual new neighbors next door, and Lester's obsession with his daughter's high school girlfriend—culminate in Lester's ultimate redemption and demise. So the film works on the level of story, with the events unfolding in time, and on the level of discourse, with the narrator taking various plot lines out of sequence and rearranging them to serve the overall narrative style that the director is after.

As defined above, the narrative functions as a large overarching category that symbolically organizes everything from the structure of a football game to the composition of a TV program. It's such a large category that it demands subdivisions, which is why narrative forms developed as a way to differentiate among and talk about the vast array of narratives. Aristotle (384–322 B.C.) in his *Poetics* first talked about generic categories in his analysis of poetry, which he divided into three basic types: "Epic poetry and Tragedy, Comedy also and Dithyrambic poetry, and the music of the flute and of the lyre. . . ."[14] Aristotle, in addition to teasing out differences between tragedy and comedy, was differentiating here among poetry that was either spoken, performed, or sung. To fast-forward to more contemporary interpretations of narrative forms, literary scholar John Cawelti in *Adventure, Mystery, and Romance* did some of the first serious analysis of commonplace popular genres or formulas such as the detective story and the western. He defined the literary formula as "a combination or synthesis of a number of specific cultural conventions with a more universal story form or archetype" and as "a means of generalizing the characteristics of large groups of individual works from certain combinations of cultural materials and archetypal story patterns."[15] In other words, Cawelti suggested that such popular story forms are archetypal: They emerge across different cultures and in different time periods, and they have distinctive features or formulas that help us distinguish one type from another.

Literary critics and popular culture scholars have tackled the problem of naming genre forms from a variety of perspectives. For example, Cawelti identified a "typology" of five popular literary formulas: adventure, romance, mystery, melodrama, and "alien beings or states." Similarly, in Northrop Frye's 1957 seminal study of traditional literary forms, *Anatomy of Criticism*, he marked four major narrative forms—comedy, romance, tragedy, and "irony and satire"—associating each of them with seasonal impulses: spring (comedy), summer (romance), autumn (tragedy), and winter (irony and satire).[16] Frank McConnell, in *Storytelling & Mythmaking*, adapted Frye's "cycle of storytelling" and offered the epic, romance, melodrama, and satire as four chief generic types.[17] He associates his four categories with dominant character types: epics (with kings), romances (knights), melodramas (pawns), and satires ("fool's mate"). McConnell draws from the original *Star Wars* film (1977) to demonstrate how these generic types saturate contemporary storytelling. He views Obi-Wan Kenobi as a heroic epic character; Luke Skywalker as the romantic hero; Han Solo, the melodramatic hero; and the droids—C3PO and R2D2—as the satiric characters. Drawing on these categories—particularly McConnell's linking of literary and visual narratives—this book uses epic, romance, melodrama, and satire as four useful formulas for discussing the central storytelling threads and character strands woven into media narratives. Rather than argue that these are distinct narrative categories marked by clear boundaries, our narrativist perspective suggests that threads of these various formulas contribute to the complex patterns of narratives in contemporary culture. Any single TV series or film narrative, then, might contain material from all four generic fabrics.

Epic Stories and Tales of Spring

Epic tales and characters are about beginnings, about the founding of cities and the establishment of law. McConnell tells us that the epic is the narrative form through which cultures and authors "imagine most explicitly how things must have come to be the way they are." McConnell uses the metaphor of the City as a way into understanding contemporary genres and forms; narratives with epic impulses are concerned with the founding of cities or civilizations, with the establishing of laws and a new order, with the birth of societies. In narratives dominated by epic concerns, "the hero is a king, the City is seen as it is founded." The central narrative tension of epics often features the conflict between civilizing impulses and the untamed forces of nature or savagery, between wise leaders trying to establish order and villains or beasts representing evil and chaos. While wise fathers and kings are central figures in traditional epics, their deeds and legacies are often carried forward by devoted sons—for example, Aeneas carrying on the work of his father Anchises in Virgil's *Aeneid*. Additional historical examples of epics include Homer's *Iliad* and *The Odyssey* (and films like *Jason and the Argonauts*), and the King Arthur legends (and films like *Camelot* and *Excalibur*), which McConnell calls "the dominant popular entertainment of their time," retaining their appeal "for perhaps longer than any set of stories in the European tradition." But think also of the first two books of the Bible, Genesis and Exodus, as among "the most complex and moving counterpoints in the history of storytelling. It is the history at once of the birth of the Law, and the succession of unwilling heroes who become, in spite of themselves, the agents of the Law's self-revelation to man."[18]

In contemporary storytelling, the Superman saga certainly resonates with the *Iliad*—"that great and bitter vision of the birth of one civilization out of the demolition of another."[19] Think of *Superman* in its various forms (comic books, cartoons,

Superman Returns (2006) represented another retelling of the Superman mythology. *Man of Steel* featured yet another version in 2013.

live-action films, and television variations like *Smallville*), containing similar story points: the demise of the planet Krypton, and Jor-El (as king/father) beginning anew through his son:

> . . . strange visitor from another planet who came to Earth with powers and abilities far beyond those of mortal men. Superman! Who can change the course of mighty rivers, bend steel in his bare hands, and who, disguised as Clark Kent, mild-mannered reporter for a great metropolitan newspaper, fights a never-ending battle for Truth, Justice, and the American Way![20]

While the epic narrative is not the dominant form of storytelling in contemporary popular culture, epic characters and themes about spring and beginnings wind through our mediated landscape—from wise king-like/father roles of Obi-Wan Kenobi in *Star Wars* (fighting the dark force Darth Vader) to Gandalf in the *Lord of the Rings* trilogy (confronting the sinister Saruman) to Dumbledore in the *Harry Potter* books and films (battling the evil Lord Voldemort). It is also revealing to track the impulses of the epic in more routine places. In TV's *M*A*S*H* (1972–1983), for example, Colonel Sherman Potter plays a benign king/father figure, charged with overseeing the emergence of civilization and a "city"—the fictional medical unit constituted by the doctors, nurses, and staff supporting the GIs fighting in the Korean War. Finally, the 2005 Disney movie, *The Chronicles of Narnia: The Lion, the Witch, and the Wardrobe*, retells C. S. Lewis's classic children's allegory. In the story, the lion figure Aslan emerges to retake the kingdom ("city") of Narnia from the evil white witch, thus restoring law and reestablishing civilization.

Romances and Tales of Summer

Romance narratives are about civilizing the city, introducing rules to live by that stitch together the fragile social fabric—living in a world where love and friendship are possible. In the romance, McConnell argues, the "founding figure of the king recedes into the background," replaced by heroic characters whose "mission is not to establish a political entity, the City, but rather to establish the secondary though essential human codes of conduct which make City life tolerable."[21] While epic tales usually feature men as champions, romances offer female characters more central roles. Historically, the heroes of romances are most typically knights and princesses—the children of the father/king of the epic world, carrying on the work of father/king figures. Codes of chivalry, loyalty, and duty ultimately represent those civilizing forces that sustain order in the world of the romance. Like the season of summer, the narrative cycle of romance promotes a world where human nature is ultimately viewed as decent and good, full of possibilities.

For McConnell, *Sir Gawain and the Green Knight* is the ultimate medieval romance. Gawain is the Round Table's "courteous knight, the valiant and definitively civilized decent man, the pure vassal or loyal retainer who brings civility into the civilization [King] Arthur has established."[22] While many traditional romances either tell the tale of macho knights rescuing fainting damsels or women requiring men for their psychic and physical completion, romances often feature more equality—a battle of wits between the sexes that often occurs in modern romantic comedies, where a man and a woman may begin as adversarial rivals before falling in love.

In the last century, Disney cartoon adaptations like *Snow White and the Seven Dwarfs*, *Sleeping Beauty*, *Cinderella*, and *Beauty and the Beast* have become a familiar model for romantic storytelling. Such narratives feature spirited princess-types as the central characters who search for, and often find, enduring love with their prince/knights.

Contemporary TV variations range from *Sex and the City* to *Desperate Housewives* to *Grey's Anatomy*. These more recent television romances often complicate the formula by sprinkling prince/knight types throughout various storylines or by withholding these male characters (to create dramatic tension), often desperately sought by the main female characters as these series evolve over a number of years. But it isn't always traditional romantic love that drives the narrative. The 1995 children's book *The Golden Compass* by Philip Pullman (the first installment in this fantasy trilogy) casts an adolescent girl, Lyra, as the main character. Although the narrative is full of epic overtones and a new city simmering in the Northern Lights, the heart of the book and what holds the adventures together is Lyra's love for her shape-changing daemon and her loyalty to her adolescent and adult friends.

On the male side of the equation, contemporary romances are also about duty, friendship, and loyalty. Take Peter Weir's 2003 film adaptation of *Master and Commander* (based on two books in Patrick O'Brian's twenty-volume naval saga). Russell Crowe plays Captain John Aubrey, carrying on the work of father/king figure and naval legend, Lord Nelson. It is partly a movie about duty, military honor, and friendship. As one reviewer suggested, Aubrey "wants to serve his country. It is his duty, in a distant corner of the Napoleonic Wars, to engage an enemy ship. . . ."[23] Aubrey above all sees duty and friendship as civilizing forces, and in the romance it is the maintenance of social order that typically resolves or civilizes the conflict between good and evil.

One of the most addictive romances of 2013, *Downton Abbey*—the story of the "upstairs" British aristocrats and their "downstairs" servants—has been among the most popular series in the history of Great Britain and U.S. public television. Downton is a place—a "city" to use our narrative metaphor "ruled by" Robert Crawley, the Earl of Grantham, surely descended from kings. He is a civilized man whose duty it is to protect Downton and pass its care and maintenance on to his "son," Matthew Crawley, who is actually a distant third cousin and, if the rules are followed, the only man (and male heir) left standing who can run the estate (Grantham and his wife have three daughters, who are technically ineligible to rule). Matthew, however, is from the professional class—a lawyer—and bristles at the rules and the class system but eventually marries the eldest daughter, Lady Mary Crawley, who is determined to carry on her father's legacy (but initially angry that she was passed over). Much of the first two seasons of the program feature Matthew and Mary's sometimes up and sometimes doomed romance.

Downton Abbey is narrative about duty, loyalty, and friendship as civilizing forces that hold a city and its inhabitants together. But it is mostly about love—between Matthew and Mary, between housemaid Anna and valet John, and between the youngest daughter, Lady Sybil, who defied upper-class rules to become a nurse during the war and defied them again to marry the family's chauffeur, an Irish activist and patriot who despises the class system. But this story is also about Downton's decline and the threats to romance and old rules precipitated by it. The narrative is set in a dark time during and after World War I when the aristocracy broke down and the working class woke up. Lord Grantham's "city" too begins to literally crumble, and he may not be able to afford the upkeep. Meanwhile, the story takes a major melodramatic turn when a disagreement erupts between old ways and new medicine—between a snooty aristocratic doctor who thinks Lady Sybil's pregnancy is proceeding normally and a war veteran doctor who argues for a relatively new procedure, a C-section at the nearest hospital. Lord Grantham listens to tradition and Lady Sybil dies. As viewers, we are left to wonder whether duty, honor, and love will restore Downton in the face of this tragedy and the loss of a central romantic character.

Melodramas and Tales of Fall

In the third narrative type, the melodrama, the city has degenerated into a corrupt place, "becoming mysterious and threatening even to the citizens whose lives it is suppose to clarify and dignify." Whereas King Arthur serves as epic hero and Sir Gawain as romantic knight, in Arthurian legend Sir Lancelot is a template for the melodramatic hero. The flawed knight, Lancelot has "both a vision of the sublime possibility of the Round Table and a vision of the human, adulterous but immensely appealing possibility of loving the king's wife." Historically, heroes of melodrama are not typically failed knights but, for McConnell, small-town marshals or sheriffs who are the complicated characters at the center of western novels and films.[24] In today's popular culture, think of the city of Los Angeles—haven for corrupt terrorist cells and evil government "moles"—and renegade terrorist-fighter extraordinaire Jack Bauer on Fox's *24* (2001–2010).

But while westerns are not as popular as they once were, they provide numerous apt examples of this cycle of storytelling. In the world of melodrama, the City (or town) "has come to be not the end of the hero's activity, but the originating problem of his dilemma." These dilemmas challenge the lone gunfighter or small-town sheriff who must stand up to opposing forces within the town or from the outside world, situations that will be familiar to anyone who has seen a western— or a parody of a western as seen in countless cartoons and comedies. Prominent examples in actual westerns include Gary Cooper in *High Noon* (1952), Alan Ladd in *Shane* (1953), and Gregory Peck in *The Gunfighter* (1950). In these narratives, the central characters not only have to clean up or civilize a town but must "live out as well as regulate the passion of the town," often finding "the conflict between . . . public and private responsibility a killing one."[25]

Like the season of fall, the narrative cycle of melodrama suggests a world that is in decay, turning brown. The city is near ruin and the social order is under siege. For example, in Clint Eastwood's *Pale Rider* (1985), the land baron/king figure in service to his own greed has taken over the town, which no longer is a civilized or hospitable place. Eastwood's mysterious preacher-loner-hero reasserts a moral code in the name of his own individual ethic and metes out justice to the bad guys. The world of the melodrama is complex; the city's rules are shaken and the former civilizing agent types (land barons) are now suspect. The heroic move in the melodrama calls for the lone gunfighter or sheriff (or Jack Bauer in *24*) to assert individual integrity in the place of the fallen "city" and social space he finds himself in.

On television, the western—with its potent hero-loners asserting their individual code of justice—served as one of the most popular subgenres in TV's early history; thirty prime-time westerns aired in the 1958–59 season alone. The popular western in both film and television, with its themes of civilization and the city confronting the frontier and wilderness, apparently provided a cultural symbol or reference point for many Middle Americans relocating to the suburbs—between town and country. The heroes of these melodramas routinely faced down corrupting influences and threats to social order, mediating the conflicts between the city and the frontier.[26]

As decades wore on, cowboys rode out and cops drove in. The detective formula, with all its variant elements and police intrigue, became another key place to find the powerful influences of melodrama. In the 1970s, police/detective dramas became a TV staple, mirroring the anxieties of many Americans regarding the urban unrest of the late 1960s. In the stories we told in our fiction and in our news, the city had become a dangerous and unruly place, with more urban problems, precipitated by the loss of factory jobs and the decline of manufacturing. Americans' popular entertainment offered the comfort of heroic police and tenacious detectives—dispensing their own brand of justice—protecting a nation from menacing forces that were undermining the economy and our cities. During this period, such shows as *Ironside* (1967–75), *Mannix* (1967–75), *Hawaii Five-O* (1968–80, and recently revived by CBS), *The Mod Squad* (1968–73), *Kojak* (1973–75), and *The Rockford Files* (1974–80) all ranked among the nation's most widely watched programs.

In contemporary melodrama, women characters occasionally emerge to play roles that traditionally belonged to men. In the Coen Brothers' remake of the film *True Grit* (2010), for example, the adolescent female character Mattie Ross teams up with aging U.S. marshal Rooster Cogburn to avenge her father's murder. She shoots and kills the bad guy (but the gun's recoil knocks her into a snake pit and she is saved by Rooster). In TV's *Buffy the Vampire Slayer* (1997–2003), an ordinary high school student, ironically named Buffy, becomes the chosen "slayer" in a city, ironically named Sunnydale. This city sits atop the Hellmouth, that dark place full of demons who continually threaten to explode upward and destroy humanity. Each week, Buffy, the good daughter, asserts her physical prowess and moral righteousness to clean up this decaying town—literally rotted out underneath—full of perverse paternal figures like the mean high school principal and evil city mayor.

Of all the generic forms, variations of the melodrama are the most pervasive storytelling tendencies in contemporary U.S. culture. They can still be found as the major organizing structure in everything from familiar cop shows like *CSI* and *The Closer* to newsmagazines like *60 Minutes* and even the evening news, anchored by star news readers who mediate their cities' worst transgressions. This is not surprising, given that individualism is probably our most persistent American value and that melodramas generally celebrate the rugged tenacity of lone moral heroes—whether they are tough prime-time detectives or cable talk show hosts.

Satiric Stories and Tales of Winter

Satiric narratives are about endings, about worlds and cities that are so dysfunctional, corrupt, or lawless that they need to start over. Think of Jesus of Nazareth as a character in the New Testament, his condemnations of evil and corruption, and the promise of redemption and a New Kingdom. Or in contemporary storytelling, think of Neo (who may or may not be "the Chosen One") in *The Matrix* (1999), a gifted computer hacker who learns that most people are pawns of evil machines and cold-hearted technology; he must navigate the virtual world of the Matrix to save us. In *Storytelling & Mythmaking*, McConnell tracks narratives as they evolve from melodrama to satire, from fall to winter. He argues that in the melodrama the hero seeks "to find out how a confusing and corrupt society operates," and in this quest, the hero "may become a more bitter figure." Under this scenario, the city "has failed to live up to the moral sanctions envisioned by its epic founders," a setting in which the hero becomes the satirist: "his relationship to the community is that of prophetic scorn, disdain, even visionary paranoia." The city too "is now inimical to the survival of the individual, rather than a means of that survival."[27] In Arthurian legend, Modred, the king's bastard son who rebels against the father, best embodies the satiric character. He is "the mocker . . . who reveals by his bitter laughter the failure of the society of the Round Table to live up to its own announced and cherished goals. . . ."[28]

These satiric stories—not always satirical in the comedic sense—can be found within familiar genres, commenting upon their conventions. For example, Clint Eastwood's *Unforgiven* (1992) is a variation on the westerns he made as a younger man. In it, Eastwood (who also directed the film) plays a former hired gunslinger, William Munny, a partially redeemed family man still haunted by a mysterious past that involved "killing women and children." Munny is called to another corrupt town by a group of prostitutes seeking revenge against the town's sadistic sheriff, an evil king figure played by Gene Hackman. In its grim depictions of death and torture, the film satirizes the myths of the Old West as wild but ultimately tamable, and as a place of rugged but decent individualism. In this film, Eastwood has already lost his wife to disease, and his best friend dies at the hands of the corrupt sheriff. While he avenges his friend's death, kills all the bad guys, and again rides out of the town, Eastwood's character is not the melodramatic hero restoring order through the power of his integrity but a sadder figure who lost his integrity long ago and remains on a restless quest for redemption and an elusive new beginning. (The real-life Eastwood attempted to take part in a satiric story within a political narrative at the 2012 Republican National Convention, with a speech endorsing Mitt Romney that attempted to capitalize on his iconic—and iconoclastic—reputation and satirize President Obama as an "empty chair" of a leader.)

In satiric stories, characters are complex, often portrayed and treated as both fools and saints. Again, let's look at how satiric impulses run through a narrative that is not essentially satiric. The popular CBS police procedural, *The Mentalist* (2008–), is a conventional melodrama in most ways, with stock characters and familiar plots that revolve around heroic but beleaguered cops finding the bad guys and restoring order. But the central character, Patrick Jane (played by Simon Baker), is both saint and fool. He is a former carnie and ex-psychic con-man whose wife and daughter have been murdered by the serial killer Red John. Jane's deductive powers rival those of Sherlock Holmes and, after his tragedy, he goes to work as a special consultant for the California Bureau of Investigation (CBI). Because of his tragic past, he is often a sympathetic and even saintly character who usually identifies with victims (but seldom anyone else). He is also mainly interested in using his CBI connection to avenge his family. But he is more often rude, insensitive, odd, and funny at inappropriate times, especially in the middle of serious murder investigations. As a result, conventional police officials regard him as a fool and a clown. He routinely upsets interview subjects and sometimes breaks the law, helping fugitives hide from his own police colleagues and even killing a character he suspects is Red John. At the end of the 2011–12 TV season, he is fired. Patrick Jane, often a comic character, is also a sad figure, haunted by his family's death and on a quest for revenge and a new beginning. Ultimately, Jane is a satiric hero trapped in a melodrama.

In addition to analyzing the satiric impulse in film and TV, let's also look at the success stories of two contemporary actors-turned-politicians who won actual governor's races playing satiric characters—Jesse Ventura in Minnesota in 1996 and Arnold Schwarzenegger in the 2003 California recall election. Ventura was a Reform Party candidate who took on the two establishment parties and won, selling the idea that the political "city" was corrupt. He was also cast as both saint and fool—a heroic Navy SEAL and a silly pro wrestler/minor actor—whose satiric persona attracted thousands of new young voters to the polls (Minnesota, in fact, had the highest turnout of eligible voters in the nation in 1996—more than 60 percent). Schwarzenegger, although he officially ran as a Republican, had married a Kennedy liberal, Maria Shriver, and offered a progressive social agenda—supportive of gay/lesbian rights and pro-choice issues. He drew 25 percent of his voters from disgruntled Democrats in the recall election against Governor Gray Davis, whose Democratic regime was toppled by a bad economy spurred by robber barons from companies like Enron, which swindled the state and drove up energy costs. Schwarzenegger too was cast

So far, two stars of the movie *Predator* (1987) have been elected governor.

as both saint and fool—the melodramatic hero of action-adventure films and the vacant movie star, former "Mr. Universe" bodybuilder, and alleged sexual predator who groped women in public. In 2003, California voters chose him as the rock their "city" would rebuild upon. In one of the great ironies of contemporary American politics, Schwarzenegger and Ventura had both appeared in *Predator*, a 1987 action melodrama starring Arnold as the leader of an elite commando unit that encounters a ruthless human-hunting alien in the South American jungle. As satirist Stephen Colbert noted at the time on *The Daily Show*: "Time was, our leaders were all veterans of World War II, the Korean conflict, or even the struggle for civil rights. But now, with the election of Jesse Ventura in Minnesota and Arnold Schwarzenegger in California, it is clear that the next generation of political leaders will all come from the movie *Predator*."[29]

Making Sense of Narrative Cycles

What the epic-romance-melodrama-satire cycle of narrative ultimately reveals is that narratives do matter—they are the chief symbolic way people make sense of social experience and articulate common values like individualism or compassion. In *Adventure, Mystery, and Romance*, John Cawelti argues that literary formulas exist and persist for several reasons. First, he says formulas or genres affirm our "existing interests and attitudes by presenting an imaginary world that is aligned with these interests and attitudes." In other words, narratives offer repeated formulas and characters that seem familiar and comforting; in a complex world, then, narratives offer reassurance and identification with shared values. So, an audience's attraction to the formulaic genres of political ads or *The Mentalist* melodramas has to do, in part, with the appearance of familiar characters doing familiar work, aligning their values with ours. Second, narrative formulas help us "resolve tensions and ambiguities resulting from conflicting interests." Narratives can grant a sense that life's problems and complexities are manageable and resolvable, and the main characters in programs like *The Mentalist* and *CSI* solve extraordinary mysteries and resolve complex crimes, just as political candidates offer themselves as straightforward solutions to the corruption and chaos of Big Government in Washington or corporate greed on Wall Street. Third, narratives enable us "to explore in fantasy the boundary between the permitted and the forbidden and to experience in a carefully controlled way the possibility of stepping across the boundary." In *The Mentalist* plots and in political campaign rhetoric, much of the portrayed criminal activity or distasteful politics resides outside the borders of normal everyday life. Yet storytelling offers a way for audiences and constituents to explore border transgressions within the safety and comfort of narrative formula whether packaged as prime-time drama or political ads. Stories help us confront the novel, the deviant, and the corrupt; they give us a way into worlds and ideas that seem alien, improbable, and horrifying. Ultimately, narrative forms provide symbolic and familiar containers for the nuances of cultural and political experience that always want to spill out.[30]

THE LIMITS OF NARRATIVE

In *The White Album*, Joan Didion says that we live "by the imposition of a narrative line upon disparate images."[31] In other words, we make sense of our world by thinking and acting "narratively," by imposing narratives on chaotic experience as a way to make sense. But sometimes words fail us; we can't always fully represent the ideas in our heads with symbols or stories. Just think of the times when teenagers come home from school and a parent asks, "What happened today?" A universal response, of course, is "Nothing." That does not mean that literally nothing happened but only that they don't have a story to tell. (Now, if there had been a romantic entanglement or a fight in the cafeteria that day, that would be a different story—with plenty of drama, conflict, and characters.)

At the level of writing, Didion describes in her reporting the problems of covering horrific or inexplicable experiences that are difficult to convert into narratives—

like the woman "who put her five-year-old daughter out to die on the center divider of Interstate 5 some miles south of the last Bakersfield exit." For Didion, this experience "did not fit into any narrative that I knew."[32] Here she confronts the limits of narrative: Sometimes events happen in the world and don't fit into a story formula. This is certainly true of any tragic event, particularly one on the scale of 9/11. Journalists had trouble imposing narratives on this event and in those first few days could only show images of crashing planes, fallings towers, and billowing ashes—over and over—and talking over the images, as though if they talked enough then some sense or meaning would emerge from their narration. But the truth is that 9/11 fit into no narrative we knew. It is probably fitting today that when people speak of that day, it is reduced simply to the numbers that mark the date. Over time, however, we did start imposing narratives, and 9/11 was explained in reflective news stories, in film, and in TV documentaries. These narratives featured variations on ideological themes and characters—as conflicts between primitive evil terrorists and innocent patriotic victims, between fundamentalism and modernity, or between the deprivation and powerlessness of developing nations and the abundance and prowess of the U.S. military and corporate might. Typically, news narratives depend on the conflict embedded in such binary oppositions, which transform complexity and nuance into more manageable two-dimensional narratives—"Every story has two sides."

Much of the limits and unimaginative quality in both our fictional and nonfictional storytelling forms has to do with TV executives and news producers finding it easier to repeat the familiar rather than tell a different tale, challenge a comfortable genre, or even invent a new story form.

Perhaps the biggest lack of narrative imagination, which has the most serious implications for democracy (which we take up in the next chapter), has to do with our national political life and the ways campaign managers (and their PR spin doctors) package our leaders. At one level, of course, many Americans make final judgments about who they will vote for based on thirty-second TV spots that the candidates produce themselves and spend millions of contributed dollars airing on local stations, cable channels, national networks, and the Internet. Like many thirty-second product commercials, political ads are often limited romantic tales that associate the candidate with wholesome virtues like decency, patriotism, and "family values." Such narrative associations operate as hegemony, attempting to convince ordinary citizens that a wealthy party and its candidate share wholesome Middle American values. At the local level, and less often nationally, candidates ambush rivals with melodramatic attack ads, which impugn the integrity of Candidate B for ruining "the city" (e.g., raising taxes) or disturbing the social order (e.g., favoring the rich) and offering Candidate A as a heroic counterpoint. But most often political ads portray candidates in some idyllic rural setting as civilized champions of honor, duty, and service. Unfortunately, though, we don't get much information on the candidate's ideas about key social problems like the U.S. role in policing world affairs or the weak regulation for the financial markets and large corporations, which, by the way, fund many of these spots and, in exchange, the problems and influence of corporate culture are often not mentioned. Like many thirty-second commercials, the slick exterior of the smartly packaged candidate emerges as an appealing product, riding a tractor or romancing a crowd. But in the end we don't learn about the characters who gave the money for the ad, what their interests are, and what the candidate's obligations are for such financial favors. The basic problem with selling candidates on TV, however, is that a generation of young voters—raised on the TV satire, political cynicism, and cultural resistance of *Saturday Night Live*, *The Simpsons*, *Family Guy*, *South Park*, *The Daily Show*, or *The Colbert Report*—are not often buying these hollow and simplistic thirty-second romances or melodramas. This doesn't, however, stop campaign managers from following the familiar and packaging politics in narrative formulas that evoke "common sense" and affirm the status quo.

| CRITICAL PROCESS 1 | Narrative in Your Favorite Film

We have described four formulas that are woven into many media narratives: epic, romance, melodrama, and satire. The goal of this exercise is to find these narrative threads in a movie or TV program that means something to you. It could be a favorite show from childhood, or something more recent; just choose a movie or program you really enjoy and perhaps have seen multiple times, or own on DVD.

Describe what happens in your favorite movie or TV program: What is it about? Who are the main characters? What are the conflicts portrayed?

Analyze the movie for its dominant narrative threads. Does your movie have elements of epic, romance, melodrama, or satire? How are these elements embodied in particular characters? Find patterns in the film or TV show that recur. Give examples of how these elements and patterns fit and don't fit each of the narrative formulas.

Interpret these patterns and threads. Is your favorite movie or TV program a "pure" formula, or have the narrative threads been woven together in a special way that somehow makes it into your favorite? What does this film or TV show mean to you? What are the roles this narrative may play in your life? What drew you to particular formulas, as a child or an adult, and how do they still appeal to you? Do your choices in other television shows, movies, video games, music, or other forms replicate your narrative preferences?

Evaluate what you like and dislike about your favorite narratives. What makes them good or bad? Be specific and use examples.

Engage with other students to create a proposal for a possible TV program (or movie) that would use each of the focus types of narrative. Draft your proposal—or "pitch"—giving the main idea behind the story.

CRITICAL PROCESS 2 | Narrative Formulas in News and History

This chapter began with a description of how politics and news use myth and narrative to tell stories, including stories about America's past, present, and future. Choose a real-life news event, and seek out two or three different accounts of it in news coverage, historical information, or even fictionalized versions in films or television.

Describe: How do these accounts depict the same event? What kind of language do they use? Are there hints of epic, romance, melodrama, or satire? Who are the main characters? Describe the conflicts portrayed in the news stories.

Analyze: What patterns do you see in the various stories? Are there similarities among the accounts? Differences?

Interpret: What narrative formula or formulas do you think these accounts use in telling the same story? Are the same formulas used repeatedly, or do they change or combine? What does it mean that the news relies on narrative techniques associated with fiction? Do you think local or national news programs operate like melodrama, as this chapter contends?

Evaluate: What is the value of these different (or similar) interpretations? Does one way of telling this news or historical story work better for some purposes than others? Is one more prevalent in a particular age group, political party, or social class? Judge these stories—what makes them strong or weak in your opinion?

Engage: Write a critique of the narrative formulas used in these news accounts. Discuss what you liked and did not like. E-mail your critique to the reporters who wrote the accounts and get their feedback. Ask them questions about how they reported and wrote the story. Try to find out how much they pay attention to narrative elements such as characters and conflict. Report your findings.

5

Political Stories and Media Messages

In an election year, stories of all shapes and sizes dominate politics and the media landscape. As President Barack Obama and former Massachusetts governor Mitt Romney faced off in the 2012 election, the president's campaign told mostly hopeful stories about saving the auto industry or providing health coverage for the uninsured, as well as stories about what the president hoped to accomplish with his second term in office. But in his political ads and speeches, he also told less positive stories that reminded voters of the mess and the wars that he had inherited from a Republican administration that was in office in 2008 when the financial crisis began. Romney, on the other hand, told mostly melodramatic stories—that Obama's "city" of Washington was still a mess and Romney was the guy who could clean it up and restore the United States to its previous grandeur. In a February 2012 speech, Romney couched his political narrative in these terms: "President Obama says he wants to fundamentally transform America. We [Romney supporters] want to restore America to the founding principles that made the country great."[1] Romney here laid out the central conflicts of his master political narrative: tradition vs. change and past vs. present. He pinned his hopes on the side of past traditions and portrayed change—and present conditions—as sinister forces that can only be overcome by returning to a time in the past when we were somehow better. The stories our leaders tell shift from election to election depending on the strategies of spin doctors and what they want us to think about our presidential candidates.

MEDIA NARRATIVES AND DEMOCRACY

To decipher the complexities of democracy, we depend on news media to provide information that helps us make decisions about our political leaders. But in close presidential elections, with so much misleading and partisan political advertising and the sometimes inaccurate or irrelevant updates on polling and projections, media are sometimes more illuminating about candidates' images than the facts of their platforms, records, and plans. We might think that TV stations, cable, and networks earning so much money through political advertising would be able to pay for good fact-checking, accurate projections, competent exit polls, and explorations of important issues. Yet how well can news media help Americans understand the national election in a TV and radio landscape littered with two-dimensional ads building up one candidate and tearing down another?

In these cases, a greater understanding of media narratives can be helpful in analyzing past, present, and future candidates. The narratives of presidential election contests can reveal more than the candidates' self-images; they can also offer examples of how politicians gain and sustain power. Though that process is ongoing throughout their terms, presidential candidates often focus most heavily on creating (and controlling) a specific narrative during campaign season.

Presidential Election Narratives

Backtracking through recent presidential elections reveals how the cycle of storytelling shapes politics. For example, in 1992, the first George Bush, former vice president to the popular Ronald Reagan, fell victim to a bad economy. His quick triumph in the first installment of the Iraq war—when U.S. forces threw the occupying military of Saddam Hussein from Kuwait but, on Bush's order, did not hunt down Saddam in Baghdad—was now a distant memory. In bad economies, voters usually won't buy romantic TV political tales about how all is right with the world. In rode Bill Clinton, a melodramatic Lancelot figure, metaphorical son of JFK and heir to the romantic Arthurian Camelot story that sprung up around Kennedy's short-lived presidency in the early 1960s. A skillful politician and charismatic speaker, Clinton also benefited from the appearance of a satiric character, Ross Perot, the 1992 candidate of the Reform Party. Like Jesse Ventura in Minnesota's governor race in 1996 and Arnold Schwarzenegger in California's governor election in 2003, Perot played a fool-saint character, telling "sane-insane" stories of potential terrorist-kidnap threats against his family. He even maintained a private army of twenty-four-hour-a-day guards with a video surveillance system hidden behind two-way mirror doors in his Texas office building that did not list his company's name in the lobby's directory. On the other hand, Perot attacked the political "city" as corrupt (run by the two bloated political parties) and badly in need of a fresh start under his Reform Party. Perot also used his wealth to buy thirty- and sixty-minute blocks of time on the national networks to explain his economic plan and disparage Bush's record, ultimately helping Clinton make his case against the incumbent president. Perot also won 19 percent of the vote, tipping the 1992 election in favor of Clinton.[2]

Following the Clinton years, the story of the controversial 2000 election featured George W. Bush, the real son of a former president, defeating Al Gore, Clinton's vice president. Although Gore won the popular vote by 500,000, Bush captured the Electoral College and the presidency after a lengthy and unprecedented postelection legal dispute—a first-rate TV melodrama—over voting irregularities in Florida, where yet another Bush, Jeb, was serving as governor and helped tip the state to his brother.[3] Ultimately, the conservative-leaning Supreme Court decided the election in Bush's favor. One of the remarkable stories of that election was how Gore lost his home state of Tennessee (which cost him the election) along with his party's hold on the presidency during a time of relative economic prosperity for many (though not all) Americans.

So what stories got told to swing the election for one candidate and against the other? First, Gore never carved out a clear, appealing identity; he chose to distance himself from the fallen knight Clinton (who had been caught in an unseemly affair with an intern), running instead as straight-laced romantic figure from a wholesome family, a man who wore earth tones and loved his wife. In a cynical age, with satires erupting all over the cultural landscape, Gore's persona seemed out of place, especially unappealing to young people. (And on top of that, Ralph Nader, the third-party satirist with a large following among college students, took votes away from the vice president, drawing the wrath of mainstream Democrats.) Perhaps Gore's abandonment of Clinton made him look disloyal, not a good move for a romantic figure who is supposed to value loyalty, duty, and friendship as prime virtues. In his TV appearances, Gore came across as smart but stiff, sharp but aloof, a far cry from his former boss's charismatic Arkansas "good ol' boy" character. Instead, Bush took up that mantle, countering Gore with a melodramatic persona who attacked the corrupt Washington big-government establishment "city" (as Reagan had done in 1980) and played another down-to-earth country boy, a Texan (by way of Connecticut and Yale) who could restore the city's moral center.

In the 2004 race, Democratic strategists told a story promoting candidate John Kerry as a strong and capable leader. This was particularly important during the early stages of the Iraq war and for a nation under the threat of terrorism and in the shadow of 9/11. At the 2004 Democratic convention, Kerry's campaign chose romantic stories full of sea and captain imagery. For the Republicans in 2004, strategists chose to continue the pre-convention melodrama of President Bush as "strong and steady," a self-proclaimed "war president," unwavering in his resolve. During the run-up to the GOP convention, this had been reinforced through stories and images of President Bush cast as a tough leader. These were often rural cowboy images of the president clearing brush or walking with his posse of advisors on his Texas ranch or stirring military images of him landing in a plane on an aircraft carrier, bounding out in a flight jumpsuit with a "Mission Accomplished" banner unfurled in the background. Between the romantic ship-captain veteran and the incumbent rugged cowboy, the Old West won out in the end. In a time of ongoing war, the majority of voters were reluctant to change leaders, and the Bush administration penchant for going it alone and fighting an unpopular war resonated among citizens who may have seen the "city" as under siege and shaky, but believed that eventually Bush's moral compass would show a way forward.[4]

In 2008, Barack Obama became the forty-fourth president of the United States. Son of a Kenyan father and a Kansan mother, candidate Obama had some things working in his favor: the ongoing and unpopular war in Iraq (it turned out that the mission wasn't accomplished), an outgoing president with a very low favorability rating, and the financial crisis that hit in mid-September 2008. Republican operatives portrayed him as an inexperienced egghead law professor with a mysterious exotic past, somehow not quite fully American. President Obama, though, also owed much of his victory to eighteen- to twenty-nine-year-old voters (also "inexperienced") who went for him 66 to 32 percent over Republican candidate John McCain. Obama strategists also cultivated both traditional media (i.e., TV commercials) and new social networks. For example, in 2008 Obama had 2.3 million "friends" on Facebook (compared to 610,000 for McCain).[5] The Obama narrative featured a romantic tale about hope, change, and overcoming racial barriers and an absent father. A Vietnam veteran and POW survivor, the seventy-two-year-old McCain had a good story too—but in the end the master narrative pitted the youthful, eloquent "son" against a war hero "father" who sometimes seemed tired and confused. It was a time for change.

Why is it that our national presidential elections continue to play out in the context of these symbolic story forms? One possible interpretation derives from the central importance of narrative in our culture, particularly narratives that celebrate heroic individuals. After all, brave heroes saving towns from villains and cities from corruption dominate mainstream fictional forms, particularly in primetime television and Hollywood movies. Political strategists, of course, want their candidates linked to these powerful story formulas—so familiar and comforting to all of us.

Indeed, while recent presidential campaigns overflow with talk of *values,* the main value that usually emerges as central is individual heroism: the notion that one person can stand in for all of us and make a difference in our lives. Of course, another limit of narrative is that our lives don't usually play out like media narratives. In fact, most progress—whether it's a small cultural change in the workplace or a major political transformation that affects our legal or military system—results from collective or community action. Rather than the initiative of one heroic person (which does occasionally happen), as played out in political ads and other consensus narratives, communities and societies usually move forward because groups and individuals work together to make such movement possible. In a nation of more than 300 million people, it is not easy for a president to effect the kinds of change and progress that are often promised in the stories spun at national conventions and in political ads, as illustrated again by the complexities of health-care reform, the auto industry bailout and resurrection, financial regulation and Big Bank resistance, and partisan budget battles between the 2008 and 2012 elections.

Media as Political Narrators

These narratives are not simply broadcast by various media; they're connected to the very survival of media industries. Through lobbying efforts on behalf of those industries, substantial amounts of ad money from political parties are turned back over to politicians running for office who vote on laws that govern media consolidation and ownership. In 2011, for example, *Politico* reported that the film, music, and TV industries spent about $100 million on lobbying efforts that year, with Comcast—the nation's largest cable company and owner of NBC Universal— spending over $15 million in 2011, 70 percent more than in 2010.[6]

So rather than upgrading journalism, today large media corporations fight regulation and invest in acquiring new properties, including additional radio stations, TV stations, and cable outlets. It is no coincidence that, over the past fifteen years, most rules restricting the number of media outlets that one company can own have been dismantled while in many newsrooms and TV stations expensive investigative reporting units (which could do stories on the impact of media consolidation on politics) have also disappeared as media managers focus on finding ways to maximize their profits.

This chapter takes up the media's complicated relationships to political culture. Rather than a conventional view that might look at politics primarily in terms of voter profiles, presidential agendas, and election coverage, we use a broader definition of politics. From our narrativist perspective, politics is about who wields power, how they use it, and how they maintain and "operationalize" it through stories. But it also has to do with how the media are implicated in this process, and—most importantly—how we think and act as citizens in relation to political power. So not only do we mean the power to shape elections and their results but also the politics of meaning: how media reflect and define the often unequal relations in power throughout contemporary society, and what kind of citizens we need to be with regard to the battles over power and meaning.

We discuss here the politics of culture and how the media insinuate themselves— through narratives—in these everyday struggles over meaning. Thus, presidential elections aren't just about the traditional political parties—about who won and who lost—but, more importantly, about who brandishes power, how mass media produce cultural meanings, how those meanings circulate in our culture's stories and champion particular values, and how we react to these as key issues that affect the quality of democracy. In other words, familiar 2012 media narratives about Mitt Romney (e.g., Harvard-educated privileged "rich boy"; ran big investment firm; out of touch with ordinary Americans) and Barack Obama (Harvard-educated former professor; isolated as president amid an "evil" Washington culture; out of touch with ordinary Americans) become powerful election-year tropes for certain pundits that helped determine real political outcomes. As citizens, we voted—or declined to vote—based on particular cultural stories about and by politicians. If we chose to vote, we probably picked candidates who, as our rulers, we thought would do the best job by serving our individual interests as well as the interests of our larger communities and democracy.

MASS MEDIA'S POLITICAL INFLUENCE

While it is easy to see politics operate at the level of daily news, press conferences, and political ads, the struggle for power also works itself out throughout society at the level of everyday culture. For example, the popular cultural storms over rock and roll and television hit in the 1950s, and their political impact was enormous. Few forms of popular media have ever been bashed as hard as rock and roll in 1950s America. This cultural phenomenon, combining the vocal and instrumental traditions of popular music with the rhythm-and-blues sounds of Memphis and the country beat of Nashville, was indeed politically charged—the first "integrationist music." Only a few musical forms have ever sprung from such a diverse set of influences, and no new style of music has ever had such a widespread impact on so many different people and cultures.

One reason for the growth of rock and roll can be found in the repressive and unsettled atmosphere of the 1950s. With the constant concern over the atomic bomb, the Cold War, and communist witch-hunts, many young people sought forms of diversion—and meaning—from the menacing world created by adults. Teens traditionally celebrate music that has a beat—music they can dance to. This happened during the 1920s with the Charleston, in the 1930s and 1940s with the jazz swing bands and the jitterbug, in the 1970s with disco, and in the 1980s through today with hip-hop. Each of these twentieth-century musical forms began as dance and party music before its growing popularity eventually energized both record sales and radio formats. Most importantly, each of these dance-music forms faced attack in its time from the ruling classes and status quo authorities. It was also a favorite tactic of politicians to condemn popular music as a way to curry favor with older constituents, often nostalgic for the old music they grew up with.

Perhaps most significant to the politics of rock and roll, the border that had separated white and black cultures began to break down. This process started with music and among the young, but it got a boost during the Korean War in the early 1950s when President Truman signed an executive order integrating the armed forces. Young men drafted into the service were thrown together with others from very different ethnic and economic backgrounds. The biggest legal change, though, came with the *Brown v. Board of Education* decision in 1954. The Supreme Court ruled against "separate but equal" laws—which had kept white and black schools, hotels, restaurants, restrooms, and drinking fountains segregated for decades—deeming them unconstitutional. Thus mainstream America began to wrestle seriously with the legacy of slavery and the unequal treatment of African American citizens. A cultural reflection of the times, rock and roll would burst from the midst of these social and political tensions and could not be understood apart from them.

In fact, as a number of historians and cultural critics have acknowledged over the years, the relative acceptance of black music that appealed to white youth provided a more favorable cultural context for the political activism that led to significant social change. The rising popularity of this music, coupled with the television news footage that, for the first time, gave many white Americans a glimpse of the segregation and inequality that many black people endured—particularly in the South—spurred important civil rights legislation in the mid-1960s. Along with the contributions of the "integrationist" rock and roll phenomenon, television played a crucial cultural role in shaping the civil rights movement in the 1960s. During this period, the major networks chose to cover important events and central issues regarding race during a complicated time in our nation's history. For many citizens, images of black people being beaten by angry whites brought home the unfairness and inequities of our social system in a way that the printed word could not.

What happens, however, when these same networks today—favoring the corporate and political needs of their parent companies—make choices *not* to cover certain issues that are also important to the functioning of democracy? Let's examine the case of the television digital spectrum space "giveaway" in the mid-1990s, an important story very few viewers and citizens knew about since it was not in the economic or political interests of the television industry to cover it.

Capitalism and Corporate Politics

One of the best examples of the confluence of hegemony, politics, narrative, and news developed in 1995–96 around the muted public debate over the landmark Telecommunication Act of 1996. The Act lifted almost all ownership restrictions in radio and television (e.g., shortly after passage Clear Channel alone bought more than 1,000 radio stations when ownership formerly had been limited to 48 stations by FCC rule). One study by two Yale professors reported that those newspapers whose corporate owners owned broadcast stations "stood to gain from the proposed loosening" of TV and radio ownership rules "offered their readers favorable coverage [of lifting ownership rules] . . . with positive consequences outnumbering negative consequences by over two to one"; however, news coverage in papers "owned by companies that did not stand to gain was overwhelmingly unfavorable, with negative consequences appearing over three times as often as positive consequences."[7]

A little-known provision of the 1996 Act concerned the "digital spectrum," which many lawmakers—both Democrats and Republicans—wanted to auction off (just as they do today to mega-companies like Verizon and AT&T when they need to extend their digital reach and frequency coverage for cell phones and smartphones).

However, in the end Congress gave away the spectrum space—a "gift" worth as much as $70 billion—to broadcast and cable industries after intense lobbying efforts on their behalf. In technical terms, the digital spectrum since the 1920s has been overseen by the government, which prevents channel and frequency interference by licensing companies (like NBC) and organizations (like universities that operate public radio) to use the spectrum space; the spectrum contains the newer digital broadcast (and phone) frequencies that provide hundreds of new cable and TV channels, including all the high-definition (HD) channels. While newspapers offered many more stories about the Telecommunication Act than did broadcast networks, through the eight-month period of debate leading up to the Act's passage, ABC, CBS, and NBC evening news programs (where most people get their news) devoted only nineteen minutes of total air time to the telecommunication deregulation act during this period. More significantly, these networks offered *no* stories about the digital spectrum issue. Why? Because network corporate owners saved billions in the giveaway and the TV news media controlled the narratives about this bill. They chose not to tell any stories about the spectrum "gift" because it was not in their economic interest to tell such stories and let American citizens in on a discussion. At the time Senator John McCain (R-Ariz.), who supported the auction to raise money on behalf of the public, said, "You will not see this story on any network."[8]

McCain was right. Charles Lewis, who directed the Center for Public Integrity at the time, said of broadcast executives: "They're going to make hundreds of millions of dollars, billions of dollars over the next several years. The last thing they want to do is have a discussion."[9] Instead, the broadcast industry ran misleading and melodramatic ads claiming that Congress wanted to "tax" Americans in a story that demonized government as the bad guy and portrayed American citizens as innocent victims who would somehow end up paying an onerous TV tax. Of course, the industry ads did not tell how much media corporations would save through the giveaway, implying instead that a "tax" would be passed along to consumers if the broadcast industry was forced to pay for the channels.

The key to understanding the synergy between politicians and media executives: Broadcasters don't tell the full story, save billions, and then charge politicians millions for the TV ads needed to win elections; politicians, on the other hand, don't want to do anything to upset an industry that could air negative editorials about them or run ads portraying lawmakers as bogeymen who would raise our taxes. The broadcast and cable lobbyists won in the end. At the time, the head of the FCC, Reed Hundt, said the failure of lawmakers to sanction an auction amounted to "the largest corporate welfare giveaway in our nation's history."[10] (Earlier in his tenure, Hundt had raised more than $20 billion by successfully auctioning off another part of the nation's airwaves.)

As citizen-critics who consume media and watch the democratic process play out, our analysis of the cross-fertilization between power and storytelling helps demonstrate how culture and politics work. As citizens, our responsibility lies in understanding this process in order to "resist, limit, alter, and challenge" stories that mislead us and misrepresent what's actually going on. Powerful politicians and media managers have the money to buy commercial speech, shape laws, and tell the stories that support political candidates and media business bottom lines. Most of the rest of us do not have this kind of money and certainly not this kind of influence. Our task, then, as engaged citizens and active critics, is to understand the narrative process that politicians and media industries exploit and to hold them accountable for the worth and substance of the stories they tell—and fail to tell.

Television can influence politics by ignoring a story; the medium can also exert influence by choosing to frame an issue or an event in a particular way. For example, in 2004 the Sinclair Broadcast Group, which owned sixty-two TV stations in thirty-nine markets at the time, banned its seven ABC-affiliated stations from airing a special episode of ABC's evening news program *Nightline*. In a tribute to the more than 700 U.S. soldiers who had died in Iraq at that point (it grew to nearly 4,500 by the time troops were withdrawn in December 2011), ABC anchor Ted Koppel read the names and displayed images of each soldier. Sinclair management, however, refused to clear the program for broadcast on the stations it owned, arguing that these simple obituary tributes constituted an antiwar position by offering "political statements . . . disguised as news content."[11] Meanwhile Sinclair executives proposed airing an anti–John Kerry documentary during prime time at the height of the Massachusetts senator's battle against President Bush in the 2004 election. Intense criticism by media reform groups and falling stock prices—the company lost $105 million in a few days—forced Sinclair to "air a watered-down version of the film"; however, management still fired its Washington, D.C., bureau chief, Jon Leiberman, for his opposition to airing the documentary on the grounds that his news division would "lose our credibility if we lend our voices and our writing and our faces to this product that clearly isn't news. It's propaganda. It's meant to sway the election—we've been told that by people inside the company."[12] At the time Sinclair banned the *Nightline* program, the Center for Public Integrity reported that 98 percent of Sinclair's presidential campaign contributions had gone to President Bush and Republicans, who had supported the continuing deregulation of the TV industry that allowed Sinclair to become the nation's largest owner of television stations. Meanwhile, Vietnam War veteran, prisoner-of-war survivor, and senator John McCain (who would later run for president as the Republican nominee in 2008) sharply criticized Sinclair, calling their executive action "unpatriotic" for preventing citizens from "an opportunity to be reminded of war's terrible costs."[13]

Once again, how do consumers and citizens respond to important issues and events that are either not reported by mainstream media or are covered only in a way that satisfies particular industry agendas? As the digital TV debate (or lack thereof) and Sinclair case reveal, the dominant messages that circulate in mainstream news media typically favor the interests of more powerful voices and agendas in society, simply because those in power have a much easier time being heard and getting their stories out than subordinate or nonmainstream organizations with alternative views—and with access to far fewer public relations resources or advertising dollars. Historian Jackson Lears contends, "It is delusional to pretend that the lumbering behemoths of the contemporary media industry have preserved any of the old republican concern for an educated citizenry."[14] As citizens, then, it is up to us to preserve this republican ideal. Through formal education, through reading multiple news sources, through everyday organizing, through holding political leaders accountable, and through critiquing the limited range of news narratives, we can check far-reaching economic agendas and test not only their veracity but how such agendas impact the quality and meaning of everyday life.

Political Bias in the News Media

All news is biased. News, after all, is primarily selective storytelling, not objective science. Editors choose certain issues and events to cover and ignore others; reporters choose particular words or images and reject others. This creates bias in favor of dramatic and conflicting quotes, in favor of telling just two sides of a story, in favor of powerful and connected sources, and in favor of practices that serve journalists' space/time limitations and deadline pressures.

In terms of overt *political* bias, recent polling data show that public perception indicates that mainstream news media operate mostly with a liberal bias. Back in 2006, a Harris Poll found 38 percent of adults surveyed detected a liberal bias in news coverage while 25 percent sensed a conservative bias (31 percent were "not sure" and 5 percent said there was "no bias"). Fast forward to 2012: A Pew Research Center survey found that the number saying there is "a great deal of political bias in the news" had risen to a new high—with 37 percent of Americans now saying there is great deal of bias—up from 31 percent in a 2008 Pew survey. The 2012 study found that very conservative Tea Party Republicans (at 74 percent) were twice as likely to see heavy political bias as any other political groups, including non–Tea Party Republicans (at 33 percent) and conservative-to-moderate Democrats (at 30 percent).[15]

Given the primary dictionary definitions of *liberal* (*adj.*, "favorable to progress or reform, as in political or religious affairs") and *conservative* (*adj.*, "disposed to preserve existing conditions, institutions, etc., or to restore traditional ones, and to limit change"), it is not surprising that a high percentage of people in these media bias polls see mainstream journalism as more liberal than conservative. (In a 2004 Pew Research survey, 34 percent of national journalists self-identified as liberal, 7 percent as conservative, and 54 percent as moderate.) After all, news media are agents of change. A profession that honors documenting and acknowledging change, checking power, and reporting wrongdoing would attract less favorable impressions from conservatives, who are predisposed to "preserve existing conditions" and "to limit change."

From a narrativist perspective, though, mainstream news media are most often in their comfort zone not necessarily advancing liberal agenda items but rather converting events and issues into simpler narrative conflicts that pit good against evil. This is, after all, a major theme in much of our popular media fiction. As the lack of serious and sustained coverage of the media business illustrates (especially in local and regional media), the purchases of news divisions by giant entertainment companies ensures that news media will not look too closely at the business and politics of their bosses. Against this backdrop, then, it is interesting to examine why one of the most enduring myths of the news media persists: that it functions with a powerful liberal bias. Where did this myth come from, and in the face of the enormous success of political conservatives in various media—Rush Limbaugh on radio, Matt Drudge and his imitators on the Internet, political columnists in newspages, and the Fox News Channel on television—how does it persevere?

Although some conservatives criticized mainstream news media for their sympathetic and favorable coverage of civil rights and the women's movement in the 1960s, the myth of liberal bias took flight in 1970 when Spiro Agnew, then President Richard Nixon's vice president, attacked "pointy-headed" liberals and intellectuals in the major media as "nattering nabobs of negativism."[16] Some critics say the myth was sustained later by the rise of conservative think tanks, financed by wealthy executives from big business, which in subsequent years remained focused on evening the score with the "liberal media" for their role in toppling the Nixon White House during the Watergate scandal. One of the roles of these think tanks was to educate conservative journalists who would champion the cause.

Sociologist Herbert Gans, however, demonstrated in *Deciding What's News*, his study of newsroom ideology back in the 1970s, that most reporters (even in the heyday of so-called liberal bias) were more shaped by a commitment to an unstated central core of values—individualism, small-town pastoralism, U.S. ethnocentrism, and responsible capitalism, among them—than to any overt political agenda.[17] (See Chapter 6.) In addition to these shared values, mainstream journalists then, as today, were socialized into a set of work rituals—getting the story, getting the story first, and telling "both sides" of a story to achieve a kind of balance—that helped them meet the daily deadline pressures and space/time constraints. In fact, this ritual commitment to "balanced" stories mandated that journalists made sure that, if they interviewed someone on the left, they had to balance their quotes by interviewing someone on the right. Ultimately, such a balancing act did not make conventional journalists objective or free from politics; rather, it made them centrist in their politics, always seeking middle-of-the-road positions in their most controversial stories. As the research suggests, mainstream journalists often hold middle-ground or moderate political positions in order to satisfy their professional training to remain superficially balanced. Sustaining that supposed balance demands that journalists' own political views be muted or moderated. For many years, this idea also supported the economic imperative of newspapers, which learned in the nineteenth century that a publication could attract more readers if it appeared not to have extreme partisan views.

In 2001, Bernard Goldberg published his book *Bias*, which attempted to sustain the liberal media bias argument. A former producer at CBS News, Goldberg, using anecdotes and stories from his days at the network, maintained that the news remains slanted to the left.[18] In 2003, Eric Alterman countered with *What Liberal Media?* in an attempt to bring hard evidence to this debate discussion.[19] Alterman's book doesn't deny that some national news stories have a liberal spin; in fact, he argues that, while many news media outlets continue to be progressive on social issues, they have become much more conservative on politics and economics, which is demonstrated in the deregulation of media and the concentration of ownership in the hands of fewer and fewer corporations, most of which are run by politically conservative CEOs. He demonstrates in *What Liberal Media?* and his ongoing column in the *Nation* (called "The Liberal Media") that conservative voices now dominate, not only in the top ownership but in everyday content in radio, on cable news, on the Internet, and on the editorial pages of most U.S. newspapers.

Despite the data, Alterman says the myth continues because conservatives keep repeating the story with such prominence—what one former chair of the Republican Party calls, "working the refs" until "you get the call." Alterman quotes key conservatives like Bill Kristol, frequent cable news pundit and editor of the *Weekly Standard*, who told a reporter, "I admit it. The liberal media were never that powerful and the whole thing was often used as an excuse by conservatives for conservative failures."[20] Dominant conservative voices in media, business, and politics have been so successful at keeping the liberal bias myth afloat that a 1999 study in *Communication Research* reported "a fourfold increase over the past dozen years in the number of Americans telling pollsters that they discerned a liberal bias in the news. But a review of the media's actually ideological content, collected and coded over a twelve-year period, offered no corroboration whatever for this view."[21]

Biases that do exist in media, then, are less likely to align with a particular political view than particular business decisions. For one example, look closely at the business sections of most U.S. regional newspapers today. Traditionally, newspapers hired labor reporters in the 1950s and 1960s to follow and document issues important to working-class Americans. These issues facing working Americans, many of them poor or lower middle class, have historically been linked to the concerns of liberal political leaders such as Ted Kennedy or Jesse Jackson. Labor reporters and the labor beat, however, except in a few union cities like Detroit, have virtually disappeared as organized unions have suffered a fall-off in membership. In Washington, when more than 1,400 reporters once covered the White House, only one was left covering the Labor Department as a full-time assignment by 2002.[22] Today only a handful of newspapers—like the *New York Times* and *Wall Street Journal*—and no major networks have full-time reporters dedicated to covering labor, union, and worker issues. Still, most adult Americans are workers whether they are in a union or not, yet the business sections of most newspapers rarely reflect their interests. Instead, they tend to represent the interests of business managers, one of the coveted demographic groups who read these papers and whose businesses might advertise in the papers. Largely ignoring ordinary workers, most contemporary business pages report the promotions and transactions of the managerial class. Many regional papers such as the Nashville *Tennessean* (which is owned by Gannett, the nation's largest newspaper chain) rarely cover worker issues even on Labor Day, which is often treated primarily as a generic holiday story with traffic problems.

Indeed, many media outlets show little interest in these issues. Throughout the 1990s, Barbara Ehrenreich wrote a regular column for *Time* (owned at the time by media giant Time Warner), until the magazine began rejecting too many of her essays on inequality and poverty, demonstrating not liberal bias but a bias in favor of corporations and upper-class economic concerns. From 1998 and 2000, Erhenreich went undercover to continue to write about America's working poor. She took jobs as a hotel maid, a nursing-home aide, and a Walmart worker, and she documented how hard it is to live off minimum-wage jobs in a book called *Nickel and Dimed: On (Not) Getting By in America.*[23] Ehrenreich has also discussed how mainstream news media largely have ignored these Americans (unless they are characters in local TV news crime stories), arguing that telling too many stories about poor Americans undercuts the media myth that anyone can become rich with a little grit and determination.

Barbara Ehrenreich

Since corporate advertisers, who primarily want to reach upper-middle-class consumers, are the economic support system for the media, there really isn't much self-interest in reporting stories about the plight of the poor. Ehrenreich also argued that most journalists use to come from working-class backgrounds and were once more sympathetic to the stories about poorer Americans; today, however, many journalists identify with middle- and upper-middle-class concerns and aspire to celebrity journalist status with a column and standing appearances on cable news programs.

The news media, then, have played a role in the misperception of political bias. While journalists are primarily storytellers, not detached scientists in pursuit of factual purity, searching for either liberal or conservative bias should not be the main focus of our criticism. Rather, investigating the kinds of storytelling that go on in media—whether they are fair or complete, whether they provide verification and documentation, whether they represent multiple views and voices—should drive media criticism. From our narrativist focus, the news media are indeed biased: biased in favor of storytelling, especially stories with obvious and dramatic conflict. This is not an overt political bias but a complex cultural one that favors the narrative form as the dominant way to make sense of experience. The mainstream media are, after all, in the storytelling business, and we should point our critical lens at how well they tell the stories that are important for citizens and democracy.

ADVERTISING AND THE CAPITALISM OF POLITICS

The glue that holds both the political and the media economies together remains advertising in various forms, whether we are talking about day-to-day print ads and TV commercials, Web pop-up ads, or the political spots that seem to take over television during local and national elections. Advertising as a mainstream profession came of age in the twentieth century, facilitating the transformation of U.S. society from production-oriented small-town values to consumer-oriented urban lifestyles. With manufacturers developing the products and advertisers providing the consumers, ads became the central economic support system for our mass media industries. Through its seemingly endless supply of pervasive and persuasive strategies, advertising today saturates the culture. In the age of social media, its ubiquity raises serious questions about our privacy and the ease with which companies can gather data on consumer habits. But an even more serious issue is the influence of advertising on our lives as democratic citizens. With only a few large media conglomerates controlling national advertising and commercial speech, what is the effect of this trend on free speech and political debate? In the future, it may not be easy to get heard in a marketplace where only a handful of large companies and two major political parties control access to that space.

As advertising has become more ubiquitous and consumers more discriminating, practitioners have searched for ways to weave their work ever more seamlessly into the cultural and political fabric of our society. Products now blend in as props or even plot points in TV shows and movies. In addition, every national consumer product now has its own site on the Web, displaying advertising on computers around the globe. With today's video technology and digital graphics, producers can even generate a TV advertising image on a wall or a flat surface—as Fox has done on the seating façade behind the batter's box during its World Series coverage—when in reality no image exists.

Among the more intriguing efforts to become enmeshed in the culture are the ads that exploit, distort, or transform the political meanings of popular music. In the 1990s and through the early 2000s, for instance, a number of formerly radical or progressive rock songs made their way into TV ads, muddying the boundary between art and commerce. "Revolution" (1968) promoted Nike shoes; the Beatles' "Come Together" (1969) morphed into the commercial theme for Nextel; and "Getting Better" (1967) accompanied Philips Electronics TV ads. Buffalo Springfield's "For What It's Worth" (1967) sold Miller beer—with the commercial stopping just short of the band's Vietnam War protest lyric, "There's a man with a gun over there." Even the ultimate 1960s protestor Bob Dylan starred in a Victoria's Secret commercial with a remixed version of his 1997 song "Love Sick." At the time, Victoria's Secret stores throughout America sold a CD of nine Dylan songs for $10.

Political Advertising and Democracy

A much more straightforward form of using culture to sell (or distort) political messages is, of course, through political advertising. Since the 1950s, political consultants have been imitating market-research and advertising techniques to sell their candidates. In the early days of television, politicians running for major offices either bought or were offered half-hour blocks of time to discuss their views and the significant issues of the day. As advertising time became more valuable, however, local stations and the networks became reluctant to give away time in large chunks. Gradually, TV managers began selling thirty-second spots to political campaigns just as they sold time to product advertisers.

In the late 1980s, a research team at the University of Pennsylvania's Annenberg School of Communication began critiquing political advertisements that reduce a candidate's ideas to a thirty-second advertising pitch. The research revealed that in using powerful visual images, these ads often attack other candidates and distract viewers through misleading verbal messages. Since the early 1990s, the major networks have been using the school's techniques in a news segment called Ad Watch. After critiquing a political ad, a commentator labeled it "true," "correct but . . . ," "misleading," or "false."[24] As a result of Ad Watch, media consultants began paying more attention to the veracity of their ads. Compared to the actual ads, however, which run over and over, Ad Watch pieces usually have run just once, so they are either missed or viewed only by people who regularly watch the evening news. Since Ad Watch, a number of political ad fact-checkers now operate on the Internet. By 2012, PolitiFact.com, operated by the *Tampa Bay Times,* had emerged as one of the most reputable sites. PolitiFact offers a "truth-o-meter" that rates political ads from "true" to "pants on fire" for ads that contain blatant lies.

Back during the 1992 and 1996 presidential campaigns, third-party candidate Ross Perot restored the use of the half-hour time block when he ran political infomercials on cable and the networks. However, only very wealthy candidates can afford such promotional strategies because television does not usually provide free airtime to politicians. As such, the debate continues over whether serious information on political issues can be conveyed in thirty-second spots that many candidates can barely afford; how a society ensures that less-financed alternative political voices are heard; and whether repeated attack ads, which assault another candidate's character, undermine citizens' confidence in the electoral process to the point of discouraging voting. Although broadcasters use the public's airwaves, they have long opposed providing free time for political campaigns and issues. Critics charge that the clear reason is because political advertising remains big business for TV stations and cable systems, which now make the bulk of their earnings in political ads sales every two or four years. Tracking the growth of political TV spots nationally, reports show that cable and TV broadcasters earned $400 million for local and national campaigns in 1996, and in 2000 that figure nearly doubled. By 2012, the two presidential campaigns by themselves spent more than $1 billion on political TV ads.[25]

For the 2012 political season, a controversial Supreme Court case—*Citizens United v. the Federal Election Committee*—upped the ante. The Court in 2010 ruled that corporations and unions have the same political speech rights as individuals under the First Amendment, thus allowing corporations and unions to use their general funds to make their own ads and unlimited election-related contributions. This gave rise to hundreds of new, highly partisan super PACs (political action committees) that raised and spent millions. In fact, six months before the 2012 election "these independent 'super' political action committees [had] already spent nearly $104 million [on TV ads] . . . compared with only $26.8 million spent in the same time period during the 2008 election."[26]

Although commercialism—through packaging both products and politicians as heroic in narrative ads—has generated cultural feedback that is often critical of advertising's pervasiveness, the growth of the industry has not diminished. Because they are almost always structured as familiar stories, ads continue to fascinate. Some consumers buy magazines or watch the Super Bowl just for the advertisements, and many people may pick a president based on a political ad. In 2011, total ad spending was roughly $450 to $500 billion worldwide ($150 billion of that in the United States)—enough money to finance the operation of several small countries.[27] A number of factors have made advertising's mostly unchecked growth possible (although it was slowed by the 2008–09 financial crisis). Many Americans tolerate advertising as a necessary "evil" for maintaining the media economy, but many others dismiss advertising as not believable and therefore trivial. As a result, because we are willing to downplay its centrality to global culture—even though we complain routinely to pollsters about negative political ads in each election cycle—many citizens do not think advertising is significant enough to monitor or reform. Such attitudes have ensured advertising's pervasiveness and suggest the need to escalate critical vigilance. As a society, we realize that without advertising our mass media and economic system would need reinvention; it is also unlikely that the commercial power wielded by corporate and political interests will diminish any time soon. So we should remain critical of one meaning that advertising has come to stand for: the overemphasis on commercial acquisitions and cultural images, and the disparity between those who can afford new products or commercial speech and those who cannot. As such, we must pay particular attention to the growing role of image advertising in politics. The inability of smart, decent third-party or independent candidates, who have a new or different point of view, to buy time needed to compete with major party candidates is a hard reality of our time. With the major parties increasingly under the influence of corporate donations and super PACs—which fund the political TV advertising that earn candidates publicity and frame them as heroes of their own stories—we need a sustained public discussion about how to get new voices and new stories into the old mix.

MEDIA AND THE POLITICS OF CULTURE

Since the early Greeks, concerns about popular culture have led to cyclical public outcries over the impact of media stories on our daily experience. The stakes are higher now, however, since mass media and popular culture play a much larger social, political, and economic role in everyday life. Many of us often feel cynical about the lack of quality in so much contemporary culture, or we feel burdened by how much information and how many options are now available.

Because mass media often function as narrators and agents of change—in everything from fashion and style to technology and politics—they are under frequent attack for assaults on "traditional values." Such value assaults can range from the increases in explicit sexual themes or depictions of violence in movies and on cable television to the portrayal of gay and lesbian themes across any number of popular culture venues. Conflating tradition and the past, some conservative critics of Hollywood (a city metaphor that has come to symbolize popular culture's decadent values) often decried the media for simply depicting contemporary changes in society that reflect new sensibilities—for instance, majority support in national polls for gay and lesbian marriages. These critics worried too that young people—much more progressive on social issues and social change—were being seduced by contemporary media into thinking about the world in very different terms from the worlds of their parents and grandparents.

Political Positions on the Media

The pervasive media cynicism, much of it understandable, that saturates blogs, radio, and cable news talk shows today is, in part, a product of a long-standing controversy over the role of culture and art in society. Those who wield power in our society, whether corporate executives, politicians and lobbyists, academic administrators and religious leaders, or mainstream cultural critics, have invested a lot of time, money, ideas, and energy in critiquing culture and arranging it into particular hierarchical categories that serve their interests. These classifications placed older "high" culture—often associated with the past—such as ballet, opera, symphony, art museums, and fine literature, at the top and newer popular, mass, or "low" culture such as television, rock music, talk radio, comics, and reality TV shows at the bottom of a cultural food chain.

Ensuing political debates over culture have continued over the years in various forms, and historically politicians on both the left and the right have used criticisms of the media (e.g., attacking Hollywood) as a popular strategy to stir the anger of many constituents. An important contemporary incarnation developed in the 1950s, the era that gave us, by some high-culture standards, the twin scourges of commercial television and rock and roll. The phenomenal popularity of Elvis Presley in that decade managed to merge both of these new media forms and set the tone for much of the contemporary debates over music lyrics and television's influence. Between September 1956 and January 1957, Presley made three appearances on *The Ed Sullivan Show*. Such was the public outcry against Presley's allegedly lascivious hip movements that by the third Sullivan show, camera operators were instructed to shoot Presley only from the waist up. Thousands of parents refused to allow their children to watch Presley's performances at all. A number of politicians, particularly in the South, were also critical of Presley, claiming that he and rock and roll, heavily influenced by black artists like Big Mama Thornton and Little Richard, "infected" white children with a low form of black popular culture. Presley and rhythm and blues were change agents they were not ready for.

While racism was the subtext for some political attacks on popular culture in the 1950s, other criticisms leveled at the media came from a very different direction—from intellectuals who worried that popular culture was undermining everything from good taste to artistic standards. In the 1950s, the debate over art and culture was usually controlled by "high culture" critics such as Dwight Macdonald, who coined the term "masscult" as a derogatory word for much contemporary culture. According to Macdonald, media industries functioned solely to produce "culture" that exploited their middle- and working-class audiences. In Macdonald's view, mass culture offered its customers neither uplifting traditions nor educational experiences.

Elvis Presley caused outcries through performances that seem tame by today's standards—controversies echoed by later musicians like 2 Live Crew, Ice T, and various heavy metal artists.

Instead, he argued, the mass media "production line grinds out a uniform project whose humble aim is not even entertainment, for this too implies life and hence effort, but merely distraction."[28] This was an argument that many politicians—then and now—have seized on either to pander to voters by villainizing media or because they genuinely believed that popular culture was society's ruination.

The intellectual critiques of popular media have had staying power. Some contemporary critics still refuse to discuss the latest forms of television and popular music as part of the same phenomena as traditional opera, ballet, literature, and classical music. As we argued in Chapter 1, many critics associate popularity with inauthenticity and with crass commercialization. The stories that these critics tell about mass media are essentially contamination tales, with popular media—especially current television and rock music—playing the role of contemporary polluters of the social environment. Such a view "from above," which has now become a popular belief about the media, both dismisses mass media products for being trivial or meaningless and, at the same time, paradoxically, assigns them tremendous power and influence. So as part of a political argument, politicians can get a "twofer"—pandering to constituents by attacking media as trivial AND creating fear by demonizing media for what they might be doing to children and the rest of us.

Yet another argument "from above"—often used by more progressive or liberal politicians—is best captured in Neil Postman's influential 1985 book, *Amusing Ourselves to Death*. In this argument, the concern is that democratic discourse has been undermined and reduced to short sound bites and a rush of images that citizens and consumers don't control. This view often reduces popular culture to a sinister, alien value system that undermines democratic ideals. Like the driving themes of some political campaign narratives, Postman offers a critique that is also nostalgic for an earlier time: "Under the governance of the printing press, discourse in America was different from what it is now—generally coherent, serious, and rational . . . under the governance of television, it has become shriveled and absurd."[29] Today various strains of this argument emerge as politicians, often running for office, critique the partisan flavor of evening cable news programs for the "shriveled and absurd" nature of how their campaigns are trivialized and portrayed. The complaints are often about the ways in which TV distorts their positions, sensationalizes trivial aspects of their past lives, or oversimplifies their nuanced stands on particular issues. They are often right.

Still another argument "from above" sees forms of contemporary mainstream media as tools of the rich and powerful in any society. In this view, popular media remain suspect because they have the potential to prevent genuine social and political change by transforming the populace into cultural dupes through the seductive allure of consumer capitalism. In this argument, mass media serve those who are in powerful positions either in government or business; they use media to mislead or distract the rest of us—including political leaders trying to reform health care or better regulate big banks—from effectively making necessary changes in society. Dwight Macdonald delivered the most succinct version of this perspective when he charged that "mass culture" was "imposed from above . . . fabricated by technicians hired by businessmen." He argued that the audiences for popular media "are passive consumers" and charged the business world—and the politicians who supported it—with exploiting "the cultural needs of the masses in order to make a profit and/or to maintain their class rule."[30]

Sex, Violence, and Headlines

In appealing to older constituents and not the young (who vote far less reliably than their parents and grandparents), political campaigns often develop common strategies for attacking the mass media. This plays well with many citizens who have increasingly come to regard mainstream media—like government—as largely negative culprits in our society: the institutional villains in the large collective narrative we tell about our nation. As such, politicians in need of an image boost might position themselves as tough individualists battling giant media—the predatory agents of sinister change. For example, in rewriting the nation's telecommunications laws in 1996 to require all TV manufacturers to equip sets with the V-chip, lawmakers scored points by approving a technology that let adults block violent or inappropriate TV programs from the view of children. Concerned about their free-speech rights, TV industry leaders at first vowed to fight the technology. But fearing government intervention (and politicians using sex and violence as wedge issues), they instead proposed an ineffectual TV ratings system that labeled violent and sexual content, similar to the self-imposed ratings codes used by both the music and the movie industries. Today, of course, we know only a small percentage of households use the once-vaunted V-chip technology. (A study by the Kaiser Family Foundation in the early and mid-2000s reported that about 40 percent of U.S. families owned a TV set with a V-chip but only 17 percent of those families used the device.) But at the time, the rhetorical hot air over V-chip legislation was fierce as family-values politicians lined up to associate themselves with the anti-violence movement and against commercial television—ironically, the medium they need most to get themselves elected.

As the millennium turned, the media did give us much to be concerned about. The 1999 killing spree at Columbine High School in Colorado that claimed fifteen lives is still partially blamed on violent video games and hard-core rock music. TV violence research continues to show some correlations between aggression in children and violent entertainment programs or video games. Radio and TV talk shows and today's reality programs still stir debate about the media's exploitation of personal problems for commercial gain. In fact, back in 2007 the season's premiere of Fox's *American Idol*, the nation's highest-rated program from 2005 to 2012, drew sharp criticism for the way some of its judges verbally assaulted untalented or naïve contestants—including one who suffered from autism.

Political and parental concerns about the state of our popular culture and mass media are often fueled by the news media's own scary headlines featuring traditional print media critics questioning reckless visual media entrepreneurs. In this story, it's often the "legitimate" print media demonizing their "illegitimate" stepchildren—the visual media. Here's a sampling from a three-month period in the mid-1990s during all the V-chip hoopla: "How TV Gets Away with Murder" (*New York Times Book Review*), "Are Movies and Music Killing America's Soul?" (*Time*), "Glued to the Tube . . . Concerns Raised about What TV Is Doing to Kids" (*Time*), and "Americans Despair of Popular Culture" (*New York Times*). At that time, our nation had not seen such intense political discussions about popular culture issues since the 1950s and 1960s spawned the twin "demons" of television and rock and roll. Today we see similar fretting by mainstream media about traditional "objective" journalism and political discourse threatened by the rise of populist radio commentators, twenty-four-hour cable news, social media networks, and the role of freelancing bloggers in shaping cultural issues and political discussions.

As we noted in Chapter 1, many occasional observers and critics of popular media face an interesting dilemma. On the one hand, they regard the media—often treated as a single entity acting with a single-minded will of its own—as frivolous and unworthy of serious attention. On the other hand, they blame the media for a plethora of ills that plague American society, from lowered reading scores on academic tests to the trivialization of American politics. If we are to charge mass media and popular culture for crimes against society and politics, then we had better take them seriously and treat them critically. Although immersed in a culture of twenty-four-hour cable news, commercial Web sites, talk-radio, shows, political ads, news blogs, and reality television, many of us are no more critically aware of everyday politics or the meaning of culture or the way power operates than we are of the air we breathe.

CITIZENSHIP AND CHANGE

What is the likelihood of actually changing this political landscape? What is our role as citizens and change agents in a contemporary democracy? For clues and context for understanding our particular time and how we ended up with our current politics, Michael Schudson's *The Good Citizen: A History of American Civic Life* provides a useful historical overview, tracing American citizenship through four overlapping eras.

The Deferential Citizen

Schudson distinguishes the time from the 1700s into the 1820s as the era of the "deferential citizen" and "the politics of assent."[31] In the early days of the nation, citizens—land-owning males—tended to defer to the wisdom of gentlemen, the elite religious, business, military, and political leaders who guided the founding of the nation. Among that leadership was a general distrust of the ordinary citizen, which is why the founders developed a representational model of government rather than trust in the direct democracy of the people. As an example, the Electoral College was established as a mechanism to check direct popular vote during presidential elections (a constitutional feature that became central to the 2000 election in which Al Gore won the popular vote but lost the Electoral College—and the election—to George W. Bush).

The Partisan Citizen

Schudson marks the period from the 1820s into the 1920s as the era of the "partisan citizen" and "the politics of affiliation." In this time, citizens—white male property

In the 2000 election, Al Gore (right) won the popular vote but lost the Electoral College and election to George W. Bush (left).

owners (until the 1920 suffrage amendment)—participated vigorously in party politics and developed loyalties to party leadership. In exchange for their loyalty and their vote in an open ballot system, these affiliated citizens would often receive jobs, money, or other forms of patronage. This particular era constituted the world's first "mass democracy" with rough-and-rowdy rivalries developing between competing parties. This period featured the Lincoln–Douglas debates, torchlight voting parades, and election sites with plenty of liquid refreshment. During this time, limited citizenship and raucous elections were "ruled by numbers, majorities of associated men organized in parties."[32]

The Informed Citizen

Schudson identifies the period from the 1880s through today as the era of the "informed citizen." In this era, citizens are expected to be knowledgeable about party politics, individual leaders, and contemporary issues. Marked by the rise of science and reforms sparked in the turn-of-the-century Progressive Era, the notion of a greater public good in theory trumped blind party loyalty. Indeed, the open ballot in front of party bosses ended, displaced by the secret ballot as the major election reform of the period. The social reforms enacted during this time "made campaigning more educational and less emotional" as citizens were expected to take their voting cues from experts knowledgeable about modern life. In this period, new civil service jobs and bureaucratic exams brought reforms that limited "the rewards parties could offer their partisans." As Schudson argues, the modern era in citizenship "prohibited electioneering close to the polling place" and "celebrated the private, rational 'informed citizen' that remains the most cherished ideal in the American voting experience today."[33] Scientific expertise, bureaucratic organization, and information dissemination would become the foundation that modern citizenship would build upon.

Schudson characterizes the difference among these first three stages in citizenship by the types of power and authority that governed society during our nation's first three hundred years. He argues that in these three periods power "shifted from personal authority (gentlemen) to interpersonal authority (parties, coalitions, and majorities) to impersonal authority (science, expertise, legal rights, and information)."[34] In terms of media during these three periods, the deferential citizen era was dominated by pamphlets and local newspapers subsidized by political interests; the party-based or partisan citizen era by the newly emerging and wildly popular penny press—the new mass medium for a new mass democracy; and the twentieth century's informed citizen by the modern newspaper with its allegiance to facts and reportorial detachment—in a print age often dubbed the "age of information."

The Rights-Bearing Citizen

But in more contemporary times, while the informed citizen model still has a strong hold on our political imagination (particularly those born in the baby-boom generation and before), competing models have emerged. According to Schudson, the last fifty years are defined as the age of the "rights-bearing citizen," which has "added the courtroom to the voting booth as a locus of civic participation." This age is marked by the triumph of individualism and individual rights. This aligns with so many of the narratives in our popular culture—from detective dramas to political ads—that emphasize the triumphant individual and acts of heroism. In terms of citizenship, Schudson traces this new model to the 1950s and particularly to the emergence of civil rights law:

> Beginning with its unanimous decision in *Brown v. Board of Education of Topeka* (1954) that found racial segregation in schools unconstitutional, the [Supreme] Court launched "a revolution made by judges." Sharply advancing a view of democracy as one which individuals can effectively claim rights against the state, the

Warren Court [of 1953 to 1969] became a leading agent and symbol of social and political change.[35]

As a further example to bolster his argument, Schudson notes that in 1935 the Supreme Court "considered questions of civil liberties or civil rights" in just 2 of 160 opinions; however, in 1989 civil rights and civil liberties concepts were at the heart of 66 of 132 cases.[36]

Outside the courts, we see other markers of this new era of citizenship—from Harry Truman's integration of the military in the late 1940s, to the GI Bill enabling working-class men to attend college after World War II, to the further democratization of college campuses by women and minority groups in the 1960s. In our own time, we have witnessed the controversy over the rights of college students to download music over the Internet in violation of modern copyright law. More significantly, in the new millennium we've watched the battle over gay and lesbian marriage and civil unions play out at both the state and national levels. Schudson argues that the rights-bearing citizen model has not replaced the informed citizen model; however, "the expansion of rights-consciousness has made the polling place less clearly the central act of political participation than it once was. The 'political,' carried on the wings of rights, has now defused into everyday life."[37]

In his conclusion, Schudson offered another evolutionary stage in development of the rights-bearing citizen and names it "a monitorial obligation":

Citizens can be monitorial rather than informed. Monitorial citizens scan (rather then read) the informational environment in a way so that they may be alerted on a wide variety of issues for a wide variety of ends and be mobilized around those issues in a large variety of ways.

Schudson sees citizens adapting to a cultural environment that is overloaded with information provided in daily conversation, cell phone chatter, twenty-four-seven cable news, Web sites, blogs, radio and TV talk shows, and regular print media. He asks us as citizens to monitor this media terrain. His ideal monitorial citizens "(1) commit themselves to dialogue and deliberation with fellow citizens recognized as moral and political equals (2) while keeping minority right in mind and (3) holding in view not only themselves but their posterity, while also (4) demanding of themselves in everyday circumstances, ordinary but not heroic efforts at information gathering and civic participation."[38]

The New Partisan Citizen

Published in 1998, *The Good Citizen* didn't fully anticipate the rise of intense partisan politics, the severe economic crisis, or the fragmentation of mass communication.

Today's media world offers more options than ever—where newspaper readers decline and TV viewers increasingly embrace cable news, social networks, blogs, and Twitter. The former mass audience has morphed into smaller niche consumer groups who follow particular hobbies, entertainment, politics, and stories. Media outlets that hope to survive appeal not necessarily to mass audiences but to interest groups, from sports fans and history buffs to conservative or progressive partisans. So, mimicking the news business of the eighteenth and nineteenth centuries, partisanship has returned with a vengeance as the best way to profit in a digital age. For the news media, concealing or tempering political leanings to reach a mass audience makes no sense when a mass audience no longer exists. CNN is discovering this as it struggles to compete with overt partisan models like Fox News and MSNBC (see Chapter 6). Instead, media now make money by targeting and catering to specialized interests. In such a marketplace, we are no longer just monitoring the landscape—we are picking sides.

Our contemporary era is also marked by a decline in the kind of journalism and news media that promoted fact-gathering, documentation, and expertise and held up "objectivity" as the ideal for journalistic practice. Rising in its place are new forms of news media that complement and encourage the new political partisanship. This era is symbolized by the rise of the news pundit, especially on cable, as a kind of opinion "expert" seemingly with more authority than actual experts. The new partisan fervor found in news outlets online and on cable has been the major catalyst for the nation's intense political and ideological divide. To move forward as citizens in the new partisan divide, it has become harder and harder to find common ground to address common problems—like home foreclosures, health care, income disparity, and higher education costs, among others.

A number of critics worry about how citizen responsibility will fare in this monitorial-partisan age when we are so bombarded with information to process and stories to interpret. In such a world, how do we balance our individual interests and preferences with a broader concern about the "common good" and shared social interests and goals?

One result could be a retreat into our own personal and individual interests, a retreat that the Internet certainly encourages. In his 1995 book, *Being Digital,* MIT's Nicholas Negroponte predicted the emergence of a kind of digital newspaper he dubbed "The Daily Me," by which he meant that each day we go online to access only our personal, customized Internet favorites, not bothering with anything else that might be going on in our world or with contrarian ideas and viewpoints.[39] In this scenario, we primarily seek out not necessarily information but confirmation of views we already hold. In technical terms, this has indeed come to pass as search engines like Google and social networks like Facebook attempt to integrate e-mail accounts, personalized news feeds, and prearranged settings into customized one-stop portals. Thus, the new partisan citizen is served and reinforced by "The Daily Me" media menu that allows us, in the words of *New York Times* columnist Nicholas Kristof, "to embed ourselves in the reassuring womb of an echo chamber."[40]

Political scientist Cass Sunstein argues in *Republic.com* and *Republic.com 2.0* that we need to counter "The Daily Me" syndrome through "unanticipated encounters"— bumping up against different ideas and other people who are not like us. He maintains that much of the polarization of views in the last decade—and the Age of the Internet—stems from people retreating to their own views, choosing to encounter media that reinforce those views. In a world like this, the chances for the give and take of democracy, for finding common ground and building consensus though compromise, become much more difficult. Sunstein's own research suggests that people who choose to live in echo chambers, exposing themselves to ideas and views they already hold, become much more entrenched in their positions without exposure to alternative ideas and outside viewpoints. He has demonstrated that "when liberals or conservatives talk about issues such as affirmative action or climate change with like-minded people, their views quickly become more homogenous and more extreme than before the discussion."[41] Sunstein also argues that we need to cultivate those aspects of the Internet and the new media world that allow us to confront experiences beyond our own "Daily Me."

In the end, monitoring our political environment and recommitting to conversations with fellow citizens, especially those not like us, offer ways to improve democracy. But how will these practices shift the balance of power? It seems that we have several choices to make as citizens. We could take a *Matrix* view of the world and simply accept the status quo political process and inequities in power as normal and natural, just the way the things are. Or, chasing our cynicism and alienation from power, we could ignore the political process, instead immersing ourselves in the individual and partisan pursuits supported by our specialized media, customized Internet services, and our own "Daily Me." We could also negotiate a middle ground, figuring out how to balance a renewed commitment to civic engagement with our individual pursuit of happiness. Finally, we could change the status quo, a daunting task in light of how much organizing would have to be done to challenge corporate interests and a two-party system that are firmly in place and powerfully in control.

The good news is that status quo power doesn't control everything in a democracy, and it certainly doesn't own the Internet. Just as in culture, the best new ideas often bubble up from below, from garage bands or independent films or unknown authors rather than corporate suits; there are ways to imagine a different kind of politics and a more equitable democracy. We could, after all, reinvigorate our deliberations from below—through cultural involvement, citizen groups, amateur journalists, local government, news-entertainment media ties, Internet communities, and the voting booth—taking more active stands in reshaping the cultural, social, economic, and political landscapes. Most of all, we need to contest and retest one of the original ideals of our founders, that "we the people" ultimately are not to be trusted shaping a direct and deliberative democracy, that we need to leave democracy up to our representatives—to the elite religious, business, military, and political leaders who know best. We now have the wide sweep of history to assess both how well that leadership has performed and what we want to do about it as we plan the future of a nation that is still near the beginning of an experiment in democracy on a grand scale.

| CRITICAL PROCESS 1 | The Narrative of Conflict

The goal of this exercise is to explore how conflict narratives characterize and inundate political coverage. Pick an issue area—something like the environment, health care, the economy, immigration, gun control, or education—and research recent coverage of it across various media: print news, TV news, and Internet stories. Pick three to four reports/stories from a representative group of media.

Describe the supposed conflict between the two sides. What do media outlets imply are the "two sides" to this issue? Who are the main "characters" in this conflict who are quoted or interviewed? Is there any attempt to portray a third or alternative side or multiple viewpoints?

Analyze the conflicts between these two sides as characterized and played out in various media sources. What patterns or similarities do you see in the coverage? How do accounts of the sides differ? Do some sources mention other positions on the issue? How does the conflict play out? How is it resolved (or not resolved)?

Interpret what seems to be at stake in discussions that are mostly two-sided. Does it have to do with legislation or government policy? If these things aren't mentioned specifically, who benefits from this constructed narrative of two sides (us and them, winners and losers, and so on)? What does it mean to represent complicated issues as two-dimensional?

Evaluate the treatment of these sides of the issue. Which story or report did the best job and which did the poorest job? Why? Do the stories you chose feel complete? If not, what seems to be missing? Are there sources (and characters) who should have been included in the report? If so, how well did the news media cover the various sides of the story?

Engage with alternative versions of this story/report: Construct another story that shows overlap between conservative and liberal positions, focusing on shared commitments and bipartisan agreement. Try to offer multiple points of view—more than two sides. What happens to the news narrative in this process? Talk to a local editor about how he or she covers complex issues that have more than two sides. Report on his or her viewpoint.

CRITICAL PROCESS 2 | "The Daily Me"

The goal of this exercise is to explore the construction of a personal news world that affirms only what we already believe—the so-called Daily Me. Examine your own favored news sources and consumption patterns as they compare to your own political views.

Describe your news consumption patterns. How do you keep up with local, national, and international news? How many sources do you use? What are they? How regularly do you check them?

Analyze these news sources and your personal news patterns. What are your chief news habits each day? Are these sources of news similar to each other or different? Do they offer unexpected or surprising perspectives, or do they mostly agree? Give examples.

Interpret your patterns and rituals of news consumption: *Why* do you make the decisions you do? What do you think it says about you and your worldview? How does it compare, do you think, to how your peers consume news? Do you think your sources have a particular political bent? How open are you to points of view that differ from your own?

Evaluate your news consumption diet. What's good and what's bad about it? Do you feel that it is complete and well-rounded? How good are you at seeking out other political viewpoints? Could you be increasing the variety of news narratives you encounter every day? Judge yourself.

Engage by conducting a survey of (or by interviewing) your friends and family, asking them about their news habits. How do they compare to you and each other? Who seems best informed among your interviewees? Who is least informed? Did you learn anything that might change your current news habits?

| 6 |

News, Culture, and Democracy

Political narratives make up only a portion of the stories told by media about our society. As forms of storytelling, most local and evening news shows function as a type of melodrama with the "city," nation, and world in various stages of crises or chaos. These narrative news displays are orchestrated by confident and all-knowing news anchors, who act as major characters in the evening news ritual, offering overviews and stories on each day's major events, usually from the comfort of hi-tech and graphically splendid command posts. Thus, an often inexplicable and conflict-ridden world is portrayed in crisp HD on mammoth flat-screen TVs under the careful supervision of local and national newsreaders. No matter how bad it is, the anchors remain well-dressed and well-groomed, stolid and solid figures comforting us—functioning as literal and figurative anchors to help us keep our bearings amid the turmoil and drama they have just presented.

From a narrativist perspective, then, news stories—like entertainment media— function as daily conversations with public audiences who search for reports that narrate and explain their world. The public is using news media, another form of consumer culture, to organize experience and evaluate the complications of modern life.

Back in a 1963 NBC staff memo, Reuven Frank, then news division president of NBC, got to the actual heart of TV news practices: storytelling. He outlined a narrative strategy integral to all news: "Every news story should . . . display the attributes of fiction, of drama. It should have structure and conflict, problem and denouement, rising and falling action, a beginning, a middle, and an end."[1] Despite Frank's insights, most modern journalists have not been comfortable thinking of themselves as storytellers, even though storytelling is the main cultural frame through which people make sense of their everyday experiences. For much of the twentieth century, in fact, journalists viewed themselves mainly as fact-gatherers or information conduits, trying to distance themselves both from partisanship and from the storytelling mandate of their daily jobs.

Today, and over the course of U.S. history, technological and social changes have altered the journalistic landscape. In order to analyze these important shifts, we first offer a narrative overview of journalism history. Next, we assess the changing economic terrain of journalism and its impact on the profession's daily practices. We then investigate the cultural habits and routines of journalists—particularly the influence of television on journalistic practice. We also argue that at the heart of news is that common ground between so-called information and entertainment cultures: stories. Finally, we discuss what kinds of journalism stories we get, we want, and we need in the twenty-first century.

A SHORT HISTORY OF JOURNALISM

Since the early 1900s, two competing models have influenced U.S. and European journalism. The first, the informational or modern U.S. model, has emphasized describing phenomena and issues from an apparently neutral point of view. The second, a more partisan and European model, has stressed analyzing experiences and advocating remedies from an acknowledged editorial viewpoint. Although the partisan model represents the earliest type of journalism practiced in the colonies and the early days of the republic, in most U.S. daily papers throughout the twentieth century the informational model dominated the front page (and TV newscasts), whereas the influences of the partisan model remained confined to the editorial and op-ed pages and an occasional front-page "news analysis" piece (or, on TV, an on-air editorial).

The long arc of journalism's history in the United States begins in colonial times with the partisan press era and continues through the emergence of a commercial era of the 1800s, objective journalism in the 1900s, and the corporate period and the new partisan era in recent times. Each of these overlapping eras or periods introduced new economic and social influences on the practice of constructing news narratives, and each of these influences continues to live on in American journalism in various forms.

The Partisan Era

Colonial newspapers were venues of debate over issues such as constitutional amendments, slavery, and states' rights. These papers generally argued one point of view or pushed the plan of the political party that typically subsidized the paper. By 1765, about thirty newspapers operated in the American colonies, including Benjamin Franklin's *Pennsylvania Gazette*, which served as a loudspeaker for contemporary issues like favoring paper money and approving the Stamp Act. Franklin was conscious of writing style and even advocated writing as a tool for thinking. According to historians Edwin and Michael Emery, the *Gazette* "soon had the largest circulation, most pages, highest advertising revenue, and most literate columns of any paper in the area."[2]

The First Amendment wouldn't be established until 1791, however, so there were limits to how much early U.S. newspapers could criticize and attack government policies before getting shut down by the British government; many papers lasted just two years or less. But after the Revolutionary War, there were 376 American newspapers, and nearly 90 percent had distinct party affiliations, with an equal balance between Federalist and Republican papers.[3] The other 10 percent served commerce, reporting ship loads, arrivals, and departures. At this time, the average newspaper cost six cents a copy and was sold not through street sales but through subscriptions. Because the annual price (roughly $10 to $12) represented more than a week's salary for most skilled workers, newspaper readers were mostly educated and wealthy men who controlled regional politics and commerce—a tiny fraction (2%) of the population.

Penny Papers and the Market Era

By the 1830s, the Industrial Revolution and the rise of the middle classes had spurred the growth of literacy, creating an explosion of newspaper and magazine sales. With the technological advance of the rotary press, publishers began to produce thousands of newspapers per hour, charging a penny for papers and telling stories that appealed to a wider range of people: scandals, police reports, serialized legends of frontiersmen like Daniel Boone, and fake stories about life on the moon. One paper, the *New York Morning Herald*, sponsored yacht and balloon races, financed safaris, and offered dispatches from correspondents covering the Civil War. These human-interest narratives aimed at nonelite audiences spurred readership growth among working folks and the emerging middle class. Penny press papers were innovative in their storytelling as well as their commercial orientation. By gradually moving overt political viewpoints to an editorial page, and by filling their pages with advertising, New York's penny papers shifted their economic base from political-party subsidies to the market. Advertising revenue, classified ads, and street sales began to finance commercial-era storytelling, and penny press papers indiscriminately printed any ad, even if the product was questionable.

The rise of competitive dailies and the penny press spawned a shift in American journalism that took sensationalism, commercialism, and tabloidism to great heights. In the late 1800s and early 1900s, two influential newspaper publishers, Joseph Pulitzer and William Randolph Hearst, became enmeshed in a circulation war that would change journalism and spur readership. Pulitzer, a Jewish-Hungarian immigrant, began his newspaper career as a reporter for a German-language newspaper in St. Louis. Working in politics, law, and journalism, Pulitzer also made clever investments and, eventually, at age thirty-one, bought the *St. Louis Dispatch*. Five years later, Pulitzer "outgrew" St. Louis, moved east, and purchased the *New York World*. To increase circulation, he ran a continuous stream of sex, sin, and even cannibalism stories, attracting immigrant populations with large headlines, maps, and graphics. Pulitzer's paper also manufactured news events and staged

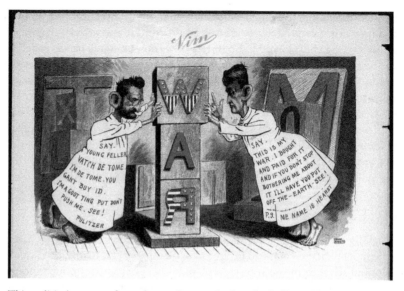

This political cartoon from the market era depicts the Pulitzer-Hearst struggle.

stunts, such as sending their star reporter—the intrepid Nellie Bly—around the world in seventy-two days to beat the fictional record in the popular 1873 Jules Verne novel *Around the World in Eighty Days.*

William Randolph Hearst was a rich-kid rebel who, at age twenty-four—after being expelled from Harvard—inherited the *San Francisco Examiner* from his wealthy father (a mining mogul and U.S. senator). In 1895, seven years into his publishing career, Hearst bought the *New York Journal,* a penny paper founded by Pulitzer's brother. Hearst proceeded to raid Pulitzer's *New York World* for editors, writers, and cartoonists, thus beginning the historic Hearst-Pulitzer rivalry. Both papers tried to outdo each other in terms of storytelling, focusing on the most lurid, sensational events, using large headlines, and pioneering graphic layout designs. Hearst's tactics, however, may have been the more dishonest of the two: To boost circulation, the *Journal* invented interviews, faked pictures, and encouraged conflicts that might result in a story. One account of Hearst's tabloid legacy describes "tales about two-headed virgins" and "prehistoric creatures roaming the plains of Wyoming." In promoting journalism as storytelling, Hearst reportedly said, "The modern editor of the popular journal does not care for facts. The editor wants novelty. The editor has no objection to facts if they are also novel. But he would prefer a novelty that is not a fact to a fact that is not a novelty."[4] A new term emerged to describe this kind of reporting: **yellow journalism,** a direct forerunner of today's tabloid papers and ubiquitous TV magazine shows like *Today, Good Morning America,* and *Access Hollywood.*

Yellow journalism featured two major characteristics: dramatic, sensationalized stories about crimes, disasters, scandals, and intrigue; and news reports that exposed corruption, particularly in business and government, and which laid the foundations for serious investigative journalism. As the less wealthy classes and immigrant populations could now both read and afford newspapers, journalism increasingly became a crusading force for the common people, with the press assuming a watchdog role on behalf of the public. Even as Hearst hired gangsters to distribute his newspapers, he was a champion of the underdog, and, like Pulitzer, his papers' readership soared among the working and middle classes, reaching 600,000 by 1897. By 1910, 30 percent of the U.S. population regularly read a newspaper.[5] What both Hearst and Pulitzer understood was that good stories sold newspapers.

Seeds of Objectivity

Although objectivity is considered a twentieth-century journalistic ideal, the early commercial and partisan presses were, to some extent, covering important events impartially. These papers often carried verbatim reports of presidential addresses, murder trials, or the annual statements of the U.S. Treasury. In the late 1800s, these journalistic practices were overshadowed as newspapers pushed for wider circulation and emphasized sensational news, especially in New York. Media sociologist Michael Schudson noted that, by the late 1890s, two distinct types of journalism were competing for readers: a **story** model, advanced by the penny and the yellow presses, which emphasized dramatizing important events, and an **information** model, advocated by papers that emphasized an approach that appeared more factual and straightforward.[6]

As the consumer marketplace expanded nationally during the Industrial Revolution, facts and news became marketable products that could be sold to consumers. Throughout the mid-1800s, the less a newspaper appeared to take sides on the front page, the more its readership base could be extended (although editorial pages were often rabidly supportive of particular political candidates). In addition, wire-service organizations, like the Associated Press (AP), were serving a variety of newspaper clients in different regions of the country. To satisfy all their clients and the wide range of political views, newspapers tried to look more impartial, softening their partisanship and focusing attention on good stories to boost sales. Jon Katz, *Wired* magazine media critic, has discussed the history of the neutral pose:

> The idea of respectable detachment wasn't conceived as a moral principle so much as a marketing device. Once newspapers began to mass market themselves in the mid-1880s, after steam- and rotary-powered presses made it possible to print lots of papers and make lots of money, publishers ceased being working, opinionated

journalists. They mutated instead into businessmen eager to reach the broadest number of readers and antagonize the fewest. . . . Objectivity works well for publishers, protecting the status quo and keeping journalism's voice militantly moderate.[7]

The ideal of an impartial, or informational, news model was partially reinvented by Adolph Ochs, who bought the *New York Times* in 1896. The son of immigrant German Jews, Ochs grew up in Ohio and Tennessee, where in 1878 at age twenty-one he took over the *Chattanooga Times*. Known more for his business and organizational ability than for his writing and editing skills, he transformed the Tennessee paper. Ochs then, like Pulitzer, moved east, and invested $75,000 in the struggling *New York Times*. Ochs's staff of editors rebuilt the paper around substantial news coverage and compelling editorial pages. To distance themselves from the yellow press, and differentiate themselves in the New York market, the editors also downplayed entertainment news and sensational features, favoring verbatim transcripts and the documentation of major events or issues.

Such distancing was partly a marketing strategy to counter the large circulations of the Hearst and Pulitzer papers. Ochs offered a distinct contrast to the more provocative newspapers: an informational paper that provided stock and real-estate reports to businesses, court reports to legal professionals, treaty summaries to political leaders, and theater and book reviews to intellectuals. Ochs's promotional gimmicks took direct aim at yellow journalism, advertising the *Times* under the motto "It does not soil the breakfast cloth." The strategy of the *Times* was similar to many TV marketing plans today that target upscale eighteen- to forty-nine-year-old viewers who spend a disproportionate share of consumer dollars.

With the Hearst and Pulitzer papers capturing the bulk of working- and middle-class readers, managers at the *Times* at first associated their straightforward reporting with people of higher social status. In 1898, however, Ochs lowered the paper's price to a penny. His thinking was that people bought the *World* and the *Journal* primarily because they were cheap, not because of their storytelling. As a result, the *Times* began attracting more middle-class readers who gravitated to the paper as a status marker for the educated and well-informed. Between 1898 and 1921, its circulation rose from 25,000 to a daily circulation of 330,000 and 500,000 on Sunday.

At the dawn of the twentieth century, with publishers interested in expanding readership and reporters adopting a more detached "scientific" posture toward news and fact gathering, the ideal of objectivity began to anchor journalism. With the standards of objective journalism, which distinguishes factual reports from opinion columns, reporters—free from political party subsidies—strove to maintain a neutral attitude toward the issues and events they covered. They also searched out competing points of view among the sources for a story.

The primary story form of objective-style journalism is the so-called "inverted pyramid," developed by Civil War correspondents whose news narratives imitated the terse, compact press releases that came from Lincoln's secretary of war, Edwin M. Stanton.[8] Often stripped of adverbs and adjectives, such reports began—as they do today—with the most dramatic or newsworthy information. Straight-forward answers to who, what, where, when (and, less frequently, why or how) led the top of the story and then tailed off with less important details. Back then, if wars or natural disasters disrupted the telegraph transmissions of these dispatches, the information the reporter chose to lead the story often had the best chance of getting through to its destination. For much of the twentieth century, then, the inverted-pyramid model served as an efficient way to arrange a timely story, which could also be trimmed from the bottom to fit available space in a newspaper. As journalism educator John Merrill once pointed out, the wire services that used the inverted-pyramid style when distributing stories to newspapers nationwide "had to deal with large numbers of newspapers with widely different political and regional interests. The news had to be 'objective' . . . to be accepted by such a heterogeneous group."[9]

The importance of the neutral pose and the reliance on the inverted pyramid signaled, among other changes, journalism's break from the partisan tradition. Although impossible to achieve any semblance of objectivity, particularly as it is understood in the natural sciences—especially given the selective process and narrative structure of news stories—the notion of a journalistic objective ideal still became the guiding beacon of the modern press. In fact, if early-twentieth-century journalists could make a convincing claim of objectivity, they could often deflect scrutiny or serious criticism that news was actually more closely aligned to narrative literature than to hard science. By the 1920s, the *New York Times* had established itself as the official "paper of record," the standard that other newspapers emulated and that libraries throughout the country stocked to document daily occurrences. The *Times* became more than just a powerful alternative to the storytelling of earlier papers; it became the official and authoritative way to practice U.S. journalism.

Storytelling in the Objective Era

One of the great paradoxes of modern U.S. journalism is its claim for detachment—a main ingredient in objectivity—as a fundamental virtue, even though journalism is primarily practiced as selective storytelling, a traditionally subjective mode of communication.

Rather than address the way news functions as storytelling, many journalists—and most journalism educators—have come to define the newsworthiness of information by a conventional set of criteria: timeliness, proximity, conflict, impact (or consequence), prominence, human interest, novelty, and deviance. Reporters manufacture these story frames to help the public make sense of prominent people, important events, and unusual happenings in everyday life. But as local newspapers are forced to fold due to declining readership, and the twenty-four-hour news cycle, and its emphasis on talking points rather than news coverage, continues to predominate, a lot is left out. What to leave out is dictated by a multitude of interests represented in the newsroom and not subject to rigorous standards of objectivity. In fact, if journalism was truly an objective practice, it should report on everything that happens on any given day—and who has the kind of time, space, and business resources to pull off that trick? Journalism, instead, is a storytelling business. Readers, viewers, citizens, and critics should judge journalists' worth by the quality of stories they choose to tell, by how they select which issues and events to transform into news—and by what they may leave out on any given day.

Contemporary Journalism in the Corporate Era

Journalism, so central to American democracy that "the press" was the only business enterprise the founders protected in the Constitution, spent the first part of the nineteenth century freeing itself from political partisanship only to find itself at the beginning of the twenty-first century under the strong influences of corporate pressures. The very process that American citizens count on to report on this phenomenon has often remained silent because it has not been in the interest of national or global corporate powers to have their journalism extensions reporting the details of the their bosses' business. After all, these kinds of complex stories of corporate influence do not fit neatly into formulas telling tales of individuals wronged by "bad guys" or by dysfunctional institutions. How do journalists tell these stories when many of these powerful institutions are their own corporate parents?

Although corporate control is strong on the newspaper side of the journalism business—Gannett, for example, operates the largest newspaper chain in the world, controlling more than ninety daily newspapers—the real impact of the current corporate era is in television. Here journalism outlets have become minor subsidiary companies in large entertainment conglomerates that all now own movie studios as well as journalism businesses. Disney, in addition to its theme parks and film divisions, owns ABC News; Viacom owns Paramount studios as well as controlling a majority stake in CBS; cable giant Comcast controls NBC, as well as Universal Pictures; News Corp. owns Fox News in addition to Twentieth Century Fox studios; and Time Warner, which operates CNN, owns Warner Brothers studios.

U.S. journalism, of course, has always struggled with this duality, trying to balance its role as public servant to democracy—a watchdog on power and corruption—and its role as profit-making business enterprise. But in journalism's contemporary corporate phase, the balance seems out of whack. Both print and TV journalism outlets today put far less money into investigative units and generally do little business reporting on media ownership issues. An early tipping point in this balance came in 1988, when Bill Kovach, the editor of the *Atlanta Journal-Constitution*, resigned after battles with the Cox Communications family, owners and business managers of the paper. In his short time there, Kovach had reinvigorated investigative journalism, doing tough stories on bank loans, real estate "red-lining," and the unequal treatment of middle-class blacks in Atlanta. But Kovach's leadership challenged the Atlanta business community; the paper served as a watchdog not just on banking but also on Coca-Cola, one of Atlanta's longtime corporate powerhouses, and its financial board, which included Cox family members. Despite using investigative journalism to help the paper realize some of its largest profit margins ever, Kovach said that ultimately he could not practice the kind of journalism he wanted to. He later said of his resignation: "I didn't leave the newsroom because I wanted to. I left because I had to. There was not a lot of beating down the doors by other news organizations to get me inside."[10] Out of daily journalism, Kovach went on to run the prestigious Nieman Fellowship program for journalists at Harvard and later became chair of the Committee for Concerned Journalists in Washington.

The Internet and the New Partisan Era

The decline of the corporate era in journalism started even before the economic collapse of 2008–09, and it is best symbolized in the bankruptcy case of the Tribune Company, owner of the *Los Angeles Times* and the *Chicago Tribune*, two of America's largest newspapers. By the turn of the twenty-first century, newspapers were losing advertising revenues, particularly from classified ads. With the rise of Internet and the emergence of mostly free Web sites like Craigslist and eBay, revenue from classified ads dropped by over two-thirds, from a peak of $19 billion in 2000 to just $6 billion by 2009, according to data from the Newspaper Association of America. Around the same time, the economic recession and housing crisis also substantially curtailed retail ads, especially from department stores, realtors, and car dealers. With fewer advertisers, newspapers laid off workers, shrank their size, changed formats, or declared bankruptcy.

On top of advertising problems, many newspaper owners like the Tribune Company had become *overleveraged.* That is, many media conglomerates borrowed lots of money in the 1990s to buy more media companies and newspapers to expand their businesses and profits. They also invested some of this borrowed money and used interest from the investments (and profits from ad revenue) to pay their debt. But when advertising tanked and their investments began losing money in fall 2008 (as the stock market crashed), many big media companies could no longer pay those debts. To raise capital, reorganize their debt, and avoid bankruptcy, most media companies had to lay off reporters and sell valuable assets.

The case of the Tribune Company's *Los Angeles Times* demonstrates best the impact of cost-cutting measures on even the most prominent national papers. Continuing demands from the corporate offices for cost reductions led to the resignation of editor John Carroll in 2005. In 2006, another editor and publisher resigned in protest over further cuts. More cutbacks in 2007 resulted in the departures of some of the *Times'* most talented staff members, including six Pulitzer Prize winners. In 2007, Chicago real estate developer Sam Zell bought the Tribune Company for $8 billion and made it private, insulating it for a time from market demands for high profit margins. However, by 2008 the company faced declining ad revenue and a tough economy and was forced to file for bankruptcy protection.[11] (The company would not emerge from bankruptcy until late 2012.)

Corporate troubles and the elimination of reporting jobs gave rise to a new era of partisan news, supplementing the traditional objectivity ideal. This trend—what Kovach and Tom Rosenstiel have called the "journalism of assertion"—is marked partly by a return to journalism's colonial roots and partly by the decline of the "journalism of verification" that serves as a watchdog over our central institutions.[12] The movement is fueled by a significant loss of newsroom workers as well as the rise of the cable TV news pundit as a kind of pseudo-expert with apparently more standing than facts, documents, and real experts. It also saves money to avoid sending actual journalists out into the field to report and document stories.

The key reason for the current return to partisanship in our news media is economics; just as a neutral stance was "good business" in the nineteenth and twentieth centuries, partisanship is profitable again. Today's media marketplace is a fragmented world where there are more media options than ever. For many in the news media business, especially in cable TV and on the Internet, avoiding political stands in favor of telling safe stories that reach a mass audience makes no sense in a world where that kind of audience no longer exists. Instead, some news media, particularly on cable television and the Internet, now make money by telling and selling stories that target niche and partisan interests.

QUESTIONING OBJECTIVE-STYLE STORYTELLING

Like lawyers, therapists, and other professionals, many contemporary journalists—even those with experience in the corporate and new partisan eras—still believe that their credibility derives from their personal detachment. Even though journalists transform events into stories, they generally believe that they are—or should be—neutral observers who present facts without passing judgment on them. After all, a long-understood assumption underpinning U.S. journalism suggests that democracy is best served when reporters present neutral facts and let citizens make judgments and decisions based on those facts. Conventions such as the inverted-pyramid news lead, the careful attribution of sources, the minimal use of adverbs and adjectives, and a detached third-person point of view all help reporters perform their work in a more neutral or supposedly "objective" manner. Because of their detachment and their discomfort with being questioned themselves, many reporters are uneasy discussing their personal values or their strategies for getting stories. Nevertheless, a stock of ritual practices underlies the modern performance of U.S. reporting and the narrative construction of news. These include getting the "good" story first, relying on expert sources, reducing events to two-sided reports, questioning aggressively politicians and leaders, and personalizing the news (the TV Effect).

Getting the Story First

According to the late Don Hewitt, creator of the long-running television news-magazine *60 Minutes*, "There's a very simple formula if you're in Hollywood, opera, publishing, broadcasting, newspapering. It's four very simple words: tell me a story."[13] Hewitt, as well as any journalist of his era, understood the tie between making money and telling stories. For most journalists, the bottom line is getting a story—an edict that overrides most other concerns. Getting a *timely* story that attracts viewers and readers fills up a journalist's day and enables him or her to meet routine deadline demands, and that task remains the gold standard against which reporters measure one another and their profession. Indeed, it is routine today for local TV stations (and some newspapers) to run self-promotions about how they beat competitors to a story: "You saw it here first on Eyewitness News!" In addition, during political elections local television stations and networks project winners in particular races and often hype their projections when they are able to forecast results before the competition does. This practice escalated into fiasco in November 2000, when all the major networks and cable news services spuriously declared Al Gore winner of the presidential election, only to later retract their predictions, declaring Bush winner, then retracting that prediction, and so on, until the Supreme Court blocked any further ballot recounts, effectively securing the presidency for Bush.

Journalistic scoops and exclusive stories attempt to position reporters in a heroic light in their news narratives: They have won a race for facts, which they have gathered and presented ahead of their rivals. It is not always clear, though, how the public is better served by a journalist's claim to have gotten a story first. Certainly, enterprising journalists can catalyze a story and effect change by calling attention to an important problem or issue. But sometimes the rush to coverage is misguided, as with the October 2009 "balloon boy" incident, in which the news media, especially twenty-four-seven cable and local news stations, chased a runaway homemade balloon that they thought carried a small boy. It turned out that the family of the boy, who was hiding in his Colorado house, had engineered the stunt for publicity, possibly hoping to get on another reality TV program (the family's mother has already been on ABC's *Wife Swap*). This is known as "herd" or "pack" journalism; it occurs when reporters follow a story in such large groups that the entire profession comes under attack for making an odd event or staged incident seem significant. Although readers and viewers might value the tenacity of reporters, the efficiency of new technologies, and the drama of their reports, the earliest (and loudest-hyped) reports are not necessarily better (or even truer) than stories written days later with more context and perspective.

With its emphasis on using technology to get the timeliest "facts," so-called objective-style news gathering de-emphasizes political discussions and historical context. As a contemporary example, news stories that referred to Al-Qaeda in the aftermath of 9/11 consistently failed to acknowledge the role of the United States in militarizing the freedom fighters in the war against the Russian occupation of Afghanistan in the early 1980s. These freedom fighters, which included Osama bin Laden, eventually became the leaders of the Al-Qaeda terrorist organization. Indeed, it would be helpful for citizens to understand the messy history of U.S. involvement in the Middle East, yet modern journalism tends to reject "old" news and important historical information for whatever new event or idea—or celebrity spat or runaway balloon sighting—disrupts the day's routines. These kinds of reports, enabled by sophisticated technology that allows reporters to appear live from even remote locations, also serve the economic interests of news by appealing to niche viewers—maybe 500,000 or so for a cable news station—who track breaking news and want immediate drama rather contextualized analysis.

Relying on Experts and the Rise of the Pundit

During the early 1900s, national politicians and opinion leaders of the Progressive movement, such as Woodrow Wilson and journalist Walter Lippmann, who distrusted mass audiences and public opinion, believed that democracy could be enhanced by cultivating ties among reporters, officials, scientists, business managers, and researchers.[14] They wanted journalists supplied with expertise across a variety of areas. Through the modern era, a wide gap grew between people with expertise and those without it, creating the need for public mediators. Reporters—first in print journalism and later in TV and online—assumed this role through the twentieth century, becoming surrogate citizens who represented both leaders' and readers' interests. With access to many experts, reporters have been able to act as agents for citizens, transforming specialized knowledge into the commonsense language of daily news stories.

In the twenty-first century, this second ritual of modern journalism—relying on outside sources—remains in place with reporters heavily dependent on experts as major characters in news stories. For much of the twentieth century, however, reporters—often experts themselves on certain issues (like politics or crime) or on various institutions (like the courts or higher education) by virtue of having covered them over time—were not allowed to display their expertise overtly. Instead, they had to seek outside authorities—characters and professionals with expertise—to give credibility to and help document their neutral reports. What daily reporters knew became generally subordinate to knowing whom to consult as an expert.

With the emergence of the culture of assertion and the appeal to niche partisan audiences, today's media marketplace features a plethora of issue-oriented Internet blogs, twenty-four-hour cable news, talk radio, and network news programs. This market is distinguished by the rise of the news pundit as a kind of expert at opinion. The displacement of Lippmann's real experts by cable "talking heads" and bloviating bloggers has undermined the role reporters played through much of the twentieth century as mediators between average citizens and genuine experts. Reporters, once upon a time, made the world more commonsensical and understandable through journalistic reports that verified and documented what was happening in individual communities and in the world.

Journalists today more and more frequently cross the line between mediator and pundit—blurring the line between remaining neutral and being an expert. While shows like CNN's *Crossfire* (1982–2005) started pitting opinionated columnists and reporters against one another as early as the 1980s, later growth spurts in twenty-four-hour cable news programs created even more demand for such relatively inexpensive talk programs featuring interviews with journalists willing to give their views (and promote their own newspapers or online sites) on the hot story or latest issue of the day. During events with intense media coverage, such as the President Clinton–Monica Lewinsky affair in the 1990s or the 2008–09 economic crisis, many print journalists appeared several times a day on various cable programs acting as experts on such stories, not only offering the facts they had gathered but providing opinion and speculation as well. Editors encouraged their reporters to go on these shows in the hope of selling more magazines and newspapers. The *Washington Post*, for example, began providing a set for their reporters' TV appearances, prominently featuring the paper's logo behind the reporter of the moment. Many critics contend that these practices erode the credibility of the profession by blending journalism with celebrity culture and crass commercialism. As the *Columbia Journalism Review* notes, two 2006 studies indicate that increasingly TV journalism had begun to rely on "live, unscripted reporting" that is "measurably thinner, more opinionated, and less densely sourced than other news forms."[15] Such live reports now make up more than half the news coverage on all U.S. cable news services. Intriguingly, one of the studies—done by the Project for Excellence in Journalism—observed, "Just as 'reality' TV is replacing scripted drama and comedy on the entertainment side, news on TV is also becoming a more extemporaneous medium."[16]

Constructing Two-Sided Stories

Embedded deep within the journalistic practice that developed in the twentieth century was the notion that news is two-dimensional—a third taken-for-granted ritual of the objective news process. A reporter sent to cover tax increases or local crime might be given this editorial advice: "Interview a Republican and a Democratic leader from the district and have them fight it out in the story." Such supposed balance, though, is a narrative device that helps generate story conflict. For most journalists, balance means presenting all sides of an issue without appearing to favor any one position. Unfortunately, because time or space constraints and narrative formulas have not always permitted presenting multiple sides or positions, in practice this value has often been labelled to "telling both sides of a story," which may, in fact, misrepresent social issues that are complex and multidimensional. The abortion controversy, for example, has often been treated as a story that pits two extreme positions (antiabortion vs. pro-choice) against one another. Yet people whose views do not fall at either end of the spectrum are seldom represented (despite being the majority of Americans).

Although many journalists claim a neutral position, they often stake out a moderate or middle-of-the-road position between the two sides represented in a story. In claiming neutrality and inviting readers to share in their "commonsense" point of view, journalists circumvent their own values. The authority of their distant, third-person, all-knowing point of view (a narrative device that many novelists use as well) enhances the impression of neutrality by making the reporter appear value-free. The claim for balanced stories, like the claim for neutrality, disguises journalism's narrative functions. After all, when reporters choose quotes for a story or TV news videographers or shooters choose camera angles, they are usually the most dramatic or conflict-oriented words or images that emerge from an interview, press conference, public appearance, or actual event. Until the recent economic downturn in the new partisan era, with its rapid escalation of small niche online audiences, the balance claim supported the financial interests of large modern news organizations staking out the middle ground. William Greider, a former *Washington Post* editor, has made the connection between good business and balanced journalism: "If you're going to be a mass circulation journal, that mean[t] you're going to be talking simultaneously to lots of groups that have opposing views. So you [had] to modulate your voice and pretend to be talking to all of them." [17]

For the news media today, of course, modulating political preferences to reach a mass audience makes less sense when that mass audience has dispersed and scattered as more and more people use media mainly to chase their individual interests. News media outlets like Fox News and MSNBC make money today by targeting and catering to partisan interest groups. They do this mainly by promoting or creating narrative conflicts between liberal and conservative positions. This journalistic shift from a kind of balance achieved by telling two-sided stories to a kind of imbalance that blatantly favors one side over another has implications for a democracy. In this age of assertion, Kovach and Rosenstiel worry that an increasingly toxic public arena will come to stand only "for polarized debate, not for compromise, consensus, and solution."[18]

Tough Questions and the Adversary Role

Complementing the paradoxical search both for balance and conflict, the fourth ritual is the one that many journalists take the most pride in: their adversarial relationship with the prominent leaders and major institutions they cover. The prime narrative frame for portraying this relationship is sometimes called a "gotcha" story, which refers to the moment when the reporter confronts a villain or corners a wrongdoer. This narrative strategy is most frequently used in political reporting. Some journalists assume that leaders are hiding something and that the reporter's main job is to ferret out the truth through tenacious fact-gathering and tough gotcha questions. An extension of the search for balance, this stance often tries to locate the reporter in the middle—again as a mediator—between "them" and "us," between political leaders and the people they represent. However, for the reporter, this is far from a neutral political position—it is a posture aligned with common sense and moderation, and a middle-of-the road viewpoint is still itself a viewpoint.

Critics of the tough-question style of reporting have argued that it fosters a cynicism among journalists that actually harms the democratic process. Although journalists need to guard against becoming too cozy with their political sources, they sometimes go to opposite extremes. By constantly searching for what politicians may be hiding, reporters may miss other issues. News critic Jay Rosen argues that "the essential problem is that the journalist's method of being critical is not disciplined by any political vision."[19] In other words, the bottom line for neutral or conventional journalists, who claim to have no political agenda, is simply maintaining the adversarial stance rather than improving the quality of political stories and democratic discussions. When journalists employ the gotcha model to cover news, being tough often becomes an end in itself. Thus, reporters believe they have done their job just by roughing up an interview subject or by asking the limited "What is going on here?" question. Yet the Pulitzer Prize, the highest award honoring journalism, often goes to reporters who ask ethically charged and open-ended questions, such as "Why is this going on?" and "What ought to be done about it?"

Personalizing Journalism: The Rise of Television News

Since the early 1970s, the annual Roper polls have indicated that the majority of viewers get their news from television and, in general, have found TV news more credible than print news. Part of the appeal of TV news, however, has always been its

Edward R. Murrow, anchor and reporter for *See It Now*, used his investigative approach to speak out against Joseph McCarthy's communist witch-hunt.

intimacy and the power of visual imagery. Unlike more distant print journalists, who try to remain detached and impersonal as a means to establish ties and credibility with readers, TV reporters and news anchors are more visible and more present to viewers. People can identify with them as characters more easily than they can identify with anonymous "bylines" at the top of a newspaper story.

In the early days of TV journalism, the most influential and respected news program was CBS's *See It Now*. Co-produced by Fred Friendly and Edward R. Murrow (both portrayed in the 2005 George Clooney film *Good Night, and Good Luck*), *See It Now* served as the conscience of TV news in its formative years. Murrow also worked as the show's anchor and main reporter, introducing the investigative model of journalism to national television—a model that programs like *60 Minutes*, *20/20*, and *Dateline* would later imitate. Generally regarded as "the first and definitive" news documentary on U.S. television, *See It Now* sought "to report in depth—to tell and show the American audience what was happening in the world using film as a narrative tool."[20] Friendly affirmed the importance of the narrative tradition to *CBS Reports*, the successor to *See It Now*: "Though based on truth, the programs still have to have stories of their own, with the basic outline of beginning, middle, and end."[21]

Over the next sixty-plus years, TV news narrated America's key events and provided a clearinghouse for shared information. Civil Rights activists, for instance, acknowledge that the movement benefited enormously from televised pictures that documented the plight of southern blacks in the 1960s. Other enduring TV images, unfurled as a part of history to each new generation, are embedded in our collective memory: the Kennedy and King assassinations in the 1960s; the turmoil of Watergate in the 1970s; the space shuttle disaster and the Chinese student uprisings in the 1980s; the Gulf War, the bombing of the Oklahoma City federal building, and the Clinton impeachment hearings in the 1990s; the 9/11 tragedy, the wars in Iraq and Afghanistan, Hurricane Katrina, the historic election of Barack Obama, and the financial crisis in the 2000s; the Sandy Hook Elementary School shooting and the Boston Marathon bombings in the 2010s. During these critical events, national TV news has been a cultural and social reference point. TV's enduring images indeed seem personal and intimate to us.

Although TV news reporters have shared many values, beliefs, and conventions with their print counterparts, television has transformed journalism in significant ways. For example, whereas modern print journalists are expected to be neutral or detached, TV news derives some credibility from live reporting, believable imagery, and viewer trust in the familiar reporters and friendly anchors who read the news. During the rise of TV news, our culture's news storytellers became viewed as much more central characters in the main narratives of the day than their print counterparts, who buried their personas in detached third-person quasi-objectivity. Through these differences, though, arises the question of how well TV news serves citizens in a democracy. Unfortunately, for the past several decades, local TV news has devoted more effort to treating its audience as news consumers instead of engaged citizens, exemplified by several common TV conventions.

The Problem of Crime-Driven News. By the mid-1970s, the public's fascination with the Watergate scandal—combined with the improved quality of TV journalism—helped local news realize profits. In an effort to retain high ratings, stations began hiring consultants, or so-called news doctors, who advised news directors to invest in one of the national packaged formats, such as "Action News" or "Eyewitness News" (sometimes satirized as Eyewitless News). Traveling the country, viewers might notice similar theme music and opening visuals from market to market. Consultants also suggested that stations lead their newscasts with **crime blocks**: a group of stories that recount the worst local and national crimes of the day. Even today, most regional TV stations still lead their evening newscasts with local isolated crime stories more than

40 percent of the time, even though such stories have very little connection to the vast majority of viewers.[22] Formulaic crime stories dominate local TV news and serve as a kind of a reality programming—not unlike the long-running *Cops* program—and as a complement to the popular fictional TV franchises like *Law and Order, CSI,* and *NCIS,* which have been a consistent narrative presence on prime time over the last two decades. The bottom line is that crime stories, whether headlining local TV news or driving prime-time programming, are essentially melodramas that tap into ingrained ways we have of making sense of our world and its complexities. Formulaic crime melodramas appeal to our sense of narrative structure and often portray social issues without complex shading. As more and more people migrate to the Internet for their news coverage, it remains to be seen how network television will respond to declining viewership and how or if it will attract an audience with different narrative expectations.

The Problem of Happy Talk. In addition to news consultants (and prime-time programmers) pushing crime stories, another strategy they have favored historically—in part to counter the grimness of crime coverage—has been "happy talk": the ad-libbed or scripted dialogue (satirized in *Anchorman,* the 2004 Will Ferrell film) that goes on among local news anchors, reporters, meteorologists, and sports reporters before and after news reports. During the 1970s, consultants often recommended such narrative chatter to create a more relaxed feeling on the news set and to foster the illusion of conversational intimacy with viewers. The overarching narrative they wished to present was news structured to feel like we were sitting around our living rooms, hearing stories from our favorite well-groomed uncles and aunts. Some news doctors at that time also believed in happy talk as an antidote to that era's "bad news," which included coverage of urban riots, campus protests, and the Vietnam War. A strategy still used heavily today, happy talk often appears forced and creates awkward story transitions, especially when anchors must report on events that are sad or tragic. Although the situation has improved slightly at some local news stations, national news consultants, such as Frank Magid Associates, continue to set the agenda for what local reporters should cover—lots of local crime—as well as how they should look—conventionally attractive, and blandly pleasant, with little or no regional accents. Essentially, news doctors have tried to replicate in modern local TV news the ad images of young attractive models that have dominated TV advertising since the 1960s—to create continuity between the look of news and the look of the advertising that the news interrupts.

Enduring News Values

Internalizing this depository of rituals and conventions discussed above has been a routine part of most journalists' education and socialization. Yet while many journalists still may think of themselves as neutral agents, these rituals mask a series of subjective choices that shape the stories they tell. Moreover, the process of producing news that appears neutral or balanced is also governed by a set of subjective beliefs that are not neutral. Sociologist Herbert Gans, who studied the newsroom cultures of CBS, NBC, *Newsweek*, and *Time* in the 1970s, generalized back then that most American reporters and editors shared several basic "enduring values." The most prominent of these values were—and certainly remain—ethnocentrism, responsible capitalism, small-town pastoralism, and individualism.[23]

By **ethnocentrism** Gans meant that in most news reporting, especially foreign coverage, reporters judge other countries and cultures on the basis of how "they live up to or imitate American practices and values."[24] Even though media mogul Ted Turner once outlawed the term *foreign* in the CNN newsroom (to downplay the U.S. perspective and create the outward show of neutrality), critics outside the United States pointed out that CNN's international news channel and other U.S. news outlets portray world events and cultures from an American point of view. In fact, the U.S. war in Iraq illustrated this point as cable news network MSNBC adopted the Pentagon's own term for the war—Operation Iraqi Freedom—as their main news title, labeling any coverage of the war with this phrase prominently displayed in red letters at the bottom of the screen. No news service outside this nation used the U.S. government's own language as their regularly recurring graphic title for the war.

Identifying **responsible capitalism** as another underlying value in news stories, Gans claimed that journalists usually have assumed that businesspeople compete with one another not primarily to maximize profits but "to create increased prosperity for all." Gans pointed out that, although most reporters and editors condemn monopolies, "there is little implicit or explicit criticism of the oligopolistic nature of much of today's economy."[25] In fact, today almost all journalists work in monopoly newspaper towns or for oligopoly parent companies. Thus writing about the limitations of such economic structures constitutes biting the hand that feeds them. Indeed, historically many publishers have preferred that reporters not cover the business operations and holdings of their parent companies. But this changed in 2008–09 when the decline and failure of media companies, especially newspapers, became part of the larger economic crisis narrative and coverage of media-related businesses increased.

Another journalistic value that Gans found threaded throughout conventional news stories was **small-town pastoralism**, that is, favoring the small over the large and the rural over the urban. Reporters and editors, like most Americans, tend to prefer and romanticize natural, rural settings over their manufactured municipal counterparts. Many journalists equate small-town life with innocence and are suspicious of cities, their governments, and daily urban experience. For example, stories about rustic communities with drug or crime problems are usually framed as good vs. evil—with the purity of bucolic country living contaminated by degenerate city lifestyles.

Finally, **individualism**, according to Gans, remains the most prominent value underpinning daily journalism. Many idealistic reporters are attracted to the profession because of its own powerful master narrative that celebrates the adversarial tenacity needed to confront and expose corruption. Beyond this, individuals who overcome personal hardships are the main characters in many enterprising news stories, and certainly our culture's interests in individual achievement and notoriety help nourish news media's (and audiences') obsessions with particular celebrities. Often, however, journalism that focuses mainly on the personal fails to explain the public dimensions of issues or events—and the workings of larger and more complex institutions. Many conventional reporters and editors are often not sure how to tackle the problems or tell the complicated stories raised by institutional wrongdoing or decay. So instead, journalists favor stories about prominent or extraordinary individuals over narratives about social problems or institutional complexity. In addition, because journalists are accustomed to working alone, many dislike cooperating on team projects or participating in citizen forums in which community members discuss community problems and their own interests. Many modern reporters view themselves as mere neutral channels of information rather than as engaged citizens or nonfiction storytellers.

REINVENTING JOURNALISM: REPORTING AND THE LIMITS OF STORYTELLING

Reporters today are often regarded with suspicion. They can be thought of, among other terms, as grim doomsayers who only report on life's seamy underbelly, as invaders of celebrity culture and personal privacy, as plagiarizers who make up quotes and fabricate sources, as cynical critics of revered national leaders, as smug semiprofessionals disconnected from the everyday problems of working people, or as opportunistic polarizers of politics interested only in profiting by pitting left against right in superficial dramas. In fact, in various public opinion polls measuring people's confidence in journalism commissioned in the 1990s and into the new millennium, respondents who said they had "a great deal of confidence in newspapers" dropped from more than 50 percent to less than 25 percent.[26]

As recently as the 1970s, most newspapers were more highly regarded—particularly the *Washington Post* and the investigative journalism of Bob Woodward and Carl Bernstein, acknowledged as major players in toppling a corrupt White House administration during the Watergate scandal. Fallout from that crisis led to the resignation of President Richard Nixon in 1974, and by the mid-1970s, journalism schools overflowed with students eager to take up careers in a profession that had such clout as watchdog over citizen interests and concerns. Since those heady days of Watergate, though, journalism has become mired in the often ho-hum formulaic storytelling of the old objective model, constrained by the self-censoring culture of giant media corporations, and accused today of promoting mean-spirited partisan politics in blogs and on cable. In recent years, several movements have tried to address some of journalism's most pressing problems, refocusing its role in democratic life, bringing in the color of partisan argument, and making daily journalism more accessible for people's postmodern lives.

Activist Journalism

Even in the corporate and new partisan eras of journalism, many traditional reporters, editors, and even publishers will still fight ferociously for the actual and assumed principles that underpin some of the profession's basic tenets—freedom of the press, the public's right to know, and the proverbial two sides to every story. In general, though, most traditional journalists do not acknowledge any moral duty to improve the quality of daily life or question the fundamental economic structures that journalism rests upon. Rather, these journalists value their important news-gathering capabilities and the well-honed news story, leaving the improvement of public life to political groups, nonprofit organizations, business philanthropists, and individual citizens. This raises the question of whether we want journalists to help improve the quality of democratic life or merely observe that life and report on it.

Although reporters have traditionally thought of themselves first and foremost as observers and recorders, some journalists have acknowledged broader social responsibility. Among them was James Agee in the 1930s. In his book *Let Us Now Praise Famous Men*, which was accompanied by the stark Depression-era photography of Walker Evans, Agee regarded conventional journalism as dishonest, partly because the act of observing intruded on people and turned them into story characters who newspapers and magazines then exploited for profit. Agee also worried that readers would retreat into the comfort of his writing—his narrative—instead of confronting what for many families was the horror and deprivation of the Great Depression. For Agee, the question of responsibility extended not only to journalism and himself but to the readers of his stories as well: "The reader is no less centrally involved than the authors and those of whom they tell."[27] Agee's self-conscious analysis has provided insights into journalism's hidden agendas and the responsibility of all citizens— including journalists—for making public life better.

When reporters are unwilling to claim any agency for improving public life or for questioning the creeping corporatization of the profession, democracy suffers. *Washington Post* columnist David Broder, writing in 1992, argued that national journalists—through rising salaries, prestige, and formal education—had distanced themselves "from the people that we are writing for and have become much, much closer to people we are writing about."[28] In 2004, this view was echoed by the George W. Bush administration. Ken Auletta, writing about the press and the president for the *New Yorker*, pointed out that, according to the administration's top political advisors, President Bush—himself a Northeast-bred millionaire and ex-oil executive—viewed "the press as 'elitist' and thinks that the social and economic backgrounds of most reporters have nothing in common with most Americans."[29] For his part, Broder maintained that journalists needed to become activists, not for a particular party but for the political process and in the interest of reenergizing public life. For the news media, this might mean spearheading voter-registration drives or setting up pressrooms in public libraries or even in shopping malls, where people converge in large numbers. More radically, leading national journalists—who command TV time, print space, and top blog sites—could rouse and lead a debate on the breakdown of balance between journalism's business demands under capitalism and its watchdog role for democracy.

Using the potential of new technologies like social networks and by advocating a more activist role for reporters and the news media, journalists, at their best, promise to reinvigorate both reporting and politics. Journalism, at its best, aims to improve our standard representative democracy, in which most of us sit back and watch elected officials and superstar journalists act (and act out) on our behalf, by reinvigorating deliberative democracy, in which citizen groups, local government, and the news media together take a more active stand in reshaping social, political, and economic agendas. In a more deliberative democracy, larger segments of the community would discuss public life, social policy, technological change, and media ownership before advising or electing officials who represent both individual and community interests.

Public Journalism

In the wake of widespread cynicism regarding journalism, a number of regional newspapers experimented with ways to "fix" journalism and to more actively involve readers in the news process. Beginning in the late 1980s, experiments surfaced primarily at midsize daily papers, including the *Charlotte Observer*, the *Wichita Eagle*, the *Norfolk Virginian-Pilot*, and the *Minneapolis Star Tribune*, that purposefully tried to involve both the public and journalists more centrally in civic and political life. Rejecting the objective model's neutral stance, public journalism embraced a mission of "helping public life go well," and moving "from detachment to being a fair-minded participant in public life."[30] In an effort to draw the public into discussions about community priorities, journalists began sponsoring reader and citizen forums where readers would have a voice in shaping aspects of the news that directly affected them. This movement, which began to wane in the late 1990s, drew both criticism and praise. Although not a substitute for investigative reporting or the more routine coverage of daily events, public journalism directly attacked objective-style reporting, asked journalists to be invested in their communities, and offered a way to involve both the public and journalists more centrally in civic and political life.

Ultimately, traditional reporters and other news critics began to consider public journalism as merely a tool of marketers and news managers, as the movement did not seriously address the rapidly changing economic structure of the news business. Despite its shortcomings, though, the public journalism movement remains a valuable lens for focusing on aspects of those fundamental news values—like reportorial detachment—that so powerfully shaped the practice, culture, and stories of American journalism throughout the twentieth century.

The Journalism of Assertion and the Fragmented Audience

Another response to objective-style journalism has been the rise of opinion and analysis that emerged with the rise of 24/7 cable news and development of the Internet. Now a major facet of journalism's new partisan era, the growth of the evening cable channels has ushered in reporters as pundits, commenting on the news as well as reporting it, giving these journalists a sort of celebrity status in the process. As *Columbian Journalism Review* editor Neil Hickey has noted:

> More than ever, journalists are delivering not just news but opinion as well. In print, the sacred line that traditionally has divided editorial page (and op-ed) columns from news columns is being blurred, as reporters add generous portions of analysis to their delivery of the facts. That trend is most apparent in television. Many print journalists appear on broadcast and cable channels, national and local, to engage in punditry—some of it enormously speculative, unsourced, and, at times, emotional—that they would never attempt in their customary roles as reporters on a beat. Some are paid for that service, either by the TV news outlets on which they appear, or by their own employers.[31]

Besides reporters taking on roles as pundits, nonjournalists (or pseudo-journalists) from talk radio or tabloids also chime in, often aggressively and flamboyantly, making minor stars of Glenn Beck, Anne Coulter, Rush Limbaugh, Arianna Huffington, Rachel Maddow, Chris Matthews, Lawrence O'Donnell, Bill O'Reilly, Joe Scarborough, and Ed Shultz. News scholar Darrell West has noted: "Ironically, as new 'journalists' appeared, the public became increasingly unable to distinguish professional journalists from their poorly trained and unprofessional colleagues."[32]

But while some may not like the 24/7 cable "yelling heads" or the millions of new news blogs, this journalism of assertion hearkens back to the partisan model of colonial America. Back in 1989, historian Christopher Lasch argued that "the job of the press is to encourage debate, not to supply the public with information."[33] Although he overstated his case—good journalism does both and more—Lasch made a cogent point about how conventional journalism had lost its bearings. Under the guise of objectivity, mainstream journalism lost touch with its partisan roots during much of the twentieth century, relegating advocacy and debate to alternative magazines, the editorial pages, and cable programs starring elite East Coast reporters. Lasch even connected the gradual decline in voter participation, which began in the 1920s, to more responsible conduct on the part of journalists, contending that with the modern objective model of the press, the public had deferred to the "more professional" news media to watch over civic life on its behalf. While some see the rise of the twenty-four-seven cable news cycle and Internet blogging as the demise of the modern objective ideal, those coming from Lasch's perspective might welcome the rowdiness and openness of new media and their impact on conventional forms of news storytelling.

Not surprisingly, some of the draw of punditry has been economic and not out of a sincere desire for critical civic debate. With an eye on the bottom line rather than the public's access to key information, news executives find it far cheaper to hire entertaining personalities who are good at agitation and opinion rather than journalists who spend long hours investigating and verifying social problems and key issues. But if neutrality, and appealing to the largest audience possible in service of it, was a profitable strategy for journalism for such a long time, what changed, economically, to encourage a return to more overt and contentious partisanship?

The economic answer resides in today's media marketplace. Network TV evening news over the last ten or fifteen years has lost far more than half its viewers to cable news, social networks, blogs, and Twitter. Newspaper readers also continue to age and decline, as young readers turn to Facebook, online news aggregators like Google, and their smartphones for up-to-date information. The former mass audience is morphing into smaller niche users who chase particular politics, hobbies, and forms of entertainment. Media outlets that hope to survive must design and produce narratives that appeal not to mass audiences but to interest groups: to conservatives or progressives or sports fans or history buffs or reality TV addicts.

One effect of this transition is that we now watch the news media—cable and the Internet in particular—transform important debates over health care or financial reform or gun control into highly partisan narratives of good vs. evil in an effort to pander to their smaller specialized audiences. Depending on our political persuasions, then, we can find a media source that targets "bad guys": either big government, greedy insurance companies and hedge fund managers, inept doctors, posturing politicians, crazy pundits, town hall agitators, or evil HMOs and big banks. The result is often news coverage that becomes two-dimensional and sensationalized, rather than complex and nuanced.

Online Journalism and Blogs: Pros vs. Amateurs

As the experiment with public journalism waned in the late 1990s, the Internet began its rise as a news medium. Initially, news organizations treated their Web sites as minor promotional venues and, in turn, treated the Web audience to free recycled print or broadcast stories and, perhaps, a few images. Instead, it was the amateurs—with a nod to the partisan press publishers of the colonial era—who began to attract the most attention. Early bloggers like Matt Drudge, creator of the highly partisan *Drudge Report*, challenged the status quo by mixing conservative politics with recycled news, rumor, and occasional scoops. Because Drudge ran a one-person blog operation from his apartment, he didn't have to worry about editors. So, in the late 1990s as *Newsweek* magazine was still fact-checking a story about President Bill Clinton's alleged affair with a young White House intern, Drudge published the report.

While some blogs coarsen public discourse with partisan rants, others have challenged "neutral" conventional journalism. The informal, first-person tone of blogs led to discussions among journalists about the value of the objective ideal in news reporting. Indeed, instead of rejecting blogs, many journalists have been inspired by them—writing their own, experimenting more with first-person storytelling in their general reporting, and sharing behind-the-scenes information that illustrates how good journalism is often a subjective, ethically strenuous, and demanding process. In some cases, bloggers stream the entire audio from their interviews so that readers can read or hear the unedited conversation and judge for themselves the fairness and accuracy of the blog.

For Bill Keller, former editor of the *New York Times*, the new era of transparency is a welcome development, like shedding a cloak of mystique:

> I know there are a lot of people in our business who feel nostalgic for the days when you weren't called upon to justify your reporting methods or defend a line of reporting. . . . it's a healthy thing to let readers know how much work we put into things to get them right and to get them fair.[34]

To take transparency even farther, media scholar and blogger Jeff Jarvis recommends journalists reveal their own backgrounds, prejudices, financial ties, political leanings, and other relevant beliefs. "Why not reveal your religion if you're covering the abortion debate? Or come clean if you're covering the auto industry and gave money to the National Audubon Society?" he asks.[35]

Blogs have liberated journalism in other ways. The practice of linking to outside news stories and other sources—a common feature of blogging—has now spread to online news sites as well. Initially, editors feared that providing outside links would encourage readers to leave their site, but it became clear that links kept people reading: They provided essential context to a story. If one mandate—and problem—of objective-style journalism was to focus on the present and de-emphasize historical context, links brought this context back and generally made a story richer without necessarily sacrificing timeliness. Even as online journalists upload stories minutes after they happen, they can also provide an ongoing discussion of how the story developed over days and call up the same story weeks or months later through links, reducing some of the pressure to both get the story first *and* get it right. A new ethic of storytelling has thus emerged: Obtain the most accurate version of events, then update as new details emerge and participate in the larger online conversation, acknowledging your sources through documentation that can be accessed through links.[36] (Traditional news organizations like the *New York Times*, CNN, and the *Washington Post* are no doubt happy to learn that their sites are those most often linked to by bloggers.[37])

Blogs have also challenged mainstream reporting by presenting a variation on public journalism that is accessible to nearly everyone. Whereas public journalism projects had to stage public forums to try to connect with readers, hundreds of readers can immediately respond to online stories, creating a sense of community and shared interest in each story. The Internet and mobile reporting technologies have also upended the news industry and notions about a free press. The American journalist A. J. Liebling famously noted that press freedom is guaranteed only to those who happened to own a newspaper or magazine. That has largely been true since the commercial age of news began in the mid-1800s. But now, reporting technology and a domain on the Web are so inexpensive that nearly anyone can own a slice of digitized media—without the space and time constraints of print and broadcast news.

For journalism, these new voices can offer analysis, present additional sides of the story, and expand the range of expert commentary—potentially solving several problems of objective-era reporting. Moreover, because bloggers have little overhead, they can play an adversary role indefinitely, keeping a story alive even as news sites are pressured to be more current and timely. For example, the reporting of Josh Marshall (from *Talking Points Memo*) and other bloggers sustained the story of federal attorneys being sacked by the Bush administration in 2007 for political reasons. As bloggers unearthed more information, the mainstream press revisited the story and furthered the investigation, which later led to congressional hearings and the resignation of the U.S. attorney general.

News sites are also incorporating elements of the blogosphere into their offerings. Through comment sections, readers can share what they know and feel, participate in compelling debates, and offer a range of insights unheard of in the age of time- and space-constrained journalism. They can also upload digital photographs and video of an event that they personally witnessed and shot themselves, offering a richer range of vantage points and helping us get closer to understanding more of the events and issues that are represented in a news story. The *Wikipedia* entry for the Virginia Tech massacre, for example, was updated every few minutes as interested, volunteer editors logged details and built more up-to-date and factual versions of unfolding events.

A question remains, though: If anyone can take text and images and upload them to a blog, *is this news?* Some, like journalism scholar Jay Rosen, envision a new era of citizen journalism. He calls the public "the people formerly known as the audience," who now have their own printing presses (and online radio and TV stations) and who share in the creation of news.[38] Others, like former Columbia University journalism dean Nicholas Lemann, see citizen journalism as a promising alternative to conventional models, but only if it is supported by informed reporting and hard work:

> [Reporting] is a powerful social tool, because it provides citizens with an independent source of information about the state and other holders of power. It sounds obvious, but reporting requires reporters. They don't have to be priests or gatekeepers or even paid professionals; they just have to go out and do the work.[39]

Lemann even sees the possibilities for new kinds of news narratives on the Internet:

> Potentially, it is the best reporting medium ever invented. . . . A few places, like the site on Yahoo! operated by Kevin Sites, consistently offer good journalism that has a distinctly Internet, rather than repurposed, feeling. To keep pushing in that direction, though, requires that we hold up original reporting as a virtue and use the Internet to find new ways of presenting fresh material—which, inescapably, will wind up being produced by people who do that full time, not "citizens" with day jobs.[40]

Still, with more than 80 million blogs, it's likely that more full-time citizen journalists will emerge, doing real reporting. As Rosen wrote in an essay directed to corporate media, "You don't own the press, which is now divided into pro and amateur zones. You don't control production on the new platform, which isn't one-way. There's a new balance of power between you and us."[41]

CONCLUSION: THE FUTURE OF JOURNALISM

As the advocates of Internet and public journalism, and critics of contemporary democracy, acknowledge, citizens have grown used to letting their representatives think and act for them. Reformed and reformatted journalistic models—whether in public journalism, blogs, or YouTube videos—ask the mainstream press to reconsider its role in deliberative democracy. For many traditional journalists, this may include paying more attention to the historical context in news stories; doing more investigative reports that analyze both news conventions and social issues; participating more fully in the public life of communities; including more viewpoints in the news; investigating the impact of economics on news media; inventing new kinds of news narratives; and, in general, taking more responsibility for their reporting and their news narratives.

In the quest to reinvent contemporary journalism, it has become clear that new technologies can help to tell better stories. But technology alone won't do this. Journalism needs to break free from static older formulas and reimagine ways to tell those stories. Local TV news programs—and to some extent the network evening news—have changed their narrative formulas and news presentations very little over the past forty years or so; only the technology of weather radar has really improved. But because there is little economic incentive to change, the tired formulas of TV news with their crime blocks and happy talk remain intact.

In fictional TV, though, storytelling has evolved over time, becoming increasingly dynamic and complex. Comparing the 1970s mega-hit TV show *Dallas* to more recent shows like *The West Wing*, *The Sopranos*, and *24*, Stephen Johnson argued back in 2005 that "one of the most complex social networks on popular television in the seventies looks practically infantile next to the social networks of today's hit dramas."[42] If fictional storytelling has changed, will TV news stories eventually change too? There is hope. After all, how long can any business continue to lose market and audience share and stay profitable? The hope here is that a new generation will drive change in TV news. It is no wonder young people are looking to *The Daily Show*, *The Colbert Report*, blog sites, citizen journalism, and social network venues for news and information. Perhaps they want something to match the more complicated storytelling around them, in everything from TV dramas to interactive video games to their own conversations. The world has grown more complicated, and we as citizens should demand significant news stories that better represent that complexity than formulaic TV news packages.

Another important strategy for championing better journalism—a "journalism of verification" that covers stories of real social significance—is to encourage commercial-nonprofit partnerships between newsrooms and universities, as Leonard Downie and Michael Schudson have advocated.[43] The Poynter Institute offers several strategies for successful news organization and university partnerships. For example, the journalism school at NYU has partnered with the *New York Times* to cover "hyperlocal" news for the East Village in Manhattan. The faculty member, an ex-*Times* reporter, has worked with a *Times* metro editor to ensure the quality of the students' work. Similarly, the *Bay Citizen* has partnered with the UC–Berkeley business and journalism schools "to develop a 'test kitchen' for innovation and experimentation in journalism."[44]

Stephen Colbert (left) and Jon Stewart (right) are comedians, but many younger audiences turn to programs like *The Daily Show* for news mixed with biting satire.

These projects are what some call a "pro-am" model: a partnership between professional newsrooms and amateur students. Journalism students should no longer be writing just for their teachers; in an online world hungry for content, they should be writing for newsrooms and engaging with their communities.

One key narrative strategy in the move to tell better stories in journalism is moving from the individual to the social, from a small illustration to the big picture. It isn't enough just to tell the story of an out-of-work father or a struggling family living in a cheap hotel after losing their home to foreclosure. The individual characters in these kinds of stories can serve as a narrative hook, allowing readers and viewers to identify, as individuals, with other individuals. But they are also catalysts for advancing the story to the more ambitious social level, presenting broad data on joblessness or on foreclosures and using experts to document local and national trends. Because online journalism has eliminated the space constraints of print news and the time limits of TV news, these kinds of complex narratives have become easier to construct—and should be constructed more often. This type of complicated storytelling also serves readers and viewers by not implying that individuals in news stories are the sole agents responsible for fixing their circumstances. Joblessness and foreclosures are not just personal crises for individuals or families—or melodramas for the evening news—but social problems whose solutions require collective action. Good news stories can move beyond melodramas and serve as a change agent—a catalyst for democratic action.

CRITICAL PROCESS 1 | Journalism Routines

The goal of this exercise is to compare local and national news outlets. This chapter discusses a "stock of ritual practices" that supposedly characterize mainstream U.S. reporting: getting the story first, relying on experts, reducing events to two sides, questioning leaders aggressively, personalizing the news, and focusing on crime. Over a two- or three-day period, watch a local newscast as well as a national newscast. For the same days, look at a local newspaper, if available, or take a look at a national newspaper site and one more local to your geographic area.

Describe the rituals discussed in this chapter that you see in these news media. Which ones can you find? Which ones are harder to locate? How do local and national news media differ? Make a list.

Analyze the differences, if any, between the local and national news outlets. How does coverage of similar events differ between the sources? Do you see any patterns? Any differences between TV and print news?

Interpret the reasons for these differences. How might these practices work to frame and define the relationship among the journalist, the readers or viewers, and the events themselves? What does it mean that news outlets rely on these routines and formulas to construct the news?

Evaluate the news sources. Which engage in more "stock ritual practices" described above? Do these differences affect their journalistic usefulness? How do these professional rituals enhance and impede good journalism? Which do the best and worst job? Why?

Engage with alternative news practices. Can you find other news sources in print, on TV, or online that rely less on reporting rituals? Talk to editors and news directors at these newsrooms and ask them why they covered certain stories and reported them in particular ways. Ask them if they are satisfied with the way they cover crime? Why or why not?

CRITICAL PROCESS 2 | Blog Journalism

The goal of this exercise is to explore how news blogs separate themselves from more traditional sources of journalism. Blogs are a relatively new form of news dissemination and commentary that, in some cases, has made new rules for itself. Pick three or four popular news blogs. You might consider examining blogs at the *Huffington Post*, the *Daily Beast*, the *Drudge Report*, or *Talking Points Memo*, or others. If they have an identifiable political leaning, try to find a mix of left-leaning, right-leaning, and centrist sources.

Describe the approach to news reporting on these blogs. Is it mostly narrative? Opinion? Analysis? How do their approaches compare to more traditional news outlets? Make a list.

Analyze their narrative techniques. Are they using mainstream "ritual" practices like those described in the previous exercise? Do they rely on evidence to support their claims? Do you see other patterns among blogs that don't conform to those rituals but do conform to one another? Do they have their own set of ritual news practices?

Interpret the reasons for differences between news blogs and more traditional news outlets. Is this traditional journalism done by nonjournalists, a new kind of journalism pioneered by bloggers, commentary on journalism, or something else entirely? Are both kinds of journalism valuable? Why or why not?

Evaluate the effectiveness of these sites as news sources. Would you return to them for news? Are they adding new perspectives and information? Are they reframing or affecting political debate? Which blogs are the best and worst? Why?

Engage with a political blog by posting informed comments. Can you participate in or shape the debate, or are you more of an audience for the bloggers' perspectives?

7

Media Economics

Two days before Valentine's Day 2004, a battle for the Walt Disney Company—among the world's most well-known corporations—ensued that had wide ramifications for the future of media consolidation. Comcast, the largest cable provider in the United States, had put out a $66 billion unsolicited bid for Disney.[1] Michael Eisner, then Disney's chief operating officer, was under attack for the company's poor financial showing since 2000. He fought back for months to keep Disney a separate corporation. Although Eisner would eventually be forced out by Disney's unhappy board of directors in 2005, the company rebuffed Comcast's takeover plans.

But Comcast did not give up. In late 2009, Comcast paid more than $13 billion to General Electric for a 51 percent interest in NBC Universal. Then in 2013 Comcast bought the rest of NBC Universal for $16.7 billion. Comcast today earns the bulk of its revenue from television, Internet, and digital phone services offered in forty states; with eighteen million subscribers to its broadband Internet and cable services, it far outpaced second-place cable company Time Warner by 2013.

Who owns the media, how they operate these corporations—for profits—and how they fit institutionally into our democracy tell us that business takeover attempts matter. The Comcast/NBC Universal deal pushed to the forefront questions about how Disney, GE, and Comcast operate in cultural, political, and social arenas. Comcast owning NBC and the Universal movie studio means fewer owners controlling fewer companies. (Similarly, Comcast acquiring Disney would have changed not only Disney movies but also ABC-TV, ESPN, and all the other Disney and Comcast networks and properties.) Adding Comcast's control of NBC to Disney's ownership of ABC and New Corp.'s ownership of Fox means that fewer powerful companies control the distribution of information on network television—the place where most Americans still go for their national and international news. This could mean that negative news concerning a company's holdings might not get reported at a time when we need to know what corporate control of news and stories means in our digital age.

Mass media corporations are everywhere, and we spend considerable time using their products. For instance, the average home still has a TV set on more than seven hours per day. We measure the costs of creating media in millions of dollars: $500 million for a high-tech movie like *Avatar*, over $1 million per episode for Charlie Sheen when he starred in *Two and a Half Men*, and multimillion-dollar annual contracts for newscasters like Brian Williams, who is mainly paid to read twenty-two minutes of network news five nights a week, attracting about five to six million viewers each evening in 2013. For consumers, the media cost more and more to acquire—for example, $70 to $80 per month for a cable broadband connection, or $500 for a new high-definition TV set. To reach us, advertisers spend billions of dollars each year on television. The hardest of the corporations to analyze are media conglomerates—that is, many media under one corporate umbrella. For instance, various versions of *CSI*, the most popular TV franchise of the early to mid-2000s, were made by the Paramount Pictures studio in Hollywood, under a CBS productions unit, and shown on CBS. All of these units (and more) were owned and operated at the time by one media conglomerate: Viacom, Inc. But in late 2005, Viacom split into two separate companies, although Viacom chairman Sumner Redstone still held controlling interest in both companies in 2013. More intriguing, Viacom was actually created by CBS in 1970 when the Federal Communication Commission (FCC) made the network get rid of its syndication business. Viacom became that new business and made a fortune in the early 1990s syndicating old *Cosby Show* reruns, which helped it swallow (or at least control) its original parent—CBS.

In this chapter, we consider how to understand the economic aspects of mass media in society, primarily at the level of the corporation. Our goals are to understand what economic control and operation mean for the diversity of voices that speak to us all and for the operation of democracy, examining in particular who owns the corporations that provide us with the entertainment, news, and information; what is at stake when media operations change; and what forms of media ownership and operation consumers should expect in our mass mediated world. In examining media industries as collections of businesses, we pose questions to help understand how media companies—structured as money-making business enterprises—interact with our democratic and cultural interests. So why do corporations offer us, for example, particular types of television or music or movies or Web sites? Can media companies make a profit covering political events and key social issues related to the functioning of our democracy? And if not, who will report on these events and issues? And in the end, what kinds of media businesses would we like to have?

MEDIA CORPORATIONS AND ECONOMIC ANALYSIS

Usually we see types of media corporations defined by their technology, such as the broadcast television corporation, the film company, or the music business. But that confuses the functions of the corporations. A more productive way of thinking about media corporations is to divide them by the three most common types of industry structures (i.e., collections of corporations offering similar products or services):

1. monopoly (domination by a single company)
2. oligopoly (domination by a few—usually four to seven—big corporations)
3. competition (many companies vying in the marketplace)

Over the post decade, mass media corporate power and influence have increased as fewer and fewer corporations face true competition; the most typical media market structure today is oligopoly. Local or regional monopolies exist, as in the one cable company (or newspaper) most of us have in our communities, but we must also consider other multichannel television services such as direct broadcast satellite or WiMax. How do we best go about analyzing the economics of the mass media industries? In this section, we offer three approaches to critiquing media business: Marxist analysis, free-market analysis, and industrial analysis. We find industrial analysis the most appropriate model, but discuss the other two for context.[2]

Marxist Analysis

Although Marxist forms of criticism have been adopted by many critics and meandered in many directions since the mid-nineteenth century, the basic idea is captured in the preface to Karl Marx's *A Contribution to the Critique of Political Economy*, first published in 1859: "The mode of production of material life conditions the social, political, and intellectual life process in general. It is not the consciousness of men that determines their being, but on the contrary, their social being that determines their consciousness."[3] To illustrate this, Marx created a "base/superstructure" model or metaphor to explain the idea that the quality of the social life of a people or nation is driven by their economic conditions. This economic foundation or "infrastructure" for Marx supports a "superstructure" that includes the ideas, laws, politics, religions, ethics, art, literature, and various media in a society. But according to Marx, the superstructure also houses "social consciousness," or what is most frequently referred to as **ideology**. As literary critic Terry Eagleton has explained: "The function of ideology . . . is to legitimize the power of the ruling class in society; in the last analysis, the dominant ideas of a society are the ideas of its ruling class."[4] All sorts of able critics have since deployed Marxist ideas and theories to study the ways dominant groups and ruling elites in any society maintain their power (and oppress subordinate groups) by controlling the "modes of production," or economic conditions.

Offering some of the most penetrating analyses of modern society, Marxist criticism has long viewed the influential cultural industry—that is, a collection of media corporations—as a classic example of monopolistic capitalism in which the economic control over media production determines the type of media any society gets. Many critics coming from this perspective, however, do not analyze or try to understand the full complexities of media corporations but simply assume they possess negative characteristics associated with the kind of capitalism that Marxists generally oppose (negative, in part, because capitalist managers, in order to sustain their control, conceal their machinations from their workers and the masses, who are exploited as the managers and bosses rake in profits). They focus on how these long-lived corporations have colluded to devise ways to maintain their economic power and cultural imperialism. So, for example, while capitalist corporate leaders and Hollywood celebrated Twentieth Century Fox and Paramount's co-financing of the blockbuster film *Titanic*, many Marxist critics saw this movie mega-hit as yet another example of studios working together—not competing—to best exploit their product and maximize profits, which they would share. So the film's producers cared not at all about the film's social, cultural, or democratic implications.

Marxist economists generally focus on the corporate propensity toward concentration of ownership that they consider central to monopoly capitalism. Marxist analysts stress the inevitable rise and continuation of giant corporations and how they seem to take over more mass media production, distribution, and use. They assume corporate stability and concentration and ignore that companies do fight for profits against one another: Think of the ongoing cable war that rages between Fox News (owned by News Corp.) and MSNBC (owned by Comcast). Look too at the recent fights between Fox and Time Warner over how much cable companies should be paying to carry regular local and network broadcast signals.

Traditional Marxist critics may also overlook that corporations seek to differentiate their offerings and to deploy new technologies in doing so. So, for example, Marxist thinking cannot easily reconcile the rise of Amazon.com or Google because such digital companies follow different, more complicated paths to industry domination than earlier media industries. Corporations also go in and out of business. RCA, for example, was once the most influential media company in the world but now exists only as a brand name leased by other companies. Similarly, AOL's 2001 takeover of Time Warner was ultimately a catastrophic failure and the powerful Tribune Media Company ended up in bankruptcy from late 2008 through 2012. Given these few examples, we need analytical approaches that can better explain the new possibilities for configuring media and the failure of old but once-strong capitalist models (some of which failed mightily without a workers revolt). We can't assume the continuing and ever-growing power of any media company.

Although Marxist analysis often demonstrates how media companies maintain their power while revealing very little of the production process to consumers and citizens, such analyses are not as strong in interpreting how a TV show or Hollywood film tells stories and makes sense to fans and audiences—who, first of all, may ignore these cultural products and, second, may interpret them in complex ways that the managers of media never intended. In addition, some Marxist analyses are not able to account for the high failure rate among new media products in the marketplace—as high as 80 and 90 percent in most years, a figure that does not support the stereotype of duped consumers buying everything that's heavily marketed but instead says that many consumers are discerning, not so easily seduced by the slick lure of advertising and promotion. Many of us resist buying what corporations are selling.

Free-Market Economics

Competition and choice lie at the heart of the second analysis model: free-market media economics. The free-market "bible" is Adam Smith's *An Inquiry into the Nature and Causes of the Wealth of Nations*, published in 1776.[5] Smith made the key point that under the right conditions free markets will produce the greatest wealth for nations that enable them. Later advocates of free-market competition have stressed that corporations offer a wide array of choices and that in an open and supposedly free marketplace, the media products that customers want will rise to the top while inferior products (and companies) will fail. For example, they might emphasize that no one was forced to go see *Avatar* and that the movie's producer-distributor, Twentieth Century Fox, created a superior media product that rose above the pack of inferior forms of mass culture when the film premiered in December 2009. The consumers had the choice to spend their money and time reading a book, magazine, or newspaper; watching programming on a hundred cable channels; listening to dozens of radio stations; cruising the Internet; or playing their favorite CD or DVD—but they chose to watch the film instead. Free-market economists assert as the very basis of their analysis this consumer sovereignty of choice and assume that no mass media company can force anyone to do or buy anything. Following Adam Smith, Alfred Marshall focused on the forces of supply and demand, seeing movie theater box office receipts or TV ratings as classic voting booths (i.e., customers "vote" with their dollars) where top films and TV programs win and unpopular movies or television stories fail to attract audiences.

What this analysis does not acknowledge is that this product diversity will often come from the same mass media conglomerate. One can see, for example, on a Time Warner channel such as TNT, CNN, or TCM, a variety of entertainment from science fiction to westerns, from reality shows to "infomercials," from dramas to comedies, from around-the-clock news to documentaries (all sometimes airing on a Time Warner cable system). But these choices all emerge from decisions made by a handful of corporate managers reporting to a corporate chief operating officer. Not recognizing this control, free marketers' overemphasis on choice reads like a predetermined pro-capitalist assumption, where profit trumps democracy and its concerns every time, in the same manner that many Marxist-based analyses start with the presumption that capitalism is essentially a bad or corrupt system. Instead of these two choices, we need analysis that starts with no predetermined answers.[6]

Industrial Economics

Industrial economists begin with neither pro- nor anticapitalistic assumptions, and instead seek to first define who owns the media, analyze what economic conduct emerges from that industrial structure, then examine how the industry performs given specified criteria, and finally recommend—if needed—possible public policy corrections to make the industry more accountable to consumers and citizens.

Industrial economists long have recognized, for example, the common tools mass media corporations use to maintain their considerable economic power and keep out competition. The key has been to use what companies refer to as **economies of scale**—spreading costs over many outlets and thereby reducing the price of a single unit or product. If, for example, a single local TV station produced one drama series for its own schedule, it would take on the whole cost of an expensive one-hour production. But a typical U.S. TV network—like ABC, CBS, NBC, or Fox—helps produce programs that air on 200-plus affiliated stations, spreading the costs around, harnessing the best talent at a central site (the network—which usually is a subsidiary in an entertainment conglomerate that also a owns a giant film studio that can make TV shows), and commanding large national audiences for which advertisers pay top dollar rather than much cheaper ad rates that the single local TV station could charge for its smaller local drama (which would also lack the high production values and top talent that a national network can attract).

Another argument maintains that media conglomerates—those that, like Time Warner or Disney, own units in every form of media production and distribution—can cross-subsidize, extracting profits from one thriving area to prop up another less financially successful area. Their film divisions—especially with a James Cameron movie like *Avatar* (as of 2013, the highest-grossing movie of all time, taking in $2.8 billion worldwide)[7]—might have a good year that offsets a poor performance in the music or publishing divisions within the same time frame. Single-line corporations (like an independent film company that makes a very small number of films each year) do not have this luxury. Thus, aspiring single-line corporate operations are invariably rare and even when they do succeed are usually bought up by larger companies. Corporations now *vertically integrate*, a process where, say, Time Warner and Disney make movies and, after the theatrical runs are finished, run them on their cable channels—thus "selling" to themselves. Another example would be the major TV networks (all now owned by companies with film studios) producing their own prime-time TV shows, running them on their own networks (or selling them to one another, as when Twentieth Century Fox produces *How I Met Your Mother* for air on CBS rather than the Fox network). These practices cut out the middle agent and save these large media corporations, who mostly just compete with each other, some major costs.

The objective of recommending industrial media economics is not to make us all into applied economists but rather to examine how economic forces determine what corporations own, how they operate, and how they control storytelling. This understanding allows us to make social and cultural judgments about how corporations are acting as players in society—and what kinds of stories they are telling and selling. The industrial media economists do not seek to value, as Marxists and free-market economists do, one form or another of corporate action. Instead, the industrial economist can suggest an array of public policy alternatives to correct identified deficiencies. Logically, the question industrial media economists turn to is how to judge the economic actions of media firms—from the largest, like Disney and Comcast, to the smallest, where a single individual runs an informational Web site.

MEDIA CORPORATIONS AND PERFORMANCE NORMS

In the end, industrial analysis of the ownership and operation of media corporations requires us to develop criteria for how corporations are performing in our economy, society, and culture. Developing explicit criteria helps us examine whether the media marketplace is working or not and to judge how corporations should behave in a democracy. If the industry is not performing well, we label this "market failure" and need to propose remedies to force better performance. Scholar Denis McQuail has suggested media performance norms that encompass most judgments. Some are easy to apply; others do not lend themselves to easy judgments. In the following section, the first criteria considered are easier to apply than those further down on the list. These are all value judgments, and the order does not reflect our priorities as authors—and perhaps not yours, as readers. We believe these values ought to promote democratic priorities, as much as possible, to work as well as possible.[8]

Facilitating Free Speech and Political Discussion

First, citizens in democracies ought to argue that media industries should facilitate free speech and political discussion. A democracy needs freedom of expression to make it work, and both noncommercial and commercial media ought to be open enough to promote debate of all points of view. The marketplace of ideas calls for criteria in which information and data are evidence-based, accurate, and comprehensive. But is this best done by letting media corporations pursue profits first and foremost—never considering noneconomic issues? Probably not. This is the cause of debate over the sensitive issue of government intervention in political speech supported by wealthy donors and companies versus the needs of a profit-maximizing economy.

For example, the ongoing loss of traditional reporting jobs and news companies led in 2010 to congressional hearings and major debates over the possible need of government support in subsidizing journalism at a time when the old advertising-based business models had broken down. Unlike toothpaste or Hollywood movies, good journalism is not just a product but an actual requirement for healthy democracy—and one that may not be able to sustain itself in a business world over the long term. The "press," in fact, is the only business that is specifically protected in the U.S. Constitution.

While political debate and excellent journalism are essential to any healthy democracy, they are not inexpensive to produce and raise a number of issues. Rules that encourage forums to which everyone can have equal access seem desirable. But today's political candidates spend more time raising money to advertise their stories on TV and the Internet than actually debating key social issues. Government subsidies for failing newspapers (or even bailing them out as we did with the auto industry and banks in 2009) might save some sectors of journalism, but such action would also raise questions about the danger of government interference in content. Early in our nation's history, though, the federal government heavily subsidized postal costs for newspapers and magazines, and since the late 1960s, the government has supported NPR and PBS, whose journalistic output and independence have usually been praised.

Our society could require government-licensed but commercially independent TV stations to provide free time to promote political debate. But free debate for all would limit our media institutions' ability to maximize profits, presenting a vexing problem that thus far has been resolved in favor of TV stations maintaining their right to charge for advertising. The next time a political debate airs on television, consider that the media enterprise broadcasting it is giving up profits at the expense of serving democracy (although some critics would argue that only the two main party candidates are taken seriously and allowed to participate in most national debates). It is a matter of debate as to whether they should be required to do this, if it should be left to their judgment, or if we should support government channels to broadcast all debates—paid for by our tax dollars.

Not Wasting Resources

Second, media corporations ought to avoid wasting resources; that is, they should be as efficient as possible. But monopolies do waste resources—they do not always care if they are wasteful—in order to maintain their monopolistic position of power, which allows them to set prices for their products. Indeed, the wastefulness of monopolies is one characteristic on which all analysts agree. We see this waste in excessive salaries and benefits (especially for top managers and CEOs), excessive advertising, and excessive claims they make about their own benefit to society. How often in the past has a local media monopoly (which may have owned the top newspaper, radio, and TV stations in the same market) claimed to have its community at heart (even as it controlled much of the broadcast ad revenue and most classified advertising in its region) as it opposed any regulation that might affect its bottom line? But if a company controls a media industry in a region, citizens should be asking for alternatives. While free-market economists focus on only this performance criterion, Marxists take it for granted and assume as normal corporate neglect of democratic, social, and cultural concerns. Industrial economists, however, seek to determine whether a corporation is truly a monopoly. For example, in some small towns alternative or free advertising–supported newspapers have broken the monopoly hold; certainly, in many areas today, the Internet and the impact of craigslist, eBay, Monster.com, realtor.com, and auto trading Web sites have broken a regional media company's hold over classified ads.

Free-market economists might argue that regulation was never necessary because these new developments in the market—the Internet and other alternative media—checked the local media monopoly and eventually provided competition, and will continue to do so. However, this competition hasn't stopped the rapid decline of

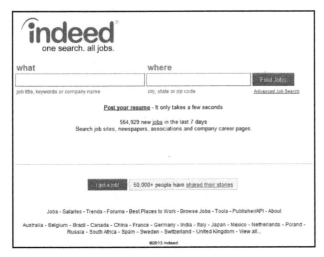

Job sites like Indeed.com have diminished the power of
traditional classified ads, which used to be a major money
maker for newspapers.

traditional print media and its commercial business model that had supported for so long much of the nation's best journalism. So key questions remain: Are the local news organizations still covering government and business in the region and doing the kinds of watchdog journalism that hold those in power accountable? If not, then should we be subsidizing journalism in particular areas to ensure that people are informed? These vexing questions lie at the heart of media economics and market failures—and urge a strong public policy response.

Facilitating Public Order

Third, media industries ought to facilitate public order, especially with regard to war, violence, and crime. For example, news media often report on crime and violence that threaten communities. Implicit in their coverage is that crime and violence disrupt order and the common good. War is tricker, often pitting citizens' need for information against a government's desire for secrecy. Governmental leaders often pressure the mass media to censor certain stories during wartime. In 2005 and 2006, for example, the Bush administration officials criticized major news organizations, particularly the *New York Times* and network news, for revealing that they were spying on U.S. citizens—without court approval—who may or may not have links to terrorist organizations. The administration had argued that they needed wide latitude in conducting a global war on terror. Indeed, war offers a classic example of how governments withhold information from media corporations in the name of national security. We need to come together as a society in times of war, but with how strict a set of restrictions on speech and communication? These restrictions are hotly debated as to where the line should be drawn.

Protecting and Maintaining Cultural Quality

Fourth, media corporations ought to protect and maintain cultural quality and offer diversity of opinion. This raises the question of whether companies that depend on advertising-generated revenue can develop quality programming—and not simply dish up one more season of worn-out formulaic rip-offs and assorted pandering—and if the government should force them to raise their standards (raising further questions about the subjectivity of the term "quality"). When government officials have sought to regulate content on television, radio, or film, they have run up against First Amendment protections. In 2006, the Bush administration served subpoenas to Internet search companies like Google and Yahoo! in order to perform random searches for individuals and companies trafficking in child pornography. We have rules and laws about obscenity, libel, and slander, but how should we regulate corporate and individual behavior to limit pornography and controversial speech when we have difficulty coming to a consensus over what constitutes obscenity and free expression?

Promoting New Technology

Fifth, media industries ought to bring new technologies to the marketplace as quickly as possible. Economists have long recognized that monopolies resist the innovation of new technologies in order to protect their highly profitable status quo positions. In fact, part of the problem in the decline of newspapers was how slow corporate executives and managers were to embrace the Internet and develop strategies that would have ensured a smoother transition into the Digital Age. If the newspaper industry itself had come up with ideas like craigslist, it might be in better financial shape today. It was, after all, fairly easy to see that classified advertising looked a lot better on the Internet without time and space restrictions than it did in the tiny typeface in most newspapers. In terms of television, should the government set and mandate standards, as the FCC actually did by mandating the end of analog television sets and signals in 2009? Or should buyers choose what is best for them individually, resulting in several standards and the higher costs of interchangeability these multiple standards set? Indeed, the media regulation approach in recent times in the United States—called deregulation—has usually left it to corporations to set the standards.

Applying these five criteria consistently, fairly, and equitably across all the mass media is difficult to do. We, as citizens, and our elected officials must make judgments. Consider, for example, the 1996 Telecommunications Act that promised more choice, more diversity, and more equity in the media. But instead this law led to concentrated ownership and higher prices. Although the growth of the Internet and the 2008–09 financial crisis has exposed many media corporations as **overleveraged** (too much debt on top of the collapse of investment earnings, so not enough capital to pay the debt bills), these large companies still dominate the production and distribution of mainstream media content. With such corporations still seeking new and increased profits, they prompt questions about how we can best organize as a democracy to match the economic interests of big business with the coverage of different points of view in matters of politics and social affairs. This is why we must understand the ownership and operation of the mass media: So we can look for governmental support and civic strategies that make sense in making the media benefit society as a whole.

MEDIA CORPORATIONS AND PROFIT

Once we have established democratic criteria for media corporations, how do we balance the paramount goal of most corporations—profit maximization—with a plan to encourage democracy and diverse voices in the media marketplace? This is important because mass media are primarily organized as corporations; while, say, NPR may be many listeners' choice as the nation's most credible news service, it is supported by tax dollars and donations, and only a small portion of the radio audience listens to this noncommercial programming. On the other hand, in 2012, Clear Channel Corporation—a profit-making entity and the nation's largest radio conglomerate—owned 850 stations that reached roughly ninety million people. One of its subsidiaries, Premier Radio Networks, now produces syndicated radio content for more than five thousand stations, about half of the nation's commercial stations. (The company also owns 90 percent of Clear Channel Outdoor Holdings, among the world's largest billboard firms with nearly one million display ads worldwide.)

Before the 1996 Telecommunications Act removed most ownership restrictions, our government, operating on behalf of citizens and championing diversity of ownership, limited the number of radio stations one corporation could own to fewer than fifty. Clear Channel took advantage of the 1996 act and bought up hundreds more radio stations, and although they've struggled with debt since then (and resold more than 400 stations), the company still benefits from the economies of scale that earn them substantial profits—perhaps to the detriment of democratic interests and a diversity of owners in the marketplace. For example, Clear Channel offers a number of soundalike formats and prepackaged digital programming that it circulates on many of its stations, which undercuts local flavor and discourages individual radio stations from reflecting the unique characteristics of their particular communities in favor of maximized profits for the parent corporation.

Profit is defined as the difference between revenues taken in by the corporation and the costs it takes to produce a product or service. For example, a newspaper has traditionally made its money from what readers pay for street sales and subscriptions and what advertisers pay to have their ads run in the paper. These are the paper's revenues. On the other side, the newspaper counts as costs the salaries of reporters and editors, buildings to work in, computers, delivery trucks, paper, ink, and so forth. Managers hope that these costs add up to an amount less than the revenues; if so, the newspaper makes a profit. If there is no profit, the paper accepts a loss. No corporation can lose money too long or it will be sold or go out of business. In addition, as newspapers—at least the print versions—look more and more irrelevant in the Internet era, their stock prices can plummet even when they still make money. For example, in 2005 the *Los Angeles Times* made more than $1 billion in gross revenues and roughly $200 million in profits, yet its owner, the Tribune Company, declared bankruptcy late in 2008. This happened in part because few stockholders thought newspapers had a future following the decrease in (though not elimination of) many papers' profits.[9]

Costs can be high even in more potentially lucrative media, like film and television production. Brad Pitt can earn $20 million or more for one film role. Jerry Seinfeld, Ray Romano, Jennifer Aniston, and Charlie Sheen all became multimillionaires based on what they earned from their TV sitcoms. The stars of a hit TV show can make $100,000 to $1 million or more per episode, but if the revenues generated through advertising, cable fees, and international sales far exceed this, they are worth it to their corporate managers. A newspaper with less impressive profit margins might, theoretically, stay in business for the good of its community. But study after study has confirmed that corporations, when given the choice, choose to maximize their profits rather than seek what might best serve a community (or democracy as a whole). If benefits come along for society, they come as secondary effects. This is a problem with the profit-maximizing corporations that dominate the media world in a democratic society.

Still, profit maximization is the touchstone of our market economy. Like Michael Eisner and the attempted takeover of Disney by Comcast in 2004, shareholders who own the company will band together to oust managers or at least remind managers of what they want: profits. As such, they often ignore the effects on democracy, causing the friction and occasional public outrage over policy decisions that corporations make. It's worth noting, as mentioned in Chapter 5, that journalists who might cover these issues are often employed by corporations whose profits could be threatened by revelations of daily business practices, high profit margins, and CEO incentives. On the upside, however, the economic crises of 2008–09 and their lingering effects have focused more attention on the business of media companies, their role in a depressed economy, and alternatives to doing business.

Indeed, profit maximization is not the only way to run mass media. There are many nonprofit media outlets, such as the radio and TV stations, newspapers, and Web sites run by colleges and universities. Florida's biggest newspaper, the *St. Petersburg Times*, is owned by a nonprofit company, the Poynter Institute. At the government-supported level, NPR and PBS do not seek to make a profit. They seek to simply—at the end of each year—make sure revenues from government funds, donors, and grants equal costs spent to produce their programming. In such nonprofit media, education, quality storytelling (especially stories that commercial media don't think are profitable), and public information are most often the goals, not maximizing profits. But in the twenty-first century, media companies remain primarily profit maximizers.

Direct and Indirect Revenue Streams

Although profits are the main goal of most commercial media corporations, not all revenues are the same. On the one hand, consumers pay directly for some products and services—whether going to a movie, purchasing a book, or buying a song online. This is called **direct revenue** and measures directly what books, movies, or music customers prefer.

But many media seem free. Buy a radio, plug it in, and there is no cost other than the electricity. Buy a computer, find a newspaper site—no charge. Advertisers pay the radio station and Google, and we get the music and news for "free." The advertisers must add in this advertising cost as part of their profit-making calculations, so in some ways it is more realistic to think that we pay for "free" broadcast radio and television when we buy the products and services that advertise on them. When a consumer sees a TV ad for a Ford SUV and that helps to spur the purchase of one, part of the price of the SUV is the cost that Ford has spent advertising. This is called **indirect revenue**, and it can confuse economic analysis because the media corporations are seeking to appeal to advertisers, not to customers. For an NFL game, a network media company's chief "product," then, is really the audience—both its overall size and its demographics (eighteen- to forty-nine-year-old males who might buy the beer that's advertised during the game being the most valuable in this case). In television, media corporations use data such as Nielsen ratings to determine the audience they can sell to advertisors.

Advertisers, of course, prefer audiences who might buy their products, and this preference involves two criteria that leave out a vast section of our population. First, advertisers prefer customers who will continue to buy new products and services; they have determined that those customers are part of the demographic group ages eighteen to forty-nine. This is why mainstream ads in mass media are generally not intended for the old and the very young—unless they're selling products like toys, sugared cereal, Viagra, or Life Alert. Secondly, advertisers exclude more of the population by targeting those customers who can afford to buy new products; this eliminates the lower-income populations. So we end up with, say, golf shows on weekends with ads for high-end sports cars because advertisers want to reach well-off men in the eighteen-to-forty-nine group who play golf. We see less news coverage of poverty or homelessness, or few sitcoms about working-class families, because this programming does not serve the audiences that advertisers want to reach. This hardly could be called helpful to a robust democracy.

Institutional Economic Model

In the end, we posit an **institutional economic model** with the mass media corporation at its center. We begin by recognizing that mass media corporations are not simple firms reducible to equations but large and complicated social, cultural, and political institutions. These mass media corporations rank among the most complex and important institutions in our lives. They do not simply make TV shows, magazines, or gadgets; they make and distribute the communication and culture that define and represent the major values of our society and democracy. Their status demands that we analyze the connections among society, culture, and these corporate institutions. Economic behavior and cultural actions are intertwined, and people are conditioned by culture and resist, change, or respond based in part upon the actions of corporations.

We should also acknowledge that the history of corporate institutions plays a central defining role in social life and that corporate institutions vary by ownership, market conditions, and technological possibilities. For example, the politically conservative

Rupert Murdoch and his News Corp., in addition to the *Wall Street Journal*, own both the Fox TV network and Fox News cable channel—a news source that mostly champions a conservative point of view, even while claiming in its ad slogan to be "fair and balanced." The institutional output and goal are profit, but the corporate owners and managers also operate in a social context as well as an economic one, with key cultural and societal effects. Central are considerations of where social, economic, and political factors intertwine. As an example of this complexity, an episode of Fox series *The Simpsons* or *Family Guy* generates profits for Murdoch at the same time the cartoon often satirizes conservative politics and Fox's corporate culture or the poor working conditions under which an animated network series is produced. In other words, Murdoch has accepted certain kinds of resistance to his politics or criticism of his authority as long as his products generate revenue and help maximize News Corp.'s profits. In fact, he is *selling resistance* to his cultural influence and conservative values. One of the keys to the durability of capitalism is its ability to co-opt criticism and package it as a narrative product. Consider the long history of NBC's David Letterman and *SNL* criticizing and satirizing their corporate parents—first GE, then Comcast.

MEDIA CORPORATIONS AND COMPETITION

The greatest corporate profits accrue when a company can dominate its competitors—or ultimately become a monopoly with no competition. One way for a firm to become dominant is to distinguish itself from its competitors. Beyond making desirable products, a firm may strive to win the hearts and minds of consumers by developing a distinct image for their entire product line—ensuring that the firm's identity or logo (and, by extension, its products or services) becomes synonymous with quality. This marketing strategy is known as **branding**. No one needs to know that ABC originally stood for American Broadcasting Company because ABC is a brand so well known to TV viewers that the logo and acronym are all that are needed. When that brand becomes synonymous with a media product audiences will enjoy, a company will do its best to portray that product as part of a larger brand from which consumers can expect similar quality or content. Following the success of shows like *Lost* and *Grey's Anatomy*, for example, ABC has branded subsequent programs in ads that refer to ABC's *The Bachelor* or ABC's *Revenge*.

To establish a brand, corporations try to become the first in the market and set up a vast network of outlets to reap economies of scale and thus make it harder for other players to compete. The corporation can recognize historical change and technical inventions and respond to the market demand they create by diversifying or **vertically integrating** (i.e., controlling production, distribution, and exhibition within the same company) or combining business strategies to continue industry domination and profit maximization over the long run. It is not easy to rate these elements in importance, but branding would seem to rank at the top of most lists.

Since its resurgence in the mid-2000s ABC has branded its new shows, making sure viewers know which network airs *Once Upon a Time* and *Revenge*.

Media Monopolies

Corporate owners and managers embrace monopoly because it has historically assured success and often secured vast profits, but true media monopolies, where a lone firm dominates a media industry, are rare. The single daily newspaper provides an example of media monopoly at a local level that many people will recognize— though with newspaper companies posting content online for free, even those monopolies have become less common. Newspaper readers in communities where one paper dominates often think back and ponder the "good old days" when cities as small as El Dorado, Kansas (population 10,000 in 1950) had three newspapers.

Monopolies obviously limit consumer choice. If a reader does not like the lone local newspaper owner's offerings, and local radio and television do not offer extensive or alternative coverage, then he or she gets little in the way of local news. A monopoly newspaper cannot always cover all subjects of interest to a community and thus makes choices—often for economic reasons—that some (or a lot) of the readers in its local area may not like. These choices may skew the paper's content to appeal to the well-off because advertisers like to reach those who have the means to buy their products. For example, in 2007 the *Louisville Courier-Journal*, a Gannett company, shut its bureau coverage of poor mining counties in Kentucky and shifted resources to better serve Louisville's affluent suburbs. If low-income neighborhoods get mentioned in local news, this typically involves only crime stories because that's what consultants say sells and because it is inexpensive to do this kind of reporting. A monopoly paper may have built its reputation on strong coverage in certain areas of local news, but under contemporary economic conditions the diversity of coverage and viewpoints has decreased. A local monopoly paper may also be bought or owned by a larger company like Gannett, attracted to owning a profitable monopoly enterprise in the local market without much interest in fully serving the community.

Until about 2005 and 2006 when their stock values started dropping, most publicly owned monopoly newspapers were highly profitable—as is expected from a monopoly—often earning 20 percent pretax profits. So why didn't more people enter the newspaper business prior to the economic downturn? An analysis of economies of scale helps explain why most towns came to have only a single newspaper with a monopoly on the local-news audience. Critical here is understanding the notion of **first copy costs**, or **fixed costs**. All manufacturing operations can generally assign the costs of production to either fixed costs, which are needed for any level of production (e.g., printing presses)—or **variable costs**, which change as levels of production change (e.g., the need for more or fewer reporters).

In newspaper publishing, the fixed or first copy costs include the machinery, office building, and sales staff salaries, and all other costs associated with printing a basic number of words and photographs, including advertising copy. Before the presses roll each day, the publisher has incurred substantial baseline costs, which are most easily recouped if the paper is a monopoly. As a monopoly, the single owner can also choose to limit its variable costs, for example, by limiting coverage of local events or keeping fewer reporters on staff. As a monopoly, these owners can maximize profit, unafraid of a challenger, and offer a single news voice. Most monopoly newspapers have been subsidiaries of even larger media conglomerates, like Gannett or News Corp., companies that own many newspapers. Thus, local coverage can suffer because, as leading media economist Robert Picard has argued, "locally owned papers tend to do a better job of covering community controversies as news" than monopoly newspapers from out of town.[10] Chain-owned newspapers can simply take advantage of their monopoly position, creating larger profits with smaller staffs.

At the outset of the twenty-first century, cable TV providers also appeared to represent a media monopoly not particularly supportive of democratic ideals. In nearly 99 percent of communities, despite the threat of direct broadcast satellite (DBS) and other alternatives, the incumbent cable operators faced no real cable competition. In situations where DBS services, phone companies, or a second cable company do compete, the contrast is remarkable: A second competitor helps to lower prices and to provide more channels. But for consumers—even in limited competitive environments—rising monthly cable fees are simply a given. Up until the Internet started providing access to channels via cell phones, iPods, iPads, and other emerging technologies, we longed for more channels—and cheaper prices. But multiple-channel TV has not been cheap, nor do we get a voice as to which channels are available to us. Historically, decisions have most often been determined by a city's cable monopoly owner with a single goal in mind—profit maximization. Community access channels—free channels open to community programming—surfaced only because they were required by renewable franchise contract so that a cable company could maintain its fifteen-year (on average) legal monopoly.

Into the 2000s, Government Accountability Office studies reported the expected actions of a monopolist: that cable rates rise far faster than the core rate of inflation. The average yearly rise in overall prices was about 1 to 2 percent, but the average cable price increases came to 5 to 10 percent because consumers generally had just one choice for a cable provider. Providers also refused to allow consumers to select à la carte menus where they pay for only the channels they watch. In fact, in 2010 when consumer groups pressed for à la carte choices, cable companies suggested that they would raise the prices on these individual channels and that their current tiers of service menus would remain cheaper. Over the years, when monopoly cable companies in particular areas have added one or two channels, they then use that as an excuse to increase the basic consumer monthly bill by five to ten dollars.[11]

The two largest cable companies, Comcast and Time Warner, cover half the United States and together take advantage of significant economies of operation. Local monopoly corporations are collected under one larger corporate umbrella (similar to "chains" in the newspaper business), creating a **multiple system operator (MSO)**, where a number of cable franchises are group owned. An MSO can have a single accounting department, a single sales force, and a single repair division, for example, spreading these and other fixed costs across the various franchises to yield lower per franchise costs and higher profits. Thus, the illusion of multiple operations masks the truth of a single owner. And that single owner makes millions of dollars per year. That is why Comcast—the largest MSO in the United States by the mid-2000s—could make a serious offer to take over a larger, more famous company—the Walt Disney Corporation—and nearly succeed and then just a few years later purchase NBC Universal.

Corporate Competition

On the opposite end of the ownership scale sits corporate competition, where there are so many companies that no one really has an accurate list of which corporations are in business or not. Each is small relative to the others and there is constant changing of choice. These competitive industrial situations are, like media monopolies, quite rare. Currently, only two such media industries in the United States could boast a corporate competition model: magazines and the Internet. For example, while there have been a few large magazine chain owners like Meredith or Time Warner (which once owned more than seventy titles), there are so many magazines—in excess of 10,000 regularly published—that the precise number can only be estimated. The magazine industry ranges from hobbyist quarterlies to the *National Enquirer* to serious journalism to the *Progressive Farmer*. The range of topics and interests available via Internet publications (including online-only magazines, online versions of print titles, blogs, and more) is even more formidable. In terms of the magazine and Internet industries, consumers have real choice—a very different picture of the media than one in which the product and the storytelling are in the hands of an oligopoly or monopoly.

Yet choice is not always what corporate owners want. The magazines and Internet sites are rare examples of real choice in today's mediated society. Companies that run magazines, for the most part, are far smaller (and easier for us to envision starting) than either of its print brethren—newspapers or book publishing—and much cheaper to start than television, music, or movies. Not many media conglomerates, which own media enterprises of various types, choose to operate magazines because there's little hope of gaining domination. Constantly, entrepreneurs start new magazines, usually around five to seven hundred per year, aimed at special interests or new niches. There is little overhead: The U.S. Postal Service handles delivery; design is done using digital desktop publishing programs; and freelance and part-time writers offer much of the content. The actual up-front investment in staff often consists of hiring a dozen people, renting a small amount of office space, investing in technology, and subcontracting the printing. Contrast this with the newspaper industry, where virtually no new daily print papers start up in a given year (although digital papers on the Internet are multiplying). There are today only about 1,400 daily newspapers in the United States (down from a high of 2,600 in 1910).

There are other advantages to corporate competition. Magazines and the Internet offer advertisers direct targeting of interested customers. Network television can supply national advertising, but often its reach is wasted on viewers with no interest in the products being hawked. In contrast, magazines and Web sites serve discrete interests and niche markets within the population. Specialization covers not just consumer concerns, but also the diverse information needs of business professions through a steady number of trade magazines and specialized Web sites. Consumer magazines, professional/business magazines, and Internet start-up companies serve the need of advertisers who wish to reach a smaller well-defined audience interested in specific products and services. In the magazine industry and on Web sites, individual voices can be easily accessed and specialized needs accommodated.

In following the magazine model, the Internet has evolved as an alternative delivery system for content currently published in magazines and many other media. Web sites like Hulu.com deliver network TV programs online. Recent developments like blogging and Twitter have become a popular way to easily publish content or interact with a community of readers. The Internet has exploded with services that provide a digest of articles and commentary circulated over e-mail or through comment boards, delivering added specialized features that no magazine can provide, including related links. One of the most profitable Web sites, eBay, includes many features previously found in magazines and newspapers but adds interactivity and real-time bidding—something older media can't offer. In addition, today one person can start a Web site cheaply about any one of her or his passions and update it daily by simply collecting messages from contributors who are also passionate about the subject. No advertising, no profit: just the will and time to assemble the messages day after day. If the site proves popular, advertising and profits may follow, as might interest from larger companies wanting a piece of the action.

While Web sites are not like traditional media, they are used for the entertainment and information functions we have long associated with older mass media such as newspapers and magazines. For example, eBay on the surface seems like an auction site, but many people consult it as if it were a magazine or newspaper simply composed of advertising; it offers more information for collectors than a single magazine could provide, with the added ability to purchase products instantly. While eBay seems to be creating and dominating a unique niche, Internet industries are changing so quickly that we can only speculate on the digital future and on how much online media will continue to transform older mass media forms. For now, though, it seems that, like magazines, there is no way for a handful of giant media companies to dominate the Internet's open architecture.

Typically, large media companies look for market power to help whittle down the number of other competitors so they can keep track of and react to new market trends. But in a competitive business environment this is not possible because, as with the 10,000-plus regularly published magazines or with nearly a half billion Web sites, there are too many to track to see what the competition is up to. In the end, however, real media economics are not represented by this competitive model, even if many citizens might prefer it for our democracy. The magazine and Internet models are exceptions. Under most economic arrangements in our mediated world, the typical media corporation faces but a handful of competitors. Still, the Internet is driving many changes in older business models and has proved to be the most difficult media enterprise in history to monopolize.

Media Oligopolies

Older media industries like film and music are in the hands of a few corporations; this environment is defined as an **oligopoly**. In an oligopoly, a handful of firms dominate a market or industry. One prominent example is the group of three major longtime

U.S. television networks: NBC, ABC, and CBS (although this was later expanded to include Fox; the CW, which emerged from UPN and the WB; and Univision, the popular Hispanic network). Another example is the movie business, which is in the hands of the six commanding major Hollywood studios. Despite all of the choices available on cable and satellite TV, these six Hollywood companies—Disney, Time Warner, Sony, NBC Universal, Twentieth Century Fox, and Viacom/Paramount—produce and distribute most TV shows and movies. Given this landscape, we need to learn not only about the basic corporate institutions themselves but also about how they interact. The economic outcomes of oligopolistic corporate behavior depend on how many firms there are, how big they are in relationship to one another, past corporate histories, changing ownership structures, and sometimes the whims and politics of individual owners. At times this economic organization might help democracy; at other times it won't. As media consumers, we should study these arrangements corporation by corporation.

What makes this analysis so difficult is that corporations collude to monopolize some operations while competing in other agreed-upon arenas. For example, the five major corporations that controlled the music business—Viacom/Universal, Time Warner, EMI, Sony, and BMG/Bertlesmann—colluded to keep the price of CDs inflated. (Despite European Union opposition, Sony and BMG merged in the late 2000s.) The development of Internet file-sharing and illegal downloads and Apple's new business model (charging 99 cents, at the time, to download a song) put a dent in the old model, but the remaining four major music companies remain both in control and mutually interdependent, at least for now. When powerful corporations like these cooperate, they can act like monopolies, work together to lobby for positive governmental policies toward their industry, and thus thwart most potential competition. Nothing unites a media oligopoly more than a threat from the outside. Simply put, oligopolists tend to seek and agree upon an informal set of rules for "competition"—for instance, controlling the price of music downloads—thereby restricting the game of profit maximization to themselves. Since many media industries are controlled primarily by oligopolies, it is hard to analyze monopolies or corporate competition models on their own. Analysis of oligopolies requires that we examine the historical development of the oligopoly and how the companies that make it up cooperate, or fail to.

Here is where we confront the media conglomerate, a media corporation that holds a number of subsidary media businesses. To maintain their positions of power in recent decades, these companies have diversified, both vertically and horizontally. **Vertical integration**, in the media industry, means a company owns the production, distribution, and public presentation or exhibition of its product. For example, Time Warner makes a movie, distributes it to theaters, and then later shows it on its wholly owned premium cable network—HBO. **Horizontal integration** means a conglomerate owns one kind of product or service in multiple markets. So, for example, the

Disney movie studio demonstrates horizontal integration by producing not only Disney films, marketed at children, but films under brands it has developed for general audiences such as Touchstone Pictures, and former independent studios it has acquired, such as Miramax or Pixar.

Both vertical and horizontal integration seek to minimize the risk the company faces. Disney not only owns and operates a famous movie studio and set of theme parks but also a television network (ABC), a score of successful television and radio stations, the cable sports colossus ESPN and all its related channels, book and magazine holdings, and more. Because of this diversification, Disney is a classic media conglomerate that is not dependent on the business cycle of any single operation. Unprofitable subsidiaries can be reconstructed and repositioned with funds generated from other profitable ongoing businesses. Disney's only real competitors are a small number of media conglomerates, like News Corp. or Time Warner, with the resources to compete in the same markets and industries. This gives rise to an oligopoly that creates a high barrier for legitimate competitors trying to enter the same market. Many potential rivals lack these conglomerates' level of diversification that protects business operations across multiple media ventures.

The best way to predict the behavior of an oligopoly is to recognize that its members operate in reaction to one another. If these conglomerates were truly competitive, they could not acquire the information necessary to predict the behavior of their competitors; if they were a monopoly, they would not care. But an oligopoly is like a poker game with five or six players. Each player knows a great deal about what the others are up to but does not possess full knowledge. Take the case of the four dominant U.S. television networks. When NBC (owned by Comcast) offers a new comedy at a particular time on a particular day, its rivals counterprogram with, for example, a reality program or drama that might appeal to another large segment of the audience. This leads to some experimentation, but all too often only means a numbing generic sameness where similar program genres (for example, more of the same kinds of sitcoms, reality programs, or dramatic procedurals) face off against each other. Because media viewership is largely determined by fickle audiences with varied cultural tastes in search of their favorite kinds of narratives, no calculable, consistent, mathematical model predicts audience and consumer behavior. Indeed, economic theorists have a great deal of trouble modeling oligopolistic behavior and consumer response.

Despite potential unpredictability, the oligopoly has developed into the most common market structure for ownership in the mass media. For example, the Hollywood film industry remains an oligopoly of six. All compete to produce and release the top box office hits, but all cooperate to make sure the game remains primarily among themselves and that the price of movie tickets adjusts upwardly as audiences decline in the age of the Internet. The Big Six premiere the vast majority of possible blockbuster hits in multiplex theaters—and surely will continue to do this well into the future. Some may complain, but film fans generally don't seem to mind on a large scale; worldwide business at the box office has remained quite healthy since the dawn of the wide-release blockbuster in the late 1970s, with Paramount and Fox's co-production of *Titanic* in the 1990s having grossed more than $2.1 billion in ticket sales over the globe, and a dozen years later Fox's *Avatar* besting even these sizable numbers with $2.8 billion in sales.

Indeed, the Hollywood oligopoly is one of the tightest in the media business. We can most easily see this power in the activities of the Big Six's trade association—the Motion Picture Association of America (the MPAA)—where the six corporations deal with common concerns from rating films to smoothing the way for international distribution to protecting their valuable copyrights around the world. Here the collusion by corporations—an agreement about the best interests of all—helps shape the oligopoly of six more along the lines of a monopoly. And, as we have argued before, when one entity is the sole power and the sole voice, democracy and consumer choices may not be as well served. In such a system there may be little support for important films that might appeal to smaller audiences.

With the TV, music, and movie industries, as well as other oligopolies like them, the only real question at the close of each year is: Who ranked where in terms of revenues? Yet while this oligopoly is surely dominant, there does exist some room on the margins for minor companies. Strong examples arrived in 2004 with Mel Gibson's *Passion of the Christ* and Michael Moore's *Fahrenheit 9/11*, both rejected by the major Hollywood Six but both highly profitable. Both were considered too risky for Big Six backers; in these cases the media controversies surrounding the films led to higher revenues, but in many cases this kind of success does not happen. As such, the Hollywood oligopoly tolerates occasional success outside of the Big Six; if they permitted no independents on the margin, they would risk government antitrust action, which they want to avoid. The Big Six also need independent companies to develop new kinds of narratives that seem too risky, quirky, or innovative for the conventional industry. However, once an "independent" company (and even independents usually need the Big Six to distribute their film) has developed a track record of producing commercially successful films, a Big Six firm may buy them out or enter into a partnership. Because of their occasional outside-the-mainstream successes and distribution partnerships with independents, the MPAA and Big Six executives can preach to governmental officials that they have competition and thus do not break any antitrust laws.

Similarly, the music-business oligopoly tolerates a certain margin of independence and outsider work in order to gauge trends and innovation, and independently run music labels have seen increased success in the past decade (especially for the artists working for these labels) as the major-label system has been slow to adapt to technology changes and online opportunities in the industry. But the major music labels will still adopt musical acts or labels that began as independents or at least imitate

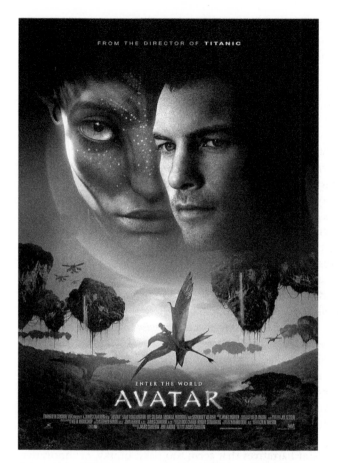

After cofinancing James Cameron's *Titanic* with Paramount, Twentieth Century Fox released Cameron's next film, *Avatar*, twelve years later. Like *Titanic* before it, *Avatar* cost an enormous amount of money to make and market—and also became the highest-grossing movie of all time.

them with the resources and power of the oligopoly structure to ensure higher success rates than less powerful independent companies.

The media consumer needs to pay close attention to changes in the oligopoly mix. That monopolies are bad for democracy is an easy case to make; but the claim that oligopolistic "competition" is not capable of serving both business's bottom line and democracy's ideals is more problematic. Thus, media oligopolies are what we live with, but what we need are regulations that offer them incentives to act for the benefit of democracy—even as they go about their priority task of maximizing profits. The 2008–09 financial crisis is a good example in which the risky practices of a handful of giant banks, including Bank of America and Citigroup, considered "too big to fail," catapulted the world into an economic mess, with unenforced or missing oversight and lax regulations at the center of the debate. Even now, the big bank oligopoly continues to lobby against the very regulations that would have prevented the crisis in the first place.

Fahrenheit 9/11 was not a James Cameron–size hit, but it was a big money-maker—the highest-grossing documentary ever—and none of the Big Six Hollywood studios were interested in releasing it.

Yet the oligopoly mix is constantly in flux. Mergers, break-ups, and over-leveraged corporations make the front page of the *Wall Street Journal*, the *New York Times,* and the evening network and daily cable news shows. The development of a successful oligopoly in a media industry or across media industries can mean greater profits for the players (though not as much as a monopoly) and more stability than a competitive media marketplace could offer—but at what cost? This is where the media consumer must be diligent. If service falters and choices become limited, it may be time to declare that an oligopoly is colluding and acting too much like a media monopoly. What to do? Seek help from government oversight groups that regulate nearly all mass media industries. Complain to the trade organizations that lobby on behalf of media oligopolies—such as the Recording

Industry Association of America (RIAA) or the National Association of Broadcasting (NAB). Apply our media performance criteria. This means we have to carefully study media oligopolies, cite their failures, and then argue for antitrust action to break the conglomerates apart or regulations to prevent collusion among them. Citizen activism and the simple threat of government action can often change oligopoly behavior. But this requires us to pay attention, to hold our representatives (who are incessantly lobbied to and supported by media corporations) accountable, and to analyze media industry behavior corporation by corporation.

MEDIA ECONOMICS, PERFORMANCE, AND DEMOCRACY

As oligopolies have become the norm under capitalism, among the areas in which they are most effective are lobbying to protect their interests and supplying donations to help sympathetic lawmakers stay in power. Since the deregulation of corporations that began in earnest in the late 1970s and early 1980s, Washington lobbyists have increased exponentially. In one study, the *Washington Post* documented that between 2000 and 2005 alone "the number of registered lobbyists" in our nation's capital "more than doubled . . . to more than 34,750 while the amount that lobbyists charge their new clients . . . increased by as much as 100 percent."[12]

But historically, it wasn't always this way. Certainly the rise of industry in the nineteenth century featured entrepreneurs such as John D. Rockefeller in oil, Cornelius Vanderbilt in shipping and railroads, and Andrew Carnegie in steel creating monopolies in their respective businesses. But in 1890, Congress passed the Sherman Antitrust Act, outlawing the monopoly practices and corporate trusts that often fixed prices to force competitors out of business. In 1911, the government used this act to break up both the American Tobacco Company and Rockefeller's Standard Oil Company, which was divided into thirty smaller competing firms. In 1914, Congress passed the Clayton Antitrust Act, prohibiting manufacturers from selling only to dealers and contractors who agreed to reject the products of business rivals. The Celler-Kefauver Act of 1950 further strengthened antitrust rules by limiting any corporate mergers and joint ventures that reduced competition. Historically, these laws have been enforced by the Federal Trade Commission and the antitrust division of the Department of Justice.

By the 1980s, tough government oversight began melting away as industry oligopolies and deregulation favored by free-market advocates became the business norm across many industries. But for democracy and our media to work well, we need to rationally adopt public policies to facilitate citizens' ability to have access to varied channels and sources, offering differential content and alternative voices. We need to know how the common structures of message production, distribution, and presentation affect audiences. We need, on an industry-by-industry basis to examine the structure, conduct, and performance of changing media ownership and economics. As history has demonstrated, market failures will continue to happen. Even the most rabid free-market economist would argue that allowing monopolists to sustain barriers to entry and thus to prevent effective competition is not in the long run in the best interest of democracy. The Sherman and Clayton Antitrust Acts and the Federal Trade Commission Act still exist as part of U.S. law. Thus, when a monopoly problem is identified or when oligopolistic practices collude to short-change consumers and citizens, alternative solutions ought to be considered and tested. But as politics change, interpretations do as well, and policies to deal with the effects of mergers on competition and policies to deal with restraints of trade have increasingly come through case law precedents.

Consider the case of trying to prop up a second newspaper in a city that once had a fiercely competitive news market. The Newspaper Preservation Act was passed in 1970, in effect providing an exemption to the antitrust laws and eventually foster-ing twenty-eight joint operating agreements (JOAs) to share costs of all business operation except for news/editorial staffs. Approved by the Justice Department, a JOA usually allowed a larger newspaper in a city to support a smaller struggling one and maintain editorial competition. But with the rise of the Internet, the decline of newspapers, and the financial crisis, by 2010 only six of these remained in place. For example, the *Detroit News* (owned by MediaNews Group) and *Detroit Free Press* (owned by Gannett) represent the largest JOA, sharing all business operations while maintaining separate news divisions. This JOA once published independent papers during the week and joint editions on Saturday and Sunday. By 2010, the Detroit JOA was delivering printed newspapers to homes only on Thursday, Friday, and Sunday. The proponents of JOA legislation argued that two separate editorial voices were a better alternative than the single voice that would exist if an otherwise mar-ginal paper were forced out of business or taken over entirely by the stronger paper. For a number of years, an opposing view had been voiced not only by many small, independent dailies but by the *New York Times* and the Newspaper Guild union as well, contending that daily and weekly papers in suburbs offered effective substitutes for failing city newspapers and thus government assistance should not have been necessary. Critics of JOAs and the Newspaper Preservation Act have diminished, though, as many JOAs began failing in the in big market cities like Houston, Seattle, Denver, and Cincinnati, where the weaker city newspaper either went out of busi-ness or converted to an online-only operation.

In another historical example, the Justice Department in 1938 sued the then "Big Eight" major film studios, and in 1948 the U.S. Supreme Court forced the majors to sell their theater chains and thus, it was hoped, to open the market to more competition. This decree remained in existence until the Justice Department of President Reagan's administration—in its deregulatory zeal—declared that new competition from pay TV and home video constituted effective competition and vacated the decree. In the long run, however, Hollywood simply took over these pay-TV and home video "rival" venues, and instead of offering competition, the current Hollywood Big Six took back the entire movie business and gained more power than they ever had in 1938.

In another move in the spirit of deregulation, the FCC in 1996 lifted the ownership limits for radio so that single companies could take in more than half of all revenues going into radio advertising in a given market. The U.S. Department of Justice under President Clinton first objected under antitrust statutes and pressed several cases opposing such mergers. Indeed, FCC rules had once limited radio ownership to no more than forty-eight stations nationwide—twenty-four AM and twenty-four FM (up from just seven each in the 1970s). But the Clinton administration succumbed and with the passage of Telecommunications Act in 1996, most radio ownership restrictions were lifted, and soon Clear Channel owned more than twelve hundred stations. In the early 2000s, the Department of Justice negotiated a number of consent decrees to reduce how many ad dollars one company controlled in a given market. In one example, CBS, as a result of its Infinity Broadcasting takeover in nine separate radio markets, agreed to divest stations to push down its dominant share of the radio advertising revenues. For a time, economies of scale made these radio consolidations profitable, but radio turned out to have few efficiencies of scale. Thus, chains of stations increased but at a more modest level than Clear Channel's more than one thousand stations.

The 1996 Telecommunications Act anticipated that for the most pervasive of the mass media—television—new technological delivery systems would challenge the oligopolistic power of the broadcast networks and monopolistic power of the cable TV industry. But, direct broadcast, or direct-to-home satellite, television provided only one alternative, and so customer choice was improved, but hardly competitive. Indeed, the conundrum today rests no longer with the expanding universe of broadcast television, but that most people watch the broadcast networks not through broadcasting but from cable delivery, DBS, and increasingly a variety of "third screen" technologies like smartphones, iPods, and tablets. The first decade of the twenty-first century saw media industries deal with the portability of mass media as one could access the Internet, radio, and television from a single small digital device.

Indeed, cable has been working on new methods to capture more power, led by clustering, a process by which MSOs consolidate system ownership within particular geographical regions. While clustering provides a means of reducing costs and attracting more advertising, it also significantly raised barriers to entry to other potential competitors. By 1999, there were more than one hundred such cable transactions with a total market value of approximately $22.2 billion. A similar pattern continued into the twenty-first century, reflecting even greater power through economies of scale. Comcast's cable properties, for example, aggressively pursued clustering, and so in and around Chicago, through swaps and acquisitions, the nation's biggest cable corporation gained control of nine of every ten cable subscribers in the Chicago metropolitan area.

At the heart of all TV legislation has been a public interest obligation first established in the 1934 Communications Act. In the interest of democracy, this act mandated that in exchange for their licenses, broadcasters must operate as trustees over the public airwaves and were legally required to operate in "the public interest, convenience, or necessity." Such an obligation could be extended to cable companies and the DBS operators like DISH and DirecTV. Then this obligation would have to be enforced. However, what defines the "public interest" has always been controversial, with at least three considerations at work: ownership restrictions, content restrictions, and protections of certain spaces for political debate. The 1996 Telecommunications Act did not revoke broadcasters' public trusteeship, thereby continuing a trend of the 1990s that began with the 1992 Cable Television Consumer Protection Act, which contained a clause (47 U.S.C. 335) intended to impose traditional public-interest obligations in the new world of DBS. This debate over existing obligations of public interest ought to define the debate for appropriate radio and TV policy and ownership in the twenty-first century that faces the new portable electronics that offer twenty-four-seven access to the mass media and the Internet.

As a final example of influencing policy, let's return to the case of newspapers—where this chapter began. Daily newspaper circulation fell by more than 10 percent in 2009, with the number of daily newspapers sold nationally dropping to forty-four million copies—"fewer than at any time since the 1940s."[13] Three papers—in San Francisco, Newark, and Dallas—lost more than 20 percent of their circulation in 2009, while *USA Today* saw a 17 percent drop to fewer than two million weekday copies. Meanwhile, the *Wall Street Journal,* helped by interest in the economic crisis and 400,000 paid subscriptions to its online service, replaced *USA Today* as the nation's most widely circulated newspaper. With ad revenue falling by 30 to 40 percent at some newspapers, the number of reporters cut by half or more at many papers and TV stations, and the economy still in crisis, the journalism business was in deep trouble.

In response to this crisis, the dean of Columbia University's Journalism School (started once upon a time with money bequeathed by nineteenth-century newspaper mogul Joseph Pulitzer) commissioned a study from Leonard Downie, former executive editor of the *Washington Post,* and Michael Schudson, Columbia journalism professor and media scholar. Their one-hundred-page report, "The Reconstruction of American Journalism," focused on the lost circulation, advertising revenue, and news jobs in 2009 and aimed to create a strategy for local reporting that would hold public and government officials accountable and to provide basic access to the kinds of information and documentation that citizens in a democracy need to be well-informed.[14]

They suggested that philanthropic organizations and foundations "should substantially increase their support for news organizations that have shown a commitment to public affairs news and the kind of reporting that hold local leaders, politicians, officials, and government agencies accountable but not at the expense of profit motives." Such organizations should be run as nonprofit corporations. Public radio and TV, through federal reforms in the Corporation for Public Broadcasting (CPB), should reorient their focus to "significant local news reporting in every community served by public stations and their Web sites." Operating their own news services or supporting regional news organizations, public universities "should become ongoing sources of local, state, specialized subject and accountability news reporting as part of their educational mission." Using the Internet, nonprofit organizations and government agencies should "increase the accessibility and usefulness of public information collected by federal, state, and local governments."[15]

The journalism industry needs to reinvent itself and try new economic avenues that better balance seeking profit and serving democracy to ensure its future. Some of the immediate backlash to this report raised questions about the government getting more involved with traditionally independent news media. As both discerning consumers and engaged citizens, we must all confront profit maximizing as the sole driving force in corporate behavior. Since media corporations will continue to fail in providing the best results for democracy, critics will continue to struggle with how to regulate, or break up, corporations. The Columbia report offers but one model for how to rethink the news media landscape so that it better functions to provide us with the information and stories that our communities and nation need. But the driving impulses of capitalism, especially profit maximization, will not change anytime soon. Media economics drives and fashions this consumer culture. Its implications for all of us are profound—and basic.

| CRITICAL PROCESS 1 | Media Performance Norms

The goal of this exercise is to apply McQuail's evaluative schema (Media Performance Norms) to a news medium. You can pick a large company, such as Disney or News Corp., or apply these standards to a news outlet in your own town or city.

Describe the company or medium you've chosen in terms of McQuail's performance norms. Describe how the company facilitates free speech. Does it waste resources? Does it facilitate public order by providing relevant information and stories? Does it maintain high-quality products? Does it introduce new technology as quickly as possible or does it hold on to old ways of operating?

Analyze the results of the company according to those norms. What patterns do you see? What seems to be the company's short- and long-range plan?

Interpret the company's strengths and weaknesses. Why do you think it fares better with regard to some standards than others? What might be some contributing factors?

Evaluate the company as a whole using McQuail's schema. In which areas is the company strongest? In which is it weakest? How well is the company performing, based on these ideas? How well does it balance its profit concerns with its role in serving its community?

Engage with the company by researching their performance and earnings; or perhaps by making contact with managers, editors, or reporters to ask about its successes and failures in these five areas. Find out what seems to guide the company. Talk to employees and get their insights. What do they like and dislike about working there?

| CRITICAL PROCESS 2 | Who Owns Your Favorite Media?

The goal of this exercise is to trace ownership of a form of media you enjoy or follow. Pick a favorite TV show, album, movie, book, or Web site and figure out what, if any, parent companies are involved in that product's ownership, funding, and distribution.

Describe the product you've selected and what you're able to discern about its parent company from packaging or outside knowledge. Then describe its actual parent company. What else does it own or distribute? What are its chief competitors in the market? Check Hoover's database on media company history and performance.

Analyze the parent company. Based on its holdings and competitors, is it part of an oligopoly? A monopoly? Or part of a larger spectrum of corporate competition? Examining the product you've chosen, *what* stories, music, or other cultural products get to market. Do you see any patterns here?

Interpret the company's reach. Does it seem to be concentrating on one medium or expanding into other media? Does it have a diverse output of products? *How* do stories, music, or other products from your company get to market? Who decides? What does this all mean?

Evaluate the parent company and its presence in the news. Does it seem to engage in fair business practices? Would you be more likely to try a new show or musician affiliated with this company? Is this a good company? How do you know?

Engage with media ownership issues by doing more ownership research. Do other television shows, albums, movies, or books you enjoy tend to come from the same companies? How many of them come from independent companies, and how many come from larger media conglomerates? Talk to a manager from the company about the process by which a product gets into the marketplace. What roles do consumers play in the process?

8

Entertainment and Popular Culture

When we think of art, we think of museums—large, silent spaces where people come to be inspired by great works. For the artists of the Renaissance, the greatest works of art were those of Classical Greece, especially their marble-white statues. For centuries these simple, elegant statues have represented a vanished world of aesthetic excellence. So it comes as something of a shock to learn that, apparently, those marble statues were once painted in bright, even garish, colors. According to recent archaeological research,[1] the pure white world of classical Greece actually looked kind of like Disneyland—more like a circus than a museum.

If Greek statues were originally painted gaudy colors, can they still represent aesthetic excellence? Maybe we should take them out of the museums, paint them accurately, and put them out on the streets, where they once were. So much of art's revered place in many societies has come from its supposed difference from everyday popular culture. Yet how different, really, is art from entertainment? Both are forms of our shared cultural heritage, yet we have traditionally taught art in school and put it in museums, and kept entertainment separate, in the media. How and why do we keep these two forms of cultural practice separate?

Making distinctions between art and entertainment is one way that we identify the quality of the culture we believe we had in the past, we currently experience in the present, and we want to create in the future. Whenever we talk about cultural quality, we address still unresolved questions about how art is defined, and whether and how it is different from entertainment. Questions about how we can improve the media, our primary purveyors of popular culture, have shaped concerns about mass communication since the early twentieth century.

As we have seen in the discussion of media metaphors in Chapter 2, the act of entertaining is often considered more suspect than the act of distributing information. There is a mistrust of what happens when we enter the imaginative world of a video game, reality show, situation comedy, or movie. Many societies see important differences between the world of reason and the world of emotion, and we apply that distinction to cultural forms whenever we try to keep the news (information) separate from entertainment (pleasure). But art, like entertainment, is not information. It too can be pleasurable and emotionally provocative, though, at least to most twenty-first-century media commentators, art is (and must remain) crucially different from entertainment.

So when we consider entertainment, we explore the supposed differences between high culture (art) and popular culture. The division between museums and circuses—between versions of culture that are imagined to be pure and inspiring, and those that are imagined to be hybrid and diverting—keeps being readdressed. Figuring out how art and entertainment connect or don't in the mass media has been central to how people understand the role of popular culture in modern life.

In this chapter we explore entertainment media and address concerns raised in the creation, distribution, and consumption of popular culture through the media. We begin by exploring the notion of cultural bifurcation—popular versus elite or high art. We then turn to particular issues raised in the 1950s and 60s about the effects of a then new mass medium (television) on elite as well as traditional cultural forms. Our present-day concerns about cultural bifurcation and blending—specifically, what kinds of culture a democracy needs, how commercial values permeate and determine cultural content, and how new technologies refigure what kind of culture is available to us—were already present in the mid-twentieth century.

We then explore how we have organized ourselves (and are being organized) into "taste cultures." Through fandom—our choice of particular popular culture forms—we create and sustain identity, connection, and meaning. But this process also allows us to be identified and targeted as demographic markets. New media technologies are blurring the boundary between our roles as citizens and consumers and could be making us easier to exploit.

Given lingering notions of cultural hierarchy and the realities of taste cultures, we consider some scholarly analyses of popular culture forms that help us recognize our own imaginative relationship to particular interpretive communities. What we think of as mere entertainment is, from a narrative perspective, the construction of imaginative worlds in which to live. Cultural and critical approaches to media content help us understand more about how particular forms of popular culture may actually work in our lives.

But these kinds of interpretive analyses do not fully address continuing concerns about the role of entertainment in a modern democratic society. In the final section of the chapter, we return to the themes of the mass culture debate that can still trouble us in the Internet Age. We end by reframing some of these themes using reflectionist, constructionist, and narrativist perspectives.

DRAWING CULTURAL LINES

We use categories when we tell stories about the world. These categories seem real and immutable until something happens to disrupt them. Categories that once seemed unremarkable and natural are shown to be interesting and constructed. As we have noted, assumptions once taken for granted have been challenged, over and over again, by both the form and content of contemporary media.

This is especially true about the categories of information, entertainment, and art. We may believe these are (or should be) separate categories, and therefore believe we need to keep news and art from becoming too entertaining. But as media culture develops, category boundaries keep getting challenged. The result has been a fascinating history of redrawn cultural lines—efforts to rethink and redefine distinctions.

Cultural Bifurcation

Entertainment is understood by many people to be crucially different from art. As New Humanist critics like Irving Babbitt argued in the early twentieth century, and as conservative critics argued in the Culture Wars of the 1980s, art is something elite, special, maybe even sacred, and entertainment is something popular, run of the mill, and sometimes, at least, profane. This is **cultural bifurcation**—the separation of culture into two distinct categories. We need to understand whether culture is intrinsically bifurcated in this way, and then explore how and why we continue to categorize (even if uneasily) culture into these two separate spheres.

In his 1988 book *Highbrow/Lowbrow*, historian Lawrence Levine traces how Shakespeare was transformed from a popular entertainment figure into a twentieth-century high-culture icon. Because Shakespeare today seems so entrenched as high art, it is surprising to learn that in nineteenth-century America, in small towns and big cities, Shakespeare was fun, familiar entertainment for all and edited, revised, and parodied to the delight of the masses. Shakespeare too was more like a circus than a museum.[2]

And of course, this was true in Shakespeare's own time: His work was considered entertainment, not high culture. His plays were performed for groundlings and aristocracy, drawing from and contributing to the popular culture of his era. Shakespeare, then, offers us an avenue into the first questions we want to explore: How is art different from entertainment? Does it matter if the boundaries between art and entertainment get blurred by the media?

Using the example of Shakespeare, Levine details how these two categories— sacred art and profane entertainment—have been constructed for particular historical, social, and political purposes. Just as technologies do not drop from the sky, neither do the categories of art and entertainment. They are socially constructed: made by us, for us and our own historically situated purposes.

Levine argues that, as America became increasingly industrialized and mass mediated, "sacralizing" culture became increasingly important. This was because (during the late nineteenth and early twentieth centuries) democratization was blurring the historical distinctions between the educated elite and the less educated masses. The production of cultural forms was becoming increasingly capitalistic, identifying immigrants and workers as a potential market rather than relying mostly on the exclusionary patronage of an aristocratic class.

The new technologies of radio and film were offering recorded rather than live performance, across time and space, to anyone who could afford them. So democracy, capitalism, and technology were combining to reconfigure the cultural hierarchies that relied on the divisions between classes in premodern eras.

A bifurcated culture tries to distinguish the elite from the rabble. The elite are defined as educated, leisured, and old-school; the rabble are ignorant, working, and modern. So Shakespeare, along with symphonic music, opera, painting, and sculpture needed to be redefined, Levine argues. The elites took over these formerly populist forms so they could use them as cultural markers to distinguish themselves from the lower orders. By making Shakespeare into high culture, Levine argues, the wealthy and powerful upper class used cultural taste to enact their social superiority.

In the nineteenth century, there was little intrinsic to Shakespeare's plays that required reverence, careful study, or historical knowledge to appreciate. But Shakespeare, once given the status of elite art, needed to be treated with respect and presented with seriousness to disciplined audiences deemed educated enough to appreciate him, to help re-create cultural hierarchy. Everyone else—the emerging masses—could make do with movies, vaudeville, and jazz. These entertainment forms were for working people who could now be assumed to lack the intelligence or cultivation to appreciate someone as exalted as Shakespeare.

In short, cultural bifurcation was constructed and maintained to deal with what felt most unsettling about late-nineteenth-century life. And by the early twentieth century, the emergence of new commercial media technologies gave audiences new cultural forms like movies and radio that continued to challenge the social location of theatrical and orchestral performance. New and cheaper print technologies gave wider audiences easier access to magazines and books. As democracy, capitalism, and technology combined to create modern society, the separation of elite art and mass entertainment, museums from circuses, became one way to maintain social hierarchy, protect class distinctions, and contain the influence of new technologies.

Cultural Blurring

The mass culture debates of the 1950s and 60s can be seen as the mid-twentieth-century version of the same effort that separated Shakespeare plays from their popular-culture origins. These debates were sparked by the widespread adoption of television. But they were really about the influence of the post–World War II media on American culture, and they engaged the energies of most of the best-known American social and cultural commentators.

In 1952, the intellectual magazine *Partisan Review* published a symposium called *Our Country and Our Culture* that included essays by influential intellectuals of the period like Jacques Barzun, Sidney Hook, Irving Howe, Louis Kronenberger, Norman Mailer, C. Wright Mills, Phillip Rahv, Arthur Schlesinger, Delmore Schwartz, and Lionel Trilling. Collections of similar essays by other authors were published with titles like *Culture for the Millions?*, *Mass Culture*, and *Mass Culture Revisited*. These intellectuals were deeply worried about how the mass media—particularly television—were reconfiguring the cultural landscape of post–World War II America. They felt that cultural forms that could truly benefit modern society were being corrupted, diluted, deformed, or displaced by a new "mass" culture that was commercially successful but aesthetically suspect. They wrote their essays to explore what could or should be done in response to the cultural influences of mass media on postwar America.[3]

The mass culture debates dissolved by the mid-60s, as intellectuals began to focus instead on understanding the counterculture of the 1960s and 70s. But the mass culture debates' concerns about cultural levels and cultural quality, in relation to the influence of mass communication, were prescient. Nearly all of what we worry about today in the Internet Age is an updated version of what worried mass culture debaters back then.

What on the surface was an attempt by intellectuals to respond to the social and cultural impact of television can also be seen as a more general response to perceived dangers in democratization, capitalism, and technological innovation. These three themes were collapsed into a category called "mass society," and the mass culture debates were about how mass media influenced and supported mass society.

In the post–World War II era, mass society was imagined as an unprecedented form of social organization. The cultural, political, and moral values of small-town life and agrarian societies were disappearing, replaced by the cultural, political, and moral values of urbanism and industrialization. These mass-society replacements were imagined as aimless and individualized, creating an atomized and alienated public, with people left rootless, disconnected from custom and tradition.

In this reading of mass society, the public becomes more like a mob because the individual is isolated, vulnerable, and therefore easier to manipulate. When people are cut loose from true community, mass society critics maintain, they are in even deeper need of cultural guidance, and the traditional folk art that once oriented a more pastoral, agrarian, communal society can no longer speak to and for them. Instead, they seek alternative ways—often through mediated culture—to form modern identity and connection.

This is where the mass culture critics took up the debate—focusing on media content and exploring the meanings and values offered, through the media, to rootless, disconnected members of modern mass society. As particular intellectuals looked at popular culture—comic books, 50s television, and popular music in particular—they felt deep concern. Rather than popular art, they found mass culture, and for a number of different reasons, they believed that mass culture was making mass society even worse.

The specter of Nazi Germany deeply shaped the mass society/mass culture perspective. The transformation of a relatively cultivated, inclusive, tolerant, and cosmopolitan Germany into an aggressive, anti-Semitic, intolerant Nazi state demanded explanation, and Jewish-German émigrés like Theodor Adorno, Max Horkheimer, and Hannah Arendt spent the rest of their careers addressing (directly and indirectly) this fundamental question. Among their explanations were the failures of popular entertainment to do the kind of cultural work they believed could and should be done by art.

In their classic essay "The Culture Industry," Adorno and Horkheimer consider the mass media in relation to our ability to understand and escape capitalism. They find that the popular culture offerings of the 1940s and 50s merely deepen the ways that capitalism keeps us mystified and dependent. The formulaic, sentimental content pre-hears and pre-feels for us, they argued, offering solace and escape but never the possibility of truly questioning or escaping the status quo. Their indictment of mass media content—as an extension of capitalism into culture and thereby consciousness—has shaped the constructionist perspective on media in society ever since.[4]

The philosopher Hannah Arendt made a different case, illustrating how and why art and entertainment should be kept separate in our society. In her 1960 essay "Society and Culture," she argues that modern society needs both art and entertainment—art to uplift, inform, guide, and inspire, entertainment to divert, delight, soothe, and enliven.[5]

Arendt argues for the necessity of cultural bifurcation—art and entertainment must remain separate spheres. She believes, along with many others, that the two areas have fundamentally different characters. Art is designed, she says, to "grasp and move us across the ages," while entertainment is instead designed to be metabolized—used up in everyday life.[6] As long as entertainment and art maintain their separation, they can each do their distinctive, necessary social work. The problem, she says, comes when the media—in their insatiable quest for content—"ransack the past" and turn art objects into entertainment forms.[7]

What worries Arendt about the mass media is that they are relentless reproducers, revisers, and adapters. Media take all kinds of cultural forms—art, trash, and everything in between—and turn them into entertainment. Art forms can "survive centuries of neglect, but not an entertaining version of what they have to say."[8] This explains why, in her view, cultural blurring—confusing art and entertainment—is so dangerous. Art can no longer speak its truths, offer its insights, or guide a civilized society when it has been turned into fun, entertaining, mass culture.

We replay Arendt's concerns whenever we realize that using Monet's water lilies on Kleenex boxes makes his original picture look like a big Kleenex box, or when we finally make it to the Louvre to see Leonardo da Vinci's *Mona Lisa* and she looks like a replica—so familiar that she should be an advertisement for something. When we hear classical music and recall cartoons set to that music, we are

"What's Opera, Doc?" the 1957 Looney Tunes short, widely considered one of the best cartoons of all time, both satirizes and takes artistic cues from the "high art" of opera.

demonstrating exactly what worried Arendt: We can't grasp or be moved by the original intentions of past artists once we've experienced their work in a popularized or commercialized way.

A related concern about how the media offer us ersatz, watered-down art can be found in Randall Jarrell's poignant 1961 essay "A Sad Heart at the Supermarket." In this essay, Jarrell argues that the media forms of the 1950s simultaneously starve and stuff us—they stuff us with cheesy approximations of art, while we remain starved for (and, in Arendt's terms, perhaps unable to appreciate) the meaning that true art can and should have. We keep going back to the media supermarket yearning for the genuine nourishment of art, but we end up stuffing ourselves with the junk food of entertainment.[9]

Cultural Levels

The possibility that, through cultural blending, mass media both ruin art (through Arendt's popularization) and drown us in mediocre, distracting junk (Jarrell's supermarket) shapes the related commentary of mass culture critics like Edward Shils,

Dwight Macdonald, and Oscar Handlin. These three critics, among many others, distinguished levels of culture—sorting out what made art and folk culture different from mass mediated culture but also what made "respectable" cultural forms like books, theater, and classical music different from television, movies, and popular music.

Shils was the strongest and most unapologetic voice for three basic levels of culture—what he called superior, mediocre, and brutal—being connected to three levels of audiences. He argues that societies contain people of varying degrees of intelligence, refinement, and ability to comprehend complexity and ambiguity. Each level of people deserves the level of culture that they most want, so that Shils ends up arguing for what he calls "cultural dissensus"—modern culture that accepts and makes room for all three levels.

For Shils, superior people deserve superior culture, and it is the job of educated intellectuals to look after and protect their cultural forms from being overwhelmed by mediocre and brutal culture. The mass media can keep offering mediocre people mediocre culture, and that's fine with Shils. Brutal people, pretty much ignored by the new mass media, also deserve their very own forms of brutal culture.

The emerging mass media aren't giving superior or brutal people the cultural fare most suited to them, Shils argues; instead, they are providing an excessive amount of mediocre culture. In his view, highbrow novels are written by respected authors, read by literate and educated people, and taught in college courses. They are difficult, challenging, and require intellect and effort to appreciate. Middlebrow novels are best-sellers, written by commercially successful writers, "page-turners" that have exciting plots and exotic settings. They are easier to understand but still require some basic literacy skills. Lowbrow novels are "genre" fiction—formulaic, with anonymous authors, like romance novels and detective fiction. They are simple, formulaic, and appeal to our basic instincts, not our intellect.[10]

Dwight Macdonald remains known for his stinging indictment of "midcult"— media-based cultural fare that aspires to be elite, or (in Shils's terms) mediocre culture that pretends to be superior. Macdonald used the term "masscult" to describe what the mass media mostly purveyed, but he was more concerned about midcult— mediocre culture that masquerades as art. He mistrusted educational television, book clubs, and broadcast symphonic music because he believed they offer pretend art—designed so that the educated elite can feel superior. Midcult aspires to (but can never offer) the valuable worthiness of true high culture. Macdonald was convinced, as was Edward Shils, that there is a measurable difference in content quality among cultural levels and that higher-quality culture makes for higher-quality experience and thereby (somehow) better people and citizens.[11]

There is plenty of debate about which novels fit in what category, as Macdonald's concerns about midcult prove. And—like Shakespeare—one era's low fiction can become admired and taught as high after enough time has passed; jazz and comic books are two clear examples of this.

But it is still possible to organize things into categories of high, middle, and low. If we turn to sports, we can see that high sports are moneyed activities like polo and tennis, middle might be football and baseball, and low could be boxing and NAS-CAR. In music, high might be classical and jazz; middle could be pop, rock, and rap; and low is more problematic. There was a time when certain forms, like country or rap, were dismissed as low culture, but as views and the genres themselves evolve, they become more mainstream and respected. So for some, the lowest kind of music might be pop music, advertising jingles, or amateur efforts like the 2011 YouTube sensation "Friday"—any kind of music that the critic thinks is unoriginal and point-less, yet popular.

No matter what terms are used to define high, middle, and low or what kinds of culture fill the categories, it becomes clear that at least one way that cultural lev-els get assigned is based not on the inherent quality or complexity of the cultural content but instead on the educational and economic level of the audiences and producers. The more elite and exclusive the producers and consumers, the higher the perceived quality of the content.

But Macdonald and Shils weren't just snobs, trying to shame those who liked things like NASCAR or romance novels. They were trying to figure out what televi-sion (and before that radio and movies) was doing to us as citizens and as consum-ers. Their answer was that both high culture and folk or traditional culture—created with honesty and effort for a responsive, known audience—were being threatened by a growing tide of commercialized media fare.

Shils's argument is softened and deflected by the historian and scholar Oscar Handlin. Handlin studied immigrants and was interested in how folk culture can be used to support identity and community once people leave their country of origin. His contribution to the mass culture debates was to focus on how pro-ducers and consumers connect in the various levels of culture. He was concerned that the mass media don't produce cultural material that emerges from a genuine connection between people. In both the disappearing folk cultures and in the dis-appearing high arts, Handlin argues, the creators knew and understood their audi-ence, and created cultural forms that they truly believed in. But in mass mediated entertainment, producers cynically create formulaic pieces for a distanced audience for whom they have contempt, so the material itself is dishonest and should be mistrusted.[12]

When we look closely at the mass culture debates, what may seem like outdated and arrogant concerns about cultural levels is, instead, an early version of ques-tions that still trouble us: questions about whether the media can turn civilized culture into a propaganda-vulnerable mass society, as theorized by Adorno and Horkheimer; about whether turning culture into entertainment really ruins it, as thought by Arendt; about the relationship between producer and consumer and what produces trustworthy culture, as asked by Handlin; about whether the media starves or stuffs us, as in Jarrell's metaphor; and about the differences between high or low culture and meaning, as debated by Macdonald and Shils.

Now we are dealing with similar worries about the effects, relationships, and differences made by the Internet. Even though we may have updated the language and shifted some of the emphasis, we are still drawing cultural lines, worrying about cultural effects, and trying to distinguish between worthy and unworthy cultural forms.

CULTURAL TASTE RECONSIDERED

Sociologist Herbert Gans reassessed the legacies of the mass culture debates in his 1974 book *Popular Culture & High Culture: An Analysis and Evaluation of Taste.* In this book, he treats the intellectual concerns of the 1950s as the most recent version of a two-hundred-year-old critique of modern culture and suggests that it is limited in three fundamental ways: It relies on an idealized notion of the past; it has disdain for the ordinary people; and it is an attempt to defend high-culture status.

If we look realistically at the past, Gans argues, and respect the tastes of ordinary people rather than worrying about whether popular culture is eroding high culture, then we see not a hierarchy of content but a world of varying taste cultures. We see different forms of culture connected with different social groups—groups he calls "taste publics." So rather than begin with notions of content (as did the mass culture debaters), Gans begins with questions about audiences: What kinds of culture do people choose, and why?

Much as he tries, Gans can't leave behind the high-middle-low hierarchy that characterizes most discussions of media content. But by exploring five taste cultures—high (art for intellectuals); upper middle (for the well-educated); lower middle (white-collar media fare); low (blue-collar media fare); and then a confused category of "quasi-low folk" that included ethnic, youth, and black cultures, he draws attention to why people like what they like and choose what they choose. He assumes people choose what works best for them and respects the possibility that ordinary people have good reasons to enjoy whatever cultural forms they like best.

This is a question of taste, but taste is never simple. As a sociologist, Gans is particularly interested in how cultural taste is socially and politically conditioned. This is sometimes a difficult point to grasp—it is easy to shrug and say, "It's just my taste," when someone asks why we like or don't like a kind of music, a style of clothing, or a particular movie. But what we like and don't like is not random or arbitrary. When we meet someone new and realize that this person's taste is very different from ours, we make judgments about who they are, what they believe, and where they fit in our social and cultural world; we are acknowledging that taste, at the very least, is used to sort us into categories. Our taste is a form of identification, and it tells us who we are and, more crucially, who we are not.

Obviously our tastes change over time (what we liked at age eight is probably different than at age eighteen, which will probably be different from age twenty-eight, thirty-eight, and so on), and we form our tastes against an ever-changing backdrop of cultural options. We will usually have cultural tastes somewhat different from our parents, and what we wear, listen to, watch, and play will have some kind of connection to our age; gender; sexual orientation; geographic origins; family background; and social, economic, and educational heritage. That connection is complicated, of course, because it is both voluntary and involuntary. Taste is ascribed to us and chosen by us, but it feels natural. Some kinds of culture are "ours" and other kinds are "theirs."

That's what Gans is getting at with his descriptions of taste cultures and taste publics. We define ourselves by the popular culture we like and choose—and by what we dislike or ignore. In a sense, the culture debaters of the 1950s were doing just that: Intellectuals were standing up for their high-art preferences against what they perceived as the threat of mediated mass culture. That's what parents are up to when they criticize the music their kids enjoy as "sounding like noise," just as their own parents probably did. That's what makes it newsworthy when Obama is bad at bowling or orders arugula in a salad. Bowling is associated with a blue-collar taste culture, and arugula is seen as an upscale leafy green. Our tastes in hobbies and foods, as well as media fare, mark us as belonging to particular taste cultures, which are associated with particular ideas, values, beliefs, and political positions.[13]

The Avengers was a huge hit movie based on comic books, it was also one of the best-reviewed mass-media entertainments of 2012.

Knowing this, we choose how to present ourselves—and also, more deeply, choose and feel chosen by particular kinds of cultural fare. Our favorite movies, shows, music, and games all tell others about us but also tell us about ourselves. Our tastes feels very deep and fundamental. Some kinds of popular culture speak to us, and some do not. Some feel rich and meaningful, and others seem dull, stupid, and pointless. This works across the cultural hierarchy; it's not just about high and low.

One of the big advantages of seeing popular culture as taste cultures and publics, rather than as differing levels of content quality, is that it reduces the arrogance and contempt that so permeated the mass culture debate. But it doesn't abandon the important questions about the meaning of cultural content for those who choose it. If those who love high culture and those who love popular culture are simply different taste publics, then we can start asking more interesting questions about the meanings of particular cultural forms to those who choose them.

Taste Publics as Interpretive Communities

Scholarly research on popular culture fans is where we can get the best sense of how particular cultural forms matter to their taste publics. Starting with Richard Hoggart's seminal 1957 book *The Uses of Literacy*, which detailed British working-class culture, various scholars have explored what 1950s intellectuals and aspirational midcult types once dismissed as mass culture. What they find is that cultural forms that seem (to outsiders) to be formulaic and simplistic and a waste of time are experienced by insiders as interesting and meaningful and worthwhile. At least part of the problem is that we are often unable to understand or appreciate the forms we don't like.[14]

So when Dick Hebdige spends time with 1970s punks, or when Janice Radway studies romance novel readers and later Book of the Month Club members, or Ien Ang interviews viewers of the popular prime time soap opera *Dallas,* these scholars are exploring how and why particular kinds of popular entertainment are meaningful to their particular taste public. They are taking seriously the content and reception of the very forms that were dismissed in the 1950s as formulaic, prefabricated, commercialized mass culture.[15]

Interpretive audience researchers have found a lot more going on in these forms of entertainment than some of their initial critics may realize. As we discuss in the next section, fans of particular cultural forms are informed and aware of how their genres work, how their formulas operate, and why they enjoy their chosen form and find it meaningful. Far from being mindless entertainment, popular culture, just like high art, can be analyzed, dissected, criticized, compared, and evaluated—by fans and by scholars.

Gans uses the term "taste publics" to describe the ways that people group themselves around particular kinds of cultural forms. In doing so, he attempts to move beyond a simple high-middle-low cultural hierarchy of cultural content and explore how particular groups of people choose to ally themselves with particular kinds or styles of culture. Taste publics can be understood as interpretive communities— groups who share ideas, values, beliefs, language, and meaning. These interpretive communities have flourished in the electronic age, as the Internet has made it possible for fans of particular cultural forms to find each other.

Video games offer us an example of how interpretive communities can work. Gaming, to nongamers, can look like an addictive waste of time—but it looks very different to gamers themselves. We can consider gamers to be an interpretive community—not merely fans, but a self-defined group of people who participate in a particular kind of cultural act: gaming. Within that world of gamers, there are many smaller, interpretive communities, based on various evaluative hierarchies. The casual game player of *Angry Birds* or *Tetris* has opinions about the dedicated player of *World of Warcraft*, and vice versa. Players of one kind of game can look down on those who choose different styles or versions. What makes a "good" game and who is a "real" gamer are questions endlessly debatable, as are questions of whether video games are an art (creative, inspiring, uplifting), an entertainment (diverting absorbing, pleasurable), or an addiction (dangerous, destructive, degrading). Nongamers can't grasp the artistic or entertainment elements prized by gamers; gamers can't take seriously the fears of nongamers. They are members of very different interpretive communities.

Journalist and gamer Tom Bissell offers evidence for all three perspectives in his gaming memoir *Extra Lives* (2010). He argues that video games can be seen as art forms because they are original, innovative, creative achievements, as well as effective, absorbing entertainment (especially, in his example, *Call of Duty IV*), yet video games are eerily similar to his own cocaine addiction, which would lead him to "binge game" for thirty hours or more. As a member of the gamer interpretive community, he evaluates what is good about the games and the experience of gaming. But this could raise questions about whether he has the right critical distance to make these judgments.[16]

The concept of interpretive communities suggests that those who are most involved with a particular cultural form know best what those forms mean to them. Insiders to any form of culture—including the often-maligned video games—can offer rich interpretive perspectives. High-art lovers, like video game lovers, have lots to say about what makes a good, mediocre, or bad version, and a good, mediocre, or bad experience. But as in all communities, there will not be a single unitary perspective, though there will still be a clear distinction between those "in the know" who love the cultural form and those outside the community who do not.

Popular culture scholarship since the 1970s has demonstrated that much of what worried mass culture debaters and continues to worry parents, social critics, and some scholars about popular culture, is based on an outsider's rather than an insider's view. Many scholars come from a high-culture perspective: They are part of an educational system that identifies particular forms as worthwhile and then seeks to instill appreciation of them in students. Both students and teachers can then become part of a self-validating system dedicated to cultural bifurcation, contrasting the allegedly fun, trivial entertainment of the outside world with the supposedly more serious, worthwhile information and art within the educational system.

Even though popular culture scholarship has become increasingly present in academic settings, it is still easy to dismiss media processes as unworthy of scholarly attention. Majoring in literature, history, or politics is assumed by some to be more challenging and worthwhile, and perhaps less fun, than majoring in media studies. Vestiges of the art/entertainment bifurcation, as well as cultural levels, mean that communication majors (and professors) often have to defend their belief that they are doing real scholarly work when they analyze contemporary cultural forms. Film studies is currently the most successful media genre to achieve scholarly respectability, perhaps because film is among the oldest of the electronic mass media forms. But video games and YouTube videos are accorded far less academic respect.

What popular culture scholarship shows us is that the techniques used in universities to understand high culture can be applied to commercial entertainment. Beyond this, the techniques fans use to understand their entertainment can help us understand how and why different people choose different kinds of culture. The pleasure of well-crafted narrative; the delight of stories, familiar or new; the power of performances, whether live or recorded, operate across taste cultures and levels.

Internet Support for Fandom

The Internet has made it much easier for media studies scholars to find and study fans. For much of the twentieth century, fans were stereotyped, at least in the popular imagination, as aberrant oddballs. As scholars began to take fans more seriously, this characterization of fandom as a kind of pathology was challenged.[17] Portrayals of fans as outcasts living to attend Star Trek conventions gave way to more thoughtful interpretations of fans as committed and engaged audience members.

Interestingly, our three perspectives on media in society—reflectionist, constructionist, and narrativist—can be found in the growing field of fan studies. From a more reflectionist perspective, fans are examples of modern media consumers, choosing celebrities, shows, and genres just as they choose other consumer brands. From a more constructionist perspective, fans are responding to hegemonic processes, either by resisting or supporting the dominant order through their fandom. And from a more narrativist perspective, fans are active participants in imaginative worlds, through their chosen cultural forms.

The Internet has also made it possible for fans of particular genres, shows, or other cultural types to find one another. There were fans before the Internet, of course, but they had no easy ways to connect, except at particular events or through small magazines, fan clubs, or mailing lists. As the Internet develops, it is becoming an ideal home for a burgeoning world of interactive fandom. What was once private has become public. What was once difficult to do—find others who shared your tastes and enthusiasms—has become easier, and what was once invisible—the world of deeply engaged and analytical popular culture fans—is now seemingly everywhere. The gulf between producer and consumer that characterized mass mediated culture—and so troubled Handlin—has lessened.

Before the Internet, television writers worked in a vacuum, with a few reviews and occasional letters from viewers the only feedback from their audience of millions. Now they can get direct fan feedback—if they want—as soon as their episodes air. Internet sites dedicated to particular shows offer fans multiple ways to comment and respond to story lines, plot twists, or character development in specific detail, almost immediately. On collective sites like Television Without Pity—originally a fan-created site but now owned by Bravo, an NBC-Universal subsidiary—fans summarize, recap, and evaluate episodes of their favorite shows, with sarcasm and insider humor. In fact, the TWoP motto is "Spare the snark, spoil the networks." As media scholar Mark Andrejevic notes, this kind of fan participation is a form of creative activity, but it is also an opportunity for producers to harness fan labor: "Creative activity and exploitation coexist and interpenetrate each other within the context of the emerging online economy."[18] Fans voluntarily post evidence of their savvy reflexivity, sharing their insight and knowledge and enjoying the online recognition of others who love the same shows. But these same fans, Andrejevic and others note, are giving away their creative work for free. The fan sites offer media producers demographic information and focus groups that they once had to pay for. They can also be used for viral advertising—to create and spread buzz. Fan participation may even, ultimately "divert the threat of activism . . . into marketing and market research."

Using the Internet to enact fandom offers new ways for audience members to creatively connect with each other and with cultural producers. And this may also mean that mediated culture is much less "mass" than it used to be. Some might even argue that media production, with the Internet as a feedback loop, makes today's media fare more like the close connection between producer and patron that Handlin valued in both folk and high art.

Subcultures as Taste Cultures

In *Popular Culture & High Culture*, Gans called for media content that was less homogenized—less dominated by the television networks, the big movie companies, and the big record companies. He wanted to "de-massify" media offerings. So he advocated for what he called subcultural programming—different cultural forms designed to address every different taste public, no matter what their size or economic clout.[19] In the 1970s, this sounded like a utopian dream. After all, mass media was characterized by its mass appeal. Cultural products were made for a wide, distant audience, whose desirability was based on their appeal to advertisers. Content usually involved vast expense, and if you were someone with odd or eccentric taste, you were out of luck in the mass media marketplace.

The subcultural programming that Gans called for did not seem likely to emerge, as it was not economically feasible in the pre–Internet media world. But now the Internet has become that subcultural programming mechanism. If you can create it, you can post it; if it can be posted, it can be found through a search engine; if it can be found, it can develop audiences and fans; and if it finds fans, it can be monetized

Even within a particular level of culture, an artist or entertainer might produce works that appeal to tastes outside of his or her cultural niche. Some might consider a Picasso painting from his cubist period (left) more provocative than his painting on page 213, which is from his blue period; others might consider the same painting more accessible, or even "lowbrow."

The Guitar Player, 1910 (oil on canvas), by Pablo Picasso

by you or someone else (at least in theory)—and more importantly, it's out there as a narrative, an interpretive world, a mediated cultural form.

Years ago media studies professors would say something like, "The media will produce whatever the audience wants. If enough people want Balkan folk dancing, then it will be on TV." Students would laugh! Balkan folk dancing? There were only

The Old Guitarist, 1903 (oil on wood panel), by Pablo Picasso

so many channels, so many hours, so many production companies. Airtime was a scarce and expensive resource, and there was no way Balkan folk dancing would ever have enough of a fan base to warrant programming it.

The Internet has made it possible for the world of Balkan folk dancing fans to post, find, and share their beloved form, and for others to discover it, with a simple Google search.[20] We may never have heard of Balkan folk dancing up to that point, but in a few minutes we can see the best the form has to offer, as well as comments on what makes it good, bad, or indifferent; its history; varieties; costumes; and products. We can go from clueless outsider to tourist, even to insider, thanks to the Internet's ability to make even the most obscure taste cultures accessible.

This kind of transparency helps us realize that issues of "good" and "bad" are within generic constraints—maybe there are not, as the mass culture debaters believed, essentially different levels of culture. Fans evaluate good and bad kinds of country, pop, rock, and rap just like fans evaluate good and bad classical music. There is good and bad black-velvet painting just as there is good and bad oil painting. Cultural experts are fans and vice versa—they can tell the difference within a particular form.[21]

The good news, then, is that Gans's dream of a rich, varied, pluralistic cultural mix has actually come true. The bad news, if you agree with Adorno and Horkheimer, is that capitalism is figuring out how to use that same technology to market Balkan folk dancing—and anything else it can find.

EXPLORING POPULAR CULTURE PLURALISM

Walt Whitman's famous 1871 essay "Democratic Vistas" imagined an amazing new American culture, one that was robust, healthy, energizing, and ideally suited to support democracy.[22] This culture would not be composed of genteel high art or the cheap amusements of Whitman's day. It would be an imagined third kind, much like Whitman's own poetry—vernacular, confident, idealistic, and designed to awaken the public and make them into the kind of citizens Whitman wanted America to have.

Similarly, the mass culture critics of the 1950s had faith that quality cultural forms could somehow protect against the tyranny that they saw as genuine dangers to post–World War II society. They, like Whitman, worried that the entertainment forms of their time were turning us into passive, unquestioning, distracted citizens, unable to lead meaningful lives or recognize threats to a democratic society. During the 1960s, much was made of television's "vast wasteland" and the notion that mass mediated culture was homogenizing. It was turning us all into imitations of each other, critics feared, offering us seemingly different versions of the same general mainstream, lowest-common-denominator culture. In order to garner wide appeal and therefore make money, culture had to be dumbed down, watered down, or otherwise diluted.

Are these worries still worth exploring? Clearly. YouTube is not full of Whitmanesque poetry, but its content is not all homogenized or dumbed down, either. It is a vast array of democratized creative effort, which delights and amuses many people, even as it bores or troubles others. Today's television includes the mass-appeal variety shows and sitcoms that so concerned the mass culture critics, but a little time on Netflix, the Internet, or even some television channels reveals an impressive variety of media fare: individual efforts from "outsiders," shoestring independent productions, exciting styles of programming, works of the past that haven't always been accessible, and international productions that few could have viewed thirty years ago. Critics have gone from worrying about a homogenized society to worrying about a fragmented one—where we have no common, unifying cultural programming.

Gans argued for the democratic value of cultural variety—what he called cultural pluralism—and believed that democracy thrives when it allows multiple perspectives and tastes to flourish. In the 1970s, he worried that taste publics stayed separate and distinct, unable to recognize or appreciate the meanings and values of material other than their own. In today's more pluralized, Internet-enabled world, we might instead wonder whether we are taking full advantage of our unprecedented access to varieties of taste cultures or if our cultural fragmentation alienates us and locks us into our own separate enclaves.

At this point in our cultural pluralism, marketers have found that—at least so far—we are remarkably predictable in our tastes, our buying habits, and our political preferences. Now that every site we visit on the Internet can be recorded and tabulated, marketers can use algorithms to predict what we might want and offer it to us, even before we know it exists.[23] On the one hand, this is an amazing presorting mechanism, a way to tame the sometimes overwhelming variety of Internet offerings. We can sit back and let someone else help us find what we might want. On the other hand, it can also potentially deepen our divisions, keeping us ever more deeply entrenched in our own limited tastes.

It is also a way to sell us products that we may or may not actually need—and just as it can sell us products, it can sell us political candidates, finding out what (or who) we will "buy" and micro-shaping messages to us that cater to our preexisting patterns and prejudices. In this way, selling products (or candidates) on the Internet can be dramatically different from the marketing that goes on through omnibus newspapers and networks, with their programming and ads designed for the vast middle-class audience. Newer forms of target marketing identify us in very precise demographic terms and basically give us more of what we already seem to be interested in.

It may be, then, that Gans's idea of cultural pluralism is as unrealistic as Whitman's dreams of a new kind of democratic culture. And it may be that Adorno and Horkheimer's fears of mediated culture deepening the hold that capitalism has on us is the more accurate prognostication. While the basics of the mass culture debates—cultural levels of differing quality and complexity—have been challenged, many of the troubling implications remain.

Even with the Internet's proliferation of user-created content, some critics remain just as concerned about the value and worth of the material being generated. Fears that we are still being "amused to death" continue, now in relation to video games or Twitter rather than comic books or horror movies, but with the same notions of "worthwhile" uses of our time.

These fears have adapted to what some have characterized as our modern kaleidoscope culture. For example, fragmentation could lead to a more contentious, politically partisan culture. On the Internet, society can seem more vicious, given the ability to interact with and respond to taste publics different from our own, in ever more inflamed ways. When marketers and pollsters can segment and brand us, democracy could be hurt in the process. Similarly, capitalism's penetration into our consciousness remains a worry to many critics, especially as capitalism gets ever more deeply woven into what once seemed a "free" Internet. Media content has always been connected to the marketplace, but we now need to figure out if the new economic patterns of the Internet have deepened or loosened the connections between creativity and commercialization.

One of the most intractable concerns of popular culture theorists is the question of value: figuring out which cultural forms give us a meaningful experience and which do not. This is what Jarrell was getting at with his "Sad Heart at the Supermarket." We are surrounded by abundance, more entertaining popular culture fare than anyone has ever had access to ever before in the history of civilization. Is it good for us or not? Are we being starved *and* stuffed?[24]

Narrativists, reflectionists, and constructionists have different but overlapping responses to these important questions. If we imagine entertainment and popular culture not as cultural levels, but as interpretive communities (as those who study popular culture fans have done), we can and should ask what it means to spend time in particular taste cultures, as a member of a particular taste public.

For reflectionists, concern will focus on how realistically and completely the taste culture represents the real world. It is scary to imagine people deeply immersed in media forms that distort reality, and that is why violent video games, for example, worry so many critics. But that is also why particular networks, talk shows, or reality shows can seem dangerous—they offer a view of the world that can make everything seem tawdry or petty or cynical, critics say. Given these concerns, it would be important to seek out taste cultures that offer counternarratives, and varieties of perspective that seek to represent actual lived experience rather than partisan or confirming accounts.

For constructionists, the media forms offered for profit under a capitalist system are automatically suspect, and the ever more elaborate demographic refinements are deepening the penetration of commercialization into our lives. Without privacy, without independent analysis, without the challenge of culture made for meaning, not profit, we become ever more unable to think in truly independent, creative ways. In this sense, the Internet has potential to offer subversive, alternative forms of culture that can liberate us from capitalist ideology, but these forms quickly become co-opted and commercialized—repackaged as products to sell back to us.

Narrativists share the concerns of reflectionists about the need for true cultural pluralism and those of constructionists about the commercialization of cultural expression. But this point of view is, on balance, more optimistic about the possibilities of the Internet to increase cultural diversity and innovation in ways that help all of us develop our interpretive abilities. As long as we realize that it is up to us to explore and understand cultural forms of "theirs" as well as "ours," of the past as well as the present, of so-called high culture and low culture, our time with popular culture can be made worthwhile.

Returning to the example of Shakespeare: It is possible that turning something into high culture is in fact a way to deaden, dull, and eviscerate a cultural form. Treating Shakespeare as high art—putting him in a museum—may well ruin his work for some students. But turning Shakespeare into popular entertainment in just the ways that Arendt fears hasn't always worked either. A common high school assignment is to act out the story of The Three Little Pigs in Shakespearean verse, supposedly making Shakespeare more accessible in the process. But turning Shakespeare into "fun," whether as a comic book, a classroom exercise, or even rewritten as *West Side Story*, *The Lion King*, or *Ten Things I Hate About You*, can obscure what is time-bound, complex, and truly interesting about his work.

Perhaps, instead, Shakespeare can come alive for us today through Shakespeare fans—members of Shakespeare's taste public—showing us what they love about him and why they love it. Taste publics, at their best and most instructive, can help us "get" their cultural forms. The legacy of interpretive audience research is the recognition that fans are scholars of their favorite cultural forms. We who are not fans, then, can learn from them. This is true of Shakespeare's fans as well as fans of comic books, television comedy, video gaming, and more.

Giving up concerns about cultural hierarchy and cultural blending lets us commit to cultural understanding instead. Ancient Greece was not a museum of art, nor does learning that the statues were painted in bright colors mean that we need to imagine it instead as a circus of entertainment. These are cultural categories we've invented, and we can discard them in favor of understanding (as best we can across time) what Greek culture actually meant to the variety of people who participated in it.

If we seek to understand entertainment as popular art, we can let ourselves learn from fans about what they love and why. In doing that, we enrich and educate ourselves about more than what we already know and already believe. That kind of cultural cosmopolitanism is what the Internet makes possible, and it has refigured at least two hundred years of hopes and fears of cultural democracy.

| CRITICAL PROCESS 1 | The Art–Trash Divide

The goal of this exercise is to explore how hierarchical cultural categories operate in our lives. Gather at least six people to fill in what you think most people would call high, middle, and low cultural forms in various categories. Call one category "art," one "middle," and the lowest "trash." Cultural categories like painting, music, film, television, newspapers, magazines, books, sports, and cities are all categories that work well. Be sure to leave an extra "question mark" category for examples that for some reason don't seem to fit.

Describe the examples you've come up with for each category. What fits in "art," "middle," and "trash"?

Analyze each of the categories and its examples. What production, content, and consumption traits does each level have in common? Does this seem to work across all the categories, from books to paintings to music?

Interpret the category placements. Why do many people believe some forms are better or worse than others? How does the question mark category reveal what is unsettled about cultural levels?

Evaluate whether you agree with conventional wisdom—or what your group thinks "most people" would say about these cultural forms. Why do you agree or disagree? What makes something good culture or bad culture to you?

Engage by brainstorming ideas about how you can (or whether you should) help increase the quality of cultural material available. Could you advocate for certain cultural forms using online forums?

| CRITICAL PROCESS 2 | Subcultural Tourism

The goal of this exercise is to become familiar with a cultural genre that you dislike, mistrust, or hold in contempt. Choose a kind of culture that you can't stand—for whatever reason. For some this may be opera, or country music, or live theater, or wrestling, or reality TV. Find someone who really loves this form, and ask him/her to be your cultural tour guide—go to an opera or concert or theater production or wrestling match or watch a favorite reality TV show with him/her.

Describe what you are seeing, listening to, or otherwise experiencing—and have your guide describe what he/she is experiencing too.

Analyze the differences between your descriptions. Do you see differences between a fan's perspective and an outsider's perspective? What are they?

Interpret the reasons for these differences—as well as the qualities that attract your guide to this cultural form—and the reasons it may or may not attract you. Does your guide's interest seem effortless or learned over time? How might you react to more exposure to this cultural form?

Evaluate what makes this cultural form good or bad to you, and whether that has changed through this process. Trade evaluations with your guide. How does he/she evaluate what you've experienced? How are your evaluations similar and different?

Engage in the process by reversing it: Invite someone who hates a cultural form that you love to share it with you, and see if you can get him/her to see what you love about it or what he/she is missing. You can also engage by visiting a Web site or reading a book or magazine that discusses the cultural form in greater detail and reacting thoughtfully to those discussions.

9

Representation in the Media

When we walk through a Toys R Us or the children's section at a Walmart, colors clearly and symbolically mark which aisles are for boys and girls. Typical signifiers for girls' products are various shades of pink and purple; a much greater color variety marks the boys' aisles, although darker earth tones and camouflage prevail. These colors, over time, have become identity signals in our culture, symbols and social constructions marking boundaries and helping shape identity. These boundaries, in part, constrain what it means to be a boy or a girl in our culture.

So why is our culture like this, and what role do media play in nurturing these symbols and identity markers?

In contemporary society, we derive our sense of self and place through social interactions, as well as our experiences with mass media. Understanding who we are and how we make sense of the world requires an exploration of the media's creative influence, as well as a critical analysis of how media are dominated by powerful industries that influence identity, experience, and events. The media use language, visuals, codes, and conventions to tell us stories about who we are and how we are supposed to behave and not to behave. They provide us with representations—narratives that represent us as individuals, as members of society, and as global citizens.

Because our media system is a commercial system, media also represent us as consumers with specific demographic profiles. Sometimes we closely identify with the representations conjured up by the mass media, while other times we resist representations that don't capture the essence of who we are, how we behave, or how we experience and make sense of the world. In order to better comprehend the media's influence on our identity and our understandings of the world, we need to study the political, economic, and ideological power of media producers. By asking who has the power to represent or "re-present" identity, meaning, and experience, and how such stories are constructed through narratives, we are able to examine how creative meaning-making emerges from this process and how it is influenced by cultural, ideological, political, and economic factors.

Because cultural representations contain visual codes of meaning, this chapter on representation complements the work on visual literacy in Chapter 3. As British art critic and cultural historian John Berger explains, "seeing comes before words."[1] As children we recognize pictures even before we speak; seeing provides us a way to understand the world and our place within it. Visual cues in our culture convey meaning through methods that are different from the written word. Therefore, we analyze the interconnections between visual literacy and representation. Specifically, we explore how visual culture and media re-present social experience and identity through the matrices of gender, race, class, and sexuality as they intersect with commercial (for-profit), mainstream productions. We also study how identities and experiences are re-presented according to ideological, political, and economic interests. As Chapter 1 suggests, our narrative approach requires asking: Who gets to tell the stories of our culture? What are the goals and objectives in producing such narratives? What is the content of these stories, and how do they produce social discourses? How do these stories influence audiences, and how do audiences interact with these stories? To answer these questions, our approach will include analyzing:

- how representations change over time
- how "reality" is socially constructed across different media
- how representations both reflect and shape the culture from which they emerge
- how representation is both a socialization influence and a form of transformative possibility

This combined approach allows us to better understand the media's power in shaping our "reality" and social experience. The goal is to provide multiple theories and perspectives about media in society to better understand, critique, conceptualize, and reconceptualize our own ways of seeing and shaping culture. Since race, class, gender, and sexuality function as markers of identity through their intersections rather than in isolation, this chapter explores how these categories of identity are formed through a variety of narratives and representations, from the past to the present.

IDEOLOGY, HEGEMONY, AND MASTER NARRATIVES

In today's media-saturated environment, our ideas are relayed through social **discourse**—how through our socialization and our institutions (family, education, work, etc.) we learn to speak about and represent our thinking. Social discourses reflect the values, beliefs, and ideas that are part of the culture, including the work of those who produce media content. When social discourses are repeated in a variety of media, they eventually form patterns of thought that emerge as **ideologies**—

systems of meaning that circulate the dominant ideas of a society, helping us to process and make value judgments about the world. For example, being exposed to cultural messages that define us as consumers instead of citizens supports a capitalist ideology that defines us through what we buy over other characteristics, values, or behaviors.

Because these systems of meaning affect so many people, it is important to examine who makes them, and how ideologies serve the interests of those who wield political and economic power. Mainstream mass media are owned and controlled by a few transnational global conglomerates, so it's helpful to examine who owns that media and whose interests they serve, better preparing us to assess how certain narratives champion some attitudes and behaviors over others. Given that our culture's main storytellers occupy a privileged space through their social, political, and economic power, it's not surprising that narratives about gender, race, class, and sexuality often mirror the values of the socially dominant groups in a given society.

In addition to referring to values, belief systems, and worldviews, ideology signals commonsense understandings that are solidified in the culture. Going beyond a Marxist emphasis (discussed in Chapter 7) on economic factors that reproduce social hierarchies, it is important to analyze how dominant ideas and belief systems shape our understandings through social texts that have **hegemonic power**. When a text has hegemonic power, it refers to those ideologies reflecting the established mainstream values—and, as such, the dominant social order. However, when ideologies do not hold that power, they are often marked as marginal or subordinate. Accordingly, when mainstream media privilege certain ideas and belief systems over others through images, visuals, and texts, they represent a dominant ideology—one that is carried in **consensus** or **master narratives**. For example, the American dream represents a master narrative in U.S. culture and is predicated on the idealized notion that everyone can equally attain wealth and power by working hard and playing by the rules. Historically, examples of dominant ideologies of identity might include erroneous assumptions that males are rugged leaders and cultural heroes, women are sexual objects or nurturing homemakers, whites are more worthy and intelligent than minorities, and heterosexuality is morally superior to homosexuality.

One powerful example of dominant ideologies uniting in various forms across time is the animated films from the Walt Disney Company. Disney films are known as family-friendly, all-ages entertainment; they offer influential stories of male heroism, female dependency, heterosexual norms, and the power of whites in society. Classic Disney narratives like *Snow White* (1937), *Cinderella* (1950), and *Sleeping Beauty* (1959) maintain heterosexual and sexist norms in which women pursue the love of a desired male over their own professional or personal ambitions. Even in a newer film like *The Little Mermaid* (1989), Ariel's father provides patriarchal rule over his daughters (sons are interestingly absent). Although in defiance of her father's rules, Ariel gives up her voice and is instructed to use her "body language" to win over a desired male human. Such depictions uphold the feminist mind/womb dichotomy in which girls and women are valued for their bodies over their brains. In *Beauty and the Beast* (1991), the female protagonist Belle is initially shown as smart and independent. However, she is forcefully kidnapped and separated from her father by a brutal beast. Rather than reject this form of oppression, Belle learns to love her abuser in order to bring out the prince in him. Cultural critics and feminist scholars have argued that the film's story underscores a dominant cultural ideology of male power and control over women through a love story predicated upon physical and domestic violence. Moving beyond gender, cultural critics have argued that *The Lion King* (1994) underscores the dominant ideology of white supremacy in its racial caricaturing. In the film, African American actors and dialects are embodied in the cartoon as antagonistic hyenas, who plot to murder the king and destroy the ideals of white rule and civilization.

Some newer Disney representations do include alternate depictions. *Mulan* (1998) was an important deviation from the theme of romance and male heroism through the depiction of a young Chinese girl whose heroism saves her country from barbarians. As a young and unconventional female warrior, Mulan emerges victorious despite the dangers associated with her daunting battles. Notwithstanding, critics were disappointed by the film's ending, as it shows Mulan returning home to her village in a culture that pressures young girls to conform to more traditional ideals of romance and domesticity. A more recent attempt to diversify the Disney formula is illustrated by Princess Tiana, the first African American Disney princess, featured in *The Princess and the Frog* (2009). However, since all media texts are subject to cultural battles over identity issues, the film remains controversial. On the one hand, Disney spokespersons praise the film for providing "a breakthrough black icon" supporting a "sea of cultural change" in black communities globally. On the other hand, some critics characterize Tiana's role as just another example of Disney's racial insensitivity. Concerns include the depiction of Tiana as a frog for much of the film rather than as a human, Prince Naveen's racial whiteness, and the commercial opportunism of merchandise marketing alongside the global popularity of Oprah Winfrey and Michelle Obama.[2]

When media use consensus or master narratives to prescribe messages about how to behave and engage with society, they cultivate "normative" ways of seeing and behaving through the acceptance of dominant attitudes and behaviors. For example, social discourses that cultivate normative female gender roles through Western standards of beauty (thin, buxom, blond, young) are mediated through a variety of sources including magazines, film, television, social networking sites, newspapers, fashion, and advertising.

The Roots of Master Narratives

There are historic, political, and economic reasons for such normative representations. Art scholar John Berger examined the art form of the European nude to identify how the people who owned or viewed these forms were usually men while the nudes represented in the paintings were usually women. He explained how the unequal relationship between men and women is "so deeply embedded in our culture that it still structures the consciousness of many women," making it so that women judge their own femininity as masculine culture does.[3] Feminist scholar Laura Mulvey has explored visual pleasure in narrative cinema to explain how the "male gaze"—men looking at woman in a sexual way—projects itself onto women who are simultaneously looked at and displayed.[4] Often used in advertisements as well as other visual media, the male gaze holds psychological power over young girls and women as they learn to conceptualize their body image from a male spectator's point of view. Conventional uses of the male gaze in media include women sexually dolling themselves up in the presence (or assumed presence) of a voyeur, as well as the camera sweep or close-up of a woman's body parts as a male passes by her. The theory holds that over time, the media's exemplification of the male gaze serves as a source of internal judgment for women who hold themselves and other women up to what were originally male standards for idealized beauty norms.

These historic and structural underpinnings of representation of gender continue today. Visual codes in a variety of media texts draw upon gender norms, relegating women to objectivity or passivity, and men to subjectivity and activity. When exploring the continuum of normative gender representations in contemporary culture, Berger explains, "Women are depicted in a quite different way from men—not because the feminine is different from the masculine, but because the 'ideal' spectator is always assumed to be male and the image of the woman is designed to flatter him."[5] Within historical and economic contexts, males have often been the primary target audience because they are deemed to have the strongest "purchasing power" for big-ticket consumer items alongside cultural authority. To be clear, women represent important niche markets for fashion, soap operas, talk shows, daytime radio, much of prime time, and new cable reality programs. However, female beauty and accommodation are emphasized in these genres in ways that reinforce women's economic and cultural subordination. For these reasons, coupled with the historical fact that males have been the primary producers of mainstream media, there is continuity in cultural representations that can be traced to traditional power structures. Analyzing how these structures frame social discourses is one way of exploring how the ideologies and hegemonic power of the media affect our ways of seeing.

That is to say, analyzing the historic, social, and economic structure of representation is not merely about making judgments about media producers. We may derive pleasure from, and identify with, dominant discourses; we may question and resist them; or we may do both. Moreover, as new technologies and media texts emerge through mainstream and alternative venues, it is harder for consensus or master narratives to retain their exclusive cultural power. Deconstructing or analyzing mediated representations through media criticism is a means to explore how our ways of seeing are altered by the values and perspectives we bring to visual texts. This approach enhances our understanding of how representational conventions and social rules emerge; how they are recreated and reproduced through structures, choices, and point of view; and how we as audiences might interpret such codes and visuals.

Despite the power of the media in cultivating certain attitudes and behaviors, they cannot fully control or account for our beliefs, preferences, or behaviors. In fact, depending on all sorts of variables (including age, education levels, gender, race, sexuality, and nationality), we engage with and interpret media texts differently. Such audience variations affect the ability of media producers to define normative behavior and advance dominant ideologies. It may be better to think of media as cultural texts that compete for our ideological acceptance as well as sell us master narratives. Cultural skirmishes between media producers and audiences seek to gain control over meaning and social engagement. For example, the producers of a political ad for Barack Obama during the 2008 presidential campaign meant for us to agree ideologically with the ad's message that is carried through a powerful and romantic master narrative, offering Obama as a heroic character who stands for hope and political reconciliation. Of course, this is a message that worked much better for Democrats or independents than for many conservative Republicans, who may have rejected the ad's intended meaning because of their own ideological take on the election and their own economic and political interests.

NARRATIVE ANALYSIS: WHAT DO OUR STORIES OF IDENTITY SAY?

In popular representations and in the culture at large, identity politics have become increasingly important markers of the individual and collective self. For example, during the Republican presidential primary race in 2012, Michele Bachmann was often identified as the "woman candidate," Herman Cain as the "black candidate," Rick Santorum and Newt Gingrich as the "socially conservative candidates," and eventual nominee Mitt Romney as the "rich candidate." Political pundits at the time often told stories about these candidates only in terms of these narrow identity markers, and the candidates themselves often struggled to escape or broaden these characterizations. As representations along lines of gender, race, class, and sexuality manifest themselves through a variety of media channels and cultural artifacts, they construct powerful narratives about personal and collective experiences and perspectives.

The politics surrounding the media construction of such narratives remain contested. Mainstream representations are usually judged by critics according to how they perform one of two functions within society. One is a **reflective** function, whereby representations are judged according to their ability to reflect the culture from which they emerge (i.e., assessing whether re-presentations mirror "real" subjects and experiences); the other is a **socializing** influence, whereby representations are seen as the products of powerful industries designed to shape the culture either through harmful means (e.g., power, propaganda, stereotyping, and commercialization) or as instruments of constructive, transformational outcomes (e.g., educational or artistic expression). A balanced model of media criticism considers the media as agents of both functions and is more likely to produce a compelling evaluation of the media's influence in society. As media scholar Sharon Willis explains, ". . . identity politics is likely to go both ways, to become either a site for the progressive use of diversity or an opportunity for the conservative management of difference within existing power structures."[6]

When it comes to representing identities, the mainstream media usually take on the point of view of the normative subject, an identity that is taken for granted or rendered invisible through its privileged position in the culture. Within American media, those who wield political and economic power are most often white, male, middle to upper class, and heterosexual. The perspectives that come from these dominant identities form powerful, hegemonic narratives. Often, when non-dominant subjects are represented, they are portrayed in ways that create "issues"— but only for dominant subjects such as business managers or affluent consumers. For example, TV news stories about labor strikes typically employ a narrative featuring inconvenienced and irritated consumers rather than in-depth profiles of why workers are striking and why work and labor issues matter to the larger public. Within these popular narratives, nondominance signifies difference—often conveyed in an "us vs. them" narrative package. This crisis of difference is commonly used as a hook to lure mainstream audiences, while neat resolutions restore normality through the celebration of white, masculine, heterosexual, and middle-class family values that reassure audiences of the stability of master narratives. Notwithstanding, there are times when the media provide alternate representations of difference as a means to gain the loyalties of new emerging identity-based markets. For instance, the Calvin Klein brand has produced fashion campaigns that used models whose sexuality could be interpreted as gay or straight.

Understanding Identity Stereotypes

When stories of identity are told, individuals and groups are usually reduced to easily identifiable categorizations, or **stereotypes**, so that audiences can label them, often on the basis of simplistic characteristics like gender, race, class, and/ or sexuality. For example, think of how characters in TV and movie narratives like *Saved by the Bell*, *Freaks and Geeks*, *Grease*, *Buffy the Vampire Slayer*, *Mean Girls*, *Glee*, and *Juno* both stereotype and challenge the stereotypes of high school students as jocks, dumb blonde cheerleaders, wise guys, nerds, slackers, and druggies. While some stereotypes help develop our understanding of group dynamics, they often fail when we apply them to individuals who compose those groups. One of the reasons stereotypes are so common in mainstream media is that they provide a familiar or common set of stories for the largest segment of the audience, who are comforted by reduced complexity and nuance. They are also used as a means to reassert dominant ideologies and hegemonic power (e.g., men are tough and emotionally detached; women are submissive and overly emotional). Some of these stories can also carry subplots and character portrayals that resist and challenge stereotypes, but the stereotypes themselves are still commonplace. When groups are pigeonholed according to simplistic narratives, this leads to generalizations and misrepresentations that affect identity politics. While stereotypes have changed over time due to changes in the sociocultural landscape and audience resistance, they are often thinly veiled reproductions of older hegemonic narratives. Therefore, it is not enough for us to ask, say, if minorities are represented more than they were in the past or if women are portrayed in more complex ways than in the 1950s. We need to analyze and evaluate how stories of identity are told within contemporary media through an informed framework of media criticism. The following stereotypes are commonly employed in media narratives and help explain how identity politics remain contested within contemporary media.

Gender. Although women continue to be represented within the domestic sphere, particularly during daytime television and within women's magazines, representations of women in public realms have increased in the last twenty years through politics, news, sports, business, law, medicine, and education. As a result, a new generation of empowered girls and women has led to the inclusion of strong role models in the media, such as physically assertive girls and women who solve their own problems. Contemporary examples include Hermione Granger from the *Harry Potter* book and film series, *Buffy the Vampire Slayer,* and Lara Croft in *Tomb Raider* video games and films. Yet media portrayals of girls and women continue to emphasize thinness, the body over the mind, hypersexualization, victimization, and ultimately cultural marginalization. Consider the fact that 39 percent of characters on prime-time television are female and that only 30 percent of actors in children's programming are women.[7] Even on PBS's long-running *Sesame Street,* there are only a handful of female Muppets.

Mainstream media provide another gendered stereotype: the hypermasculine, hypersexualized, violent male. In sports, steroid use and body enhancers have increased as men are pressured to outperform and break records through super-human strength and muscularity. In film, violent male icons range from Sylvester Stallone in the *Rambo* movies of the 1980s to Matt Damon in the newer *Bourne* film trilogy. In addition to sports and film, video games, television, some music genres, and the Internet all regularly feature stereotypical masculinity depicted through violence and hypersexuality. Males are also regularly caricatured in their roles as chumps, idiots, losers, buddies, male chauvinists, and studs.[8] For most mainstream commercial media, sustaining a narrow range of narrative stereotypes creates familiarity and reduces complexity to a few categories.

Race and Ethnicity. Although images of race and ethnicity have flooded mainstream media to a greater extent than before, the narratives have not strayed far from old stereotypes and racist themes. Historically, black males have been represented regularly as either comic entertainment or as thugs and criminals, whereas black women have often been portrayed in sassy comic roles or, worse, as characters denigrated through sexual insults. Asian male characters have routinely attained their command over technology as nerds and techno-geeks, while Asian women have been frequently eroticized as geishas and subservient females. Latino characters often have been depicted through a brand of cultural "machismo" that has combined violence and sexuality with survival in a hostile, anti-immigration environment, while Latina characters have been shown as interlopers who should be grateful for domestic work and low-paying jobs. Regardless of sex, and despite their growing visibility in the population at large, minorities remain marginalized and underrepresented in mainstream media. Even the long-standing stereotype of the Italian Mafioso endured through HBO's hit series *The Sopranos.* As Peter Bondanella describes in his book *Hollywood Italians: Dagos, Palookas, Romeos, Wise Guys, and Sopranos,* Italian American stereotypes have evolved through contemporary depictions, such as *The Sopranos* and *Everybody Loves Raymond.*[9]

Though Lara Croft (of the *Tomb Raider* franchise) is physically assertive and mentally sharp, she is also defined in part by her unrealistic body and outfits. The most recent Croft game, titled simply *Tomb Raider,* attempted to downplay her male-fantasy image.

Whereas Tony Soprano is a psychologically distressed mob leader, Raymond appears as the suburban dupe dominated by meddling parents who live across the street. In all of these portrayals, "whiteness" remains central to the master narrative in terms of racial representations. Since the dominance and privilege that come from being white are hardly ever the subject of the stories, the point of media criticism is to call attention to what's missing, how stereotypes are constructed, and how mainstream media narratives come to be taken for granted as "just the way things are."

Class. One of the subtle ways hegemony can work in major media is to marginalize working-class concerns. For example, at many regional newspapers struggling to maintain their profit margins, editors have decided not to cover poverty or working-class issues regularly—in part because the groups affected by economic concerns couldn't afford newspapers and because more affluent suburban readers, who subscribe to papers at much higher percentages, indicated in focus group studies that they would rather read about economic issues that "affect them." In 2006, the *Louisville Courier-Journal*, a Gannett paper, disbanded its Hazard, Kentucky, bureau, which for years covered Appalachia, coal mining, and issues related to that state's poor and rural demographics; the paper, at the time, said it was putting more resources into covering Louisville's suburbs.

In television, popular prime-time network programs rarely wrestle seriously with issues related to economic hardship. Working-class characters dealing with financial marginalization are found most often in network sitcoms, and while shows like *Roseanne* (1988–1997) and the earlier seasons of *The Simpsons* (1989–) have covered these issues with serious shadings, economic hardship is usually treated comically, as on *The Honeymooners* (1955–56) or *My Name Is Earl* (2005–09). When working-class characters appear in the media, they are often depicted as lazy, ignorant, and ill-mannered. In contrast, the American middle- and upper-middle classes have often played a role in a romanticized socioeconomic narrative that privileges those who have either pulled themselves up by their proverbial bootstraps to thrive within capitalism or who never seem to face economic struggle in their daily lives. These narratives often feature the individual, not the community, who achieves greatness through savvy and hard work. This scenario plays out in news stories about successful CEOs (Steve Jobs and Bill Gates), in movies (*The Social Network*), in episodic TV series (*Gossip Girl*), in almost all reality shows (*Secret Millionaire, Undercover Boss*), and in advertising. Meanwhile, as a foil for the middle class, the very rich and famous are also often shown in a negative light: as narcissistic and greedy, even though the world they inhabit is idealized as the epitome of the American dream that is ever-attainable by the savvy, hard-working middle-class characters.

Sexuality. In most mainstream media narratives, the dominance and "normalcy" of heterosexual orientation are typically taken for granted. When gay, lesbian, bisexual, and transgender persons have appeared in prime-time TV programs over the years, their sexual differences—usually portrayed comically—are often part of the narrative intrigue, setting up conflicts with so-called "normal" characters. With gay and lesbian characters, most frequently portrayed as not normal, mainstream values and characters can test their normalcy against so-called "abnormality." Over time, even on more gay-friendly programs like *Will and Grace* (1998–2006), common TV caricatures have included gay men as effeminate, lesbians as chic, bisexuals as confused, and transgender characters as comedic anomalies. Drawing from an informed historic and institutional analysis, a critical approach allows us to question and analyze such depictions by identifying how dominant narratives disguise and support hegemonic values through representations of identity and experience.

INSTITUTIONAL ANALYSIS: WHO GETS TO TELL STORIES OF IDENTITY?

In addition to narrative analysis, our understanding of cultural identity and the power of representation is contingent upon our analysis of the politics and economics of media ownership, production, distribution, and advertising. By examining institutional power in the media, we are able to see how representations of identity are shaped by the perspectives and ideologies of those who fund, write, and transmit stories within society, just as those stories are shaped by the cultural contexts in which they are produced. This means that, in addition to analyzing how stories are represented, we need to correlate such findings with political and economic factors affecting the narrative process.

While media are in the business of producing stories that attract audiences and advertisers, such stories might frequently be told in ways that may not best represent the personal experiences and identities of others. In other words, those who get to tell stories in the media often draw on their own experiences while telling stories about those who are different from them. This can lead to the portrayal of the "Other" as different, as outside of the consensus or master narrative. Since men historically have dominated cultural production, their stories about women often correlate with their own experience rather than with the experiences of women. Likewise, when stories have been told about African Americans, Latinos, or Asian Americans, their narratives are usually mitigated by their perceptions and identities as white rather than through direct or personal experiences from within the communities they are trying to represent. While these narratives and fantasies may not be easily measurable with comparisons in "the real world," they do tell us a lot about the producers. Across media outlets and genres (e.g., news, business, politics, sports, prime-time TV, pay-per-view, video games), many representations have centered the narrative around the experiences of white, straight, middle- to upper-class men. Most other characters in these narratives—including women—tend to serve as foils against which men test their own values, interests, and experiences. It is not surprising then to find patterns of identity stereotypes within mainstream media. In the age of reality TV and cable, however, new stereotypes around privileged upper-class women have mushroomed in series like *Keeping Up with the Kardashians* and various versions of the *Real Houswives of New Jersey* or *The Real Houswives of Atlanta*—just pick a city.

Institutions by the Numbers

According to industry statistics about gender and race in media operations, women and minorities have made some professional advances, although they remain marginalized in media ownership and production. Men maintain the upper echelons of power by comprising roughly 66 percent of supervisory roles, 58 percent of all copy editors, nearly 62 percent of reporters, and 75 percent of photographers.[10] According to the Associated Press Sports Editors' Racial and Gender Report Card, member newspapers received a "C+" rating for racial hiring practices and a "D+" for gender hiring practices in 2012. White males continue to dominate sports journalism, with women serving as 9 percent of sports editors, 17 percent of assistant sports editors, 10 percent of columnists, 12 percent of reporters, and 20 percent of copy editors/designers.[11]

Within American broadcasting, women own less than 7 percent of U.S. commercial broadcast TV and radio stations, and people of color own even less, with 5 percent of TV stations and 8 percent of radio.[12] African American station ownership has decreased to less than 1 percent.[13] According to the Center for Media and Public Affairs, less than a third of evening newscasts (ABC, CBS, NBC) were reported by women in 2007. Their statistics also show that since the 1990s, women have stayed at roughly 40 percent in the television news workforce, with a decrease in radio from 24.4 percent to 22.7 percent.[14] According to the Radio Television Digital News Association, women occupy only 30 percent of news directorships.[15]

According to the *Columbia Journalism Review*, bylines in America's top intellectual and political magazines are predominantly male. A study of eleven magazines published from October 2003 to May 2005 showed favorable male differentials, with thirteen-to-one at the *National Review*, seven-to-one at *Harper's* and the *Weekly Standard*, and two-to-one at the *Columbia Journalism Review*.[16]

In television, the number of women writers on prime-time broadcast programs declined from 29 percent in the 2009–10 season to a mere 15 percent in the 2010–11 season of writers for prime-time dramas, comedies, and reality shows on ABC, CBS, NBC, Fox, and the CW. Women directors also declined to 11 percent from 16 percent in the previous year.[17]

In film, a 2010 study by USC Annenberg Professor Stacy Smith revealed that "females in Hollywood continue to be just as significantly marginalized, hypersexualized and underrepresented as they were thirty years ago,"[18] with males holding 83 percent of positions as directors, writers, and producers. The study also found that the number of female characters increased dramatically when women were given control of film production.[19] A female filmmaker did not win the Academy Award for Best Director until 2010, when Kathryn Bigelow broke through the film industry's glass ceiling by winning for *The Hurt Locker*; in over eighty years of Oscars, she was only the fourth female nominee in that category. Additionally, men write 70 percent of all film reviews published in the top U.S newspapers.[20]

In all of these media categories, when nondominant groups do not hold the political or economic power to tell their own stories about their identities and experiences, gaps in the reflective function of master narratives appear. Likewise, nondominant groups often have little control over the socializing influences that come from the media since they cannot compete with the attention received by commercial media messages. If more diversity existed among artists, scriptwriters, and cultural producers, it wouldn't necessarily lead to an overnight revolution of identity politics in the mainstream; other political and economic structures would likely keep dominant narratives in place. For instance, many women are socialized into male value systems in business, politics, and media production in order to thrive in these industries. However, increasing the pool of cultural producers across gender, race, ethnicity, age, class, and sexuality would help diversify the perspectives from which mainstream images and representations of identity emerge.

There are signs of progressive change in identity narratives in cultural storytelling. Undoubtedly, the representations of race, class, gender, and sexuality are far more diverse today than they were two to three decades ago. Programs like *George Lopez Tonight* (2010–11), *The Ellen Degeneres Show* (2003–), *Modern Family* (2009–), and *Everybody Hates Chris* (2005–09) represent advances in the depictions of minorities. As new technologies and advances in media lead to more expansive and diverse channels, genres, and global perspectives, there is growing evidence that the cultural dominance of the American broadcast networks and film studios has diminished amid shifting economic realities and a more diverse political landscape, altering identity politics.

HISTORIC ANALYSIS: HOW ARE STORIES OF IDENTITY SHAPED BY CULTURE?

It is often harder to critically examine how identities are constructed within contemporary society because, like fish in water, we have become accustomed to the visual and textual cultural codes surrounding us. This makes it harder to detect the process of how and when such images were created and whose visions they represent. One important way of understanding how representations of identity are socially constructed is to look to the past. A historic approach allows us to see how the representations of today have evolved as a result of adaptations in cultural beliefs, events, and institutional power. In this section, our historic analysis will take place within two of the most potent message purveyors of our time: advertising and television. Both offer us ways of exploring narrative storytelling devices through a variety of media texts. Through critical historical analysis, we will better understand how these forms of media simultaneously create powerful narratives and adapt to emerging changes in society.

Going back to John Berger's analysis of women as they have been visually represented in paintings, we will begin with representations of women within the mid-twentieth century, as these narratives coincide with the emergence of television as a groundbreaking medium. Since television's origins in the mid-1950s, producers and executives have often courted their audiences by appealing to an idealized image of the quintessential, wholesome American family. Women have figured prominently in this idealized narrative, particularly in their role as mothers. Although images of women have changed considerably over the course of the last fifty years, the iconography of women continues to carry profound implications within visual culture and our social lives. Exploring these images of gender as they intersect with race, class, and sexuality will help us better understand how representations of identity both reflect the culture from which they emerge (the reflective power of media) and shape the culture through their power as dominant storytellers (the socializing influence of media).

Happy Homemakers, Power Moms, and Superwomen

In early- to mid-twentieth-century ads, women were portrayed in traditional roles—as happy and attractive housewives, homemakers, and mothers who were predominantly white—within a domestic realm that honored suburban femininity. Ads praised women's virtues of family caretaking through household goods and appliances. A 1925 advertisement for Perfection Oil Cook Stoves & Ovens extolled a product that "makes mother a companion" as she can now turn "kitchen time into playtime with husband and children."[21] Westinghouse appealed to women's modernity in 1935 by inviting them to "Interpret the modern spirit of beauty and efficiency" through a washer that would replace their hard toil with "Electric servants for modern homes."[22]

Notice how, in the second ad, the term "electric servants" served as the idiom through which race and class were conjured. As Lynn Spigel explains, when the then-emerging technology of television became a national medium, "the networks continually drew on the image of the white, middle-class family audience when devising programming and promotional strategies."[23] In addition to analyzing such ads within a historical context as post-industrialization celebrations of consumer-oriented caricatures, we can explore how the production of such media representations was about maintaining hegemonic power or leaving undisturbed the "normal"—that is, portraying white, middle-class women in the home, rearing their children and supporting their husbands—inasmuch as it was about the capitalism of selling goods.

This approach also includes a socioeconomic critique that analyzes how these idealized notions of femininity and motherhood promoted the mythic ideal of the middle-class, white, suburban, American family, and how minorities were generally excluded in such representations since they were not perceived to be economically viable or integral to the myth of the American Dream—nor were they in positions of power with any control over who got to tell the culture's stories.

Prior to the 1970s, TV programs and commercials rarely represented women outside of the domestic environment. But when economic changes led to an increase in women's work outside the home, post-1970s constructions of the modern woman within the media assumed that women were only beginning to enter the paid labor force as a result of social progress. Historic analysis helps debunk this media myth. According to feminist scholars and historians, although women were not the dominant gender in paid labor, they were among the first to earn wages in this country as a result of increased urban industrial production after the early-twentieth-century transition from farm and small-town economies. Over time, the proportion of women in paid employment has grown: Women's participation in the paid workforce increased from 10 to 20 percent between 1850 and 1900, and from 30 percent to over 50 percent between 1947 and 1980.[24] Despite the plethora of cultural images of married mothers who stay at home, two-thirds of all mothers have been in the workforce since the mid-1980s, and 58 percent of all married couples with children have both parents working.[25] In addition, according to a 2008 study by the U.S. Bureau of Labor Statistics, employed adult women spent nearly an hour more per day than employed adult men doing household activities and caring for household members.[26]

Even with the great strides women have made in the twenty-first century within the workplace, representations of professional workers favor men in the culture. In an important study of 128 programs that examined one episode of every situation comedy, drama, and reality program airing on the six broadcast networks (ABC, CBS, NBC, Fox, UPN, WB) during the 2005–06 prime-time season, network television was found to reinforce gender stereotypes: Female characters enacted interpersonal roles involved with romance, family, and friends, while male characters were more likely to enact work-related roles. The findings of this study contradict media-induced hype that "women are back," as "broadcast webs have rediscovered the joy of the fairer sex," or that "the New Woman"[27] represents a more progressive type of character. Unfortunately, media claims of fairer representations of women are not supported by social scientific research. One reason for this schism:

> [In] their zeal or perhaps desperation to find a new angle for reporting on television programming, critics and writers often overstate the magnitude of change in portrayals . . . rely[ing] often on high-profile yet anecdotal examples of the fortunes of just a few programs, such as *Grey's Anatomy*, to make their case.[28]

The findings of this study support the conclusions of previous research on prime-time programming airing on the broadcast networks from 1990 to 1998 in which male characters were more likely to work than female characters, with males also having a wider range of jobs than females.[29]

While most early depictions of women kept them at home, important shifts have since taken place in media, echoing (if perhaps belatedly) historical changes. For example, representations of career-driven females in the 1980s and 1990s reflected a change in the status of women. A popular article in *Working Mother* magazine described how women drastically altered the American workplace in that decade:

> They've led the entrepreneurial boom, starting businesses at twice the national average. They've raised their family's standard of living and American's gross national product, increasing median income by 25 percent over the last three decades, according to the Census Bureau. They've redefined the office environment, compelling companies to introduce child care and flextime initiatives. And they've altered the look of the boardroom, with a 79 percent increase over the last four years in the number of companies boasting three or more female directors, according to the nonprofit research group Catalyst.[30]

As for the rise of the TV career woman, as Andrea Press explains in her 1991 book *Women Watching Television*: "Changes in television images have not always paralleled actual changes in society . . . particularly with regard to the depiction of women."[31]

Although Press's research had its roots in the decade prior to the new millennium, this important study was one of the few to explore issues of gender, class, and generation in the American television experience. Using categories that help situate women's roles historically, Press used three distinct modes of feminism to examine women and television from the 1950s to the 1990s. First, "prefeminism" emerged from images of family women almost exclusively in the domestic or private realm. Examples include *I Love Lucy* (1951–57), which on the one hand, showed Lucy—and sidekick Ethel—as resourceful and rebellious to the expectations or rules laid down by their husbands Ricky and Fred but, on the other hand, showed them at home with their ambitions deflated. Although women often demonstrated their authority and competence over their husbands, the middle-class programs of the prefeminism era of television—for example, *I Love Lucy*, *The George Burns and Gracie Allen Show* (1950–58), *I Married Joan* (1952–55), *The Dick Van Dyke Show* (1961–66), *The Donna Reed Show* (1958–1966), and *Father Knows Best* (1954–1963)—nevertheless assigned family authority primarily to the husbands, while women held sway over issues concerning the home. Press notes that only in a few programs depicting the working class were families shown to be "governed by strong, decisive females"— for instance, Alice in *The Honeymooners* (1955–56) or the title character in *Mama* (1949–1957).[32]

In the "feminism" era (late 1960s to the early 1980s), television offered women some new roles, but not without setbacks. In 1968, *Julia* presented what was considered at the time to be an anomaly: an African American, single-parent, professional nurse who succeeded gracefully—but not without embodying traditional Western standards of beauty and white middle-class sensibilities. In 1976,

Lucy and Ethel often conflict with the expectations of Ricky and Fred on *I Love Lucy*.

Charlie's Angels showed that strong career women could seduce audiences, even when occupying roles traditionally allocated to men, but not without flaunting their sexuality and following the orders of an omnipresent off-screen patriarch (much like the disembodied voice in domestic product TV ads—that deep-voiced male narrator who seemed to know his way around a woman's kitchen better than she did). Like *That Girl* (1966–1971), *Mary Tyler Moore* (1970–77) afforded a new image of the city-bound career woman. Yet a glass ceiling prevented Moore's career as a news producer from surpassing her male colleagues or her male boss. Her body image, emotions, and insecurities created a contradictory story about the ability of women to succeed as professionals. In the working-class sitcom *Alice* (1976–1985), a working mother is shown in more complexity. As is typical of many shows in this feminist era, women are shown together working in unison rather than as isolated individuals. Thus, Alice and coworkers Flo and Vera collaborate to overcome the patriarchal tendencies of their boss, Mel.[33]

Finally, the "postfeminism" era (1980s to 1990s) of television constitutes a backlash against the social gains obtained in the women's movement. As feminist scholars Andrea Press, Susan Faludi, and Susan Douglas explain, media representation of this version of postfeminism has occurred in three forms: first, through the proliferation of negative images of the women's movement; second, by personalizing or individualizing solutions to the problems of women; and finally, by commercializing femininity. But the portrayals in network sitcoms of professional women, such as the title character of *Murphy Brown* (1988–1998) and Clair Huxtable in *The Cosby Show* (1984–1992), as well as characters on *Designing Women* (1986–1993), are hyperfeminine. In the case of Clair Huxtable and Murphy Brown, these are "supermom/superwomen" who embody a feminine mystique for the 1980s and early 1990s. While both supermoms are always in control of their familial or work domain, Clair is hardly ever shown at work and Murphy is hardly ever at home.[34]

Herein lies the need for the representation of both possibilities—professional women shown at home and at work in all of their complexities. Such images are virtually absent from traditional network sitcoms, as cable and network TV in general have become overrun with less expensive reality programs. Joanna Powell in 2000 explained the network sitcom dilemma in the lead article for *Working Mother* magazine: "Alice. Roseanne. Cybill. Murphy. Grace. There used to be lots of working mothers on TV. These days, we've all but vanished, and when we do show up we're often job-obsessed, kid-neglecting harridans. What's up with that?"[35]

Hence, whereas *Roseanne* (1988–1997) and *Cybill* (1995–98) once occupied opposite working positions on the TV sitcom dial in terms of socioeconomics (one was working class, one upper middle class), real-life working moms began being replaced by attractive single gals (HBO's *Sex in the City*) who only have their personal aspirations to worry about. Which cable creating more opportunities and competition with successful shows like *Rizzoli and Isles* and *The Closer*, the networks countered with strong and often complex female characters in dramatic hits such as *CSI*, *Grey's Anatomy*, *Bones*, and *The Good Wife*. The slew of reality shows like *Extreme Makeover*, *American Idol*, and *Dancing with the Stars* also feature strong and talented women, although characters in these programs sometimes play out dramatic conventions or to embody normative cultural standards.

One of the few programs to address the sacrifices of working moms at home and the workplace is *The Middle*, featuring Patricia Heaton as Frances "Frankie" Heck. Frankie's character breaks two important stereotypes associated with TV moms: She has a full-time job as a member of the working class and her employment as a car salesperson is within a male-dominated field. Whereas Patricia Heaton's character in *Everybody Loves Raymond* demonstrated the struggles associated with raising a family as a stay-at-home mom, her current role shows a working mom providing for the family. On the program, Frankie is the quintessential middle-class Midwestern American supermom who is overworked at home and at her job. There is little glamour for Frankie, who stresses over her school-age children's lives, her husband's inconsistent employment, elder care, and the buffoonery of her boss and coworkers.

Long-time matriarch of the cartoon world, Marge Simpson (*The Simpsons*, 1989–) has repeatedly tried to follow her heart and pursue a career on and off for over two decades. Yet personal guilt combined with the ineptitude of her son Bart and her husband Homer oblige her to stay at home to keep the family intact. Likewise, on the long-standing comedy series *Everybody Loves Raymond*, the only Top 10 sitcom from 1996 to 2005 to feature parents with children, wife Debra Barone is clearly the rational stronghold of both the nuclear and extended family. Despite her strength as a strong mother who regularly outfoxes Raymond and his family, she also struggles to find a career and often competes with her mother-in-law.

After deconstructing the narrative elements of such programs and applying evaluative criticism of their socialization function, postfeminism programs may seem more problematic than the depictions of stereotypical women, such as Donna Reed of *The Donna Reed Show* and Carol Brady of *The Brady Bunch* (1969–1974). While the judges, attorneys, investigators, news reporters, forensic anthropologists, and actresses on television and in advertisements often can delude us into believing that gender stereotypes are a thing of the past, and that *women can do it all* in much the same manner that Nike ads once encourage us to "Just Do It," such roles also assert a contradiction: that women must remain dedicated nurturers or sex symbols at all times, even if it means denying their own personal and professional ambitions. Joan Peters explains that, "whereas the feminists of the sixties and seventies rejected the

Donna Reed model of womanhood, many of their daughters, rejecting in turn the feminist model, have become 'power moms' or 'super-moms'":

> Power moms may have been sales reps or run companies before their children were born; now, cell-phones in hand, they run their homes. Super-moms can spend the day trading bonds or processing, but they still preside over their homes, making birthday cakes and Halloween costumes even if it takes staying up all night. Believing themselves to be the equals of men, and their motherwork to be more important than any job, these new moms hardly identify with that icon of domesticity who never troubled her pretty little head with bottom lines. They resemble her nonetheless.[36]

Given the reemerging cultural contradictions for women on television, newer representations of women provide complex identities within alternative gender role depictions. Contemporary programs disrupt the evolutionary trajectory for women from prefeminist to feminist to postfeminist representations through self-reflexive critiques of traditional gender roles. For instance, ABC's *Modern Family* (2009–) provides a diverse set of family types and representations across gender, generation, and sexuality (if not class). In a show with perhaps one of the most diverse cast of characters, *Grey's Anatomy* (2005–) portrays a set of strong and qualified professional women in a medical drama. The show's producer, Shonda Rhimes, has stated that her intention was to reflect the broader spectrum of America's diversity on network television.[37]

Although innovative identities do not always emerge consistently across the traditional broadcast networks, cable television and the Internet have become alternate venues for exploring identity. For example, AMC's multiple-award-winning drama *Mad Men* has promulgated a significant amount of discussion and debate about the program's unadulterated sexism in the 1960s workplace. In spite of complex female characters represented in the program, "the men dominate with their infidelity, overt double standards and unchecked sexual harassment."[38] The program fuels gender politics as the men working in the show's ad agency are preoccupied with what women want and how to sell it to them in sexist and stereotypical representations in advertisements. Interestingly, a 2008 study underscored the fact that, even today, few women reach the top levels of advertising agency creative departments, despite the fact that there are a relatively equal number of women and men who enter the field as copywriters and artists.[39]

Similar disparities exist in film; there are only a handful of active female writer-directors making big-studio movies. In a 2009 *New York Times Magazine* feature about women in film, Daphne Merkin wrote "in Hollywood, the glass ceiling is more shatterproof than many in other industries, giving way only when the pressure of accumulated evidence is brought to bear."[40] As an exception to the rule, the article featured the successes of Hollywood director Nancy Meyers, whose films speak to an important demographic usually ignored in film: middle-age women. Despite the predominance of Caucasian characters, Meyers's films, such as *It's Complicated* (2009) and *Something's Gotta Give* (2003), celebrate middle-age women who embrace feminist independence alongside romance and sexuality. Meyers unabashedly explores the sexual appeal of middle-age women in domestic and workplace settings, moving beyond a movie culture dominated by depictions of youth sexuality (e.g., superheroes, vampires, werewolves, and slackers). Although they are in the minority, Hollywood directors such as Nancy Meyers and Nora Ephron have pushed the boundaries of gender and age through films that have grossed well over $200 million each worldwide.

As with fictional depictions, network news, commentary programs, and cable comedy shows (especially *The Daily Show with Jon Stewart* and *The Colbert Report*) cannot ignore identity politics within contemporary contexts. For example, in the 2008 election, there were tensions between race and gender as older generations of feminists who supported Hillary Clinton could not understand why younger generations of women supported Barack Obama. In turn, a younger generation of women—many of whom uphold feminist ideals—could not understand why gender (and race) mattered more than the strengths and qualifications of a presidential leader. Regardless of generational or ideological perspective, the media will undoubtedly continue to shape society's understandings of race, class, gender, sexuality, and other markers of identity as well as reflect the evolution of identity politics in years to come.

Trophy Wives, Masculine Heroes, and Metrosexuals

Whereas women were often judged according to their familial roles and professional ambitions in previous decades, today beauty and sexuality are the new, more pervasive standard by which women—and increasingly men—are judged within media representations and culture at large. In the family, the shift from domestic nurturance to sexual fulfillment is best embodied in the new media iconography of "hot mamas" and "trophy wives" whose sexuality affords husbands libidinal satisfaction within domestic realms and sanctioned heterosexual marriages. The term "trophy wife" conjures up the image of a powerful man's wife who is younger, beautiful, and sexual while retaining the successes of the superwoman/ supermom incarnate of the previous generation. Perhaps the most visible if not extreme trophy-wife image to circulate in the mainstream media was the tabloid stories surrounding oil magnate J. Howard Marshall's marriage to former *Playboy* playmate Anna Nicole Smith: He was eighty-nine years old and she was twenty-six at the time of their marriage.[41] While excessive, the icon of the trophy wife suggests

Anna Nicole Smith

that some women's moral strengths as nurturers and perseverance as superwomen/ supermoms may not be enough: They must now be physically attractive and sexually pleasing within both the domestic and public spheres, regardless of marital or childbearing status.

Such sexualized iconography is the by-product of an infantilized, sexualized ideal within the media at large. Naomi Wolf, author of *The Beauty Myth*, has explained how contemporary media representations exploit younger girls as the new sexualized ideal:

> The notorious Calvin Klein ad campaigns eroticized sixteen-year-olds when I was a teenager, then eroticized fourteen-year-old models in the early nineties, then twelve-year-olds in the late nineties. GUESS Jeans ads now pose what look like nine-year-olds in provocative settings. And the latest fashions for seven- and eight-year-olds re-create the outfits of pop stars who dress like sex workers.[42]

Wolf documented in 2002 how the mainstream media are part of a system of powerful industries that profit from myths of perfection, beauty, and eroticism that annually procure $33 billion through the diet industry, $20 billion through the cosmetics industry, $300 million through the cosmetic surgery industry, and $7 billion in the pornography industry.[43] Pamela Paul noted a similar trend in her book *Pornified* (2005), documenting how the mass media have contributed to a "pornified" culture as a result of hypereroticized sexual representations:

> It's on *Maxim* magazine covers where even women who ostensibly want to be taken seriously as actresses pose like *Penthouse* pinups. It's in women's magazines where readers are urged to model themselves on strippers, articles explain how to work your sex moves after those displayed in pornos, and columnists counsel bored or dissatisfied young women to rent pornographic films with their lovers in order to "enliven" their sex lives. It's on VH-1 shows like *The 100 Hottest Hotties* where the female "experts"—arbiters in judging the world's sexiest people—are *Playboy* centerfolds (the male experts are pop stars and journalists), and on *Victoria's Secret* prime-time TV specials, which attracted a record nine million viewers in 2003. Soft core pornography has now become part and parcel of mainstream media.[44]

This development has been especially prevalent in the music industry, where rock, rap, and pop musicians have used porn as standard vernacular in their marketing. As Paul documents, performers such as Eminem, Kid Rock, Blink 182, Metallica, Everclear, and Bon Jovi have included porn actresses in their music videos. Younger female artists, such as Britney Spears, Katy Perry, and Christina Aguilera mimic porn star moves as part of their media performances.[45]

The fact that the pornography industry is predominantly supported by men is not just a measure of women's subjugated position in the culture: It also attests to new standards men are pressured to strive for in order to assert their heterosexuality. It's important to keep in mind that changes in media representations often signal a change in the sociopolitical/socioeconomic culture. In much the same way that hypermasculine body types emerged in sports, media, and commercialism at a time when women were entering the workforce and demanding equality, the representation of hypersexualized males in media products has transpired at the moment that images of gay, lesbian, bisexual, and transgender identities have become more mainstream in popular culture, but especially in advertising imagery.

Within media narratives that appeal to a heteronormative audience, ads for Viagra and Cialis are now standard fare, and men are routinely measured by their sexual potency and physique through idealized male models and body-builders. Shari Lee Dworkin and Faye Linda Wachs explained in "The Morality/Manhood Paradox: Masculinity, Sport, and the Media" that in sports, male athletes with muscled bodies have been associated with moral superiority and heroism, which brings about social and economic privileges in addition to those of gender. Yet a gender paradox persists with the heterosexual male athlete:

Print media coverage rarely if ever acknowledges norms in sports or in U.S. culture at large that equates masculinity with sexual prowess. Sexual access to women is a cultural privilege associated with being a [heterosexual] man, yet, in turn, the powerful then use this privilege to stigmatize subordinated masculinities [gay men] and women [while dominant men remain invisible to the watchful media eye].[46]

There has been a shift in media coverage of high-profile cases featuring the sexual misconduct of athletes, coaches, and politicians. Added scrutiny to such male figures reflects important shifts in media coverage of gender and sexuality. Even so, some men accused of sexual misconduct, such as Tiger Woods and Newt Gingrich, eventually get a "pass" by returning to male-dominated realms of sports and politics, while members of nondominant groups often find it more difficult to overcome such privilege.

While the dominant masculine hegemony is predicated on old clichés of sexual potency and muscular physique, the acceptance of gays and lesbians in the media has changed to some degree with the advent of the "metrosexual"—an urban male with a strong aesthetic sense who spends a great deal of time and money on his appearance and lifestyle. The alliance between and among identity groups regardless of sexual orientation signals a growing acceptance of gays among younger generations. In fact, according to media scholars, gays and lesbians have achieved an equality far greater in mainstream media than that found in the political and social realm.[47] Communications scholar Katherine Sender examines how advertising and marketing geared to the gay community since the early 1990s have helped members of the LGBT community gain visibility while also constituting an imagined community through a commercially driven media system. While she acknowledges that niche marketing leads to problems of stereotyping and commodification, she explores how gay marketing has ultimately helped advance a sense of community and political activism within the gay, lesbian, bisexual, and transgender community.[48]

Despite such gains in queer visibility, such positive depictions enhance profits also. As Fred Fejes explains:

> While in the past other marginalized groups have attained political power through the marshaling of economic resources, for lesbians and gay males it is not in their role as producers or controllers of capital, but in their role as consumers, particularly as a defined market niche attractive to advertisers, that they are offered the surest route to equality.[49]

Marguerite Moritz goes further in her critique by analyzing trendy discourses of "lesbian chic" in mainstream media that glamorize lesbianism through a focus on normative standards of beauty, appearance, and sexual attractiveness as a means to titillate straight male viewers instead of validating marginalized identity. She explains how such strategies are part of the mainstream media's attempt not only to "deny lesbians a real voice in the culture but also to construct them in the same sexualized and sexist ways that [images of] women in general have been formulated."[50] She warns that, while we may want to celebrate lesbians' inclusion in the media as a sign of social progress, they can just as quickly disappear from mainstream cultural representation if they are not viewed as a viable market or demographic.[51]

BECOMING THE MEDIA: PARTICIPATORY CULTURE AND NEW IDENTITIES

As we have learned, master narratives offer powerful stories that can colonize our conceptions of identity—but also liberate our imagination as we explore new possibilities for our "selves" as individuals and community members in the twenty-first century. The emphasis in this chapter has been to offer this broad analysis of media's representational power and to affirm an approach that recognizes the media's reflective and socializing influence. We've suggested that, through the prisms of gender, race, class, and sexuality, the media often reproduce master narratives using stereotypes and exclusion. We have examined the ways in which historic traditions, practices, and perspectives of marginalized groups, in relation to dominant cultures, are represented in popular culture. This process has allowed us to identify, analyze, and understand how these structures of identity politics are interpreted, created, manifested, represented, and claimed in contemporary commercial culture.

Although identity exclusions and misrepresentations in mass-produced culture remain visible, there are discernible shifts that serve to loosen the media's grasp of traditional femininity, hegemonic masculinity, middle-class ideals, privileged whiteness, and normative heterosexuality. First, media scholars recognize that identity politics are products of media representations and are therefore unstable and subject to change. Second, attention to diversity and multiculturalism have prompted new social discourses of inclusivity and visibility for nondominant groups in mainstream media, even if propelled by the commercial quest for increased ratings, niche marketing, and profitability.

As a result, while stereotypes persist across media, there are openings in the seamlessness of dominant narratives and representations. "Sensitive new-age guys" (SNAGS) are more prevalent across media, as more and more men are interested in family life and meaningful relationships. Men—often portrayed as dummies and losers in advertisements and TV programs—suggest the need for competent women to save both them and the world from their idiocy! Minorities are more visible as leaders and equals, particularly in reality shows, news reporting, and niche marketing. Homosexuals are afforded their share of representation through niche marketing and specialty programming. And the poor and working class are often shown as deserving of government aid when disasters like Hurricane Katrina and the subprime loan crisis occur or when hard times prompt the media to participate in community-based charitable causes (e.g., ABC's *Extreme Makeover* and *Oprah*). While dominant discourses are in place as the primary structures of power in mainstream media, these alternate narrative texts—especially enabled by the wide-open and noncommercial sectors of the Internet—offer a more nuanced way of negotiating identity politics and modeling real cultural change.

Third, in addition to cracks and fissures within mainstream texts, audiences play an important role in determining the impact of media discourses. They can rely upon the media to define their own sense of self and view of the world (the preferred hegemonic reading), they can be skeptical and savvy about their content and influence while also relying on them to help them navigate their social understandings (negotiated readings), or they can contest and reject them (resistant readings).[52] Increasingly, newer generations view the mainstream media as straitjackets that restrict mobility and creativity in defining oneself and others. Through media literacy and a proficiency in media production, today's generation is increasingly "becoming the media" rather than solely depending on it. New technologies—computers, smartphones, Web sites, online social networking, wikis, blogs—have complicated identity politics, as individuals and subcultural groups create more complex and detailed selves through interconnectivity and play.

From Facebook to iMovie to YouTube, people are using popular music, films, TV episodes, clips, and sites from mainstream and alternative media to express themselves and create multiple identities. This influences the function and meaning of mainstream culture: Audiences interact and play with social discourses and media content, while simultaneously altering meaning through collage, poetry, parody, and personalizing the narrative elements that shape cultural stories. Using a mélange of alternative and mainstream media from both original and borrowed fragments of culture, our selves and our identities are continually constructed in the practices of everyday life by active, participatory audiences who consume and interact with a variety of media texts. Today's audiences—often aided or driven by newer forms of social media—are electronic global trekkers who venture to new territories to discover innovative identities and cultural influences where they can interact with others across new temporal and spatial lines.

While the power and pervasiveness of mainstream media will forever shape our cultural understandings of ourselves and others in society, participatory cultural production will undoubtedly continue to alter the course and terrain of identity politics, cultural representation, and master narratives in the coming years.

| CRITICAL PROCESS 1 | Disney Representations

The goal of this exercise is to understand more about how movies aimed at children or family audiences represent women, men, and relationships. Pick a favorite Disney movie—or a popular family film made by another company—and make notes about the male and female characters in the movie.

Describe their gendered traits of the characters. Make lists of each.

Analyze how the male/female relationships in the movie change over the course of the story. Are there common threads and patterns in the portrayals of male and female characters? Are there shifts in the male/female dynamics or do they remain more or less the same? If they shift, what kinds of changes happen in service of the story? Does the story follow any of the narrative patterns or formulas discussed in Chapter 4?

Interpret the larger stories that this movie tells about gender and love. How might the world of the movie be applied to real-life notions about men, women, and romantic relationships? In this movie what does it mean to be a women, to be a man?

Evaluate the movie's ideas about women and men. Are they true for you or people you know? Did you once believe these suppositions about gender but now question them? Or are they still an ideal? What characters are portrayed in the most positive light? What characters are portrayed in the worst? Why do you think the film makers chose to depict these characters this way.

Engage with classmates about the influence of this movie (or similar ones) on their understanding of love and gender. Compare your list of gendered character traits with theirs.

| CRITICAL PROCESS 2 | Representations in Parody

Parody and satire are ways that we recognize and play with representation. The goal of this exercise is to analyze both an original narrative and the parody of it to explore how narratives work in our lives. Choose an original song, advertisement, or movie scene that has been parodied. For example, Weird Al Yankovic has spent his life parodying popular songs; the "Campaign for Real Beauty" by Dove Soap spawned multiple parodies on YouTube; Star Wars has offered multiple opportunities for imitation and ridicule; and *The Colbert Report* opening sequence parodies a stereotypical Fox News opening sequence using images of flags and eagles accompanied by soaring music to "out-patriotize" the originals.

Describe the original narrative and then the parody. What are the differences between the serious, original representation and the mocking one? List them.

Analyze those differences. What patterns emerge? Does parody work as a new form of a narrative? Why or why not? What does this parody have in common with the traits of satire outlined in Chapter 4?

Interpret how the authors of the parody or satire felt about the original work. Does their rendering feel affectionate? Angry? What is the effect of parody on the original—does seeing the parody make the original somehow seem different?

Evaluate the parody's success in imitating and spoofing the original work. Consider ways that parody and satire are now shaping media, news, and politics—is everything up for grabs, available for ridicule? Should it be? What does the parody do well? What does it do poorly?

Engage by trying to construct a parody of something that you currently take seriously and value. This exercise might work best as a group project where you parody an ad or a news story with classmates. Notice how parody requires a deep familiarity with narrative style and convention—it may be an act of homage and respect as well as ridicule.

10

Technology, Convergence, and Democracy

In the run-up to the presidential election in 2012, a major narrative in campaign speeches and political ads was articulated by GOP candidate Mitt Romney in the wake of the Nevada primary caucus "President Obama wants to fundamentally transform America. We [the GOP] want to restore to America the founding principles that made the country great."[1] The central conflict driving the political spin in this narrative is the pitting of change against tradition. Such a narrative also explains, in part, why the "mainstream media" often face persistent criticism from conservative political leaders and media figureheads. If the media act fundamentally as narrators of change in our society—which is a central argument in this book—then it is easy for them to be seen not only as agents of modern change but as agents of liberal causes.

The paradox of this particular narrative, however, is that even as some politicians champion reactionary politics and resistance to change, they embrace technological innovation—certainly a major agent of change in our contemporary world. Conservative politicians still set up Twitter accounts and Facebook pages. They have smartphones. They read the news online. They embrace raising money via the Internet, a centerpiece in any modern political campaign.

This political paradox is part of society's paradoxical relationship with technology. We might criticize the way some people sit glued to their screens, losing themselves in a video game or checking their cell phones during in-person conversation. We revere words like *natural, real,* and *authentic,* while we are suspicious of words like *synthetic, artificial,* and *manufactured.* On the other hand, most of us like gadgets. We like the ease of e-mail and texting, and fast access to Internet information. We like our handy smartphones when we can't remember that grocery store item or when we're driving late at night and seek the comfort of a familiar voice. We like our NPR news or our audio books on those congested drives to work or school. We like watching whatever *Simpsons* episode we want, whenever we want; we like catching up with old friends on Facebook; we like checking our up-to-the-second

Twitter feeds. We like our satellite TVs, our printer-scanners, our digital display exercise bikes, our microwave popcorn, our Blu-ray discs, and our DVRs that can skip through commercials. We like our cars. And we like the way technology can keep us informed in terrible times, whether it's tracking missing soldiers during wartime or relaying stories about natural disasters like Hurricane Katrina or human tragedies like the Boston Marathon bombings.

Everyday life has become so technically complex that we use one machine to blot out another. We put on headphones to block out street noise and the rumble of traffic. We call a state or federal agency to ban those exasperating telemarketers from interrupting our favorite TV show. We grab the TV remote to mute that annoying local used-car salesman. We get in our cars to escape to the country and away from the neon hustle of urban living.

This love-hate relationship with technology marks one key paradox of contemporary society. We are nostalgic for the pace of the past at the same time we drive headlong into the future, overloaded by our gadgets—most of them having indeed made our lives, if not better, at least more convenient. As mentioned in Chapter 1, Amazon.com represents this paradox as a giant digital retailer that started out selling the oldest mass medium, the book. But another paradox of contemporary life—one that speaks to the state of democratic life—is the way the Internet potentially fragments us. That is, we now live in a world where there is no longer the shared common culture of the daily news or shared stories aired on just three major networks. Whereas a large percentage of Americans once relied heavily on such similar cultural touchstones, today our media use—except in those times of national tragedies or cultural ritual (108 million of us in the United States tuned in to the Super Bowl in 2013—among the largest TV audiences in U.S. history)—is marked mostly by our individual interests.[2] Has a shared sense of community or nationhood been undermined by the ways our cultural pursuits are now driven by personal choice, whether it is the specialty magazine about golf or a particular chef on a satellite-delivered channel or the narrow politics of a news blog or cable news talking head? In a nation as diverse, stratified, and politically divided as ours, technology has made it possible to pursue only those things that interest us as individuals, which may obscure the daily common cultural ground we require to talk about the kind of society and democracy we want.

In this chapter, we address the ways new technologies have enhanced or harmed our lives both as consumers and as citizens. First, we trace the history of our transformation from a production-oriented to a consumption-driven society, relying on the concept of media convergence and the stages through which new media technology develop. Next, we examine closely the impact and influence of our newest media—particularly the Internet—inspecting issues ranging from technical convergence to economic consolidation. Finally, we return to questions surrounding the complicated and paradoxical relationship between technology and democracy.

FROM AN INDUSTRIAL AGE TO THE INFORMATION ERA

In Europe and America in the late nineteenth century, the rise of modern industries and new machines revolutionized social life as factories replaced farms as the main centers of work and production. During the 1880s, roughly 80 percent of Americans lived on farms and in small towns; by the 1920s and 1930s, much of this population had shifted to urban areas, where new industries and economic opportunities beckoned. The city had overtaken the country as the focus of national life. The gradual arrival of the modern Industrial Age usually refers to the period spanning the development of the steam engine in the 1760s to mass assembly-line production of the early to mid 1900s, an era that transformed and was transformed by manufacturing and consumer culture.

In America, this major shift from an industrial, print-based society to an Information Era began with the development of the telegraph in the 1840s. Telegraph technology made four key contributions to communication. First, "it permitted for the first time the effective separation of communication from transportation," making media messages instantaneous—unencumbered by stagecoaches, ships, or the pony express.[3] Second, the telegraph, in combination with the rise of mass-marketed newspapers, transformed "information into a commodity, a 'thing' that could be bought or sold irrespective of its uses or meaning."[4] By the Civil War, news had become a valuable product, foreshadowing its contemporary role as a communication form that is both enormously profitable and overwhelmingly ubiquitous. Third, the telegraph made it easier for military, business, and political leaders to coordinate commercial and military operations, especially after the installation of the transatlantic cable in the late 1860s. Finally, the telegraph prefigured future technological developments, such as the fax machine and the cellular phone. The dot-and-dash symbols of Morse code telegraphy foreshadowed the one-and-zero binary code combinations of digital communication in our own time.

The rise of film at the turn of the twentieth century and the development of radio in the 1920s were early signposts, but the electronic phase of the Information Age really developed in the 1950s and 1960s. The dramatic impact of television on daily life marked the arrival of a new visual and electronic era. With the coming of the latest communication gadgetry—cable television, DBSs (direct-broadcast satellites or services), fax machines, ever smaller personal computers, cell phones, electronic mail, DVDs, DVRs—the modern Information Era entered its a digital phase. In digital communication, images, texts, and sounds are converted (encoded) into electronic signals (represented as varied combinations of binary numbers—ones and zeroes), which are then reassembled (decoded) as a precise reproduction of, say, a TV picture, a magazine article, a song, or a telephone voice. Electronic innovations, for instance, included hand-cranked and later rotary-dial telephones, whereas digital innovations handed us Touch-Tone technology. On the Internet's multitudinous Web pages, image, text, and sound are all digitally reproduced and transmitted globally.

New electronic and digital technologies, particularly cable television and the Internet, have developed so quickly that traditional business and political leaders in communication have faced challenges to their control over information. For example, in the 1992 and 1996 presidential campaigns the news networks first began to lose their influence and audience to cable's CNN, Comedy Central, and MTV as well as to radio talk shows and Internet communities. Moreover, the technology of e-mail, which has assumed much of the functions of "snail-mail" postal services, has outraced attempts to control it within national borders. A professor sitting at her desk in Tulsa, Oklahoma, can instantly send a message to a research scientist in Zagreb, Croatia, who can now respond without fear—most of the time—of government agents opening the mail. As recently as the early 1990s, written letters between the two might have taken months to reach their destinations.

Converging and Evolving New Media

As the millennium turned, the merging of the electronic and digital eras fostered a whole new direction in mass media—the age of **media convergence**. Media convergence refers to the appearance of older media forms on the newest media channels—for example, magazine articles or TV programs now accessible on the Internet. But this convergence is not particularly new. Back in the late 1920s, the Radio Corporation of America (RCA) purchased the Victor Talking Machine Company and ushered in machines that could play both radio and recorded music. Then in the 1950s, the radio and recording industries again teamed up, with radio using records to replace the content—quiz shows, sitcoms, dramas, national sponsors—that it had lost to television. Meanwhile, the new magazine *TV Guide* made television its content and reached multimillion print circulation figures rivaled at the time only by *Reader's Digest*.

Media convergence is also much broader than the simple merging of older and newer forms along an information highway. In fact, the various eras of communication are themselves reinvented in the Age of the Internet. An older era of oral communication, for example, finds itself reconfigured, in part, as e-mail, instant messaging, and Twitter. Print communication finds itself re-formed in the thousands of newspapers now available worldwide in digital formats for our tablets and computers. Meanwhile, electronic communication forms such as television and radio are being reimagined in the form of YouTube clips and video blogs and podcasts, as well as excerpts from traditional TV or cable programs recirculated with streaming online video.

Although convergence offers the promise to citizens of wide choice and flexible control over how we use and access media, another definition of media convergence describes a particular business model that is favored by corporate interests. In this model, convergence is about consolidating various media holdings—say, cable connections, phone services, television transmissions, and Internet access—under one corporate umbrella. Here the goal is not necessarily to offer consumers more choice but to better manage resources, cut staffs, and maximize profits. For example, a company that owns TV stations, radio outlets, and newspapers in multiple markets—as well as in the same cities—can deploy a reporter or producer to create three or four versions of the same story for various media outlets. So rather than each radio station, TV station, newspaper, and online news site all generating diverse and independent stories about an issue vital to a community or city, a converged media company can now use fewer employees to generate multiple versions of the same story. This means a company employing a convergence model needs fewer reporters, producers, and editors—not more. So fewer stories generated under this business arrangement means less citizen choice in terms of news coverage. This model offers more profits to those companies that figure out how to downsize—or converge—their workforce, and at the same time they increase their media holdings in many markets.

Marked then by both the technical and economic convergences, our so-called Information Era has barely begun. Most mass media do evolve through various stages, which are initiated not only by the diligence of smart inventors, such as Thomas Edison, but by social, cultural, political, and economic circumstances. For instance, both telegraph and radio developed as newly industrialized nations sought to expand military and economic control over colonies and to transmit information more rapidly and conveniently. The phonograph too emerged in part because of the social and economic conditions of a growing middle class with more money and leisure time. Today, the Internet is a contemporary response to similar sets of concerns: transporting messages more rapidly and conveniently while appealing to middle- and upper-middle-class consumers.

NEW MEDIA: INNOVATION, IMPACT, AND INFLUENCE

Typically, media innovations emerge roughly in four phases. First is a **development stage** in which inventors and technicians try to solve a particular problem, such as making pictures move, transmitting voices across space without wires, or sending mail electronically. Second is the **entrepreneurial phase** in which inventors and investors determine a practical and marketable use for the new technology. The Internet, for instance, was originally developed by the military as a widely distributed communication system—that could survive natural disasters or, more importantly, nuclear attacks on a central command post like the Pentagon.

The third phase in a new medium's development involves a breakthrough to the **mass medium stage**. At this point, entrepreneurial managers figure out how to market the new technology as an appealing product for the home or office. In the case of the Internet, Pentagon and government researchers developed the prototype, but commercial interests extended its reach nationally and globally. With the release of the World Wide Web in 1991, and the introduction of user-friendly graphic browsers like Mosaic in 1993 and Netscape in 1994, the Internet entered its mass medium stage.

Finally, the fourth and latest phase in a medium's evolution is the **convergence stage**. In this stage older media like magazines are reconfigured in various forms like digital tablets. But this does not mean that these older forms disappear. For example, we can still get the *USA Today* in print, but it is also now accessible on laptops and smartphones via the Internet. During this stage, we see the merging of many different media forms onto online platforms, but we also see the *mass* in mass media dissipate as the large so-called mass audience fragments into smaller targeted market segments. For example, at the height of TV's Network Era in the 1960s and 1970s,

Mass media of today can reach us in an ever-expanding variety of formats—often converged into single multimedia devices.

the bulk of the mass audience watched one of the three major networks. But as cable and satellite TV programmers developed hundreds of new channels and services, and as millions of new Web sites exploded on the Internet, the audience—now with thousands of choices beyond the three original TV networks—spread out in many different directions.

For media in society, the central questions raised by the evolution of contemporary media and technology have to do with their impact on democratic life: whether we are more or less involved in the political decisions of our nation, especially in times of national crises; whether we all have fairly equal access to this technology; and whether that technology has so fragmented us that, while we seem interconnected, we are also isolated from one another in totally new ways. In this section we take up these questions, focusing primarily on our newest medium, the Internet, as a case study for what the digital world has wrought and how it has impacted not only our other mass media but the very nature of democratic life.

Media, Military, and Technical Solutions

Just as radio developed in part as a solution to get messages to military ships at sea (which, of course, could not be reached by telegraph poles), the Internet too had military origins. The "information highway," like the physical interstate highway system, originated with military-government planning and with national security as one of its goals. Begun in the late 1960s by the Defense Department's Advanced Research Projects Agency (ARPA), the original Internet—called ARPAnet (and nicknamed the Net)—enabled military and academic researchers to communicate on a decentralized network system. The design of what would become the Internet differed from the centralized style of telephone communication at the time, whereby calls were routed through a central switcher. A more decentralized and broadly distributed network system offered two advantages to the researchers and military units developing the Internet. First, because multiple paths linked one computer site to another, communications traffic would be less likely to get clogged at a single point. This helped convince computer researchers in the 1960s to sign on to the network project—they could share research and data on the new network without their computers becoming overrun by the traffic of others' messages. Second, because this network was like an interconnected web, the Internet offered a communication system that seemed more impervious to technical errors, natural disasters, or military attacks. If a bridge was out on one road of the highway, Internet traffic could be rerouted.

Ironically, one of the most hierarchically structured and centrally organized institutions in our culture, the national defense industry, created the Internet, probably the least hierarchical and most decentralized social and technical network ever conceived. Each computer hub in the Internet has similar status and power, so nobody can own the system outright and nobody has the power to run all others off the network. There's no master power switch, no Internet police force that can shut down the Internet (although some authoritarian nations do control computer hubs and servers).

During its developmental stage, the military computer network permitted different people in separate locations to communicate with one another. By simply leasing existing telephone lines, they used the system to send e-mail and to post information on computer bulletin boards, sites that list information about particular topics such as health issues, computer programs, or employment services. At this stage, the Internet was primarily used by universities and government research labs, and later by corporations—especially companies involved in computer software and other high-tech products—to transmit and receive text information.

By 1982, the Internet hit its entrepreneurial stage: The National Science Foundation invested in a high-speed communications network designed to link computer centers around the country. This innovation led to a dramatic increase in Internet use. Then, after the dissolution of the Soviet Union in the late 1980s, the ARPA-net military venture officially ended. By that time, however, a growing network of researchers, computer programmers, commercial interests, and amateur hackers had tapped into the Internet, creating tens of thousands of decentralized side roads and intersections. As the military had predicted, the absence of a central authority meant that the Internet could not be knocked out. By 1993, the Internet had developed its convergence capabilities, enabling users to transmit pictures, sound, and video. This technology slowed down computer performance at first, but with the emergence of high-speed cable broadband and rapid DSL lines offered by telephone and electric companies, we have come to expect our Internet access today to be instantaneous. And we are annoyed when it is not.

Just as most radio pioneers did not foresee the medium's potential, many innovators of the Internet did not predict how rapidly its mass appeal would spread beyond military and research interests. They also did not foresee that the convergence stage of this medium had the potential to both connect us and insulate us from one another. During the 1990s, the number of Internet users started doubling and then tripling each year, and this growth drew the attention of commercial interests who did see the potential of creating all these new smaller niche markets that could be isolated and targeted. Companies searching for ways to profit from the increased traffic on the Internet hoped to turn each user into a consumer by hawking products, providing services, and selling ad space. Governments also established Internet sites, providing information online, posting important documents, and distributing such items as tax forms.

In the United States, the Internet has also been heralded for embracing the public's right to know, with thousands of government documents posted for easy public access. However, after 9/11, that effort was severely curtailed, as the U.S. government moved to restrict seemingly benign public information, such as Clean

Air Act reports on industrial sites, for fear that such information would be used for terrorist purposes. Elsewhere, in nations such as China, the world's millions of online users have generally circumvented attempts to block some information. In fact, many users take advantage of the Internet's ability to cross borders, circulating banned or controversial writing or art that may have been suppressed by authoritarian governments. This ability to subvert centralized authority is one of the early democratic promises that Internet technology has actually delivered on.

A New Media Model

Preceding the development of the Internet, cable television had begun altering the media landscape by redefining the concept of **narrowcasting**—moving away from the mass audience by providing specialized programming for diverse and fragmented groups. This development slowly cut into traditional TV "broad"-casting's coveted and large prime-time audience. For the advertising industry too cable TV programs provide access to specific target audiences that could not be guaranteed by the big broadcasting giants. For example, golf-equipment manufacturers can buy ads on the Golf Channel and reach only golf enthusiasts. Or Fox News executives can market their own brand of "fair and balanced" news and opinion that appeals to more politically conservative viewers. Because the audiences are now smaller and specialized, ads are sold at a fraction of the cost of a 1980s network ad; they reach only the targeted viewers and not the larger general public. As cable channels have become more and more like specialized magazines or radio formats, they have siphoned off viewers from ABC, CBS, and NBC, undermining the networks' former role as programmers-in-chief, providing shared stories in our common culture (particularly during the period from the mid-1950s to the early 1980s).

So when cable emerged to challenge traditional broadcasting in the 1970s, expectations were high, not unlike today's expectations for the Internet. Offering more than new competition, cable's increased channel capacity provided the promise of access. With more government, educational, and public-access channels, cable at first seemed to promise the possibility of vibrant debate, allowing ordinary citizens a voice via television. Local nonprofit access channels have, in fact, provided some opportunities for citizens to participate in democracy and even create their own programs. But by the late 1990s, political leaders in major metropolitan areas like Kansas City decided that access channels were no longer required for cable franchises. For the most part, cable and now direct broadcast satellite, or DBS, services (like DirecTV or Dish TV) have come to follow the one-way broadcast model: Their operators choose programming from hundreds of for-profit service providers like CNN and ESPN, with little input from citizens and consumers. This means most of us purchase monthly subscriptions to expensive packages or tiers of programming (most of which we never watch) rather than just paying for those services and channels we actually watch.

The Internet improves enormously on the cable subscription model, offering mostly free services and delivering on the early interactive potential of cable. Considering the information highway metaphor allows us to imagine our more traditional media—books, newspapers, television, and radio—as an older interstate highway system now outdated and overrun by sprawling growth and under-construction new developments. In addition, many side roads along the highway are virtually unregulated, open to all kinds of opportunities, mischief, crime, and pornography.

Unlike highways built by federal and state governments, however, the information highway has been taken over and expanded by private enterprise, although it was initially established and subsidized by the government. What difference does this make? If we look to the history of another medium, we know that, when private commercial managers took over radio broadcasting in the 1920s and 1930s (through the creation of RCA), they helped build the United States into the world's foremost producer of communication technology and content. At the same time, though, they dramatically thwarted the growth of nonprofit (labor, religion, civic groups, etc.) and educational broadcasting. They did this, in part, by linking their commercial interests to "America's interests" and by portraying nonprofit radio operators as "special interests." In other words, they conflated capitalism with democracy and persuaded the newly created FCC that market agendas had priority over noncommercial concerns and the "special interests" of labor, religious, and educational institutions.[5]

Certainly the Internet, like cable, demonstrated early democratic promise, primarily because it was so decentralized and so interactive. With the opportunity for anyone to send an e-mail, blog, or enter a chat room, the Internet offers a voice to the voiceless—an early ideal that drove cable's development of government, education, and local public-access channels. But the full impact of the Internet and the expanding information highway, like that of radio and other mass media, has not yet played out. Cable TV, for example, which operated in only 13 percent of American households in 1975, took nearly twenty years to reach 60 percent of U.S. homes. The Web has had a much more rapid ascent to mass-medium status: More than 60 percent of U.S. households were connected to the Internet by 2002, just ten years after the introduction of the first Web browsers. By 2012, more than 90 percent of U.S. households had Internet access.

Though it has echoes of cable and other earlier mass media, the Internet is unique in that few limits exist on how much content it can support. For example, the last print edition of the *Encyclopædia Britannica* had 65,000 articles that came from 4,000 expert sources; *Wikipedia* in 2012 had over 3.8 million articles—and 750,000 contributors.[6] Although it's difficult to fully assess how the Internet is changing the world, it became very clear after the 9/11 terrorist attacks how ingrained online communication had become in global economies, politics, and cultures. Millions around the world turned to the Internet that day to find information on the attacks and communicate with others. Later, it became clear that while it has worked to help relief agencies in aiding victims of terror, the Internet has also served as a covert message conduit and recruiting tool for global terrorism. Then, when Katrina hit in 2005, the Internet served as a message board to help reunite scattered evacuees from New Orleans and other small and large communities ravaged by the hurricane and flooding.

The Internet remains a major medium for the global economy. But the slowing of the dot-com business world in 2000 and the 9/11 attacks a year later led to new cautionary tales about the Internet. In October 2001, the United States enacted the Patriot Act, an antiterrorism law that granted sweeping new powers to law enforcement agencies for tracking Internet banking and transfers of money and for intercepting computer communications, including e-mail messages and Web browsing activity. Although there was widespread public criticism that the Patriot Act was a response to fear and made us less free, Congress renewed the Act in 2006. Other nations followed the United States' lead on increasing Internet surveillance. Today, the debate over security measures versus civil liberties continues and will shape communication on the Internet and in the entire world for years to come.

As governments, corporations, and public and private interests vie to control the evolution of this relatively new medium, answers to many questions remain ambiguous. Who will have access to the Internet, who or what will attempt to manage it, and what are the implications for democracy? The task for critical media consumers is to sort through competing predictions about the Internet and new technology, analyzing and determining how the "new and improved" Information Age can best serve the majority of citizens and communities.

These rapid technological advances pose a major challenge to cable TV and other more traditional media. With its ability to support both personal conversation and mass communication, Internet convergence with other mass media has broken down conventional and historical distinctions among media and between private and public modes of communication.

Internet Innovations and the Web

The Internet embodies convergence, and three innovations in particular make the Internet a distinct medium. First, it is interactive, enabling receivers to respond almost immediately to senders' messages. Second, its various sites enable many traditional media, such as books, magazines, and films, to appear on computer or smartphone screens. Third, it allows individuals inexpensively to create and distribute their own messages, authorizing users to become significant producers rather than just passive consumers of media content.

The Internet has blurred the boundary between point-to-point communication (like the telephone) and mass communication (like television). It has linked home, school, and business computers, TV sets, radios, iPods, CD and DVD recorders and players, DVRs, digital cameras, e-mail, video games, scanners, newspapers, fax machines, magazines, communications satellites, smartphones, and tablets. This capability makes it theoretically possible for anyone to become a player—from cable TV companies and regional telephone providers to computer-software firms and individual entrepreneurs. But the new convergences have had the greatest impact on two more personal communications media—the telephone and the personal computer—that both developed primarily as forms of point-to-point or personal communication, not as mass communication. Both, however, have become central players in the digital media revolution.

The key innovation in taking the Internet from its developmental and entrepreneurial phases to the mass media and convergence stages was the introduction of the World Wide Web. Developed in the 1980s by software engineer Tim Berners-Lee, the Web was initially a text-only data-linking system that allowed computer-accessed information to associate with, or link to, other information no matter where it was on the Internet. Known as "hypertext," this data-linking feature of the Web was a breakthrough for those attempting to use the Internet. Hypertext is a nonlinear way of organizing information, enabling a user to click on a highlighted word, phrase, picture, or icon and skip directly to other files related to that subject in other computer systems.

The millions of pages, or sites, on the Web can be designed on an ordinary word-processing program that has a feature for writing hypertext commands and can communicate everything from a point of view to a job résumé to consumer product information. To navigate the Web, directory services like Yahoo! or search engines like Google help us find our way around; they rely on people to review and catalogue Web sites, creating categories with hierarchical topic structures that can be browsed. Search engines and directories maintain staffs of paid editors to review the sites, whereas open directory projects like *Wikipedia* depend on armies of volunteers from around the world to stay credible and up-to-date. Search engines offer a different route to finding content by allowing users to enter key words or queries to locate related Web pages. Google has emerged as the key search engine to the Web. Developed by two Stanford University students in the mid-1990s, Google is today among the most valuable brand names in the world. The company's motto—"Don't be evil"—worked well in the early days when Google was a small search engine taking on the near monopoly power of Microsoft. But things are different today as Google has grown into a multibillion-dollar corporation, facing its own charges of monopoly, as well as concerns about its ability to guard privacy rights. Critics worry that as the company expands globally it has been more willing to make compromises that have co-opted its motto. For example, Google's cooperation with the Chinese government's attempts to censor its critics has drawn worldwide attention. When it first began doing business there, Google made a controversial agreement with China's political leaders to censor search results. But after several years of feuding with the government over these issues, in 2010 Google set up a link on its censored and China-approved ".cn" domain, Google.cn, to an uncensored Web site located in Hong Kong—Google.com.hk.

Google is so ubiquitous today (5 billion searches per day in 2012) that it is beginning the transition from well-loved innovator to corporate icon. On this trajectory, the pioneering search engine has achieved a status that has surpassed McDonald's, Walmart, and, of course, Microsoft. Google is accomplishing this by using the Web browser as the central application on the computer, instead of Microsoft's dominant operating system, Windows, and accompanying application Office. Office came out in 1990 and by 2013 held a monopolistic 95 percent market share for desktop office software.[7]

In keeping up with the newest technology breakthroughs in software, Mircosoft has struggled. Despite efforts to develop smartphone software with its Windows Mobile products, Microsoft has gained little traction in a mobile operating systems market dominated by Google's Android and Apple's iOS. In efforts to also play in the search engine game, Microsoft has tried to acquire Yahoo! several times. Microsoft's main interest in acquiring Yahoo!, of course, was to challenge search engine leader Google. The company did overhaul its own struggling search engine Bing in 2009. Shortly thereafter, Yahoo! and Microsoft reached a ten-year agreement in which Microsoft took over the search engine responsibilities on Yahoo!, which received 88 percent of all search-related ad revenue for the deal's first five years.[8]

Comparing Microsoft and Google*

MICROSOFT

(Millions U.S. Dollars)	2012	2011	2010
Revenue	$73,723	$69,943.0	$62,484.0
Net Income	$16,978	$23,150.0	$18,760.0
Net Profit	23.0%	33.1%	30.0%
Employees	94,000	90,000	89,000

• One Year Sales Growth: 5.4%

GOOGLE

(Millions U.S. Dollars)	2012	2011	2010
Revenue	$50,175	$37,905.0	$29,321.0
Net Income	$10,737	$9,737.0	$8,505.0
Net Profit	21.4%	25.7%	29.0%
Employees	53,861	32,467	24,400

• One Year Sales Growth: 32.4%

Source: Hoover's Company Records—In-Depth Records, accessed February 24, 2013.

Corporate dominance aside, today's Internet search engines, led by Google, can do more than offer instant access to millions of Web pages related to cruising for certain information. These engines will be able to search TV programs and movie archives by image, personalize searches by remembering our specific interests, and retrieve data from searches of both local information held on our home computers and broader databases available on the Internet. We often use search engines to find answers—for example, how many copies the last Harry Potter book sold, what movies Spike Lee directed, and how much advertisers pay for a TV ad in prime time. Initially, our queries came back mostly as a giant list of Web pages that might lead us to the answers. However, as search engines get better and more refined, the Internet now delivers not merely a list of popular Web sites but actual focused answers to specific questions.

But corporate concerns could short-circuit the enormous retrieval power of the Internet. Because search engines are popular entry points, or portals, to the Web, the home pages of search engines now offer not only a search button but also several "channels" that provide shortcuts to the day's news stories, up-to-the-minute sports scores, and links to advertisers' Web sites. The idea behind these channels is to keep users connected to the search site for as long as possible and thus offer an attentive audience to Web advertisers. The channel locations on the search engines' Web pages are also typically paid for by the content providers, creating another revenue stream for search engine sites. In the pursuit of greater revenue, many search engines have compromised their usefulness as locators of Web content. By accepting payment for listing certain Web sites at the top of a result list—and not always notifying users of this practice—search engines are increasingly ensuring that the best-financed sites on the Web get the most visitors, whereas nonprofit Web sites that can't afford priority placement become increasingly marginalized. Although this practice generates funds for commercial search engines, it does not bode well for search engines as research tools for the Web.

TECHNOLOGY AND DEMOCRACY

Back in 1993, media critic Marc Gunther offered an analogy for access to virtual and real highways: "If the information highway becomes a vital communications link in the 21st Century, who will be able to ride? . . . The interstates of the 1950s helped relocate jobs to the suburbs and beyond, leaving city folks stranded unless they owned cars."[9] Whereas traditional broadcast media served the public interest statute of the Federal Communication Act of 1934 and made the same information available to everyone who owned a radio or a TV set, the Internet creates economic ranges and disparities in service. This is similar to the development of cable in the 1970s when that industry began offering different tiers of service—from stripped-down basic cable to deluxe offerings that included a number of premium channels like HBO and Showtime.

Like deluxe cable packages, parts of the Internet have become toll roads rather than freeways, with wealthy users buying different levels of privacy, specialty access, and Internet capabilities. The *Wall Street Journal*, for example, has a paid service that successful business costumers subscribe to, and the *New York Times*, after several experiments with pay systems, has settled on a system where readers can see a limited number of articles for free, but must subscribe (digitally or to the print version) for regular full access. Policy groups, media critics, and concerned citizens are debating the implications of limiting media access for democratic societies, which have traditionally valued the equal opportunity and open access to the knowledge and information required to make decisions in any robust democracy.

Who Owns the Internet?

With the increasing convergence of owners and players in mass media industries, large media firms continue to expand. Corporations such as Disney, Comcast, Sony, Time Warner, News Corp., Viacom, CBS, Microsoft, and Google have been buying up or investing in smaller companies and spreading their economic interests among books, magazines, music, movies, radio, television, cable, Internet channels, and digital technology. Time Warner and News Corp., however, have been divesting themselves of their less profitable print media.

As with the automobile or film industries of an earlier era, many players and companies are jockeying for positions of prominence. With the passage of the sweeping overhaul of the nation's communication regulations in the 1996 Telecommunications Act, many regional and long-distance phone companies now participate in both cable and Internet-access businesses, and as cable and phone companies gradually converted older wiring into high-speed fiber-optic lines, they wrestled for Internet supremacy—sometimes without clearly foreseeing the coming of Wi-Fi. Phone and cable companies spent billions upgrading wires but by 2012 wireless connections were the present and not the future.

Given the paucity of regulations governing the Internet and the industry's rapid growth, it is not surprising to see an explosion of mergers, joint ventures, consolidations, and power grabs. Although these mergers have attempted to find a dominant position in the Information Era, some companies have loomed larger than others. Microsoft, for example, built monopoly dominance of its Windows operating systems and Internet Explorer browser software throughout the 1990s. Then the U.S. Department of Justice brought an antitrust lawsuit against Microsoft in 1997, arguing that it used its computer operating system dominance to sabotage its competitors. But Microsoft prevailed in 2001, when the Department of Justice dropped its efforts to break Microsoft into two independent companies.

The desire of corporations to tap into the untamed and unpredictable Internet economy is clear. Increasing commercial interests are affecting the way in which the Internet—once an unassuming nonprofit, government-subsidized medium known for freely accessible information—is evolving. Indeed, the 2000 phenomenon of the fifteen-year-old Internet dial-up service provider AOL merging with Time Warner, then the world's largest media conglomerate, certainly spoke to the power of the Internet in the twenty-first century. But then high-speed cable service developed as great competition for AOL, and investors grew increasingly disappointed with AOL Time Warner's subsequent poor financial performance in the following years. Eventually, by 2002, AOL's inability to keep expanding saddled the company with more debt and the AOL tag was quietly dropped from the giant corporation's name.

Discussing the economic implications of the "information highway" back in the mid-1990s, critics Daniel Burstein and David Kline associated the Internet with a series of personality traits: "Free. Egalitarian. Decentralized. Ad hoc. Open and peer-to-peer. Experimental. Autonomous. Anarchic."[10] They contrasted these traits with the personality of modern business organizations: "For profit. Hierarchical. Systematized. Planned. Proprietary. Pragmatic. Accountable. Organized and reliable."[11] Given this clash of values, the development of the Internet remains in many ways unstable and dynamic, despite attempts to control and commercialize it. Unlike other media and communication businesses, where ownership has become increasingly consolidated in the hands of a few powerful firms, many parts of the Internet have eluded centralization. Moreover, it still remains fairly easy for individuals or groups to start up everything from a for-profit company to a political organization through their own Web sites. In fact, the Internet is less likely to suffer from the same economic limitations of other mass media because it was not designed to be an efficiently managed, hierarchically controlled, or tightly monitored system. Unlike a Hollywood movie and or prime-time TV program, its starting production costs are also very inexpensive.

The current Web 2.0 and 3.0 movements have been trying to keep alive the initial promises of the Internet with second and third generations of Web-based services that include blogging, social networking (e.g., Facebook and Twitter), and "wikis"—Web sites, like *Wikipedia,* that encourage collaborative writing and joint authorship by allowing individual users to add, remove, edit, and change existing content, usually anonymously and without registering.

Although the open, interactive, and democratic process of *Wikipedia* has wide appeal, there are downsides, including postings that are plagiarized—blocks of material lifted from other sources and pasted into *Wikipedia*—or simply wrong. For example, in 2006 *Maclean's* magazine provided this example:

> On Wednesday, July 5, Ken Lay, the former chairman and CEO of Enron Corp. died in Colorado. The news first hit the wires around 10 a.m., and at 10:06 Wikipedia, the online encyclopedia that allows users to update and modify entries,

proclaimed that Lay had died "of an apparent suicide." Two minutes later, somebody changed the entry to say Lay had died "of an apparent heart attack or suicide." Less than a minute later, some cooler head intervened and corrected the entry to say the cause of death was "yet to be determined." At 10:11 the entry was changed again, this time asserting that "The guilt of ruining so many lives finally led him to suicide." A minute after that, someone cited a news report that "according to Lay's pastor the cause was a 'massive coronary heart attack.'" Then, at 10:39, one of the Internet's anonymous, self-taught cardiologists wrote: "speculation as to the cause of the heart attack lead [*sic*] many people to believe it was due to the amount of stress put on him by the Enron trial." Finally, a few hours later, the entry was set straight, noting simply that Lay had died of a heart attack in Aspen.¹²

Open sites like *Wikipedia* lack the journalistic filters and often enough seasoned editors to oversee a more thoughtful and careful process for reporting breaking news. As *Maclean's* noted at the time, "The real problem is that, with the spreading influence of the Internet, we are trading in authoritative and accurate for cheap and convenient. *Wikipedia* is only one example."¹³

The Web 2.0 movement also featured **social networking** and swapping services—sites for storing, sharing, and classifying media content from words to images to music, much of it user-generated. For example, in 2006 Yahoo!, once trying to keep up with Google, bought Flickr, a service for photo-sharing; del.icio.us, a service for storing and sharing Internet bookmarks; Jumpcut.com, a site for uploading and editing photos and video; and Bix, an entertainment polling and contest site. While debate remains over the meaning of the next Web generation, one critic made this distinction back in 2006:

> In Web 1.0, we went to the Web to see pages someone else created. We went to Amazon to buy books and music. We went to Google to find things.
> In Web 2.0, surfers go to MySpace and create a page that contributes to a social network. Without the users, there would be no content.
> Generation Web 2.0 goes to Blogspot to share deep thoughts or vent spleens and to link to others with similar thoughts and venting. They go to Wikipedia and help build a grass-roots encyclopedia.¹⁴

All of these services and technologies have shared the desire to make information free and to make the Web more socially aware, creating communities based on tagging—labeling pieces of the Web so that other users with similar interests can better connect with them. This movement has a distinctly open-source flavor to it and, again, tries to reclaim the original egalitarian and participatory spirit of the Internet. **Open-source software** referred originally to the early days of computer code writing, when amateur hackers collectively developed software by freely sharing the program source code and ideas to upgrade and improve programs. Beginning in the 1970s, Microsoft ended much of this activity by making software development a business in which programs began with private business financing and users were required to pay for them—and all the necessary upgrades.

Part of this open spirit includes an anti-authoritarian strain—from the easily downloadable shareware and freeware to the work of self-described "hacktivists," who use their hacker skills to bring political protest to the Internet. Even though studies have found that more than 80 percent of the Internet serves commercial purposes, not all efforts to commercialize the Internet have been effective, and to a large extent the Internet ethos of free information is alive and well. The terrorism attacks of September 11, 2001, changed this to some extent, as subsequent antiter-rorism laws and the Patriot Act increased government surveillance of the Internet. Nevertheless, the free trade and circulation of information continues.

The Internet and the Digital Divide

Even as that information trade continues, though, a key economic issue for our times is whether the cost of getting on the Internet or buying cable and DBS packages will undermine equal access to information. Mimicking the economic disparity between rich and poor that grew more pronounced starting in the 1980s and continues today, the term **digital divide** refers to the growing contrast between information "haves," or digital highway users who can afford to acquire multiple media services, and information "have-nots," or users who may not be able to afford cable, a computer, and the monthly bills for service connections, much less the many options now available to more affluent citizens. For example, examine the ongoing annual studies commissioned by Pew Internet and its Internet & American Life Project, which have traced the U.S. audience for Internet use by several demographic categories, including gender, age, race, ethnicity, household income, and formal education levels.

Many communities and organizations have addressed the access problem by installing computers equipped with Internet connections in libraries, banks, schools, and other public locations; this gives most community members some Internet access. As late as 1996, only one in four U.S. libraries offered access to computers and the Internet, but with money generated from Microsoft profits, the Bill and Melinda Gates Foundation since 1997 has been the leading advocate of funding net-worked computers in public libraries. Today nearly all public libraries in the United States offer Internet access, and nearly 10 percent of all Internet users gain access to computers this way (ranking fifth as an Internet access point after home, work, school, and someone else's home). This kind of public library access has helped close the digital divide for many low-income citizens and remote rural residents. The Gates Foundation project has extended its philanthropy over the years and now

Demographics of Internet Users—April 2012

Total Adults	82%
Women	82
Men	83

Age

18–29	97%
30–49	91
50–64	77
65+	53

Race/ethnicity

White, Non-Hispanic	84%
Black, Non-Hispanic	77
Hispanic (English- and Spanish-speaking)	75

Household income

Less than $30,000/yr	71%
$30,000–$49,999	87
$50,000–$74,999	93
$75,000+	97

Educational attainment

No High School Diploma	58%
High School grad	75
Some College	90
College+	95

Source: Pew Research Center's Internet & American Life Project, *Spring Tracking Survey,* conducted March 15–April 3, 2012. N = 2,254 adults ages 18 and older, inlcuding 903 interviews conducted by cell phone. See www.pewinternet.org/Static-Pages/Trend-Data -(Adults)/Whos-Online.aspx.

offers free Microsoft software to libraries in thirty-five countries.[15] In some cases, cities have begun offering free Internet access to their entire citizenry; for example, in 2006, Philadelphia announced plans to bring a free Wi-Fi system to its residents. That same year, Google announced it would offer free high-speed Internet access to all households in Mountain View, California, its home base in Silicon Valley. At the time, this Wi-Fi network established Mountain View as the largest U.S. city with free Internet access, surpassing St. Cloud, Florida, a suburb of Orlando.

Globally, though, the information "have-nots" face an even greater obstacle in connecting to the Internet. Although the Web claims to be worldwide, countries like the United States, Norway, Sweden, Finland, Japan, Israel, Australia, Britain, and

Though personal computers and Internet-enabled smartphones have become more common, some Internet users still get access through public libraries.

Germany account for most of its international flavor. In nations such as Jordan, Saudi Arabia, Syria, Iraq, China, and Myanmar, the governments permit only limited access to the Web. In many poorer countries—particularly in Africa and parts of Asia—inadequate telecommunications infrastructure means that many endure long waits in order to participate or still have no Internet access at all. For example, by the end of 2012, only 16.4 percent of the adult population in Africa and 28 percent in Asia were Internet users compared to 79 percent in North America and 63 percent in Europe.[16]

Iran presents a particularly compelling case study for Internet use, especially in the area of blogging by both government supporters and dissenters. In 2006, the *Guardian* in London reported:

> The arrival of the religious ruling class on Iran's blogosphere is ironic in view of the harsh crackdown launched by the authorities against bloggers who have used it to voice political dissent. Scores of bloggers have been jailed in recent years while many sites have been blocked using US-made filtering technology.[17]

At the outset of 2007, Iran had one of the higher per capita rates for blogging in the world, many citizens still writing anti-government blogs critical of Iran's lack of freedoms. By the end of 2006, the *Guardian* estimated that Iran had "between 75,000 and 100,000 bloggers, most of them avoiding politics to concentrate on matters like social affairs, culture, and sex."[18] The political reform movement in Iran apparently began in 2001 "as a response to the closures of dozens of liberal newspapers and magazines on the orders of religious hardliners. It has since become a phenomenon among the computer-savvy younger generation."[19] In 2012 Iran had about 36.5 million Internet users—about 46 percent of their total population.[20]

Americans, meanwhile, have often touted emerging mass media for their potential contributions to democracy and culture throughout the twentieth century. As radios became more affordable in the 1920s and 1930s, we hailed the medium for its ability to reach and entertain even the poorest Americans caught in the Great Depression. When television developed in the 1950s and 1960s, it also held promise as a medium that could reach everyone, even those who were illiterate or cut off from printed information. But with the expansion of cable in the 1970s and 1980s, we started to see a repositioning of television as a medium that had separate levels of information and entertainment services. The more money consumers had, the more tiers of service they could buy. The Internet has extended this digital divide that separates rich and poor. Still, despite the criticisms of the Internet's accessibility and continuing national and international discrepancies, many critics and citizens have praised the Internet for its democratic possibilities, its decentralization, and its accessibility.

Decentralized and Fragmented Culture

Unlike many media industries, the Internet has developed and flourished largely from the bottom up. Just as amateur radio operators influenced the growth of wireless communication in the early twentieth century, the development of the Internet owes a large debt to amateurs—students, engineers, and computer buffs. There are several disadvantages, however, to the decentralized and widely distributed nature of the Internet. One drawback has been the increased circulation of "spam" e-mail and spurious "news"—the Internet equivalent of unwanted junk mail (especially the pornographic variety) and backroom gossip. Unlike traditional media, which routinely employ editors and producers as information gatekeepers, many individuals and newsgroups on the Internet send out data that are not checked by anyone. Most serious news media screen material for accuracy, fairness, appropriateness, and decency, but such screening is more difficult to accomplish on the Internet.

Although the Internet is subject to misinformation, it is also a source of unique and valuable information such as Web sites that disclose financial contributions to candidates for public office. As such, the Internet offers a diverse array of communication models. In such a decentralized system, millions of message groups send out bits of information, allowing millions of other interested users to receive and respond. Instead of the few-to-many model of traditional media, the Internet offers more opportunities for both one-to-one and many-to-many communication encounters.

The biggest threat to the Internet's democratic potential may well be its increasing commercialization. Similar to what happened with the radio and television media, the growth of commercial outlets and Web sites on the Internet has far outpaced the emergence of viable nonprofit channels, as fewer and fewer corporations have gained more and more control. The passage of the 1996 Telecommunications Act cleared the way for cable TV systems, computer firms, and telephone companies to merge their interests in advancing communication technology. Although there was a great deal of buzz about lucrative Internet start-ups in the 1990s, many large corporations such as Microsoft and Time Warner have weathered the low points of the dot-com economy and maintained a controlling hand in the new information systems.

At the outset of 2013, the United States had about 245 million Internet users—second to China (538 million users). This was about 78 percent of the population (compared to 40 percent in China).[21] While the spread of the Internet—up in the United States from 50 percent in 2000—greatly increases its democratic possibilities, it also tempts commercial interests to gain even greater control over it, intensifying problems for agencies that are trying to regulate it. If the past is any predictor, expect that the Internet's potential for widespread democratic use will always be partially preempted by narrower commercial interests.

On the more positive side of these issues, the new technologies may be so uniquely accessible that they offer at least the potential for enriching democratic processes. Books, newspapers, magazines, radio, film, and television widened and expanded the reach of media, but they did not generate equivalent avenues for response and debate. Defenders of the Digital Age argue that newer media forms—from the MP3 music of emerging artists to online streaming of independent short films to an enormous variety of blogs and social networking sites like Facebook, Twitter, and Tumblr—allow greater participation. Individuals, through social networking or by creating their own Web sites, now lead and encourage conversations about everything from movies, dating, or politics to the best colleges, worst bands, or least favorite pizza places. In response to these new media forms, older media are using Internet technology to increase their access to and feedback from varied audiences, soliciting e-mail from users or fostering social media discussions on how to connect better with audiences and improve their services.

Despite the potential of new media forms, there are some doubts about the participatory nature of discussions on the Internet. For instance, Internet users may be seeking out only those people whose beliefs and values are similar to their own. While sites like Facebook encourage younger generations to talk to one another, they may also alienate older generations who feel cut off from the kind of technical savvy required to negotiate the Internet. Although it is important to be able to communicate across vast distances with people who have similar viewpoints, these kinds of Internet conversations may not serve to extend the diversity and tolerance that are central to democratic ideals.

To take a critical position on the information highway and digital divide debates, we need to analyze and judge possibilities and limitations. Such a position should be grounded in the knowledge that the media are converging nationally and globally, changing the nature of mass communication. It is also no longer very useful to discuss print media and electronic or digital media as if they were completely segregated forms. We live in a world where a ten-year-old can simultaneously watch a TV episode recorded on TiVo and read *The Hunger Games*, where a twenty-year-old student can make sense of a nineteenth-century poem while wearing a twenty-first-century iPod playing downloaded music that was released that day. Moreover, it is now possible to access, say, old TV shows, horror thrillers, classic literary texts, and techno music, all through cable, home computers, smartphones, tablets, and wireless Internet connections. Media such as e-mail, audio books, DVRs, and blogging are integrating aspects of print, electronic, and digital culture in daily life.

In the broadest sense, the development of Internet technology has always posed contradictions. On the one hand, our newest mass media channels have dramatically increased the number of venues and offered previously underrepresented groups the opportunity to address their particular issues. On the other hand, they have undermined a modern era during which print culture, and later network television, worked as a kind of social adhesive, giving most of the population a common bond, a set of shared information outlets and narrative programs. This same concern remains today: Do the most recent developments of the Digital Era create a fragmented, customized culture in which individuals pursue narrow personal agendas at the expense of larger social concerns?

As more and more communities become equipped with computers, satellites, smartphones, and TV screens, such convergence may make us homebound, freeing us from traditional participation in and travel to workplaces and schools. New technologies have the capacity, of course, to simultaneously bring us together in the virtual reality of the Internet and isolate us physically from one another. Other issues democracies must face are the control of a few giant media corporations over our means of communication and how we will tie technological developments to citizens' social needs as these new and old media forms continue to influence consumer and business priorities. The gulf between the information rich and the information poor remains wide, increasing concerns about who will have access to—and who will be able to afford—the next new wave of media technologies. As the speed of technology accelerates and those stories and forms of information that most interest us become more accessible, the key question to ask is: Can our shared interests and common ties be balanced against our individual desires and cultural differences?

| CRITICAL PROCESS 1 | Internet Innovations

This chapter argues that three key innovations of the Internet are that it is interactive, it repurposes traditional media, and it enables production rather than passive consumption. The goal of this exercise is to critically process one of these three major innovations. Choose at least one of the three and work through the steps below.

Describe the nature and role of one or more of these innovative aspects of the Internet in your life. Describe how the Internet (or some accompanying form of social media) helps you interact with others; repurposes traditional media forms like movies, television, or music; or allows you to produce and share original content.

Analyze the role the Internet has in your life. How does it structure your day? How do your daily habits and routines revolve around certain Internet activities? Is this part similar to or different from the role the Internet plays in other people's lives?

Interpret what this means. Why are your interactions with and on the Internet valuable or desirable to you? What does it offer you? How has the Internet become a part of your life?

Evaluate the costs and benefits of your example. What would your life be like without this particular element of the Internet? Do you think your Internet habits play positive or negative roles in your life? Explain.

Engage with others and develop an informal survey of the positive and negative aspects of the Internet. Create a list and share this with your class. What did you discover?

| CRITICAL PROCESS 2 | Stages of Media Development

The Internet, according to this chapter, passed through four stages—developmental, entrepreneurial, breakthrough, and convergence—which can be applied to almost any new form of media culture. The goal of this exercise is to apply these four stages to another technological or cultural item. It can be something much smaller than the Internet, like a new smartphone application, genre of music, style of clothing, or a type of storytelling. Pick an aspect of media that you feel has reached the breakthrough and perhaps convergence stages in recent years, months, or even weeks. (For example, imagine you are tracking the breakthrough of reality television, starting with MTV's *Real World*. Next track what has happened to that type of storytelling today as it has dispersed through a converged and fragmented media landscape.)

Describe your example and its present trajectory. When did it seem to first develop, how has it been entrepreneurially supported, and when did it seem to break through to a larger audience or usage? Has it reached a convergence stage yet?

Analyze that trajectory and its patterns. How did these developments occur? Why did it go in one direction and not another? What forces were behind its initial development, entrepreneurial support, breakthrough status, and possible convergence? If it hasn't fulfilled all of these stages yet, analyze its current stage.

Interpret this process. How and why is this type of media breaking through and converging? When might convergence happen, if it hasn't yet? Why and how do other, similar types of media or other kinds of storytelling stay at the developmental stage or fail at the entrepreneurial stage? (Consider News Corp.'s *Daily* failing as a tablet news venture.)

Evaluate what constitute a breakthrough. How do communication technologies get invented, popularized, and adopted? Is it driven by capitalism, by innovation, by usefulness, by our needs, by advertising? Is quality a factor? Why or why not?

Engage with classmates, friends, or family about your example. Are they aware of its development? Has it affected their lives at all? Ask them for their own examples. Make a list and share with your class.

11

Media Globalization

Throughout the late twentieth century, the international expansion of U.S. culture has allowed many forms of U.S. media to flourish abroad. U.S. media companies like Disney or Time Warner may lose money on products at home, but they know they can still profit nicely in the international market. In any given year, 80 to 90 percent of U.S. movies, for instance, do not earn back their costs in U.S. theater distribution. Instead, they depend on global circulation to make up for such domestic losses. Even financially underperforming movies like Disney's *John Carter* or Universal's *Battleship* may have their financial blows cushioned by money made overseas, which can turn flops into mild disappointments or even hits—and U.S. hits into global mega-hits.

The same is true for the U.S. TV industry. Satellite transmission has made North American and European TV available at the global level. Cable services such as CNN and MTV quickly took their national acts to the international stage, and by the twenty-first century, CNN and MTV were available in more than two hundred countries. And in the past decade, the sharing of music, TV shows, and movies on the Internet (both legally and illegally) has expanded the global flow of popular culture even further.

Concerns about technology, capitalism, and democracy are also global. Most people believe that new forms of communication technology have created and continue to shape a new kind of cultural, social, political, and economic world. For the last two decades or so, **globalization** has been the term used to describe this new world order. Globalization, simply put, is the process by which the world is becoming more connected and interdependent. In this chapter we explore some key terms, concepts, and concerns about the globalization of mass communication, focusing on cultural elements, with attention to economic, political, and social consequences. Our central question is: Are U.S. media, through the exportation of our popular culture, really transforming the world?

The story of media globalization is rapidly being rewritten in the Digital Age. But our three theoretical perspectives on media criticism—reflectionist, constructionist, and narrativist—still apply. The media metaphors that operate in U.S. media criticism—characterizing media as interlopers, information sources, propaganda, distractions, and so on—are still being deployed. Concerns about the role and influence of media in American society are now being recombined and extended to explore the role of media internationally.

ELEMENTS OF GLOBALIZATION

One of the more confusing elements in the debate about globalization is that the term is applied to more than just communication content and form. The debate addresses a number of different but related processes. Globalization can be primarily political, dealing with the apparent spread of U.S.-style democracy, especially since the end of the Cold War. Globalization can be primarily economic, addressing the increasing interdependence of nations, the outsourcing of jobs to cheaper labor markets, and the influence of capitalism across the world. Globalization can also be about technological impact, which can radically alter more agrarian societies by introducing machines and electricity, as well as television and digital cell phones, to rural cultures. Or it can be primarily social, focusing on the ways in which traditional family and community relationships are coming to resemble more modern, Western ones. All these aspects are elements in a more general cultural critique: a fear (or hope) that, because of mass communication, the whole world is becoming ever more culturally modern, Western, and therefore Americanized.

In this way, the term *globalization* often ends up referring to modernization, westernization, and U.S.-exported media. Globalization doesn't usually refer to the creation of a globally interdependent economic, political, or social network but to a process of cultural (and therefore political, social, and technological) domination. If globalization was just a description for increasing world connectedness—a speedier, more interactive way to organize and share culture or information—it would not provoke so much anxiety. What troubles or exhilarates media critics is the way media globalization seems to be turning cultures everywhere into one homogenous, commercialized, westernized, consumerist global culture.

So the same ambivalence that many critics have about modern American mass media—summarized by the metaphors in Chapter 2—is also being expressed internationally. It is no longer just U.S. society that seems at risk of being shaped by the mass media, but all peoples, all over the world.

For the most fearful critics, there will no longer exist a geographical escape from the bad effects of media and consumer culture. Their nightmare is becoming global reality—the whole world may turn into a giant U.S. media-dependent network, living on reruns of every bad U.S. movie or television show ever produced. This fear has been called "the Hollywoodization of the world." It is of course important to respect these fears. We in the United States have become accustomed to being culturally dominant, so it can be difficult for American citizens to appreciate what it is like to be culturally invaded. As a nation that some describe as born in modernity, we have rarely (if ever) had our traditional ways transformed and displaced by another nation's traditions, cultures, habits, and beliefs.

We can have glimpses of this sense of invasion when we worry about how many goods we import from China or wonder about the influence of Japanese card games like Yu-Gi-Oh on our children. But even when we think we are being invaded or dominated by other cultures—with, say, animé or salsa music—these are not comparable experiences. Globally, at least up until recently, we in the United States are the ones absorbing, not being absorbed.

In the following sections, we explore global media technologies, cultural imperialism, globalized content, information imbalance, the globalized audience, and cultural diffusion as elements in the globalization of media. Once these concepts are clarified, they can be used to evaluate the consequences of globalization, including competing visions of what it means when media technology, capitalism, and democracy spread.

Globalized Media Technologies

It is much easier to focus on the spread of communication technology itself than to understand the cultural meaning and consequences of media globalization. We can draw maps, trace adoption routes, and track the use of things like radios, television, cell phones, and the Internet across the world. The new technologies become change markers—visible manifestations of presumed social and cultural shifts. But all this tracking and observing can't tell us what it really means when communication technologies spread.

Even the words we use to describe the adoption of new communication technologies imply different concerns and thereby reveal how difficult it is to find a neutral language to describe global shifts in communication, culture, and society. The terms we use carry underlying assumptions regarding media and modern life—the kinds of assumptions and associations discussed in Chapter 1 in describing the reflectionist, constructionist, and narrativist perspectives.

If we say that media technologies "spread to" or "permeate" other cultures, we imply a natural process of growth. This would be compatible with a reflectionist perspective, with the media as neutral aspects of social reality. This makes the process of global media expansion seem both benign and inevitable. If instead we say that media technologies "infiltrate" or "invade" other cultures, we imply that they cause damage or spread disease. This is more compatible with a constructionist perspective, where the media create false or toxic beliefs. This makes the process of global media expansion seem dangerous and worth fighting against. If we say that media technologies are used or adopted by other cultures, we imply that people are making choices about global media technologies, which is more compatible with a narrativist perspective. This makes the process of global media expansion seem within our control—something we can guide and shape to our own purposes.

No matter which terms we use to describe media globalization, it is clear that when communication media spread, human relationships are affected. It is not just that there are televisions in tribal huts, but that television shows serve as embodiments and inflections of modern U.S. values and beliefs that are often in conflict with different local cultures. They shape what theorist Raymond Williams called "structures of feeling," which are always linked to structures of power.[1] This is true of our current digital culture, just as it was of print, written, and oral cultures.

But communication technology theorists go even further, influenced by the Canadian communication scholar Marshall McLuhan (famous for his dictum "the medium is the message") and his teacher Harold Adams Innis. These technology theorists note how the new electronic forms of communication collapse time and space, allowing the instantaneous dissemination of symbols across the world.[2] This means that as forms, not just as content, they can and will change the ways people imagine themselves, as well as how they organize into groups, form and sustain communities, and distribute and maintain power. The influence of television and now the Internet on tribal cultures, and the infiltration of U.S. brands across the globe, have become shorthand ways to present not just cultural impact or exchange but deeper shifts in the role of time, distance, and power in society.

The consequences of these shifts are what many scholars and critics are worried about, whether they realize it or not. For example, in the 1960s McLuhan optimistically imagined the future dawning of a new, electronic-based "global village."[3] Before the telegraph, satellite communication, and various new forms of digital technology, communication was limited by either time or distance, or both. In the nineteenth century, once the telegraph started sending the first "instant messages" at the speed of light (in Morse code), McLuhan argued, the world and communication changed.

Before the telegraph, early written communication could move great distances, but only as fast as the fastest horse, carriage, ship, or train. Cultural exchange happened at a slower pace and local custom and tradition often remained insulated outside of major cities. And because the world was developing unevenly, only the so-called First World cultures of Western Europe and the United States experienced the full effects of print culture.

With mass production enabled through the printing press, mass reproduction emerged and subsequently the mass distribution of messages. But there were still distances to be traversed and time gaps limited by the speed of travel. This meant that local habits and customs—while shaped by contact with external writing, print media, trade, and other forms of cultural exchange—still had some autonomy. In fact, cultural variety flourished, as individuals, groups and societies sought to identify themselves as different from one another.

But what happens when electronic and digital media forms, from the telegraph to radio to e-mail to Twitter, are added to the mix? And what happens when there is no established print culture to disseminate electronically? Electronic communication mimics aspects of face-to-face speech. Events and experiences can happen at the same time, as they do in oral cultures, but for the first time this could happen among strangers who are not in the same place. This means that communication can happen separately from the bonds of hierarchy and authority that historically shaped communication in oral and print-based cultures. With electronic communication, there can be contact between people who do not necessarily know or care about each other's local status. Meanings are potentially made with less regard to local customs and traditions, as well as distinctions of race, class, gender, or religion.

These shifts may seem commonplace to those of us born into the digital era. The speed, simultaneity, and democratization of new forms of communication are old hat to U.S. citizens. But electronic and digital communication offers a startling and destabilizing shift in the ways in which other individuals and groups experience and interact in the world. For good or ill, the collapse of time and space made possible by electronic and digital media reorganizes inherited forms of economics, politics, and culture. Think of Arab or Israeli immigrants in Detroit communicating by Skype with close relatives in the Middle East. Or the way electronic technology, particularly cell phones, assisted the revolutionary Arab Spring of 2011, displacing long-ruling dictatorships with the possibility of popularly elected leaders.

First and Second World cultures and societies (including the United States) developed forms of commerce and trade, political systems, educational systems, towns and cities, habits, values, and beliefs more slowly across time during print-based eras. This means that we responded to new electronic communication in relation to a deeply imbedded print consciousness. But the values, habits, and social structures of many world cultures predate print influence—what are called *Third World* or *developing nations* are mostly oral cultures, with all the traits connected with that form of communication. Those less technologically developed oral cultures may have very different reactions when new digital technologies are introduced without the more gradual period of development experienced in the United States and Western Europe.

Questions of global media impact not only address the intractable problems of media and modern culture that we've considered in earlier chapters—they also address problems of tradition, innovation, and national sovereignty over politics and culture. For developed nations, the impact of electronic and digital communication forms has been profound but not nearly as revolutionary as some predicted. In spite of the hopes of futurists like McLuhan and others, the electronic era of radio and television and the Digital Age of the Internet and Facebook have not created—and are not likely to create—a utopian, harmonious global village. Indeed, all we can be certain of is that new media bring changes that are unexpected, even in the United States.

The changes that a century of electronic and digital communication has brought about are notable, but they have not suddenly made a world that is utterly different from ever before. In spite of computer-age prognostications, the United States has not become a nation of telecommuters. The Internet helps facilitate lots of new kinds of communication but did not and cannot replace face-to-face communication. Similarly, the United States of the twenty-first century has not become a paperless society. Indeed, more paper is now being consumed than ever before, as printers became cheaper and businesses demand paper copies of online transactions. Imbalances of power, social status, and wealth continue, in spite of (and sometimes because of) new forms of media.

But understandably, many see electronic and digital communication as putting developing nations at particular risk. In technologically developed societies, the changes wrought by new gadgets are evolutionary, not revolutionary—each new form of communication and technology gets overlaid on previous forms. As we have described elsewhere, since the 1830s mass printing, including newspapers and magazines, fueled mass literacy and laid a foundation for the development of the radio, records, movies, television, cable and satellite communication, and the Internet.

But in countries where printed books are rare, literacy limited, telephones scarce, and electricity a luxury, television suddenly became the most popular form of entertainment. Critics worry that the sudden adoption of, for example, television as a technology, and American television shows as content, eviscerates traditional cultures. Developing nations will be turned into America-dependent colonies, as electronic culture displaces, then erases, oral culture. So concerns about globalization range from worries about the hybridization of native languages and identity (as in Western Europe) to concerns about increased global homogenization to strong fears about the obliteration of indigenous customs and permanent cultural dependency and exploitation.

In contrast, there are some observers who applaud globalization because they see it instead as guaranteeing the spread of modern values, habits, and beliefs. A homogenous global culture is a vast improvement on what has gone before, they believe. It is time that the rest of the world becomes more "like us." This perspective almost always combines cultural with economic, political, and social benefits in relation to U.S. self-interest.

These positive accounts of globalization are often startlingly insensitive to the perspective of non-U.S. societies. Pro-globalization commentators presume that whatever is good for "us" is good for the world. In response to concerns about cultural hybridization, homogenization, and obliteration, defenders of globalization praise the benefits of economic development for the United States or the value of political democracies and modern social relationships for equality and freedom, as well as for global stability.

In this way (as in all discussions of media in society), the globalization of media technologies is about a lot of different things, all at once. It is a symptom of much bigger, more interesting, and complicated assumptions about what makes for a good society. Understanding media globalization involves again exploring beliefs about tradition, modernization, national identity, cultural relativism, social progress, and the value of diversity, as well as continuing, unresolved concerns about the meaning and value of contemporary culture. In sorting out what media globalization means, we revisit familiar issues, now in the context of international rather than national debates. We also hear some new voices: the concerns of non-U.S. citizens exploring the problems and possibilities of mass media–related transformation.

Cultural Imperialism and Assimilation

The global influence of American popular culture has created considerable debate. On the one hand, the notion of freedom that is associated with innovation and rebellion in American culture has been embraced by many internationally. The global spread of and access to media have made it harder for political leaders to secretly repress dissident groups because police and state activity (such as the torture of illegally jailed citizens) can now be documented digitally and dispatched by satellite, the Internet, and cell phones around the world.

On the other hand, U.S. media are shaping the cultures and identities of other nations; American styles in fashion, food, and media fare dominate the global market. This development is often identified as **cultural imperialism**. Today, numerous international observers contend that consumer control is minimal in countries inundated by American movies, music, television, and images of beauty. Although many indigenous forms of media culture—such as Brazil's *telenovela* (a TV soap opera), Jamaica's reggae, and Japan's animé—are internationally popular, U.S. dominance in producing and distributing mass media puts a severe burden on all countries attempting to produce their own cultural products. American TV producers have generally recouped their production costs by the time their TV shows are exported; this enables American distributors to offer these programs to other countries at bargain rates, inevitably undercutting local production companies trying to create original programs.

Defenders of American popular culture note that aspects of our culture challenge authority, national boundaries, and outmoded traditions. They believe that American popular culture can create an arena in which world citizens can raise questions about their own inherited status quo. Supporters also argue that a universal popular culture fosters communication across national boundaries, which might create the long-dreamed-of global village. They point to the role of media technologies and American popular culture in fostering the popular uprisings in Eastern Europe that led to the fall of the Berlin Wall in Germany and to the hope, in parts of the Middle East, of democratically elected leaders.

Richard Barnet and John Cavanaugh, however, in *Global Dreams: Imperial Corporations and the New World Order*, have written that although American popular culture often contains protests against social wrongs, such protests "can be turned into consumer products and lose their bite. Protest itself becomes something to sell."[4] The harshest critics have also argued that American cultural imperialism both hampers the development of native cultures and negatively influences teenagers, who abandon their own cultural heritage to adopt American tastes. The exportation of U.S. entertainment media is sometimes viewed as cultural dumping because it discourages the development of original local products.

Of particular concern to critics of cultural imperialism is the elevating of expectations among people whose standards of living are not routinely portrayed in contemporary media. About two-thirds of the world's population cannot afford most of the products advertised on American, Japanese, and European television. Yet now, more and more of the world's populations are able to glimpse consumer abundance and middle-class values through television, magazines, and the Internet. What does that seeing-without-access do to a society?

As early as the 1950s, media managers feared political fallout—"the revolution of rising expectations"[5]—if ads and products raised the hopes of poor people whose national economies could not keep pace. Furthermore, the conspicuousness of consumer culture makes it difficult for people to imagine new ways of living that are not heavily dependent on the mass media and brand-name products. We hear, in these critics, the media metaphors of propaganda and commerce.

It is difficult for many U.S. citizens to understand fears of cultural imperialism because our heritage is already one of cultural **assimilation**, or blending. That is to say, we absorb and combine various cultures because, as we learn in elementary school, the United States was founded as a nation of immigrants. In many of our master narratives, the United States is the pot into which other cultures melt, the salad bowl into which other cultures mix, the quilt that patches together diverse pieces. In this way, then, globalization is about the whole world becoming like "US," in that it is becoming an assimilated global culture. From this perspective, globalization is not imperialism (the forcing of one culture onto another) but instead about the assimilation of cultural diversity into a made-in-the-USA—pick a metaphor—pot, bowl, or quilt.

But what looks like assimilation to us is experienced as imperialism by those who feel forced to blend. What may seem mundane or natural to us is threatening to those "other" cultures being melted, mixed, or stitched. U.S. media culture readily, cheerfully, and often unthinkingly absorbs and transforms other cultures. From the perspective of other nations, we can seem a giant, self-interested amoeba that takes in, digests, and feeds off of smaller life forms. Globalization seems to be heading toward a similar hybridized standardized culture, with bits and pieces of different cultural styles, with no real or meaningful differences among them.

Both U.S. and non-U.S. critics worry about the appeal, and therefore the power, of an assimilated mass mediated culture. Just as earlier superpowers used politics and economics to create dependent colonies that they exploited, now some charge the

United States with using media and other cultural forms to create a culturally dependent global society. Through the power and appeal of its entertainment and products, the United States is creating a worldwide network of consumers dependent on its offerings. People in widely different cultures and societies are all being transformed into customers who will want U.S. culture—and products—in many forms.

In this way, globalization is seen as a form of **neo-colonialism**. We in the United States are not classic colonialists, using politics and the military to directly control other nations; instead, media technologies enable a new kind of colonialism, using cultural power to dominate the globe. To many observers, the United States is using communication technology and content to spread our values, beliefs, and products, thereby dominating other nations and furthering our own interests.

Cultural imperialism and neo-colonialism critics are strongly constructionist in their perspective. They see much of the world as vulnerable to the influences of powerful Western cultures and presume that some non–Western values will be lost. They worry about economic, social, and cultural dependencies. Western influence, these critics argue, will transform indigenous people into a vast estranged modern audience, consumers who become dependent on Western media and products. In the worst-case scenarios, the combined forces of cultural imperialism and neo-colonialism create a global market of media-influenced shoppers, with no indigenous culture beyond the desire to work in U.S.-owned sweatshops so that they can consume the products being resold to them by U.S. corporations like Walmart and Nike.

Information Imbalance

Media theorists like Herbert Schiller and Noam Chomsky believe U.S. news media are seriously limited in the ways that they cover world events.[6] They are now becoming even more concerned with the consequences of global communication inequity. If ethnocentric U.S. news media come to dominate the globe, such critics argue, the gulf between the information poor and the information rich will continue to widen, while American ideology will increasingly shape global public opinion.

As Dutch media scholar Cees Hamelink has argued, information imbalance expresses the increasing difference between what are called core (rich, powerful, developed countries like the United States) and periphery (poor, powerless, developing) nations.[7] The ability of core and periphery nations to create, distribute, and use information and new communication technologies differs, creating the imbalance. While information hardware is quickly spreading from the more technologically advanced nations, periphery nations remain customers rather than producers. This means that they remain dependent, replicating and perhaps increasing the global power imbalances that already exist.

In terms of journalism, the news wire services, including CNN, Reuters, and the Associated Press (AP), originate in rich, Western countries, and so they deal with events in relation to their impact on those core countries. Some studies have shown that, when the periphery is covered, it is usually linked to superpower conflict, to a threat to core country interests, or to a sensational drama like a flood or famine.[8] Periphery countries are presented on the world stage as passive sites for dramatic or tragic events rather than as full participants in a global community. As with the flow of cultural products, information flow maintains and legitimates the dominance of core countries.

Core-to-periphery information flow also means that periphery countries cannot easily share information or form alliances that might allow them to compete with core nations. As they seek to combat poverty or develop new programs, they do not always have the scientific or technical information they need, and they also don't have the opportunity to easily share information with other countries in similar circumstances.

What can be done about global information imbalance? Several approaches have been tried. One is to better integrate core and periphery nations. Under this development model, core countries work to make periphery countries as technologically sophisticated and as "modern" as core countries. Yet efforts to modernize or develop periphery nations often result in greater dependencies—the periphery countries simply become customers for the core countries' products, just as critics fear. And modernization almost always involves loss of traditions, which often constitute a periphery nation's cultural identity.

A second approach would be to increase the bargaining power of the periphery nations by pooling their resources. The rapid rise of the news network Al-Jazeera—called by some the Arab CNN—is an example of the pooling of news and information technology by what were once considered to be periphery nations. By addressing world events from a non-Western perspective, Al-Jazeera consciously positions itself as the voice of the Arab world, and world viewers can now compare their accounts to CNN's coverage. Were periphery nations to work together economically, sharing raw materials and technology and working toward common goals, they would be more difficult for core nations to exploit. Such an alliance could go even further—it could eventually allow periphery nations to de-link from the current core nations in communication as well as in economics, becoming more independent. A collective periphery effort toward self-reliance could end up giving each nation the information and resources needed to become independent and sovereign.

But for now—and looking toward the near future—market forces are determining the spread of information technology, and those forces do not often work to change the long-standing pattern of information imbalance. For all the talk of the power of the Internet to equalize information access, the core-periphery information flow remains unbalanced; the bulk of Internet information content is being generated by core countries in support of their own economic, political, and social interests. Unless periphery nations find ways to use new information technologies for their own benefit, most critics see large imbalances and inequities continuing.

IDEOLOGY AND INFORMATION

Concerns about globalized media technologies, information imbalance, and cultural imperialism are derived largely from reflectionist and constructionist perspectives. The information imbalance assumes that information and news circulation is a relatively linear one-way process of knowledge transmission. Cultural imperialism theories hold that people are being shaped by the ideology of consumerism contained in media fare and other cross-cultural products like fashion, cosmetics, and sports.

These models have dominated critiques of media globalization. Such perspectives share a belief that individuals (who can be unconsciously misled) are vulnerable to the shaping influence of symbols. Whether the message is presumed to be directly injected into recipients, or to subliminally seduce viewers, or to alter the consciousness of audiences, the metaphor is similar—the recipient, viewer, audience, or public is being unconsciously reshaped.

Global Audiences: Active and Passive

But how disempowered are audiences—whether modern and Western or traditional and non-Western? An important strand of mass communication research focuses on media audiences as creative, active, and selective in their search for meaningful and appropriate narratives. From this active-audience perspective, people from all parts of the world will combine and enjoy cultural forms in pursuit of what they want and believe. If individuals actively choose cultural forms and identify social values for themselves, then debates about appropriate and inappropriate culture are simply part of the process by which all people—developed; developing; Western; Eastern; First, Second, or Third World—sort out what is worth their attention and loyalty and what is not.

When we apply the perspective of the active audience to the globalization debates, we reach similar conclusions: We consider the possibility that people are not being brainwashed or seduced but are consciously choosing media fare in ways that can help as well as harm. Put simply, we must consider that people in the Third World are not mere sitting ducks for First and Second World exploitation. In their concern about cultural globalization, critics may be using the same kind of disrespectful assumptions about the audience that they have been using (as we saw in Chapter 8) about American audiences.

This can be true even for critics who are widely admired for speaking for disempowered peoples. In *The Wretched of the Earth* (1961), social critic Frantz Fanon (born of mixed-race parents on the Caribbean island of Martinique, then a French colony), wrote:

> Our people have at their disposition leisure occupations designed for the youth of capitalist countries: detective novels, penny-in-the-slot machines, sexy photographs,

pornographic literature, films banned to those under sixteen, and above all, alcohol. In the West the family circle, the effects of education and the relatively high standard of living of the working classes provide a more or less efficient protection against the harmful effects of these pastimes. But in an African country, where mental development is uneven, where the violent collision of two worlds has considerably shaken old traditions and thrown the universe of the perceptions out of focus, the impressionability and sensibility of the young Africans are at the mercy of the various assaults made upon them by the very nature of Western culture.[9]

Here Fanon—a widely admired activist for social justice and change—uses logic similar to what U.S. critics used when discussing the effect of media on children: Because they don't have the right protection, they are more vulnerable to harmful influence.

Similar logic has been deployed to "protect" women and minorities from being allowed to own property, to play sports, or to participate in politics. It is a logic that presumes that the commentator has special wisdom and insight, while presuming that vulnerable "others" need their greater wisdom and insight. Do various world peoples really need to be protected from the dangerous influence of Western culture? Or can they be counted on to interpret it creatively and effectively, in relation to their own social, economic, and political reality?

This stark question requires us to finally take a stand on how vulnerable we think people and cultures are to outside influence. One way to assess this is to look at actual examples of American cultural influence. What can communication research tell us about what seems to be happening when American culture "invades" or "spreads" or "is adopted" in other societies? The classic cultural diffusion studies focus mostly on developed nations, but we believe that their principles can be fruitfully applied to developing nations too.

Cultural Diffusion

As with the spread of media technology, it is relatively easy to document the worldwide spread of U.S. popular culture. What is harder to document is how these technologies and cultural forms actually affect the people using them. International interpretive audience research explores what an American comic book, TV show, movie, song, or Web site means to non-American audiences. Rather than relying on a critic's reading of these forms, and then assuming that the critic's interpretation is the "message" being sent, qualitative audience researchers focus on the meanings that other national peoples glean from U.S. content. What these researchers find is that American cultural content is **polysemic**—it has multiple meanings, varying across age, gender, ethnicity, and nationality. It is not possible to predict what a media text actually means to someone else—the meaning is made by the interpreting audience, not made by the producer or lodged in the text itself.

One of the earliest and most influential studies of the presumed impact of American popular culture was a book by Chilean intellectuals Ariel Dorfman and Armand Mattelart called *How to Read Donald Duck* (1971). Dorfman and Mattelart analyzed the ideas, values, and beliefs they found being promoted by Walt Disney's Donald Duck comic books. They documented the ways they believed that American capitalist values were being smuggled into the popular consciousness of their fellow citizens in Latin America.[10]

When these authors studied Donald Duck comics (but not the readers of them), they found the portrayal of "compulsive consumerism," an obsession with money, and stereotypic portrayals of foreign and exotic lands ready for exploitation. In the adventures of Donald, Uncle Scrooge, and Huey, Dewey, and Louie, they found capitalist class relationships portrayed as natural, which meant that the comics were not just entertainment or diversion, but anti-communist and anti-revolutionary propaganda. As critic John Tomlinson puts it in his book *Cultural Imperialism*, from the perspective of Dorfman and Mattelart, "the Disney comics aren't really about small, furry and feathery animals sent off by a comic uncle to have adventures

The adventures of Donald Duck and Uncle Scrooge have appeared in a variety of formats over the years; some scholars have characterized these stories as portraying and endorsing a "capitalist-imperialist worldview." Nonetheless, the comics and cartoons have a large international audience.

searching for gold in fantasy lands. . . . [T]hey are about the capitalist-imperialist worldview implicit in the narrative."[11]

This also raises a question of audience, however. What do cultural forms say to the people who choose and enjoy them, rather than to the people who make them or the people who dissect them to find evidence for their own concerns about cultural imperialism? A more audience-oriented approach to the charge of cultural imperialism has been defined by communication scholars like Ien Ang, Elihu Katz, and Tamar Liebes. Their classic interpretive research studied the meanings that different international audience groups make from the internationally popular 1980s American TV drama *Dallas*. What they found is much more complex than Dorfman and Mattelart's propaganda for capitalism. Rather than defining the media as invader, propaganda, or bad teacher, these researchers explore American media content as a narrative resource, one that international audiences use to construct their own meanings, values, and beliefs. This makes the "cultural imperialism" perspective less plausible, at least for the audiences they studied.[12]

Ang studied Dutch women and the pleasure they took in watching the internationally popular American evening soap opera about J.R. Ewing and his Texas oil-rich family. The women she interviewed knew the show was exaggerated and dramatized. Many of the viewers expressed disapproval of the intrigue, chicanery, wealth, and power that, nonetheless, made the show so fun to watch.[13] Similarly, Katz and Liebes found that various groups of Israeli citizens had complex and idiosyncratic readings of *Dallas*. The focus groups they organized included Israeli Arabs, new Russian immigrants, Moroccan immigrants, and kibbutz members. They compared the interpretations of these groups with those of ten groups in Los Angeles and found that different ethnic groups assigned different interpretations and meanings to the identical show they screened for each of them.[14]

Anthropologist Eric Michaels studied the Warlpiri people—Australian aborigines who had been forced off their tribal lands by European immigrants. In his studies of their enjoyment of Hollywood films on home video, he found that the Warlpiris' oral tradition meant that they were drawn to, and actively interpreted, the Hollywood material in the context of their own cultural norms. Michaels criticized as racist and paternalistic the assumption that the Warlpiri are vulnerable, pre-literate people who need to be protected from the ravages of media and modernity.[15]

In instances like these, global viewers seemed to be using their own ethnic values and beliefs to critique the same shows. These findings imply that the American values in our media fare are subject to critique and comment by world audiences—the content is fuel for discussion of already extant ideas and values. It is not just smuggled in as ideology. In other words, what a show means varies dramatically with who is doing the interpretation.

So perhaps U.S. popular culture, as it is spreading around the globe, is not so neatly transmitting strong Western ideology in particular messages but instead is offering meanings—stories—for people to explore, criticize, reject, or accept. We believe that concerns about the global diffusion of American culture should take the active audience into account, assuming that different people, from different national, ethnic, and religious backgrounds, will interpret U.S. offerings in relation to their own values and beliefs, based on their own lived experiences.

Raymond Williams has suggested that:

> A lived hegemony is always a process. . . . It is a realized complex of experiences, relationships, and activities. . . . [I]t does not just passively exist as a form of dominance. It has continually to be renewed, recreated, defended, and modified. It is also continually resisted, limited, altered, challenged by pressures not at all its own.[16]

In other words, hegemony may not be a one-way, ironclad, inexorable process of domination, but a negotiation. Culture is a conversation, even when one of the parties is a rich, developed nation and the other is a poor, developing one. Disempowered people have the interpretive ability, as Williams notes, to resist, limit, alter, and challenge the Western content and values that have been dominating global culture.

This active, interpretive audience may also mean that other cultures may not be hearing what we think we are saying when we "send our message" about American values and beliefs to the world. If we are not injecting messages directly into vulnerable audiences but instead are offering narratives that they interpret in their own ways, with their own particular ethnic, cultural, and/or national context, then we can't be certain they understand or believe what we think we are telling them with our popular culture. Our reputation as "the Great Satan" in parts of the Arab world tells us that what we think we are saying to other nations is not necessarily the message that is being received. We can perceive ourselves as liberators or benefactors and instead be perceived as invaders and oppressors.

In fact, what can be called the recalcitrance of media audiences is ever more obvious when our national message is being interpreted as U.S. imperialism rather than, say, humanitarian aid or our attempt to ensure world peace. World audiences are always interpreting our mediated accounts of our national interests from their own perspectives. Sometimes, no matter what we try, we can't seem to convince them that we mean well. This implies that world audiences are far less vulnerable to our persuasion than some might hope.

EVALUATING GLOBALIZATION

Beliefs about media globalization and its consequences are based in large part on our own sense of the quality of contemporary U.S. life. Whether we realize it or not, we have already come to naturalize beliefs about what is good and bad in our society. Modernization brings welcome technological advances, but at a cost—the loss of the virtues of the past. To many, traditional societies seem to offer closer and deeper familial relationships, more stability, more certainty, and more meaning. From this perspective, the costs of modernization have been high.

Traditional agrarian societies were certainly less environmentally destructive because they were less technologically sophisticated. Modern environmental destruction can seem like empirical evidence of a deeper moral or spiritual corruption; one could make a symbolic link between environmental and civic virtue. One could also make this assumption from recent concerns about gay marriage and universal health care. From the perspective of ecological activists like the Green Party, as well as from elements of the Tea Party Movement, traditional society represents a more valuable, more natural, and more virtuous way to live. From this neo-traditionalist view, modernization is to be strategically deployed and resisted when it results in the destruction of the environment, of community, of local autonomy, of family values, and of cultural authenticity.

But it may be more fruitful to evaluate globalization without imagining simple binary oppositions between an authentic past and a corrupting present. Traditional societies were not completely kind, warm, and supportive; modern societies are not completely hollow, materialistic, and meaningless. There are positives and negatives in each system; they are different. It is wise to sort out what we think the trade-offs actually are. Two commentators have written in detail about these trade-offs and their evaluations of them.

Friedman's Perspective

In *The Lexus and the Olive Tree: Understanding Globalization*, Thomas L. Friedman explores the contrast between what he calls the "age-old quests for material betterment and . . . individual and community identity," a contrast he sees being played out against an international system of globalization. He calls the "anonymous, transnational, homogenizing, standardizing market forces and technologies" the Lexus, and "the ancient forces of culture, geography, tradition, and community" the Olive Tree. His point is that the globalization of free-market capitalism is already happening, so we need to find ways to balance material progress and communal rootedness—to keep both the Lexus and the Olive Tree vibrant.[17]

Friedman famously advocates a "Golden Arches Theory of Conflict Prevention," which states that "no two countries that both had McDonald's had fought a war against each other since each got its McDonald's."[18] This is not because Big Macs have some kind of magic power to prevent armed conflict but because economically developed countries with thriving middle-class cultures that attract and support fast food don't like to fight wars—they'd rather focus on being each other's clients and customers. Though exceptions have since emerged (the former Yugoslavia and the Middle East), Friedman has stuck by his argument that economic interdependence rather than military conquest is what globalization is all about.

Friedman uses McDonald's and its global popularity to explain a stage of economic development around the world.

Furthermore, U.S. fast-food franchises, Friedman argues, symbolize a fantasy of
a U.S. way of life—"they proliferate because they offer people something they want,
and to tell people in developing countries that they can't have it because it would
spoil the view and experience of people visiting from developing countries would
be both insufferably arrogant and futile."[19] This implies that much of the developed
world's critique of globalization is self-serving. Friedman is suggesting that critics
from the West may oppose globalization because they want ways to visit "the Olive
Tree" of different cultures without actually having to live there.

What Friedman prefers is what he and others calls "glocalization," which assimilates
fast food, and forms of U.S. media, into particular countries, cultures, and ethnic sensibilities. Rather than trying to keep cultures distinct, pure, and untouched, he argues
we should accept and support cultures as they adapt to the influences of modernization. He points out that the history of civilization is the history of "glocalization,"
with successive waves of adoption, adaptation, and transformation of beliefs.[20] Nonetheless, even he has concerns about the current influence of electronic media:

> We cannot hope to preserve every culture in the world just as it is. And we cannot
> want a culture to be preserved if it lacks the internal will and cohesion to do it
> itself. As with species, cultures spawning, evolving, and dying is part of evolution.
> But what is going on today, thanks to globalization, is turbo-evolution. It is almost

not fair. In a world without walls, even some very robust cultures are simply no match for the forces of the Electronic Herd.[21]

Other critics would suggest it is definitely not fair. Friedman notes the backlash against globalization not just among fundamentalists but among peoples who now find themselves (thanks to the influx of Western media and culture) "strangers in their own backyards."[22] But in the end, he comes down in favor of a Lexus-like world with touches of Olive Tree values because he believes that most people want what material progress offers. As he puts it:

> With all due respect to revolutionary theorists, the "wretched of the earth" want to go to Disney World—not to the barricades. They want the Magic Kingdom, not Les Miserables. And if you construct an economic and political environment that gives them half a sense that with hard work and sacrifice they will get to Disney World and get to enjoy the Magic Kingdom, most of them will stick with the game—for far, far longer than you would ever expect.[23]

Friedman's perspective is exactly what constructionist critics Dorfman and Mattelart feared, however—and what mass culture critics have been saying since the 1950s. Something about U.S. popular culture keeps people "sticking with the game" far longer than is truly good for them. The game is rigged, these critics believe. It convinces people they need to work to consume and thus better supports individualism and capitalism (the Lexus) at the expense of nurturing families, communities, and traditions (the Olive Tree). Unlike Dorfman and Mattelart, Friedman believes that American society can and should serve as the role model and beacon for the rest of the world—demonstrating a way to balance the material and the communal. But notice that Friedman is presuming that we in the United States already live in the best of all possible worlds.

Barber's Perspective

In his 1996 book *Jihad vs. McWorld*, Benjamin Barber makes a very different argument. Barber sees the tension between modernity and tradition as an increasingly volatile conflict between consumer capitalism and religious or tribal fundamentalisms—illustrated so tragically when Al-Qaeda operatives took down the World Trade Center on 9/11.[24] We are currently caught in an explosive dialectic between soulless capitalism and fanatic hatreds, he argues, and in the end the possibility of peaceful, civil, democratic society suffers. The "balance" that Friedman extols and believes U.S. media represents is evaporating, Barber contends. It is evaporating because neither consumer capitalism nor fanatic fundamentalism can offer the world what it needs to thrive.

Current events support Barber's view that U.S. culture can be perceived by others as capitalistic exploitation—rapacious, self-interested, economically driven imperialism—and then countered with Jihad—fanatic, violent, religiously based fundamentalist attacks—as both ways of life attempt to vanquish each other. Barber argues that each depends upon and strengthens the other in a desperate synergy that only deepens the dilemma. Many social critics see this as the underlying story of 9/11 and the Iraqi and Afghani conflicts—elements in our current "war on terrorism."

Barber makes clear that, for him, capitalism is not democracy. This is a key point because many who believe in the value of Western culture believe that it encourages the spread of liberalism, pluralism, and egalitarianism—that "their" beliefs will come to match ours. What Barber argues instead is that the spread of "our" consumer culture (in the guise of the so-called McWorld) fuels the hatred and rage that fosters and supports terrorism (Jihad). His solution makes a crucial distinction between democracy and capitalism. Barber seeks ways to strengthen civil society, and the institutions that support democracy, internationally. As he puts it:

> We need markets to generate productivity, work, and goods; and we need culture and religion to assure solidarity, identity, and social cohesion—and a sense of human spirit. . . . With mediating civic institutions firmly in place and democracy once again the sovereign preserver of our plural worlds, Jihad can yield to healthy forms of cultural difference and group identity while McWorld can take its rightful and delimited place as the economic engine of a world in which economics is only a single crucial dimension. With McWorld's excesses under control, communities of blood and spirit will not have to make war on it and, beyond the homogenous theme parks of commerce, we may rediscover the free spaces in which it is possible to live not only as consumers but as citizens.[25]

Notice how Barber's analysis makes crucial distinctions among our three themes—technology, capitalism, and democracy—that are conflated by Friedman. Barber's perspective depends on finding ways to control McWorld and Hollywood, something that would concern those who are staunch free-market capitalists. It may be, as Friedman argued, that people actually want what Barber calls "homogenous theme parks of commerce" and are content to be consumer-citizens. As we have seen throughout this book, effectively understanding the role of media in society asks us to decide how much we can or should control the spread of capitalism and consumer culture, and how much we can trust audience tastes in culture and in politics. These are the very questions that haunted U.S.-based media and cultural critics throughout the twentieth century and now haunt internationally oriented media criticism in the twenty-first.

If Friedman is right, modern twenty-first-century U.S. popular culture will manage to balance the Lexus and the Olive Tree—a balance that other nations could emulate. In a globalized future, each country would put its own "glocalized" stamp on a modern, commercial-but-communal world. If Barber is right, we will continue to have a forced choice between a sterile wasteland of consumption and a reactionary radical response to it until we find ways to imagine, develop, and spread more truly democratic institutions that promote civil societies and support glocalized cultures.

How important is it for a nation to retain a separate, autonomous national and cultural identity? For some, it is crucial; for others, it is a prelude to endless strife, border conflicts, and social repression. Strong national, ethnic, or cultural identities underlie almost all contemporary wars. Government attempts to diminish or wash away ethnic or cultural identities, as in the former Soviet Union or Yugoslavia, have been only minimally successful. The return to ethnic diversity and religious tension brings with it complicated animosities and loyalties that seem, at least in nations today like Iraq and Somalia, to guarantee racial or ethnic strife and, in some cases, violence and genocide.

From this perspective, cultural homogenization, if it can somehow be brought about by media, may actually result in a more peaceful, harmonious world. This trade-off is the one that globalization may be asking us to make. If ethnic loyalties become "glocalized" as consumer choices in the marketplace, rather than tribal warfare and government cleansing projects, many people would see this as an advance. Some advocates of modernization even see it as the best solution to the age-old problem of war.

THE FUTURE OF GLOBALIZATION

We now have some key terms, concepts, and evidence to analyze the international impact of new media forms. In combination with the ideas in previous chapters, we can now analyze the consequences of globalization and how they might affect the future of media and society. What is at stake? What do we think should be done, politically, economically, socially, and culturally, in response to globalization?

Freedom of Choice

Capitalism is not structured democratically but arranged vertically, with powerful corporate leaders at the top and hourly wage workers at the bottom. In fact, as Steve Brill reported in the *New York Times* in 2010, over "the last 50 years, the ratio of top pay to average pay at public companies has multiplied roughly 11 times (24:1 to 275:1). That's more pay in one workday for the chief executive than his average employee makes in a year."[26] As the recent Occupy movement's slogan makes clear, most of us are the 99 percent who will never cross the widening economic gap into the mega-wealth of the top 1 percent.

An Occupy Wall Street protest marches through New York City's Times Square, a center of consumerism and homogenized culture.

But democracy, in principle, is built on a more horizontal model in which each individual has an equal opportunity to have his or her voice heard and vote counted. In discussing free markets, Edward S. Herman, in an article on democratic media, has distinguished between two types of consumer power, *consumer control* over marketplace goods and freedom of *consumer choice*: "The former requires that consumers participate in deciding what is to be offered; the latter is satisfied if [consumers are] free to select among the options chosen for them by producers."[27] Most Americans and the citizens of other economically developed nations clearly have *consumer choice*: options among a range of media products. Yet until recently, consumers and even media employees have had limited *consumer control*: power in deciding what kinds of media get created and circulated.

This is what is so exciting about how the Internet allows inexpensive access and distribution. The global media environment is now much more accessible to independent and alternative producers, artists, writers, publishers, and online entrepreneurs. Despite the movement toward economic consolidation throughout the latter half of the twentieth century, the fringes of media industries continued to offer a diversity of opinions, ideas, and innovative products. As mentioned throughout this book, business leaders at the top depend on independent ideas from below to generate new product lines. A number of transnational corporations encourage the development of local artists—talented individuals who might have the capacity to transcend the regional or national level and thus to become the next global phenomenon.

In the end, who should decide which cultural values, beliefs, and practices are best for a group of people, a region, a nation? Our beliefs about the power of the media, and the vulnerability of audiences, will shape our answers here. We must also consider the context for these choices. From a free-market perspective, everyone can choose whether or not he or she will read, watch, buy, believe, or participate in American culture. But critics of capitalism point out that our choices—nationally and internationally—are actually limited. They believe we are being offered only what will benefit those already in power and that consumer-citizens have little say in the range and kinds of media products that are produced.

Beyond this, we have been trained to imagine products as solutions to problems rather than finding ways to address the true sources of our discontent. This could render the supposedly free and open marketplace neither free nor open because we have been persuaded to want only those things that the marketplace is equipped to sell us. If this is true, then is any choice, under modern capitalism, really "free"? When people from other nations seem to choose to watch Hollywood-produced TV shows, are they freely choosing? Reflectionists and constructionists say probably not, while narrativists say they probably are.

Level Playing Field

Many argue that communication in general should be free and unrestricted, and that global communication should not be regulated. But this approach would probably lead to a U.S.-dominated global media environment. The playing field is far from level because not every culture has an equal opportunity—and the state-of-the-art production system—to create and distribute global media content. Media products marketed to local cultures can succeed globally only by becoming palatable to a commercial system.

In the search of cheap labor, the United States long ago outsourced, then lost control over, media hardware production (TV sets, VCRs, DVDs, etc.) to Japan, Korea, Mexico, and China, among other nations. But the United States retained its software advantage as the major producer of media content (movies, music, books, TV shows, Internet sites, etc.). U.S. media systems remain the standard for high production values, with dominant global distributions systems in place together with the ability to tailor products to local markets by reshaping American media to fit various versions of international taste. In many cases, they can easily drive out local media productions, forms, and distributions systems. As we have noted, successful U.S. TV programs, which have already earned profits in the United States, can be distributed in (or "dumped on") other nations at a fraction of the cost those nations would need to spend to create their own original programming. Still, the success of India's version of Hollywood, Mumbai's Bollywood, or Brazil's tele-novela productions suggests that indigenous media productions are becoming more and more appealing to local or native audiences.

Until undermined by the decentralizing power of the Internet, the global media system for a time resembled the U.S. commercial music market. The major record labels long used independent record labels and artists (and later new music introduced on YouTube) as a way to track innovative local musical tastes and trends, and then buy those labels and sign those artists or at least profit from them through distribution deals, helping them reach a wider audience. Independent labels and artists could make and even distribute their own CDs, but their best bet for conventional success was to sign contracts with major labels so that their music could get wider distribution, attention, and airplay.

Until the Information Age—and the infiltration of so much illegal downloading and the decline of the packaged commercial album—this process worked for the major labels and the most popular artists. It was a process that shaped music culture toward a homogenized mainstream, one that met listener expectations by guiding demographic tastes to a few hand-picked artists who were representative of a particular genre and maintained the minimum amount of variety to continue to appeal to these generic markets. Global artists and music, like global media, offered much variety but much similarity too. They needed to have enough difference to seem interesting and authentic, but they were (and remain) products oriented toward, and filtered through, a commercial process aimed at the general appeal, trimming back idiosyncrasies or local points of reference.

Before the Digital Era, the global arena for popular media really produced a Leveling Playing Field—designed to accommodate, or assimilate, varieties of cultural expression for consumption by the widest possible market. The recording industry model from the 1950s through the 1990s may be a useful way to explore what may happen globally as barriers to entry disappear, distribution costs decrease, and mainstream media content develops from independently produced content. Will the Information Era support a global culture that is not U.S. dominated but controlled by three to five major nations, so world culture looks more like a worldwide recording industry—dominated by mega-corporations that draw innovation from independent cultural producers worldwide?

The Promise of Cosmopolitanism

In the past, most people were exposed to one culture only—the culture they were born into. With the development of modern forms of transportation and communication, it became easier to experience other ways of life, at least superficially. Modernity offered the well-educated and the well-traveled access to different habits, values, and beliefs. In fact, one way to understand the origins of higher education is to see it as a route toward **cosmopolitanism**—a familiarity with cultural variety and sophistication about the parochialism of our own inherited culture. A college education is not just about getting a good job but about gaining access to the varieties of ways that the world has been analyzed and experienced across time and space.

The globalization of communication via the online revolution gives many more people the opportunity to reconsider the cultural systems they were born into. They no longer need to be privileged elites, with access to libraries and the time and money for grand tours of Europe. The newer forms of communication, including radio, television, movies, and now the Internet, have made it possible for the rich and powerful as well as the poor and the disenfranchised to recognize that their culture is only one among many. More and more people are now able to explore alternatives to the interpretive world into which they were born.

If we want to maintain a stable, hierarchical society, and our own place in it, then it is best to have a population that does not even begin to question the status quo. If we want a life without ambiguity, doubt, or surprise, then it is best to be a person who does not imagine alternative ways to live. Once people start recognizing the contingencies of their own beliefs, it is much more difficult for them to maintain faith in any one ideology. As the old song more or less asked, how do we keep them down on the farm once they have seen (or read a book or seen a movie or heard a podcast about) Paris?

Mass media can and should democratize access to alternative ways to think, speak, act, and create. In this way, media globalization—if it is not dominated only by the powerful elites—offers the possibility of cosmopolitanism on a wider scale, even though it was once the exclusive possibility of the (mostly male, mostly Western) educated elite.

This process has made cosmopolitanism more widely experienced in contemporary society, as well as somewhat rootless, without loyalty to a particular group, tribe, or belief system. It is a flexible, absorptive stance that thrives on variety. To some, this also makes it hollow and empty. In Europe before World War II, for example Jews were described—in coded anti-Semitic language—as "rootless cosmopolitans" and feared as dangerous influences on allegedly pure, traditional national culture. Today many older people raised in traditional small towns still fear the "evil" influences of urban culture on their children and their values for similar reasons.

Cosmopolitanism can seem unstable and incoherent to those who value stability and coherence. Some critics fear that lack of national or local loyalties will make people more vulnerable to persuasion—that a cosmopolitan person will more easily succumb to propaganda than will a traditionalist. There is also concern that a cosmopolitan is inherently relativist—accepting as appropriate a wide range of behaviors and beliefs, and therefore (it is feared) becoming amoral and aimless. In this view, cosmopolitanism weakens the bonds and beliefs of traditional societies in potentially dangerous ways.

But cosmopolitanism can also be an inclusive, progressive, pluralistic stance that respects and accommodates difference. Our own sense of the costs and benefits of cultural cosmopolitanism will probably stem from, and determine, how we feel about modernity in general and the global role of the mass media in particular. Whatever the costs of media globalization, it is possible that cultural cosmopolitanism is the benefit.

Up until now, cultural cosmopolitanism has been technologically, economically, and politically defined by the United States. American media have, as critics of U.S. cultural imperialism rightly note, aspired to become a dominant, assimilating, leveling cultural force. But cultural offerings have multiple meanings and are being actively interpreted around the world. A developing global problem, as Herman reminds us, is that consumer choice is not the same as consumer control.[28]

Thanks to the Internet, worldwide media consumers may have far more opportunity to create, comment on, and respond to mainstream media offerings. The rich and powerful media corporations will use consumer feedback to stay rich and powerful—this is how media industries work. But the narratives will no longer originate in the United States to be spread worldwide—control over media narratives seems to us to be moving away from corporations and toward global audiences.

Global Technology, Capitalism, and Democracy

Three themes have oriented our discussions of media in society: technology, capitalism, and democracy. In conclusion, we return to these themes in a global context. As always, we invite you to respond from your own critically developed perspective to the claims and arguments we make.

Communication technology is adopted—it does not infiltrate or simply spread—because it addresses the needs, values, and beliefs of particular groups. But electronic technologies are not neutral—as Innis and McLuhan point out, media forms can transform the ways we think, act, and govern. This Internet Age is especially fascinating on a global scale because it allows us to witness what happens when historically oral or written cultures rush headlong into cell-phone and television use, bypassing the print-era developments that have characterized Western history.

New, exciting, and valuable social, cultural, and political forms can emerge from the global spread of communication technologies, but these very same forms can also be deployed in repressive ways. We look to the critical, evaluative capabilities of those who adopt technology—whatever their race, class, gender, or ethnicity—to help ensure that new media technologies are adopted and deployed in ways that deepen and enhance the lived experience of particular nations and groups.

As for capitalism, there is much to deplore about the effect of capitalism and consumer culture as they are adopted and resisted by other countries. But there is also much to learn. We presume that global media content will incorporate narratives of capitalist celebration as well as capitalist critique if unfettered media creation is allowed. In other words, we are deeply committed to freedom of expression and trust that a globalized media world will allow people to broaden and deepen their access to multiple, conflicting discourses about everything that affects their lives, including capitalist ideology. We do not want to limit the stories that are available, and we are excited about the likelihood that every subsequent generation of media users will be less ethnocentric, less nationally limited, less content to live in only one dominant narrative.

Ours is, therefore, a hopeful perspective, one that believes that cultural democracy—equal opportunity to create and choose the stories we live by—will lead to a more just, equal, and meaningful society. The Internet, if it continues to allow democratized access and distribution of narratives, can support that process worldwide.

The cosmopolitanism that print culture began can become even more widespread and inclusive in the Digital Age. But democratic culture may not be natural, even though that is what our Founding Fathers believed. It is possible that democracy needs our conscious commitment and best efforts. Flourishing democracies need us to become informed, wise, and engaged citizens of the world. That has been a goal of our critical process exercises, and it is our underlying purpose in writing this textbook.

We believe that both the content and the study of media can help you become a wiser and more effective global citizen. As the world becomes more mediated, more people will have access to varieties of ways to think, feel, and be. We believe this is a good thing that can lead to a fairer and more inclusive world.

And as the world becomes more mediated, other people will feel the same hopes and fears of media influence that you now know so well. We hope that our discussions of media in society—nationally and globally—help you see the stake you have in these discussions. Wherever the Digital Age leads us, to be a world citizen you will need to be able to think critically about media content, form, and influence.

| CRITICAL PROCESS 1 | Experiencing Global Popular Culture

Charges of cultural imperialism have been mostly directed against American media. But American media also sometimes receives other cultural forms. For example, Asian cultural forms have become a larger part of American popular culture in recent years. The goal of this exercise is to examine American culture on the receiving end of globalization.

Describe the role of Asian media culture forms like anime, K-pop, or Asian cinema in your life—either now or at an earlier stage. (Perhaps you watched *Pokémon* cartoons when you were younger. Or played video games with an Asian origin, like *Super Mario Bros.*)

Analyze how these were introduced and whether you experienced them as alien or "foreign" and if this was a good or bad trait.

Interpret your interest in, affection for, or distrust of these forms. What did they offer you? What do they offer current American fans?

Evaluate how cultural forms can and do cross national borders. What effect has an increased exposure to Asian pop culture (or other "foreign" pop cultures) had on you, if any?

Engage with international students who experienced American culture in their childhoods. Which media forms did they like? Why? What can that tell you about how cultural globalization works?

| CRITICAL PROCESS 2 | Globalized News

International news coverage in the United States has been criticized for operating with a core-periphery model—news requirements focusing on "the West," with "the Rest" covered only as sites of natural disasters, armed conflicts, starvation, and poverty. The goal of this exercise is to examine news coverage of a non–Western nation. Pick a non–Western country and research its coverage in news media; you can use online, print, or televised news.

Describe the ways that this nation appears in a search of major U.S. news sites or sources: e.g., CNN, the *New York Times,* the major networks. What issues have been covered in relation to this country? Go back as many years as you need to in order to establish a general pattern.

Analyze any patterns you notice. Does the country appear only in relation to disaster and conflict, or does it get covered for its culture, politics, economics, or social traits?

Interpret what you've found. What are the dominant narratives being given to this non–Western nation by the U.S. news media? Is it a disaster-prone area of conflict and deprivation, or something else—perhaps an authentic or unspoiled region?

Evaluate the pattern of coverage. Does it support the core-periphery critics' charge that non–Western countries are treated as dangerous backwaters rather than autonomous nations with their own complicated histories, cultures, and politics? How could the coverage be improved?

Engage by reaching out to and contacting someone from that nation to discuss news events from his or her perspective. Do they find things missing from U.S.-based coverage of their country?

Notes

1 Introduction: Understanding Media in Society

1. Marshall McLuhan, *Understanding Media: The Extensions of Man*, critical ed. (1964; Berkley, Calif.: Gingko Press, 2003), 25.
2. The best overview of Carey's work, which includes his seminal essay "A Cultural Approach to Communication," is *Communication as Culture: Essays on Media and Society* (New York: Routledge, 1989).
3. Clifford Geertz, *The Interpretation of Cultures: Selected Essays* (New York: Basic Books, 1973), 5.
4. Allan Bloom, *The Closing of the American Mind* (New York: Simon & Schuster, 1987), 79.
5. Ibid.
6. Alvin Kernan, *The Death of Literature* (New Haven, Conn.: Yale University Press, 1990), 149–150.
7. W. Phillips Davison, "The Third-Person Effect in Communication," *Public Opinion Quarterly* 47 (Spring 1983): 1–15.

2 Media Metaphors

1. George Lakoff and Mark Johnson, *Metaphors We Live By* (Chicago: University of Chicago Press, 1980), 145–146.
2. Ibid., 141.
3. Joli Jensen, *Redeeming Modernity, Contradictions in Media Criticism* (Thousand Oaks, Calif.: Sage, 1990).
4. Stephanie Coontz, *The Way We Never Were: American Families and the Nostalgia Trap* (New York: Basic Books, 1992).
5. George Lakoff and Mark Johnson, *Metaphors*, 141.
6. Michael Schudson, *Discovering the New: A Social History of American Newspapers* (New York: Basic Books, 1978), 3.
7. Michael Schudson, *Advertising: The Uneasy Persuasion: Its Dubious Impact on American Society*, paperback ed. (1984; New York: Basic Books, 1986), xiii.
8. Steven Johnson, *Everything Bad Is Good for You: How Today's Popular Culture Is Actually Making Us Smarter* (New York: Riverhead Books, 2005), 72.
9. Malcolm Gladwell, "The Coolhunt," Annals of Style, *New Yorker*, March 17, 1997, www.newyorker.com.
10. Robert Putnam, *Bowling Alone: The Collapse and Revival of American Community* (New York: Simon & Schuster, 2000).

3 Visual Literacy and the Truth behind an Image

1. Joan Tumblety, "The Soccer World Cup of 1938: Politics, Spectacles, and *la Culture Physique* in Interwar France," *French Historical Studies* 31, no. 1 (Winter 2008): 77–116.
2. Ibid.
3. Peter Beck, "England v. Germany, 1938," *History Today* 32, no. 6 (June 1982): 29–34.
4. Philip M. Taylor, *The Projection of Britain, British Overseas Publicity and Propaganda, 1919–1939* (London: Cambridge University Press, 1981).

5. Herbert Zettl, "Aesthetics Theory," in *Handbook of Visual Communication: Theory, Methods, and Media,* ed. K. Smith, S. Moriarty, G. Barbatsis, and K. Kenney (Mahwah, N.J.: Lawrence Erlbaum Associates, 2005), 366.

6. Michael Rabiger, *Directing: Film Techniques and Aesthetics* (London: Focal Press, 2003), 77.

7. Virginia V. Kidd, "To Shape and Direct the Audience's Point of View: Production Appeals," posted April 1998, www.csus.edu/indiv/k/kiddv/ProductionTechniques.htm.

8. Johannes Itten, *The Art of Color: The Subjective Experience and Objective Rationale of Color* (Hoboken, N.J.: John Wiley, 1974), 120.

9. V. I. Pudovkin, quoted in Ann Marie Barry, *Visual Intelligence: Perception, Image and Manipulation in Visual Communication* (Albany: State University of New York Press, 1997), 201.

10. Lev Kuleshov, quoted in "The Rediscovery of a Kuleshov Experiment: A Dossier," ed. and trans. Yuri Tsivian, *Film History* 8, no. 3 (1996): 357–367.

11. Gretchen Barbatsis, "Narrative Theory," in *Handbook of Visual Communication,* ed. K. Smith, S. Moriarty, G. Barbatsis, and K. Kenney (Mahwah, N.J.: Lawrence Erlbaum Associates, 2005), 329–350.

12. Allert Tillman, *The Hitler Salute,* trans. Jefferson Chase (New York: Picador, 2009).

13. Lester, Paul Martin, *Visual Communication: Images With Messages* (Independence, Ky.: Cengage Learning, 2006), 55.

14. Sandra Moriarty, "Visual Semiotics Theory," in *Handbook of Visual Communication,* ed. K. Smith, S. Moriarty, G. Barbatsis, and K. Kenney (Mahwah, N.J.: Lawrence Erlbaum Associates, 2005), 227–241.

15. Roland Barthes, *S/Z: An Essay,* trans. Richard Miller (New York: Farrar, Straus and Giroux, 1974), 62.

16. J. Evans and S. Hall, *Visual Culture: The Reader* (London: Sage, 1999), 4.

17. Marita Sturken and Lisa Cartwright, *Practices of Looking: An Introduction to Visual Culture* (New York: Oxford University Press, 2001).

18. Paul M. Lester, *Visual Communication: Images with Messages* (Belmont, Calif.: Thomson Wadsworth, 2003).

19. The Tuborg Beer advertisement can be viewed online at http://adsoftheworld.com/media /print/tuborg_bachelor_party.

20. Tim Nudd, "Padma Lakshmi Seduces a Hardee's Burger," *AdWeek,* February 26, 2009, www.adweek.com/adfreak/padma-lakshmi-seduces-hardees-burger-14578.

21. "Padma," Hardee's/Carl's Jr. television commercial, feat. Padma Lakshmi, dir. Chris Applebaum (CKE Restaurants, 2009).

22. Ibid.

23. W. Mark Dendy, "The Science Behind Target Marketing Aimed at Men: The Santa Fe Turkey Burger," *examiner.com,* Feb. 15 2012, http://www.examiner.com/article /the-science-behind-target-marketing-aimed-at-men-the-santa-fe-turkey-burger.

24. Ibid.

25. Tim Nudd, "Padma Lakshmi."

26. Robert Harriman and John L. Lucaites, "Public Identity and Collective Memory in U.S. Iconic Photography: The Image of 'Accidental Napalm,'" *Critical Studies in Media Communication* 20, no. 1 (March 2003): 35–66. See also C. Finnegan, "Rhetorical Circulation and Visual Politics," unpublished paper presented at the 2nd Annual Kern Conference, Visual Communication: Rhetoric, Technology and Social Change (Rochester, N.Y.: Rochester Institute of Technology).

27. Kevin M. Deluca, "The Speed of Immanent Images: The Dangers of Reading Photographs," in *Visual Communication: Perception, Rhetoric, and Technology,* ed. Diane Hope (Cresskill, N.J.: Hampton Press, 2006), 79–90.

28. Walter Benjamin, "The Work of Art in the Age of Mechanical Reproduction" (1936), www.marxists.org/reference/subject/philosophy/works/ge/benjamin.htm.

29. Susan Sontag, "In Plato's Cave," in *On Photography* (New York: Picador, 2001), 3–24.

30. See Roland Barthes, *Camera Lucida: Reflections on Photography* (New York: Hill and Wang, 1982).

31. Christina Kotchemidova, "Why We Say 'Cheese': Producing the Smile in Snapshot Photography," *Critical Studies in Media Communication* 22, no. 1 (2005): 2–25.

32. Ibid.

33. Errol Morris, "The Case of the Inappropriate Alarm Clock," *Opinionator, New York Times*, October 24, 2009, http://morris.blogs.nytimes.com/2009/10/24/the-case-of-the-inappropriate -alarm-clock-part-7/#more-2335.

34. M. Andrews, "Mathew Brady's Portrait of Dickens: 'A Fraud and Imposition on the Public'?" *History of Photography* 28, no. 4 (2004): 375–379.

35. Farid Hany, "Digital Image Forensics," *Scientific American*, 298 (2008): 66–71.

36. Errol Morris, "Photography as a Weapon," *Opinionator, New York Times*, August 11, 2008, http://morris.blogs.nytimes.com/2008/08/11/photography-as-a-weapon/.

37. National Press Photographers Association, *Ethics in the Age of Digital Photography*, September 1999, https://nppa.org/page/5127.

38. Craig Johnson, creator and manager of the Web site Little Green Footballs, is credited with having come up with the term *fauxtography*. See Morris, "Photography as a Weapon."

39. Fred Ritchin, "New Standards for Photographic Reproduction in the Media," *PixelPress*, May 1, 1994, www.pixelpress.org/contents/newstandart_fs.html.

40. Morris, "Photography as a Weapon."

41. Barthes, *Camera Lucida*.

42. E. A. Hapgood, *Football Ambassador* (London: Sporting Handbooks, 1945); Stanley Matthews, *The Way It Was: My Autobiography* (London: Headline Book Publishing Ltd., 2000).

43. David Mellor, "Shameful Picture of England Squad Giving Nazi Salute Still Haunts British Sport. Why, 70 Years Later, Do We Still Suck Up to Dictators?" *Daily Mail*, February 9, 2008, www.dailymail.co.uk.

4 Narrative Formulas and the Cycle of Storytelling

1. Clark Hoyt, "Urgent Issues, Buried in the Mud," Week in Review, *New York Times*, October 12, 2008, sec. 10.

2. Frank McConnell, *Storytelling & Mythmaking: Images from Film and Literature* (New York: Oxford University Press, 1979), 3.

3. Jerome Bruner, *Making Stories: Law, Literature, Life* (New York: Farrar, Straus and Giroux, 2002), 8.

4. Raymond Williams, *Marxism and Literature* (New York: Oxford University Press, 1977), 108.

5. Ibid., 108.

6. Antonio Gramsci, *Selections for the Prison Notebooks*, ed. and trans. Quitin Hoare and Geoffrey Nowell Smith (New York: International Publishers, 1971).

7. Williams, *Marxism*, 112.

8. See Edward L. Bernays, *Public Relations* (1952; repr., Norman: University of Oklahoma Press, 1978).

9. Stuart Hall et al., *Policing the Crisis: Mugging, the State, and Law and Order* (London: Macmillan, 1978), 155.

10. David Thorburn, "Television as an Aesthetic Medium," *Critical Studies in Mass Communication* 4 (June 1987): 167–171.

11. Ibid., 168.

12. Stuart Hall, "Encoding/Decoding," in *Culture, Media, Language*, ed. Hall et al. (London: Hutchinson, 1980), 136–138.

13. For a discussion of story and discourse, see Sarah Ruth Kozloff, "Narrative Theory and Television," in *Channels of Discourse: Television and Contemporary Criticism*, ed. Robert C. Allen (Chapel Hill: University of North Carolina Press, 1987), 43–45.

14. Aristotle, *Poetics*, trans. Malcolm Heath (London: Penguin Books, 1997), 1.

15. John Cawelti, *Adventure, Mystery, and Romance: Formula Stories as Art and Popular Culture* (Chicago: University of Chicago Press, 1976), 6–7.

16. See Northrup Frye, *Anatomy of Criticism* (Princeton, N.J.: Princeton University Press, 1957).

17. McConnell, *Storytelling*.

18. Ibid., 12, 17, 44.

19. Ibid., 27.

20. See *The Adventures of Superman*, syndicated television series, 1952–58.

21. McConnell, *Storytelling*, 12–13.

22. Ibid., 16.

23. Richard Corliss, review of *Master and Commander*, dir. Peter Weir, *Time*, November 10, 2003, 84.

24. McConnell, *Storytelling*, 13, 16.

25. Ibid., 13, 17.

26. For information on TV programming history, see Tim Brooks and Earle Marsh, *The Complete Directory to Prime Time Network and Cable TV Shows, 1946–Present*, 9th ed. (New York: Ballantine Books, 2007).

27. McConnell, *Storytelling*, 17.

28. Ibid., 16.

29. Steve Colbert, quoted on *The Daily Show with John Stewart*, originally aired by Comedy Central on October 8, 2003, video, 2:35–2:52, www.thedailyshow.com/watch/wed-october-8-2003/democracy-grown-up.

30. Cawelti, *Adventure*, 35.

31. Joan Didion, *The White Album* (1979; repr., New York: Farrar, Straus and Giroux, 1990), 11.

32. Ibid., 13.

5 Political Stories and Media Messages

1. Mitt Romney, quoted in "Romney: Obama Should 'Be Apologizing To America,'" *Fox Nation*, February 6, 2012, http://nation.foxnews.com/mitt-romney/2012/02/06/romney-obama-should-be-apologizing-america.

2. Anna Sale, "Ross Perot: The Last Great Political Insurgent," WNYC, October 3, 2011, www.wnyc.org/articles/its-free-country/2011/oct/03/why-there-will-never-be-another-ross-perot/.

3. *Encyclopædia Britannica Online*, s.v. "Al Gore," accessed May 7, 2013, http://www.britannica.com/EBchecked/topic/239178/Al-Gore.

4. Katharine Q. Seelye, "Moral Values Cited as a Defining Issue of the Election," *New York Times*, November 4, 2004, p. P4.

5. Anna Quindlen, "Waiting in Line," *Newsweek*, October 31, 2008, www.thedailybeast.com/newsweek/2008/10/31/waiting-in-line.html.

6. Jennifer Martinez, "Shootout at the Digital Corral," *Politico*, November 16, 2011, www.politico.com/news/stories/1111/68448.html.

7. Martin Gilens and Craig Hertzman, "Corporate Ownership and News Bias: Newspaper Coverage of the 1996 Telecommunications Act," *Journal of Politics* 62, no. 2 (May 2000): 383.

8. See Bill Moyers, *Free Speech for Sale*, originally aired by PBS on June 8, 1999, video, http:// billmoyers.com/content/free-speech-for-sale/. See also Dean Alger, *Megamedia: How Giant Corporations Dominate Mass Media, Distort Competition, and Endanger Democracy* (Lanham, Md.: Rowman & Littlefield, 1998).

9. See Moyers, *Free Speech for Sale*.

10. Ibid.

11. See Elizabeth Jensen, "Broadcasters Move to Block Nightline Special on War Dead," *Los Angeles Times*, April 30, 2004, p. E1; David Folkenfilk, "Sinclair Steps Into Spotlight," *Baltimore Sun*, May 12, 2004, p. E1.

12. See Eric Klinenberg, "Beyond 'Fair and Balanced,'" *Rolling Stone*, February 21, 2005, www.rollingstone.com/politics/.

13. Ibid.

14. Jackson Lears, "America the Exceptional: How the Press Became the Media," *The New Republic*, July 26, 2004, 2.

15. For polling numbers on political bias in news media see David Krane, *News Reporting Perceived as Bias, though Less Agreement on Whether It Is Liberal or Conservative Bias*, Harris Poll #52, June 30, 2006, www.prnewswire.com/news-releases/news-reporting-is-perceived -as-biased-though-less-agreement-on-whether-it-is-liberal-or-conservative-bias-57036137.html; Pew Research Center for the People & the Press, "Values and the Press," *Bottom-Line Pressures Now Hurting Coverage, Say Journalists*, May 23, 2004, www.people-press.org; Pew Research Center, *Cable Leads the Pack as Campaign News Source*, February 7, 2012, www.people-press.org; and Lymari Morales, *Majority in U.S. Continues to Distrust the Media, Perceive Bias*, September 22, 2011, www.gallup.com/poll/149624/majority -continue-distrust-media-perceive-bias.aspx.

16. See Spiro Agnew, quoted in "Agnew Factor in California Race," *The Dispatch* (Lexington, N.C.), September 12, 1970.

17. See Herbert Gans, *Deciding What's News: A Study of* CBS Evening News, NBC Nightly News, Newsweek, *and* Time (New York: Vintage Books/Random House, 1979), 42–52.

18. See Bernard Goldberg, *Bias: A CBS Insider Exposes How the Media Distort the News* (New York: Perennial, 2003).

19. See Eric Alterman, *What Liberal Media? The Truth About Bias and the News* (New York: Basic Books, 2003).

20. Ibid., 2.

21. M. D. Watts et al., "Elite Cues and Media Bias in Presidential Campaigns: Explaining Public Perceptions of a Liberal Press," *Communications Research* 26 (1999): 144–175.

22. See Christopher Martin, *Framed! Labor and the Corporate Media* (Ithaca, N.Y.: ILR Press, 2004).

23. See Barbara Erhenreich, *Nickel and Dimed: On (Not) Getting By in America* (New York: Metropolitan Books, 2001).

24. Kathleen Hall Jamieson, "Truth and Advertising," *New York Times*, January 27, 1996, p. A15. See also Jamieson, *Packing the Presidency: A History and Criticism of Presidential Campaign Advertising* (New York: Oxford University Press, 1996).

25. Katharine Q. Seelye, "About $2.6 Billion Spent on Political Ads in 2008," *The Caucus*, *New York Times*, http://thecaucus.blogs.nytimes.com/2008/12/02/about-26-billion-spent-on -political-ads-in-2008/. See also "2012 Presidential Campaign Finance Explorer," *washingtonpost .com*, accessed May 21, 2012, www.washingtonpost.com/wpsrv/special/politics/track -presidential-campaign-ads-2012/.

26. Jasmine Melvin, "Broadcasters to Post Political Ad Buys Online," *Reuters*, April 27, 2012, www.reuters.com.

27. See Stuart Elliott, "Forecaster Trims Predictions for Ad Spending," *Media Decoder, New York Times,* July 12, 2011, www.mediacoder.blogs.nytimes.com.

28. Dwight Macdonald, "Masscult & Midcult," in *Against the American Grain: Essays on the Effects of Mass Culture* (New York: Random House, 1962), 5.

29. See Neil Postman, *Amusing Ourselves to Death* (New York: Penguin, 1985).

30. Dwight Macdonald, "A Theory of Mass Culture," *Diogenes* 1, no. 3 (1953): 2–3.

31. Michael Schudson, *The Good Citizen: A History of American Civic Life* (New York: The Free Press, 1998), 5.

32. Ibid., 6–7.

33. Ibid., 6.

34. Ibid., 8.

35. Ibid., 249.

36. Ibid.

37. Ibid., 8.

38. Ibid., 309.

39. See Nicholas Negroponte, *Being Digital* (New York: Knopf, 1996).

40. See Nicholas Kristoff, "The Daily Me," *New York Times,* March 19, 2009, www.nytimes.com.

41. Chris Sunstein, quoted in Kristof, *"The Daily Me."* See also Sunstein, *Republic.com 2.0* (Princeton, N.J.: Princeton University Press, 2009).

6 News, Culture, and Democracy

1. Reuven Frank, "Memorandum from a Television Newsman," repr. as Appendix 2 in A. William Bluem, *Documentary in American Television* (New York: Hastings House, 1965), 267.

2. Michael Emery and Edwin Emery, *The Press and America: An Interpretive History of the Mass Media,* 7th ed. (Englewood Cliffs, N.J.: Prentice-Hall, 1992), 85. See also Michael Schudson, *Discovering the News: A Social History of American Newspapers* (New York: Basic Book, 1978), 12–31.

3. Ibid., 27–29.

4. William Randolph Hearst, quoted in Piers Brendon, *The Life and Death of the Press Barons* (New York: Atheneum, 1983), 134.

5. Darrell West, *The Rise and Fall of the Media Establishment* (New York: Bedford/St. Martin's, 2001), 69.

6. See Michael Schudson, *Discovering the News: A Social History of American Newspapers* (New York: Basic Book, 1978), 88–121.

7. Jon Katz, "AIDS and the Media: Shifting Out of Neutral," *Rolling Stone,* May 27, 1993, 32.

8. David T. Z. Mindich, "Edwin M. Stanton, the Inverted Pyramid, and Information Control," *Journalism Monographs* 140 (August 1993). See also Mindich, *Just the Facts: How "Objectivity" Came to Define American Journalism* (New York: New York University Press, 1998).

9. John C. Merrill, "Objectivity: An Attitude," in *Media, Messages and Men,* ed. John C. Merrill and Ralph L. Lowenstein (New York: David McKay, 1971), 240.

10. Bill Kovach, quoted in Howard Kurtz, "The New Reform School; Disillusioned Journalists Crusade for Change," *Washington Post,* May 12, 1997, p. B1.

11. See James O'Shea, *The Deal from Hell: How Moguls and Wall Street Plundered Great American Newspapers* (New York: Public Affairs, 2011).

12. Bill Kovach and Tom Rosenstiel, *Elements of Journalism,* rev. ed. (2001; New York: Three Rivers Press, 2007), 78–111.

13. Don Hewitt, quoted on *60 Minutes,* CBS News, February 21, 1989. See also Hewitt's autobiography, *Tell Me a Story: Fifty Years and 60 Minutes in Television* (New York: Public Affairs, 2001).

14. Walter Lippmann, *Public Opinion* (New York: Simon & Schuster, 1922; New York: Free Press, 1997).

15. See Michael Schudson and Tony Dokoupil, "The Research Report: The Limits of Live," *Columbia Journalism Review* (January/February 2007): 63.

16. See Project for Excellence in Journalism, *State of the News Media 2005*, http://stateofthemedia.org/2005/network-tv-intro/content-analysis/.

17. William Greider, quoted in Mark Hertsgaard, *On Bended Knee: The Press and the Reagan Presidency* (New York: Farrar, Straus and Giroux, 1988), 78.

18. Kovach and Rosenstiel, *Elements of Journalism*, 86.

19. Jay Rosen, "Politics, Vision, and the Press: Toward a Public Agenda for Journalism," in Jay Rosen and Paul Taylor, *The New News v. The Old News: The Press and Politics in the 1990s* (New York: Twentieth Century Fund, 1992), 6.

20. See A. William Bluem, *Documentary in American Television* (New York: Hastings House, 1965), 94.

21. Fred Friendly, quoted in Joseph Michalak, "CBS Reports Covers Assortment of Topics," *New York Times*, December 13, 1959, sec. 2, p. 21.

22. See Tom Rosenstiel et al., *We Interrupt This Newscast: How to Improve Local News and Win Ratings, Too* (New York: Cambridge University Press, 2007), 41.

23. Herbert Gans, *Deciding What's News* (New York: Pantheon, 1979), 42–51.

24. Ibid., 42.

25. Ibid., 46.

26. See Davis Merritt, *Public Journalism & Public Life: Why Telling the News is Not Enough* (Hillsdale, N.J.: Lawrence Erlbaum, 1995), xv–xvi; Philip Meyer, "Raising Trust in Newspapers," *USA Today*, January 11, 1999, p. 15A; and, for current research statistics, Pew Research Center's Project for Excellence in Journalism, *State of the News Media 2013*, http://stateofthemedia.org.

27. James Agee and Walker Evans, *Let Us Now Praise Famous Men* (Boston: Houghton Mifflin, 1960), xiv.

28. David Broder, quoted in "Squaring with the Reader: A Seminar on Journalism," *Kettering Review* (Winter 1992): 48.

29. Ken Auletta, "Fortress Bush," *New Yorker*, January 19, 2004, 53.

30. See Merritt, 113–114. For an overview of the public journalism movement, see Jay Rosen, *What Are Journalists For?* (New Haven, Conn.: Yale University Press, 2001).

31. Neil Hickey, "The Perils of Punditry: What Happens When Reporters Deliver Opinion on TV," *Columbia Journalism Review* (January/February 1999), http://www.cjr.org/.

32. West, *The Rise and Fall of the Media Establishment*, 69.

33. Christopher Lasch, "Journalism, Publicity and the Lost Art of Argument," *Gannett Center Journal* 4, no. 2 (Spring 1990): 1.

34. Bill Keller, quoted in Rachel Smolkin, "Too Transparent," *American Journalism Review* (April/May 2006), www.ajr.org/Article.asp?id=4073.

35. Jeff Jarvis, quoted in Rachel Smolkin, "Too Transparent."

36. See Kovach and Rosenstiel, *Elements of Journalism*, 45.

37. See "How Many Blogs Are There? 50 Million and Counting," *CyberJournalist.net*, August 7, 2006, www.cyberjournalist.net/news/003674.php.

38. Jay Rosen, "The People Formerly Known as the Audience," *PressThink*, June 27, 2006, journalism.nyu.edu/pubzone/weblogs/pressthink/2006/06/27/ppl_frmr.html.

39. Nicholas Lemann, "Amateur Hour: Journalism without Journalists," *New Yorker*, August 7, 2006, www.newyorker.com.

40. Ibid.

41. See Rosen, "The People Formerly Known as the Audience."

42. Stephen Johnson, *Everything Bad Is Good for You* (New York: Riverhead Books, 2005), 115.

43. Leonard Downie Jr. and Michael Schudson, "The Reconstruction of American Journalism," *Columbia Journalism Review* (October 19, 2009), www.cjr.org.

44. Mallary Jean Tenore, "Five Strategies for Successful News Organization-University Partnerships," Poynter.org, June 13, 2010, www.poynter.org/author/mjtenore.

7 Media Economics

1. Peter Thai Larsen, "Comcast Looks to Snatch Disney with $66 Billion Bid," *Financial Times,* February 12, 2004, p. 1; and Geraldine Fabricant, "Comcast Pulls Disney Bid Off the Table," *New York Times,* April 29, 2004, pp. C1, C6.

2. For alternative methodologies see *International Encyclopedia of the Social & Behavioral Sciences,* ed. Neil J. Smelser and Paul B. Baltes (New York: Elservier, 2001), s.vv. "Film and Video Industry" and "Television: Industry," by Douglas Gomery.

3. Karl Marx, preface to *A Contribution to the Critique of Political Economy* (1859; repr., London: Beekman, 1972).

4. Terry Eagleton, *Marxism and Literary Criticism* (Berkeley: University of California Press, 1976), 5.

5. See Adam Smith, *An Inquiry into the Nature and Causes of the Wealth of Nations* (1776; repr., New York: Oxford University Press, 2008).

6. For more on the free-market approach, see Benjamin M. Compaine and Douglas Gomery, *Who Owns the Media?,* 3rd ed. (Mahwah, N.J.: Lawrence Erlbaum Associates, 2001).

7. "All Time Box Office," Box Office Mojo, accessed May 23, 2013, http://boxofficemojo.com /alltime/world/.

8. Denis McQuail, *Media Performance: Mass Communication and the Public Interest* (London: Sage, 1992).

9. See *Frontline,* "News War" (Boston: Frontline/WGBH, 2007), PBS Video, 270 min., www.pbs.org/wgbh/pages/frontline/newswar/view/.

10. Robert G. Picard, *Media Economics* (London: Sage, 1989), 80.

11. U.S. Government Accounting Office, *Telecommunications: The Changing Status of Competitions to Cable Television* (Washington, D.C.: GAO, July 1999).

12. See Jeffrey H. Birnbaum, "The Road to Riches Is Called K Street: Lobbying Firms Hire More, Pay More, Charge More to Influence Government," *Washington Post,* June 22, 2005, www.washingtonpost.com.

13. Richard Perez-Pena, "Newspaper Circulation Falls by More than 10 Percent," *New York Times,* October 27, 2009, p. B3.

14. Leonard Downie Jr. and Michael Schudson, "The Reconstruction of American Journalism," *Columbia Journalism Report,* October 20, 2009, 77–91. For the full report, see www.cjr.org.

15. Leonard Downie Jr. and Michael Schudson, "Finding a New Model for News Reporting," *Washington Post,* October 19, 2009, www.washingtonpost.com.

8 Entertainment and Popular Culture

1. See Matthew Gurewitsch's description of German archaeologist Vinzenz Brinkmann's findings in "True Colors," *Smithsonian Magazine,* July 2008, www.smithsonianmag.com/arts-culture /true-colors.html.

2. Lawrence W. Levine, *Highbrow/Lowbrow: The Emergence of Cultural Hierarchy in America* (Cambridge MA: Harvard University Press, 1988).

3. See *Our Country and Our Culture,* in *A Partisan Century: Political Writings from Partisan Review,* ed. Edith Kurzweil (New York: Columbia University Press, 1996), 115–136.

4. Theodor Adorno and Max Horkheimer, *Dialectic of Enlightenment* (London: Verso, 1979).

5. Hannah Arendt, "Society and Culture," in *Mass Culture Revisited*, ed. Bernard Rosenberg and David Manning White (New York: Van Nostrand Reinhold, 1971), 93ff.

6. Ibid., 95.

7. Ibid., 98.

8. Ibid., 99.

9. Randall Jarrell, "A Sad Heart at the Supermarket," *Culture for the Millions? Mass Media in Modern Society*, ed. Norman Jacobs (D. Van Nostrand Co., 1959; repr., New Brunswick, N.J.: Transaction Publishers, 1992), 138ff.

10. Edward Shils, "Mass Society and Its Culture," in *Mass Culture Revisited*, ed. Bernard Rosenberg and David Manning White (New York: Van Nostrand Reinhold, 1971).

11. Dwight Macdonald, "A Theory of Popular Culture," *Politics* 1, no. 1 (1944): 20–23.

12. Oscar Handlin won the Pulitzer Prize for *The Uprooted: The Epic Story of the Great Migrations that Made the American People*, 2nd ed. (Little, Brown and Company, 1951; Philadelphia: University of Pennsylvania Press, 2002). See also Handlin's analysis of folk culture in "Comments on Mass and Popular Culture," *Culture for the Millions? Mass Media in Modern Society*, ed. Norman Jacobs (D. Van Nostrand Co., 1959; repr., New Brunswick, N.J.: Transaction Publishers, 1992), 104.

13. See Herbert J. Gans, *Popular Culture & High Culture: An Analysis and Evaluation of Taste*, rev. ed. (1974; New York: Basic Books, 1999).

14. Richard Hoggart, *The Uses of Literacy*, repr. with a new postscript by John Corner (Essential Books, 1957; New Brunswick, N.J.: Transaction Publishers).

15. See Dick Hebdige, *Subculture: the Meaning of Style* (1979; repr., New York: Routledge, 2002); Janice Radway. *Reading the Romance* (Chapel Hill, N.C.: University of North Carolina Press, 1984); Janice Radway, *A Feeling for Books: The Book of the Month Club, Literary Taste and Middle-class Desire* (Chapel Hill, N.C.: University of North Carolina Press, 1997); and Ien Ang, *Watching Dallas: Soap Opera and the Melodramatic Imagination* (York, England: Methuen, 1985).

16. Tom Bissell, *Extra Lives: Why Video Games Matter* (New York: Random House, 2010).

17. Joli Jensen, "Fandom as Pathology: The Consequences of Characterization," in *The Adoring Audience: Fan Culture and Popular Music*, ed. Lisa Lewis (Boston: Unwin-Hyman, 1992), 9–29.

18. Mark Andrejevic, "Watching Televsion Without Pity: The Productivity of Online Fans," *Television & New Media* 9, no. 24 (2009): 24–46.

19. See Gans, *Popular Culture*.

20. See, for example, www.dunav.org.il; http://www.youtube.com/watch?v=Tyhcm99lwDI; http://barkend.com/davis_folkdance/dfd_balkan_dance.shtml; and www.balkanfolk.com.

21. Joli Jensen, "Fandom as Pathology."

22. Walt Whitman, *Democratic Vistas*, ed. Ed Folsom (1871; Iowa City: University of Iowa Press, 2009).

23. For more information, see Bill Bishop, *The Big Sort, Why the Clustering of Like-Minded America Is Tearing Us Apart* (New York: Houghton Mifflin, 2008).

9 Representation in the Media

1. John Berger, *Ways of Seeing* (London: BBC and Penguin Books, 1972), 7.

2. "Is *Princess and the Frog* racist?" *Week*, December 7, 2009, www.theweek.com.

3. Berger, *Ways of Seeing*, 63.

4. Laura Mulvey, "Visual Pleasure and Narrative Cinema," in *The Sexual Subject: A Screen Reader in Sexuality*, ed. Mandy Merck (New York: Routledge, 1992), 22–34.

5. John Berger, "Ways of Seeing: Representation and Art Practices," in *An Introduction to Women's Studies,* ed. I. Grewall and C. Kaplan (New York: McGraw Hill, 2006), 269–273.

6. Sharon Willis, *High Contrast: Race and Gender in Contemporary Hollywood Films* (Durham, N.C.: Duke University Press, 2002), 3.

7. Stacy L. Smith et al., *Gender Roles & Occupations: A Look at Character Attributes and Job-Related Aspirations in Film and Television* (Geena Davis Institute on Gender in Media), www.seejane.org/downloads/KeyFindings_GenderRoles.pdf.

8. Michael Messner and Jeffrey Montez de Oca, "The Male Consumer as Loser: Beer and Liquor Ads in Mega Sports Media Event," in *Men's Lives,* ed. Michael S. Kimmel and Michael Messner (Boston: Pearson, 2007), 484–497.

9. Peter Bondanella, *Hollywood Italians: Dagos, Palookas, Romeos, Wise Guys, and Sopranos* (New York: Continuum, 2004).

10. American Society of Newspaper Editors, "Employment of Men and Women by Job Category," in *2012 Newsroom Census,* http://asne.org/content.asp?pl=140&sl=144&contentid=144.

11. Associated Press Sports Editors, "ASPE Racial and Gender Report Card Shows We Have Work to Do," March 2, 2013, www.apsportseditors.org/uncategorized/apse-racial-and-gender-report-card-shows-we-have-work-to-do/.

12. Free Press, "Long Overdue FCC Report Shows Abysmal levels of Female and Minority Broadcast Ownership," November 14, 2012, www.freepress.net. See also S. Derek Turner and Mark Cooper, *Out of the Picture 2007: Minority & Female TV Station Ownership in the United States* (Free Press, 2007), www.freepress.net/sites/default/files/fp-legacy/otp2007.pdf.

13. Joe Flint, "FCC Media Ownership Survey Reveals Lack of Diversity," *Company Town, Los Angeles Times,* November 14, 2012, www.latimes.com.

14. Center for Media and Public Affairs, "2006 Year in Review," *Media Monitor* 21, no. 1 (Winter 2007), www.cmpa.com/files/media_monitor/07winter.pdf.

15. Bob Papper, *2012 TV and Radio News Staffing and Profitability Survey* (Radio Television Digital News Association, 2012), www.rtdna.org/uploads/files/vv7.pdf.

16. Hannah Seligson, "One by One, Women Count Bylines," *Women's eNews,* December 2005, http://womensenews.org/story/media-stories/051226/one-one-women-count-bylines#.UZ_ndCt363k.

17. Lee Margulies, "Number of Women Working in TV Falls," *Los Angeles Times,* August 23, 2011, http://articles.latimes.com/2011/aug/23/entertainment/la-et-women-in-tv-20110823.

18. Stacy Smith, interview by Jessica Youseffi, "Women Underrepresented in Hollywood on Screen and Behind the Camera," *Huffington Post,* March 26, 2010, www.huffingtonpost.com/2010/02/24/women-underrepresented-in_n_475128.html.

19. Ibid.

20. Martha Lauzen, *Thumbs Down—Representation of Women Film Critics in the Top 100 U.S. Daily Newspapers,* Alliance of Women Film Journalists, December 16, 2009, http://awfj.org/hot-topic/thumbs-down-representation-of-women-film-critics-in-the-top-100-us-newspapers-a-study-by-dr-martha-lauzen/.

21. Perfection Oil Cook Stoves and Ovens (advertisement), 1925, http://www.adclassix.com/ads/25perfection.htm.

22. Westinghouse (advertisement), 1935, http://www.adclassix.com/a4/35westinghousewasher.html.

23. Lynn Spigel, *Make Room for TV: Television and the Family Ideal in Postwar America* (Chicago: The University of Chicago Press, 1992), 6.

24. A. Dorenkamp, J. McClymer, M. Moynihan, and A. Vadum, *Images of Women in American Popular Culture* (New York: Harcourt Brace, 1985).

25. Arlie Hochschild, *The Second Shift* (New York: Avon Books, 1989).

26. U.S. Bureau of Labor Statistics, *American Time Use Survey,* Charts by Topic: Household activities, 2008, http://www.bls.gov/TUS/CHARTS/HOUSEHOLD.HTM.

27. Michael Schneider, "Nets on Gender Bender," *Variety*, May 9–15, 2005, 24.

28. Martha M. Lauzen, David M. Dozier, and Nora Horan, "Constructing Gender Stereotypes through Social Roles in Prime-Time Television," *Journal of Broadcasting & Electronic Media* 52, no. 2 (June 2008): 200–214, doi: 10.1080/08838150801991971.

29. Nancy Signorielli and Susan Kahlenberg, "Television's World of Work in the Nineties," *Journal of Broadcasting & Electronic Media* 45, no. 1 (2001): 4-22, doi:10.1207/s15506878jobem4501_2.

30. G. Espinoza, "Who's the Money Boss," *Working Mother*, February 1999, 16, 23.

31. Andrea L. Press, *Women Watching Television: Gender, Class and Generation in the American Television Experience* (Philadelphia: University of Pennsylvania Press, 1991), 27.

32. Ibid., 34.

33. Ibid., 37.

34. Ibid., 44. See also Susan Faludi, *Backlash: The Undeclared War against American Women* (New York: Anchor Books/Doubleday, 1991); and Susan Douglas, *Where the Girls Are: Growing Up Female with the Mass Media* (New York: Times Books, Random House, 2004).

35. Joanna Powell, "Invisible Moms," *Working Mother*, July/August 2000, 50.

36. Joan Peters, *When Mothers Work: Loving Our Children Without Sacrificing Ourselves* (Reading, Mass.: Addison Wesley, 1997), 12.

37. Berea Orange, "Shonda Rhimes: Prominent Proponent for Diversity," *Daily Toreador*, February 19, 2013, www.dailytoreador.com/opinion/article_324f0b14-7b0f-11e2-86b7-0019bb30f31a.html.

38. Joy Parks. "Mad Men Mad Women," *Herizons*, Winter 2009, www.herizons.ca.

39. Karen Mallia, "The Mid-Career Vanishing Act: A Qualitative Examination of Why So Few Women Become Creative Directors," paper presented at the annual meeting of the Association for Education in Journalism and Mass Communication, Marriott Downtown, Chicago, IL, updated August 6, 2008, www.allacademic.com/meta/p272174_index.html.

40. Daphne Merkin, "Can Anybody Make a Movie for Women?" *New York Times Magazine*, December 20, 2009, 30ff.

41. Sheri Stritof and Bob Stritof, "The Marriages of Anna Nicole Smith," About.com Guides, accessed May 24, 2013, http://marriage.about.com/od/entertainmen1/p/annasmith.htm.

42. Naomi Wolf, *The Beauty Myth: How Images of Beauty Are Used Against Women* (New York: Harper, 2002), 3.

43. Ibid., 17.

44. Pamela Paul, *Pornified: How Pornography Is Damaging Our Lives, Our Relationships, And Our Families* (New York: Henry Holt and Co., 2005), 5.

45. Ibid.

46. Dworkin, Shari Lee and Wachs, Faye Linda, "The Morality/Manhood Paradox: Masculinity, Sport, and the Media," in *Masculinities, Gender Relations, and Sport*, ed. Jim McKay, Michael A. Messner, and Don Sabo (Thousand Oaks, Calif.: Sage Publications, 2000), 469–483.

47. Fred Fejes, "Advertising and the Political Economy of Lesbian/Gay Identity," in *Sex & Money: Feminism and Political Economy in the Media*, ed. Eileen R. Meehan and Ellen Riordan (Minneapolis: University of Minnesota Press, 2002), 196–208.

48. Katherine Sender, *Business, Not Politics: The Making of the Gay Market* (New York: Columbia University Press, 2005).

49. Fejes, "Advertising and the Political Economy of Lesbian/Gay Identity," 197.

50. Marguerite Moritz, "Lesbian Chic: Our 15 Minutes of Celebrity?" in *Feminism, Multiculturalism and the Media: Global Diversities*, ed. Angharad N. Valdivia (Thousand Oaks, Calif.: Sage Publications, 1995), 128.

51. Ibid.

10 Technology, Convergence, and Democracy

1. Mitt Romney, quoted in "Romney: 'This Election Is a Battle for the Soul of America,'" NBC News video, posted January 21, 2012, www.nbcnews.com/video/nbc-news/46086088#46086088.
2. Walker, Dave, "Superb Owl 2013 attracts 108 million viewers," *Times-Picayune*, February 4, 2013, www.nola.com.
3. James W. Carey, *Communication as Culture: Essays on Media and Society* (Boston: Unwin Hyman, 1989), 203.
4. Neil Postman, *Amusing Ourselves to Death: Public Discourse in the Age of Show Business* (New York: Penguin Books, 1984), 65. See also Elizabeth Eisenstein, *The Printing Press as an Agent of Change*, 2 vols. (Cambridge: Cambridge University Press, 1979).
5. See Robert McChesney, *Telecommunications, Mass Media, & Democracy: The Battle for Control of U.S. Broadcasting, 1928–1935* (New York: Oxford University Press, 1993).
6. See Mark Silverman, "*Encyclopædia Britannica* vs. *Wikipedia*," Mashable.com, March 16, 2012, http://mashable.com/2012/03/16/encyclopedia-britannica-wikipedia-infographic/.
7. "An Overview Why Microsoft's Worth $42," *Forbes*, January 9, 2013, www.forbes.com.
8. Microsoft, *Microsoft, Yahoo! Change Search Landscape*, July 29, 2009, accessed May 24, 2013, http://www.microsoft.com/en-us/news/press/2009/jul09/07-29release.aspx.
9. Marc Gunther, "What's Your Stake in It All: Information Highway Looks Like a Rough Road," *Detroit Free Press*, November 18, 1993, p. D1.
10. Daniel Burnstein and David Kline, *Road Warriors: Dreams and Nightmares Along the Information Highway* (New York: Dutton, 1995), 104.
11. Ibid.
12. See Steve Maich, "Pornography, Gambling, Lies, Theft, and Terrorism: The Internet Sucks," *Macleans*, October 30, 2006, www.macleans.ca.
13. Ibid.
14. Jonathan Sidener, "I'm Ready to Move to the Web's Next Level," U-T San Diego, September 11, 2006, www.utsandiego.com.
15. See also Bill & Melinda Gates Foundation, "What We Do—Global Libraries: Strategy," accessed May 24, 2013, www.gatesfoundation.org/what-we-do/global-development/global-libraries.
16. See "Internet Users in the World: Distributed by World Regions—2012 Q2," Internet World Stats: Usage and Population Statistics, last updated February 17, 2013, www.internetworldstats.com/stats.htm.
17. Robert Tait, "Iran's Clerics Caught Up in Blogging Craze," *Guardian*, October 11, 2006, 17.
18. Ibid.
19. Ibid.
20. Ibid.
21. See "Top 20 Internet Countries: By Users—2012 Q2," Internet World Stats: Usage and Population Statistics, last updated March 6, 2013, www.internetworldstats.com/top20.htm.

11 Media Globalization

1. Raymond Williams, *Marxism and Literature* (New York: Oxford University Press, 1977), 133.
2. See Marshall McLuhan, *Understanding Media: The Extensions of Man* (New York: McGraw-Hill, 1964), 1; and Harold Adam Innis, *The Bias of Communication* (Toronto: University of Toronto Press, 1951).
3. Marshall McLuhan develops the concept of the "global village" in *The Gutenberg Galaxy: the Making of Typographic Man* (Toronto, Canada: University of Toronto Press, 1962).

4. Richard Barnet and John Cavanaugh, *Global Dreams: Imperial Corporations and the New World Order* (New York: Simon & Schuster, 1994), 38

5. The phrase "Revolution of rising expectations," attributed to Harlan Cleveland in a speech at Colgate University, ca. 1950.

6. See Herbert Schiller, *Mass Communication and American Empire*, 2nd ed. (1969; repr., Boulder, Colo.: Westview Press, 1992). See also Noam Chomsky, *World Orders, Old and New* (New York: Columbia University Press, 1994).

7. Cees Hamelink, "Information Imbalance Across the Globe," in *Questioning the Media: A Critical Introduction*, 2nd ed., ed. John Downing, Ali Mohammadi, Annabelle Sreberny-Mohammadi (Thousand Oaks, Calif.: Sage Publications, 1995), 293–307.

8. See, for example, Tsan-Kuo Chang, "All Countries Not Created Equal to Be News World System and International Communication," *Communication research* 25, no. 5 (1998): 528–563.

9. Frantz Fanon, *The Wretched of the Earth* (Middlesex: Penguin, 1967), 142.

10. Ariel Dorfman, *How to Read Donald Duck: Imperialist Ideology in the Disney Comic* (*Para leer al Pato Donald*, 1971), with Armand Mattelart, tr. David Kunzle (London: International General, 1975).

11. John Tomlinson, *Cultural Imperialism: A Critical Introduction* (Baltimore: Johns Hopkins University Press, 1991), 43.

12. See Ien Ang, *Living Room Wars: Rethinking Media Audiences for a Postmodern World* (London: Routledge, 1996); and Tamar Liebes and Elihu Katz, *The Export of Meaning: Cross-Cultural Readings of Dallas*, 2nd ed. (Cambridge, Mass.: Polity Press, 1993).

13. Ien Ang, *Watching Dallas: Soap Opera and the Melodramatic Imagination* (London: Methuen, 1985).

14. See Tamar Liebes and Elihu Katz, *The Export of Meanings: Cross-cultural readings of Dallas*, 2nd ed. (Cambridge, Mass.: Polity Press, 1993).

15. Eric Michaels, *Bad Aboriginal Art: Tradition, Media and Technological Environments* (Minneapolis: University of Minnesota Press, 1993).

16. Williams, *Marxism and Literature*, 112.

17. Thomas L. Friedman, *The Lexus and the Olive Tree: Understanding Globalization* (New York: Random House, 2000), 32–35.

18. Ibid., ix.

19. Ibid., 294.

20. Ibid., 295.

21. Ibid., 303.

22. Ibid., 34.

23. Ibid., 364.

24. See Benjamin Barber, *Jihad vs. McWorld: Terrorism's Challenge to Democracy* (New York: Ballantine Books, 1995).

25. Ibid., 300.

26. Steve Brill, "What's a Bailed-Out Banker Worth?" *New York Times Magazine*, December 29, 2009, www.nytimes.com.

27. Edward Herman, "Democratic Media," *Z Papers* (January-March 1992): 23.

28. Ibid.

Credits

Photo Credits

2: © Dorothy Alexander / Alamy
9: Charles Trainor / © Bravo / Courtesy: Everett Collection
14: Bill Aron/PhotoEdit
22: JGI/Jamie Grill /Getty Images
26: © Lionsgate/Courtesy Everett Collection
35: John Shearer/WireImage/Getty Images
42: Fox/Photofest
47: © Miramax/courtesy Everett Collection
52: Popperfoto/Getty Images
57: Richard Cartwright/ABC via Getty Images
61: Jonny Gawler/Fast Bikes Magazine via Getty Images; TRP/imagerover.com/Alamy
64: Ullstein Bild/The Image Works
71: Soccer photo courtesy Popperfoto/Getty Image; fairies photo courtesy The Granger Collection
72: © Print Collector/HIP/The Image Works; Getty Images
73: Stalin portraits courtesy of David King Collection, London; Hitler photos © Scherl/Sueddeutsche Zeitung Photo/The Image Works and © SZ Photo/Scherl/The Image Works
78: © Lucasfilm Ltd./courtesy Everett / Everett Collection
83: Saul Loeb /AFP/Getty Images
90: © Warner Brothers/courtesy Everett Collection
97: © Sunset Boulevard/Corbis
102: Joe Raedle/Getty Images
115: Phil Velasquez/Chicago Tribune/MCT via Getty Images
121: © Michael Ochs Archives/CORBIS
125: Mark Wilson/Newsmakers/Getty Images
132: AP Photo/NBC, Jonathan Orenstein
136: Library of Congress, Prints and Photographs Division
148: Photo Researchers/Getty Images
161: WireImage/Getty Images
164: © Ilene MacDonald / Alamy
173: Courtesy of Indeed.com
180: Donna Svennevik/ABC via Getty
188: © Twentieth Century-Fox Film Corporation/Photofest
189: © Lions Gate/courtesy Everett Collection
196: © pumkinpie / Alamy
203: Warner Bros/Photofest
207: © Columbia Pictures/courtesy Everett Collection
212: The Guitar Player, 1910 (oil on canvas), Picasso, Pablo CNAC/MNAM/Dist. RMN-Grand Palais / Art Resource, NY. © 2012 Estate of Pablo Picasso / Artists Rights Society (ARS), New York
213: The Old Guitarist, 1903 (oil on wood panel), Picasso, Pablo (1881–1973) / The Art Institute of Chicago, IL, USA / The Bridgeman Art Library/ © 2012 Estate of Pablo Picasso / Artists Rights Society (ARS), New York
220: WENN/Newscom
230: AFP/Getty Images

Index

Note: Page numbers in italics indicate illustrations